SCOTTISH MOTOR RACING AND DRIVERS

One hundred years of Scotland's involvement with motor racing

Graham Gauld

First published in 2004 by Havelock Publishing, The Coach House, Blackwood Estate, Lesmahagow, ML11 0JG, Scotland.

The information in this book is true and complete to the best of our knowledge. All recommendations are made without any guarantee on the part of the author or Publisher, who also disclaim any liability incurred in connection with the use of this data or specific details.

ISBN No.   0-9549167-0-0

Printed in Scotland by Buccleuch Printers Ltd.

CONTENTS

Dedication

In recent years many books have been planned and even written but the prospect of them ever being published has become more and more difficult, due to the vagaries of the specialist motoring book market.

This book would not have been published without the direct assistance of nine very good friends who agreed that it was important for a history of Scottish motor racing be published and to recognise the contribution Scotland has made to International motor racing.

This book, therefore, is dedicated with heartfelt thanks to :

Martin Colvill: Martin has raced historic cars for many years and is a former owner of an Ecurie Ecosse Group C2 car raced by the team in 1985.

Andrew Fletcher: In the 1970s Andrew raced Brabhams and Chevrons Internationally. His grandfather can claim to have been Scotland's first serious racing driver.

Lord Laidlaw: Irvine Laidlaw is an extremely successful Scottish businessman and historic racing driver who was enobled in 2004 for his services to business and politics.

Hugh McCaig: The current Patron of Ecurie Ecosse needs little introduction. In the past twenty five years Hugh has reformed Ecurie Ecosse and taken the team to its first World Championship. He has contributed towards the racing careers of many young Scots.

Campbell McLaren: Campbell manages to mix his passion for golf with his passion for historic motor racing. He is a former winner of the Jaguar Historic XK championship and collector of Jaguars.

Bruce Mickel: Douglas Mickel, Bruce's father, was long time Secretary of the MG Car Club in Scotland. He was directly involved with all the early Scottish motor racing developments at Charterhall and Turnberry. Bruce's contribution to this book is in memory of his father.

Dick Skipworth: Nobody in the world owns more ex-Ecurie Ecosse cars than Dick Skipworth. His passion for Ecurie Ecosse is reflected in his remarkable collection which contains everything from Sir James Scott Douglas' original Jaguar XK120 to the famous Commer transporter.

Sandy Watson: Sandy originally raced Clubmans cars at Ingliston and as a successful businessman he now races Internationally with his Chevron B8, B16 and his Lotus single seater.

Peter Windsor: Peter spent part of his earlier life in Australia where he first met Jim Clark, a meeting which virtually changed his life. Today he is a successful Television commentator on motor sport and opinionated columnist in F1 Racing magazine.

Graham Gauld

Foreword

Graham Gauld has been around motorsport in Scotland, for as long as I can remember and clearly from his writings in this, his latest book, the reader will recognise that he has been an enthusiastic historian of Scottish motorsport, in particular.

If I have any questions regarding a speech I might be giving anywhere in the world, where I have to have facts relating to the early motorsport days in Scotland, it would be to Graham Gauld that I would go.

When I first met him he indeed was a Journalist, writing in Motor World I believe at the time. Very early in my career, I recall him doing radio reporting for Scottish programs and later also for television.

Over the years he has worked within the motor trade for large companies in relationship to public affairs and been enormously active in the midst of Scottish motorsport for decades. He has always been on the scene, popping up all over the world in different roles and different projects. His commitment and enthusiasm for motoring in Scotland is probably unique; there is hardly a person who had touched a competition car that Graham Gould would not know, or has not met. He has never written for money, he has simply been the ultimate enthusiast, who felt a book, such as the one you are about to read, needed to be written. It has been chronicled for the archives, and that alone is an important and generous gesture.

I can tell you that on reading through the galleys, many happy memories flooded through my mind. I was reading of people whose autographs I collected when I accompanied my racing driver brother Jimmy Stewart, when he took me to Winfield, Turnberry, Bo'ness, Rest and be Thankful, Charterhall; not to mention racetracks I visited in England with my brother to see a multitude of Scottish racing drivers compete against some of the best names in the world.

Scotland surely has had a rich history of carmakers who have participated in motorsport, whether it has been Arrol-Johnston, Albion, and Argyll. There have also been motor racing enthusiasts who have created cars, specifically for the job. In the early days they were called specials, whether it was Joe Potts or Jimmy Gibbon, to the sophisticated Ecurie Ecosse, which produced the odd hybrid of its own.

For a small country with a very small population, the ratio of success in motorsport has been quite extraordinary. This very worthy book that Graham Gauld has put so much into, is not designed or expected to be a large volume seller, but it certainly is a book that needed to be written and is a must for any collector, who has an interest in the heritage of sport in Scotland, not necessarily motorsport.

Having said that, our wee country of Scotland has enjoyed absolutely amazing success in the field of motorsport on a global basis. Well done to Graham Gauld for registering for posterity this proud record.

Sir Jackie Stewart
September 2004.

Preface

It could be said that this book started way back in 1951 shortly after I had joined the Edinburgh Evening Dispatch as a trainee reporter. In my youthful enthusiasm I was willing to take on anything and was even appointed wrestling correspondent, principally because nobody else wanted to do it. The motoring and motor racing correspondent of the paper was an Advertising man called William Cranston Hall who worked on the SMT Magazine. He was about to start his own advertising agency, Hall Advertising, and wanted to give up his motoring column, so my involvement with cars began.

It was a strange choice, really, as nobody in our family had ever owned a car but as a result I was able to attend the first race meeting at Charterhall in 1952. Little was I to know what would follow.

From the start, I kept my photographs and many of my notes from those days and they, along with a huge archive, have been the bedrock on which this book was constructed.

This is not a technical book. It is people and their stories that make history fascinating so my emphasis has always been on the human side of motor racing. Ask anyone about Scotland and motor racing and the majority will recall Jim Clark, Jackie Stewart, David Coulthard and perhaps Allan McNish and Dario Franchitti. However, Scots have been to the fore in motor racing all over the world and have helped mould this sport, which is why an entire section is based on Scottish drivers who have raced Internationally but are generally overlooked. It is also why, in that section, Ron Flockhart, Innes Ireland and Tom Walkinshaw, for example, have longer stories than Clark, Stewart or Coulthard : the latter three having had entire books dedicated to them.

Perhaps the most poignant section covers the Phantom Circuits, for Scotland has had its fair share of new circuit plans that progressed so far and then collapsed. Indeed, only one completely new purpose-built motor racing circuit has been built in Scotland in fifty years : Knockhill. The rest were adaptations of airfields, parks or showground sites.

This then is an overview of Scotland's contribution to motor racing.

Graham Gauld
September 2004.

Acknowledgements

In the course of preparing and writing this book, a multitude of people and various articles and books were consulted. To list them all would be impossible but I would like to make special mention of Andrew Fletcher who dug out all the photographs and cuttings collected by his grandfather ninety one years ago, Lord Malcolm Selsdon, who did likewise about his father and Sandy Cormack whose father Alastair Cormack was a factory driver for Alta before the war. I am also grateful to the archivist of G & J Weir Ltd in Glasgow who provided background information on the Weir-Darracqs.

Bibliography:

Books:

24 Heures du Mans: Moity et Tiessedre.
A Record of Grand Prix and Voiturette Racing : Paul Sheldon and Duncan Rabagliatti.
Archie and the Listers : Robert Edwards.
Cooper Cars : Doug Nye.
Daytona USA : William F Nolan.
Ecurie Ecosse : Graham Gauld.
Encyclopaedia of Motor Sport: Nick Giorgano.
From Chain Drive to Turbocharger : Denis Jenkinson.
Jaguar Sports Racing Cars: Philip Porter.
The Story of Brooklands: William Boddy.
Triumph of the Red Devil : Brendan Lynch.

Magazines:

Automobile Quarterly, Autosport, Motor Sport,
Motor World, Motoring News, News from the Mews,
Scottish Clubman, Top Gear, Wheelspin.

Chapter 1

In the Beginning

Depending on which history you read, the first motor car to come to Britain was a 4 h.p. Panhard delivered to the Honourable Evelyn Ellis in June 1895. Four months later the first car arrived in Scotland for Mr George Johnstone. This car was shipped from Antwerp on October 25 1895 along with "1 barrel, essence, petroleum" by one of the steamers run by George Gibson & Company in Edinburgh. The original bill of lading for this car is one of the many items in the archives of the Royal Scottish Automobile Club, the pioneering motor club in Scotland.

The second car to be delivered in Scotland was a two-cylinder Panhard Phaeton. It was ordered by T R B Elliot of Kelso who drove the car around Roxburghshire. The red flag law, whereby any motor car driven on the road had to be accompanied by a man walking ahead with a red flag, was still in force in Britain. Elliot, however, appears to have come to "an accommodation" with the local police whereby they would do nothing unless they had a complaint from the public. Alas, early in February 1896, Elliot decided to drive across the border into Berwick upon Tweed, arriving at the town hall at three o'clock in the morning. He was immediately surrounded by no fewer than thirteen police constables. They took his name and he was fined the sum of 6d (two and a half pence). He was also responsible for the legal costs of 19/6 (close to £1) for *"using a horseless carriage without having a man on foot preceding it"*. Elliot therefore became the first of an enormous line of Scots subsequently convicted for driving a motor car.

Every motorist was concerned about that particular law and it was overturned in 1896. What it did, however, was to bring together motorists in Scotland to form a club prepared to fight any future laws the Government might impose to restrict the development and running of the motor car.

The first moves to form such a motor club in Scotland were discussed in the offices of Mitchell & Smith CA at 59 St Vincent Street, Glasgow on May 3 1899 where the guiding light was R J Smith, one of the senior partners in the accountancy business. He was to become the leading figure in those pioneering days in Scotland. Following this meeting, and various letters to other interested parties, a further meeting was convened in the Royal Hotel in Princes Street, Edinburgh on Friday December 1 1899 with the purpose of forming a motor club.

The meeting was attended by some heavy hitters of the time, including the Lord Justice Clerk for Scotland, Sir John Hay Atholl Macdonald, who was asked to chair the meeting. Amongst those present were W Lowrie Sleigh who, with T F Ross, founded the Rossleigh company that, many years later, became Jaguar distributors and were closely involved with the

Robert J Smith, seated right, was founder of the original Scottish Automobile Club. On the left is R.J.Ebblewhite the famous Brooklands timekeeper who officiated on the early Scottish Rallies.

exploits of Ecurie Ecosse. Another was John Stirling who was to become one of Scotland's pioneer car-makers. Our old friend T R B Elliot was invited to attend but sent his apologies.

One of those attending was Claude Johnson, the secretary of the Automobile Club of Great Britain and Ireland - later to become the RAC - and it was he who outlined the method of forming such a club and elucidated its objects. Dr Dawson Turner moved that such a club *"...composed of Automobilists and those interested in automobilism resident in Scotland be formed forthwith. That its objects shall be to promote, encourage and develop automobilism in Scotland."* It was further proposed that the club be called the Scottish Automobile Club and it become *"... the Scottish Branch of the Automobile Club of Great Britain and Ireland to which club a small percentage of the members' subscriptions may be paid in token of affiliation and in support of their efforts with regard to legislation and other matters of common interest."* So, from the beginning, the Scottish Automobile Club, later the Royal Scottish Automobile Club, and the RAC were linked.

In 1906 the Scottish Automobile Club moved its operations to Glasgow and by then it had 620 members. One of the first recorded runs organised by the club took place in 1902. Lord William Weir, a member of the family that owned the huge Weir engineering group, suggested that club members hold a run to his father's mansion at Ladybank near Girvan in Ayrshire.

Lord Weir, who bought his first car, a 3.5 hp Benz, in 1898, was one of the more enthusiastic founders of the Scottish Automobile Club and, one could almost say, its guiding light. He was one of the most prominent Scots to actively promote the motor car and ran his cars in all the Scottish Automobile Club events. He went further and invested in A Darracq & Co Ltd, which had been formed in London to promote and sell French Darracqs in Britain. His original investment of £750 was rapidly increased to nearly £3000.

The first true motor sporting event to touch Scotland was the 1,000 miles Trial of 1900 organised by the RAC and going from London to Edinburgh. As was the case with many early events, these were merely tests of reliability because most cars of the period were less than reliable. Manufacturers supported them vigorously as success in such an event was not only good for publicity but good advertising material. The Gold Medal Award winner

There was a remarkable turnout of cars when Lord Weir invited Scottish Automobile Club members to run to his father's mansion, Ladybank, near Girvan, in 1902

that year was a certain Mr C S Rolls who, with Mr Royce, was to become famous within the motor industry.

As one of Scotland's major exports has been human talent, one could claim that an early Scottish pioneer in racing was Alexander Winton ; not however in Scotland but in America.

Alexander Winton

Alexander Winton was born in Grangemouth in 1860 where his father was an agricultural engineer. Young Alexander was enthusiastic about the sea and took a job on the Atlantic steamers. On one trip to New York he had the chance to join an iron works as an engineer and never looked back. He was an inventor and went into the bicycle business with a bike of his own design. He eventually moved to Cleveland, Ohio, where he founded the Winton Motor Carriage Company, in 1897 to build cars.

It is interesting that one of the first cars he sold in 1898 was to two brothers called Packard who went on to found the Packard company. Winton was a feisty character. In 1902 he was staying in the Ormond Hotel in Ormond Beach, Florida, where a fellow guest was Ransom E Olds. Olds, who founded the REO company and later Oldsmobile, was keen on publicity so he drove his Olds Pirate down to Ormond beach and managed to hit 50 mph. In triumph he returned to the hotel and enthused to his friend Alexander Winton *"what a thrill it is out there. Do you know what it feels like to go 50 miles an hour ?"* Clearly Winton took this as a challenge and a few months later both of them were back at Ormond Beach, Olds with his Pirate and Winton with the Winton Bullet. They drove down to the beach and parked side by side. They saluted each other and then set off with both cars running flat out down the beach, round an improvised arc and back again, recording 57 mph and claiming a dead heat. Winton was hooked. He returned a year later with Bullet II recording nearly 69 mph. The following year, 1904, the first Winter Speed Carnival took place at Ormond Beach so starting the series of beach races that led to the eventual building of the Daytona motor speedway we know today.

In 1924 Alexander Winton gave up the motor industry, founded a company to develop marine diesel engines which he later sold to General Motors.

In 1903, another Scot became probably the first true Scottish racing driver: Andrew Fletcher. He was descended from a historically famous Scottish family and was seriously keen on anything mechanical. Naturally, he was a pioneer motorist and bought a 60Hp Mercedes for racing. He entered it for the 1903 Southport speed trials and, in a match race, defeated one of England's greatest racing drivers of the time, S F Edge.

In 1904 Fletcher continued to support Mercedes and travelled all the way to Nice for the Henri de Rothschild Cup where he finished seventh. There was an amusing incident on that occasion when the local newspaper reported *"Just after passing Antibes, three 90 hp Mercedes racers were seen waiting on the road parallel to the railway line. Andrew Fletcher and Camille Jenatzy were quickly recognised as drivers of two of the monsters whilst Braun was known, at once, to be in charge of the third. He (Braun) is generally accompanied by his collie dog chauffeur, begoggled and leather-coated! No sooner had the*

Alexander Winton with the remarkable Winton Bullet II at the start of a sprint in England in 1903.

Scotland's first true racing driver, Andrew Fletcher from East Saltoun near Edinburgh. He poses at the wheel of his Mercedes.

crawling train gone past than Jenatzy flew past, followed by Fletcher, to the excitement and delight of all."

Meanwhile, back in Scotland in 1904, the country's first brush with motor racing came about through the indefatigable Lord Weir who was now chairman of G & J Weir the Glasgow engineers. As we have seen, Lord Weir was also a director of the French Darracq company's London importers. When Darracq decided to enter for the 1904 Gordon Bennett Cup eliminating trials, they were faced with a rule that stated everything to do with the car had to originate in the country of the entrant.

The Darracqs would obviously run in the French elimination trials to select the French national team to go to Ireland for the race. However, Mr Darracq knew his cars were unlikely to beat the Richard-Brasiers and the Panhards in the French trials so the ploy was to hedge his bets and somehow contrive to enter the Darracqs as British cars for the British elimination trials.

Back in 1900, Lord Weir had watched the start of the Paris-Lyon race and was enthralled. When it was announced that the first Gordon Bennett Cup race would take place in Ireland in 1903, Lord Weir not only planned to see the race but took along with him a group of members of the Scottish Automobile Club. According to the detailed description of the race in Brendan Lynch's superb book *"Triumph of the Red Devil"* *"Scottish Automobile Club members commandeered the Gresham Hotel, their airy kilts adding a dash of traditional colour to the display of strange motoring outfits."* This was the first international race held on British soil and when Alexandre

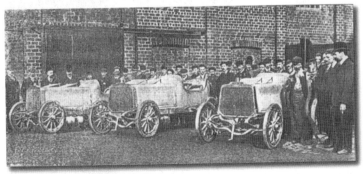

The three Weir-Darracqs lined up outside the Cathcart factory of G & J Weir before going to the 1904 Gordon Bennett Trophy elimination trials.

Darracq decided that Darracq should take part in the 1904 race they were faced with getting through these elimination trials.

The managing director of Darracq in London, Thomas Charles Pullinger, was put in charge of the construction of the team of three "British" Darracqs for the race. Due to Lord Weir's involvement in Darracq, G & J Weir were asked to solve the problem. They only had three months to build and prepare the cars. Mind you, Lord Weir had made a strong case for the decision when he wrote to Darracq's London Manager, Alfred Rawlinson, *"I consider, speaking quite frankly, that no one can do this class of work better than we can. The Suresnes works (Darracq's factory in Paris) are good, but I can show you something better here, and I think you should take the earliest chance to get down to see us"* These were brave words for at that juncture the Weir company had no experience in cars save for a prototype they had built as an experiment. To build three race cars in three months, with no experience, was, however, a monumental task.

Early in February 1904 the technical drawings arrived in Glasgow, complete with the instruction that the three cars had to be in London by noon on April 16 at any cost. The first problem was that Weirs, though they were experienced engineers, had never been faced with measurements in metric units so they had to translate everything into feet and inches before starting work on building the chassis and bodywork. Once this was done, some of the detail work was sub-contracted to firms in Leeds and Sheffield.

By operating three eight-hour shifts a day, Weirs were able to finish the job, but not without problems. The cars proved to be overweight so some parts were then made in aluminium whilst the chassis were drilled with holes. Finally the three "British" Weir-Darracq racers were taken south on a special train with dining and sleeping cars so that the mechanics could continue to work on the train! From London the cars were transported to Paris for their final road tests and check, something upon which Darracq had insisted.

Algernon Lee Guinness bought one of the Weir-Darracqs for the 1905 season and had a number of successes with the car.

Their problems were not over, however, for when they arrived in the Isle of Man for the eliminating trials, the Scottish-built Weir-Darracqs were re-weighed and the team were sent off to shed even more weight. They managed to bring one of the three cars down to the official weight so this car was covertly pushed through scrutineering three separate times so they could get the scrutineers tags for all three team cars!

As it turned out, it was all in vain, as all three cars retired on the first 52 mile lap. French drivers Henri and Edmond lost their brakes and Rawlinson retired the third car just after the start with a broken prop shaft. An interesting sidelight to the actual 1904 race was that the British cars were painted green in recognition of the fact that Britain's first international motor race had taken place in Ireland the previous year and green remained Britain's international racing colour.

It was an inauspicious start to Scotland's involvement in motor racing. Lord Weir was furious and blamed the prop shaft breakage to work done at Darracq in Paris in the final preparation. In a letter to his friend Lord Ailsa, Lord Weir fumed *"...they took out the cardan shaft and hardened it glass-*

Andrew Fletcher, left, about to start a match race at the 1903 Southport Speed trials. His opponent is in a streamlined Mors. Note the starter behind the cars with his flag raised

hard, so that at the first real shock it snapped clean away. Their reason for this I cannot tell. The experience they had in their own cars showed them that the brake attachments were defective. They altered Rawlinson's and left the other two unaltered and under the stress of racing, naturally enough, they gave way."
In truth, Lord Weir's outburst probably concealed his disappointment that the hasty building of the cars had more to do with the problems. This was partially underlined by Algernon Lee Guiness, who bought one of the Weir-Darracqs and ran it in 1905 with considerable success.

There was another interesting development in 1904, also involving Lord Weir. The Hon. Charles Rolls formed his own company in Fulham that year and was looking for an engineering partner. In March he wrote to Lord Weir with a view to Weirs building his cars and Rolls selling them. Weir was interested, and in reply wrote that they were building the Darracqs for the Gordon Bennett race and that Rolls should visit them. Clearly nothing transpired as Rolls signed up with Henry Royce in December 1904 and formed Rolls Royce. It might have been Rolls-Weir.

By 1905 the members of the Scottish Automobile Club had tired of their simple runs so the first actual competitive event took place, the Scottish Four-Day Reliability Trial. It featured hill tests all over Scotland, as far north as Huntly and Keith, but starting and finishing in Glasgow. There were 43 starters who headed out from Glasgow to Edinburgh on the first leg. Some of the competitors merely sat in the cars, whilst their chauffeurs drove.

The event included hill climb tests where an electric wire was stretched across the road. In principle, when the wire was touched by the front wheels of a car it would notify the officials at the summit to start the clock. On reaching the top the officials would telephone the start for another car to be sent on its way. However, the whole idea was scrapped as the first car, a Mors, dragged the wire away from the start and finish line and that was that. It was a lively event, one Argyll driver breaking his propeller shaft

on a hump on the Spittal of Glenshee test. This was not to be the only event around that time as one or two sporting events, including hill climbs, were held but these were not fully competitive and only provided the satisfaction of actually climbing the hill rather than how quickly they did so.

The Scottish Automobile Club, for example, held climbs at Cairn o'Mount and on the hill leading from the river Clyde up to the town of Lanark. Another venue was on the Linlithgow to Bathgate road with a start about two miles from Linlithgow. This latter was first held in 1905 and was actually timed. The club had tents at the start and finish with a telephone land-line covering the climb of just over a mile. Again, they used two wires stretched across the road to trigger the timing; something very advanced for the day. The competitors, however, took their entire families with them on the runs illustrating that it was not a serious competition. Also, it was illegal to have "races" on the public roads so the times were all "unofficial".

The fastest time was 4 minutes 46 seconds for a distance of one and one eighth miles (roughly 12 mph)

Around this time a young lad joined the Scottish Automobile Club as an assistant to R J Smith. He was to become the guiding light in developing motor sport in Scotland for the rest of his life. His name was Andrew Keir Stevenson; "AK" to everyone who knew him. Though his boss, Smith, had a slight interest it was "AK" who threw all of his youthful enthusiasm into pushing anything to do with motor sport.

In the years to his death in the 1980s he was the true "Godfather" of Scottish motor sport. It was he who organised the first British start for the Monte Carlo Rally and he was later honoured by the A.C.de Monaco for his services, with a medal presented to him by Prince Rainier. Stevenson's name will continue to crop up as he was also the link between Scotland and the RAC at the highest level.

Chapter 2
Scotland and the Tourist Trophy

The year 1905 provided another landmark in British motor racing as the Automobile Club of Great Britain and Ireland organised their first major motor race, the A.C. Tourist Trophy.

The concept of running a race for production motor cars was laudable but the problem facing the Club was that there was no established motor racing circuit on which to hold it. Brooklands had not been built at that time but the success of the Tourist Trophy race in 1905 probably planted the germ of the idea of a permanent racing circuit in the mind of H F Locke King who was to start building Brooklands the following year.

So what was the A.C. to do? The British Government had banned motor racing on the public roads and so they found an alternative that lay half way across the Irish Sea, on the Isle of Man.

The Manx Government were perhaps more enlightened, or else more commercially minded, as they were quite happy to close roads for events which would attract visitors to the island. The House of Keys passed a bill authorising both the Gordon Bennett Cup eliminating trials and the Tourist Trophy races to go ahead and gave the highway board the powers to close roads for the purpose of racing.

The road circuit chosen for the Tourist Trophy was the largest circuit ever created in Great Britain measuring 52 miles to the lap and had already been used for the Gordon Bennett Cup.

The circuit must have been stunning. It started from just outside Douglas and headed over to Castletown before going round St Johns and Peel until it reached Kirk Michael and Ballaugh. From here it wound into Ramsey and then took what is the present motorcycle TT course over the Bungalow and Snaefell and back to Douglas.

One of the 14 horse power Argylls speeds down the dusty roads that formed part of the 1905 Tourist Trophy race on the Isle of Man

This would have been a tough course for today's cars but in 1905 it was seriously daunting. The event was run for touring cars that were regulated by their fuel consumption and weight. Any car taking part had to be available for sale to the public and have proper touring bodywork. When the entry list for this first Tourist Trophy race was originally announced it contained a number of factory entered cars including two Rolls Royces entered by the Honorable Charles Rolls and two Napiers by S F and Cecil

Edge. Of Scottish interest, were two Argylls entered by Alex Govan. Later John S Napier entered two of his Arrol Johnstons.

Quick to seize a commercial advantage, the German Continental Tyre company's distributors in Britain offered 100 guineas or a trophy of equivalent value - on the presumption that a gentleman would not wish to accept cash. They also offered a back-up service of spare tyres and assistance to the competitors. As it turned out, they ended up by simply offering a trophy but its award was to create a problem for the eventual winner.

The race was for 4-seat Touring Cars costing up to £1000 and they had to average 25 miles to the gallon of petrol. A number of manufacturers were dubious about achieving this and did not enter but many of those who did resorted to over-gearing their cars, and it is said that one car had been fitted with a 6-speed gearbox, something unknown at that time. The regulations stated that each car would only be allocated nine and a half gallons of petrol for the entire race distance so it was a formidable task, bearing in mind the stone-age technology of the day.

The Arrol-Johnstons were designed by John Napier - no relation to the founder of the Napier car company - and both were 18hp models with two horizontally-opposed cylinders producing 18 bhp at 800 rpm. For the race they used special carburettors to gain the maximum fuel economy/performance ratio.

There were 49 starters for the TT and they assembled at Quarter Bridge on Thursday September 14 1905. In the final instructions, the competitors were urged to take care going through villages. To emphasise this, at places like Ballasalla and Castletown, men with red

John Napier

flags were placed at the entry and exit to both villages and competitors were asked to drive slowly between them.

John Napier powers across the finish line on his Arrol-Johnston to win the first ever Tourist Trophy race held on the Isle of Man in 1905.

Contemporary reports of this race highlight the many problems of racing a car in 1905. A number of teams of horses were on hand to tow the cars to start them but eventually they all got away for four laps of the circuit (a total of 208 miles).

As the cars were set off at intervals, the spectators were in confusion as to who actually led. The first car past the start and finish line at the end of the first lap was Percy Northey's Rolls Royce and it received a huge cheer as it sped by. However, as John Napier's Arrol Johnston was the last car to start, they had a long time to wait until the Scots car appeared and it was two minutes faster than the Rolls. Napier had averaged a remarkable 33 mph for his standing lap. However, on the second lap the exhaust started to come loose and he dashed into the service point to have it repaired letting Northey's Rolls into the lead. Once his exhaust had been repaired Napier stormed back into the race.

With a fixed fuel allowance, the race turned into one of attrition. The first car to run out of fuel was Karl Beireiz's Dixi that rolled to a halt at Ramsey on the third lap. Going into the fourth lap, Northey's Rolls was slightly in the lead and then the real fun started as one by one the other cars ran out of fuel. As an early starter in the race, Northeys Rolls was the first car to cross the finishing line and the crowd went wild. Those who knew the regulations, however, realised they would have to wait something like 24 minutes before they would know whether the Arrol Johnston had run out of fuel or had retaken the lead.

For the 1908 Tourist Trophy Race Arrol Johnston prepared these three sports cars but not one of them finished the race.

What made things worse for the Arrol Johnston team was that the organisers' look-outs at Ramsey and Snaefel, actually missed Napier's car going past and so they thought the car had hit trouble. However, by covering the entire 200 miles in six hours and nine minutes, John Napier beat the Rolls Royce by two minutes and so created history by being the first Scot to win a major racing event and also the first to do it driving a Scottish car.

The fuel tanks of all the finishers were drained and Napier was found to have 8.3 pints of petrol left whilst the Northey Rolls had 6.8. To cap it all, the sister Arrol Johnston finished 4th with 6.2 pints and the other Scottish car, the Argyll driven by W Parker Thomas, finished 8th.

Immediately the Hon. Charles Rolls protested Napier's Arrol Johnston on the grounds that when his silencer came loose the power of his engine would be increased. As the event was strictly for production cars this constituted breaking the rules by Rolls' interpretation. The stewards of the meeting threw out the protest but it left a nasty taste.

A week after the event John Napier, back in Scotland, wrote to Motor World magazine :

"I notice that in some of the London papers it is stated that the Hon C S Rolls entered a protest - which however was not upheld - to my car winning the Tourist Trophy because my silencer became loose, and therefore I was enabled to get more power from the engine than with it fixed, and presumably, it was my intention that it should become detached.

I would like to point out that this silencer, after becoming detached, dragged on the ground, thereby hindering my progress and rendering a serious accident imminent. Secondly, I designed the silencer in question to give extra power to the engine, and therefore would not wish to run in such a contest without it, the extra power gained being equal in this case to over 6% of the total power.

J.S.Napier
Underwood,
Paisley.

Two months after the race, the AC Race Committee decided to issue some special awards to the cars of entirely British manufacture. John Napier wrote to the Automobile Club to say as this had not been mentioned in the regulations, they should not give awards retrospectively. But they did and Napier, the winner, was not given an award on the grounds that he had used "foreign" Continental tyres!

To add further insult, the Club admitted they had not in fact made an actual Tourist Trophy but agreed they would have one designed and produced, possibly in the style of the sculpture of Hermes in the British Museum, in time for the 1906 event! As Motor World remarked, ironically *"So you see, that if you only give the Automobile Club of Great Britain time - plenty of time - it will do things all right"*. The winner of the 1906 event, and first recipient of the trophy was the Hon. C S Rolls!

In 1908 T C Pullinger left the Humber company to become manager of Arrol-Johnston and, believing that motor racing success sold cars, he entered three Arrol-Johnstons for the 1908 Tourist Trophy. However all three of them retired.

In April of that year (1908) the Brooklands track opened near Weybridge in Surrey. In an effort to publicise the circuit, a variety of odd races were held, including the Household Brigade Handicap, open only to officers in the various Guards regiments. The winner was Sir George Abercromby of the Scots Guards with a 58 hp Fiat – probably the first Scot to win a race at Brooklands.

In 1911 Pullinger again entered Arrol Johnstons but this time for the Coupe de L'Auto race held in Boulogne, specifically for small cars.

The three Arrol-Johnstons, with slightly modified engines and shorter wheelbases, were entered for John Reid, James Hodge and the famous racing driver Dario Resta. Incidentally, all three cars carried the Scottish lion rampant on the sides of the cockpit - as opposed to Enzo Ferrari and the horse rampant that became his trademark from the 1930s.

For the 1912 Coupe de L'Auto at Dieppe Arrol-Johnston created a stir when they arrived with their three cars painted in the Gordon Tartan. The race was run together with the French Grand Prix. The car here is Alex Crossmans.

Dario Resta was born in Italy in 1884 but was brought to London by his parents when he was just two years of age. He competed in the first ever race meeting at Brooklands, finishing third and soon became a factory driver. However, in 1909 he had virtually stopped racing to concentrate on his business and was only drawn back into it by Pullinger, who persuaded him to drive one of the Arrol-Johnstons in this race.

In addition to the scratch event for the Coupe de L'Auto in 1911, there was a team prize which Arrol-Johnston won, with Reid finishing seventh, Resta eighth and Hodge eleventh. Shortly afterwards Resta joined the new Sunbeam team and his racing career took off once more. He was later to win the Vanderbilt Cup in America and won the 1916 Indianapolis race in a Peugeot. He was the last European to win Indianapolis until Jim Clark won the Indianapolis 500 in 1965.

An interesting sidelight to the Arrol-Johnstons, was despite the fact the company were pioneers in fitting front wheel brakes to their road cars, they did not put front wheel brakes on their racing cars!

In 1912 Arrol-Johnston again entered three cars for the Coupe de L'Auto for voiturettes, run in conjunction with the French Grand Prix that year. They were all 15.9 hp models with an 8 foot 6 inch wheelbase. Two of them had live axles and the third had a final drive by side chains, but all of them had five speed gearboxes.

The circuit was now at Dieppe and the race took place on the weekend of June 25/26 . The previous year, the organisers of the French Grand Prix had a poor entry of pukka grand prix cars so to make a big field they included the Coupe de L'Auto cars, which actually outnumbered the grand prix cars,

As if to further underline how puny modern grand prix racing has become, this event, in 1912, covered 1,000 miles over two days of racing - five times the length of a modern grand prix distance.

For this race the Scottish company entered three cars: for Alex Crossman, who had raced for Sunbeam, Richard Wyse and James Reid. They were up against factory teams from Hispano Suiza, Vauxhall, Sunbeam and Darracq. To add a touch of colour to the event, all three Arrol-Johnstons were painted in the green and blue plaid of the hunting Gordon tartan!

The cars were hardly in the same racing league as some of the other marques but their performance surprised a lot of people. Richard Wyse was classified in fifth place in the Coupe de l'Auto and James Reid finished in ninth place. Crossman suffered from a cracked radiator due to a flying stone and was forced to retire.

It was to be many years before a Scottish car was to again appear at the French Grand Prix - the Stewart-Ford in the 1990s.

Later in 1912 John Reid set up thirteen records at Brooklands with one of the Arrol-Johnstons.

The special Argyll prepared for the Brooklands records.

In 1913 the Argyll company felt they needed to promote their 15/30 model as they were concerned that the motoring public did not seem to appreciate either their single sleeve-valve engine or their worm-drive back axle, so they looked around for a way to promote this to a wider public. They hit upon the idea of going for some Class D long distance records at Brooklands for the plain and simple reason that no such records existed at that time!

They engaged a professional racing driver in L G "Cupid" Hornstead, who was the official Benz racing manager and a leading driver in his own right. The 2.6 litre four cylinder engine had a cubic capacity of 2614ccs and so

the car was eligible for Class D where the capacity limit was 2868ccs. The car was prepared for the event with the help of Hornstead who reversed the fourth leaf of each of the half-elliptic springs to assist the damping. They also raised the top gear ratio to 3.25:1. The company made up some special sleeves with three inlet and two exhaust ports, modified the con rods and ran a higher compression ratio.

The factory records illustrate the improvement in performance was considerable.

Production 15/30 Argyll	Brooklands version.
28 bhp @ 1,600 rpm	34 bhp @ 1,600 rpm
32 bhp @ 2,000 rpm	43 bhp @ 2,000 rpm
	55 bhp @ 2,800 rpm

The Argyll factory in Dumbarton, meanwhile, designed and built a narrow single-seater racing body in sheet aluminium with a scoop to let cool air down to the crank case. A hand oil pump was mounted on the side of the body to assist in lubrication but otherwise the engine was relatively standard. The car weighed about 24 cwts when delivered to Brooklands and the record attempt started on May 19 1913 at 6.21 in the morning.

Hornstead shared the driving with another Brooklands regular, W G Scott. The engine's designer, Perrot, had brought everything necessary for a serious attempt with spare parts to cover any eventuality. Before the start, however, Perrot explained to the drivers that he had devised a scheme to ensure that the drivers remembered to pump oil to the sleeve valves. If no smoke showed from the exhaust he would wave a white flag to remind whoever was driving to pump in more oil; if too much smoke appeared a blue flag would bid the driver to turn off the supply ! At each stop a mechanic would produce a huge syringe and squirt castor oil into the worm-drive back axle. During Scott's initial spell the Argyll averaged over 72 mph but when Hornstead took over he suffered an air lock in the fuel feed. With Scott back at the wheel, a rear tyre punctured and he limped to the pit on the bare wheel. With the rain beginning to fall the team called it a day after 14 hours when they had covered one thousand and sixteen miles at an average speed of 72.59 mph. This exceeded, by nearly 78 miles, the world's 14 hour record set up by S F Edge's 60 hp Napier in 1907. The Argyll also chalked up 26 Class D records from one to 14 hours and 50 to 1,000 miles.

A week later they decided to try again, this time starting at 5.55 a.m. and they were quicker with a lap speed of 78 mph early on. Then they lost 7 minutes with fused plugs and a broken fuel line which meant they had to hack away the undershield with a chisel. Then came the thunder and lightning and Hornstead had a huge skid on the Railway straight. They took some more records including one held by Sunbeam but it all came to an end when a track rod end came away. The Argyll spun on the Home banking and collided with the barriers on the Railway Straight demolishing a telegraph pole. Scott was slightly hurt and Argyll went back to Scotland satisfied with their performance.

What is not well known is that Argyll planned to go back to Brooklands the following year with a poppet-valve 2840cc engine. The company had advanced to the stage where the engine was put on test and it produced a remarkable 75 bhp at 3,300 rpm. Chief engineer Perrot was confident they could take back their 1913 record that had meanwhile been broken. Unfortunately the first World War broke out in 1914 and the whole plan was abandoned.

Chapter 3
The 1920s and 1930s

During the 1920s and 1930s there was little or no high speed activity in Scotland but there were a few ex-patriate Scots involved in racing, one of which was the famous "Bentley Boy" Glen Kidston whose family owned the Clyde Shipping Company in Glasgow.

The Beardmore company started in Glasgow in 1920 and three years later introduced a sports model with a 1656cc engine rated at 11 hp. This was so successful they then enlarged it to 2 litres, calling it the Super Sport. It became quite popular for sprints and hill climbs. One of Britain's leading racing drivers, Cyril Paul was engaged to race the factory car and lowered the Shelsley Walsh hill record in 1925 beating such cars as Raymond Mays' Brescia Bugatti and Humphrey Cook's TT Vauxhall. Beardmores flirtation was brief: one season.

Scotland was later pushed into the limelight with Sir Malcolm Campbell's decision to attack the Land Speed Record in South Africa

In 1928 Campbell had commissioned Vickers to design a streamlined body for his Bluebird which then went to Daytona and set a new land speed record of 206.956 mph. He was followed by a phalanx of other cars including Ray Keech with the Triplex Special, powered by no fewer than three Liberty aircraft engines, Frank Lockhart with the Stutz Blackhawk Special - in which he was killed in final attempt - and Sir Henry Segrave who set the new record. For a 1929 record attempt he commissioned Arrol-Aster in Dumfries, formerly Arrol Johnston, to redesign his 1928 record car with the radiator mounted once more at the front and with better streamlining, particularly at the rear of the car. Once it was completed the Napier-engined car was shipped to Verneuk Pan in South Africa for a further record attempt. The trip was a disaster for on April 12 his fastest speed through the kilometre was 217.6 mph; nearly 20 mph slower than Seagrave's existing record of 231.44 mph set just one month before.

Beardmore had a short-lived flirtation with motor sport to promote their sports model. They gave it to the experienced Cyril Paul to drive, here seen sliding round Shelsey Walsh hill climb.

Two years later Campbell had Bluebird completely rebuilt, this time by Thompson and Taylor at Brooklands and so Scotland's involvement with

the land speed record was short and sweet. The Royal Scottish Museum in Chambers Street, Edinburgh has, amongst its archives, the wind tunnel model of the Dumfries-built Campbell car.

The year 1934 saw the arrival of Peter Mitchell-Thomson, grandson of Sir Mitchell Mitchell-Thomson, a former Lord Provost of Edinburgh. The Mitchell-Thomsons were founders of "The Scottish Shipping Line" based in Glasgow. Peter's interest in racing started when he was at Winchester school. His mother bought a TT Replica Frazer Nash in 1933 which spurred his interest and in 1934 she bought another one which was the first car he raced. At the same time he commissioned Frazer-Nash to build him a single seater to race at Brooklands.

Various private entrants had converted their sports cars to offset single seaters but this was the first pure single seater built by the factory. The car used a sports car chassis modified with the steering and pedals set in the centre and a narrow body. The engine was the new overhead cam engine with a Marshall supercharger. The car was completed in August 1934 in time for Peter Mitchell-Thomson to race it in the Brooklands 500 Mile race. It retired with a blown head gasket. He raced the car until 1938 when it was sold to an Australian and spent part of its life down under.

There were comparatively few Scots participating in motor racing events in the 1930s. However, one who was to make a name for himself within motor racing both before and after the war, was John Eason Gibson from Glasgow.

In an article for Country Life magazine in 1967 he wrote of his early days in the late 1920s.

"...I acquired my first car, a magnificent second-hand 1926 Chain-gang Frazer Nash. This was an example of the Boulogne sports model that had been raced. With the assistance of the foreman of the local garage it was tuned and titivated until we were convinced it was better than factory fresh. Motoring and motor racing had become my fetish.

"Back in those days of little traffic, there was a pleasant custom of setting up unofficial records from Glasgow to the various venues of the leading speed-trials and hill climbs. My Frazer Nash figured often enough in this pastime.

"It is amazing, looking back, to discover that most of the fun one had out of motoring pure and simple was obtained out of the difficulties and inconveniences, rather than from the occasions when everything went with utter smoothness. I can recall on one occasion the first-gear chain drive breaking in a sodden Devonshire lane on my Frazer Nash, and it being necessary for my wife and me to manhandle the car upward while wedging second gear in its oily nakedness, into position. Incidents like this served to help my wife, of but two weeks duration, to learn some of the more 'likeable' sides of my nature."

It was not long after this that John Eason Gibson moved to England to be closer to the racing scene and so began many adventures with racing cars. He eventually completed his career as the firm but amiable secretary of the British Racing Drivers Club.

Then there was William Leslie Innes.

Bill Innes was born on July 17 1915 in Hawick. The family owned A P Innes & Co, a knitwear firm that traded as Braemar. He was educated at Merchiston Castle, Dumfries, and later at Morges in Switzerland before joining Harrods in London. However, this did not fit in with his interests and he joined the Riley Motor Company in Coventry as a trainee. In 1935 he bought a second hand Ulster TT Replica and later traded it for another

Riley. In 1937 he competed in the Monte Carlo Rally with a Riley Sprite with his brother Riddell Innes as his co-driver. They finished third in the up to 1500cc class.

The following year, 1936, he ordered a brand new Frazer Nash-BMW 328. This car came about when the Aldington brothers, who owned Frazer-Nash, saw the tremendous potential of the then-new BMW 328 and came to a licensing agreement with BMW in Munich to build the car with right hand drive in Britain. It proved to be quite a popular car for motor sport, particularly in Scotland. Indeed, the first three FN-BMWs to be built in Britain were sold to Scots. John Flint in East Lothian bought the first, followed by Johnny Millar in Glasgow and Tom Meikle in Perth. They were followed by David H Murray, Captain Grant of the Scots whisky company and then Bill Innes who took delivery of his car in January 1938. Innes competed in the Paris-Nice rally that included speed tests up the La Turbie hill climb, just outside Monaco, finishing 8th overall, a tremendous performance. He also won the cup for the highest placed foreign driver.

Bill Innes was very friendly with another Scot, David Hugh Murray from Edinburgh (not to be confused with David Murray of Ecurie Ecosse.) who had moved to England. Murray had independent means and took a ten per cent shareholding in Frazer Nash alongside the Aldington brothers. Murray was a regular racer with Frazer Nash models from Chain Gangs to BMW's and in 1950 he bought a Bristol 400 to compete in the Monte Carlo Rally with Bill Innes as his co-driver. They both ran in the Monte and the Daily Express rally in 1951 in the Bristol. William Innes' last competition event was the 1952 Monte Carlo rally when he co-drove in a Ford Consul.

David Hugh Murray left Scotland in the mid-1930s and bought a garage in Pinner. He became friendly with the Aldington brothers who, with Archie Frazer Nash, were the mainstays of the Frazer Nash company. He bought a chain-gang version which he raced and was one of the first owners of a Frazer-Nash BMW. He entered the car for the 1937 Le Mans 24 hour race with one of the most famous racing drivers of the day, the South African, Pat Fairfield. Fairfield had made his name racing ERAs and had his own car (R4A) with which he was very successful.

Fairfield's racing experience made him the obvious first driver and eight laps into the race he came upon an accident involving one of the German BMW 328s at Arnage. Fairfield's Frazer-Nash BMW plunged off the road and cartwheeled, killing Fairfield. David Murray rebuilt the car and went on to race it both before and immediately after the war, before buying a Le Mans Replica Frazer Nash. In the 1950s he came back to his native Scotland and raced his Frazer Nash giving commentators nightmares when the "other" David Murray, of Ecurie Ecosse, also raced.

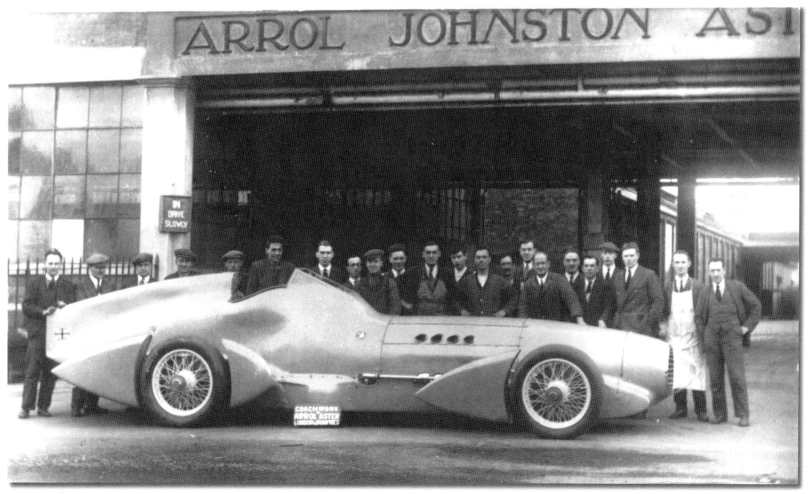

Sir Malcolm Campbell's Bluebird was sent to the old Arrol Johnston/Arrol Aster factory in Dumfries to have this new body built for record attempts in 1937. (Courtesy Dumfries Museum)

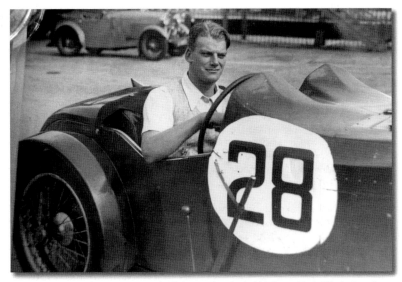

Peter Mitchell-Thomson, later Lord Selsdon, at the wheel of his Frazer-Nash "Chain Gang" at Brooklands in 1938 (Courtesy Lord Selsdon Archive)

In 1932 the Scottish Sporting Car Club was formed in Glasgow and the members enthusiasm to find somewhere to hold true speed events led them, in 1934, to the East of Scotland and the little town of Bo'ness. They were able to persuade the local town council to let them use a small and narrow hill that led from the main road to Grangemouth up through the Kinneil Estate. The hill climb course itself was tarmac but after the finish line all the competitors had to return to the grass paddock beside the main road by way of an unsurfaced track that wound round Kinneil House. This same unsurfaced piece of road was still being used in the 1960s when the local council decided it needed the land for a new housing estate and stopped the Bo'ness Hill Climbs.

The winner of that first Bo'ness Hill Climb was Jimmy McCredie with a Model 90 Sunbeam. He was five seconds quicker than Arthur Clarkson's Ford V8 but at that time they only used a shorter section than was to be used after the War.

The Kinneil Estate was originally owned by the Duke of Hamilton, a diplomat and sportsman. In 1936 he was a British official at the Berlin Olympic Games and met Hitler's deputy Rudolph Hess. During the war Hess flew to Scotland in an attempt to arrange a peace treaty and parachuted out of his Messerschmitt near Eaglesham on the outskirts of Glasgow. He was attempting to get to the Duke of Hamilton apparently in the hope that he could help him to negotiate a peace deal between Hitler and Churchill.

Many years later, in the 1960s, the Duke's son, Angus, took up motor racing and, as Angus Clydesdale, raced a 2 litre Lola sports car and a 250F Maserati in historic events. Angus Clydesdale is the present Duke of Hamilton.

Back in 1924, however, the Duke sold the Kinneil estate to Bo'ness Town Council. Once agreement had been reached with Scottish Sporting Car Club, the Council built the safety banks and corrected the cambers of the road.

As for the hill climb course itself, it started from the main road with a short straight into First bend followed by a dark alleyway between the trees to the tighter right hander at Second bend. This led into the esses of the Courtyard with buildings and walls to avoid. Once out of this it was a straight line uphill to the top save for Snake bend, a right-left

curve half way up. It was this curve that saw the only fatality ever recorded at Bo'ness when, in 1951, John Struthers touched a bank and his Allard overturned.

Generally speaking, motor cycle speed events were more prolific than car events but in June 1933 a sprint was held on the wide promenade sands in Kirkcaldy. It was basically a motor cycle event but there were two classes for cars. Edinburgh driver Alastair Cormack entered a special bodied Speed 20 Rover Meteor and won the scratch race with ease. However, in the handicap event, the low tension lead broke and left him stranded.

The 1935 Le Mans 24 Hour race saw two Scots to take part, Margaret Allan from Perth, in an all-woman MG PA team and Peter Mitchell-Thomson with a "Chain-Gang" Frazer Nash. The Mitchell-Thomson car retired with oil problems but Margaret Allan finished 26th out of 28 finishers.

The Diminutive Margaret Allen from Perth is almost dwarfed by the wheel from the Bentley she raced at Brooklands and with which she won her 120mph badge.

In the 1930s competition cars often had to compete in different types of event. The Austin Company developed a new car for competition in 1935 that they used for the Lands End Trial. Then they developed a team of them to run at Le Mans with special alloy cylinder heads designed by supercharger specialist, Murray Jamieson. After this, the three Le Mans cars were supercharged and run in trials and hill climbs. They had been given the name "Grasshoppers".

Left Behind. Peter Mitchell-Thomson's Frazer-Nash (15) is left behind at the pits at the start of the Ards Tourist Trophy race of 1935(Courtesy Lord Selsdon Archive)

For the 1936 Le Mans another four new cars were built but all four of them retired. One of them, COA119 was raced by Kay Petre in the Donington 12 hours and finished fifth. Two years later, three of the factory Grasshoppers were sold to Scottish competitors, two of whom happened to be Austin dealers. One was George Valentine in Perth and the other Benbie Carlaw in Glasgow. A short time later a fourth Grasshopper came to Scotland for Jack Wilson the Austin dealer in Dunoon. Jack had been an Austin apprentice at the time and phoned his mother to see what could be done to buy one of the Grasshoppers. The car survived the war and Jack - or Jock as he usually calls himself - still brings it out on the Royal Scottish Automobile Club veteran car runs. He brought it to the Mount Stuart Classic in September 2002 where two of Britain's leading racing car designers, Peter Stevens (BMW - Audi - MG Le Mans cars) and Tony Southgate (B.R.M. Ford etc) could not believe their eyes as it was the first Grasshopper they had ever seen in the "flesh".

In 1938 the Scottish Office, in developing a better road programme, decided to bypass a notoriously narrow and hilly road between Arrochar and Inveraray. Part of this road, which, weaves up Glen Croe, was originally built in the middle of the 18th century by the famous English General Wade and his sappers. It was built so that the English army could make a rapid response to any insurrections by Highlanders opposed to the result of the Battle of Culloden. The road was called "Rest and be Thankful" This road was a killer for both horse drawn traffic and early motor cars. The gradient, overall, was around 1 in 8 but the final hairpin was nearer 1 in 3 making it tough to get round. Indeed there was always a wide space at the top where motorists could stop and let their radiators cool down and take water from the stream. A roughly hewn stone, placed by the sappers just beyond the final tight hairpin bend, marks the spot.

With the new road, the old road was left to wrack and ruin, the land being turned over to the Forestry Commission.

Alastair Cormack prepares to take his factory Alta racer up Shelsey walsh hill climb. (Sandy Cormack)

It was not until 1947, two years after the end of world war two, that the Royal Scottish Automobile Club, led by the indefatigable A K Stevenson, made an approach to the Commission to have the use of the old "Rest" as a hill climb venue. The deal was that the club could run their hill climb provided they patched up the surface of the old road to a reasonable state and respect the young timber the Commission had planted. Two years later the Rest and Be Thankfull hill climb opened for business with some of the leading hill climb drivers in Britain taking part. The event was to continue in this role well into the 1960s when a number of near misses - including Peter Lawson taking his four wheel drive BRM over the edge and down the hillside - saw the climb closed as a competition venue.

The 1938 Le Mans 24 Hour Race saw the young former Glaswegian T A S O Mathieson running a Talbot T150C with Freddy Clifford. They had a great race and were lying in 17th place after 159 laps, when the car lost its electrics. The following year Mathieson was back at Le Mans in another Talbot but this time there were two other Scots running in the race. Rob

BRIGHTON AND HOVE MOTOR CLUB LTD.

SPEED TRIALS : BRIGHTON.

This is to Certify that *a super charged Alta*

driven by *A. J. Cormack*

attained an average speed of *70·98* m.p.h.

from a Standing Start, timed over half a mile.

R.A.C. Timekeeper.

September 26ᵗʰ 1936
Date

Hon. Secretary of the Meeting.

The Certificate given to Alastair Cormack when he set his record at the Brighton Speed Trials in 1936. (sandy Cormack)

Alastair Cormack with the Alta sports-racing car he ran in the 1930s. (Sandy Cormack)

Walker was sharing a Delahaye with Ian Connell and they finished strongly in 8th place overall.

Rob Walker was always a colourful character and a true gentleman to boot. His father was heir to the Johnny Walker Scotch whisky company. Rob was a very competent racing driver and was later to become the successful entrant of Stirling Moss, Jo Siffert and many others in motor racing.

At Le Mans in 1939, Rob displayed all of the "Bertie Wooster" elements of the British gentleman. When he took over for the evening driving stint from Ian Connell at 8.00 pm, Rob took the wheel wearing a beautifully-cut dark blue pin-striped suit and tie. The following morning, when he was called upon to drive again, he had changed to his Sunday morning dress of a suit in Prince of Wales check. When his co-driver's feet were badly burned on the pedals, Walker raced to the end of the event in rope-soled plimsolls that had been soaked in buckets of cold water. When Rob married in 1940, he promised his wife he would only do sprints and hill climbs and would never race again.

The other Scot in the 1939 Le Mans race was Peter Mitchell-Thomson, now Lord Selsdon following the death of his father. He finished fourth overall, an incredible performance, partnered by his friend Lord Waleran in one of the huge V12 Lagondas. He little realised that he would return ten years and a world war later as a winner of the race.

The Lagonda team that finished third and fourth at Le Mans in 1939. Left to right, Arthur Dobson, Charles Brackenbury, Earl Howe, Lord William Waleran, and Lord Peter Selsdon. The Dobson/Brackenbury V12 Lagonda is in the background (Photo courtesy Lord Selsdon Archive)

Bill Innes from Hawick taking part in the La Turbie Hill Climb in 1939 with his Frazer Nash-BMW 328. (Graham Gauld Archive)

Chapter 4
The War Ends and Racing Begins.

In 1946 the Scottish enthusiasts began to return from the war and started searching around for venues on which to race. There were very few actual racing cars about but Scottish Sporting Car Club decided to reopen the Bo'ness hill climb and on Sunday September 7 1946 the first post-war event took place. What was significant about this, save for the polyglot selection of cars, was a strange little car brought northwards by Colin Strang, the Strang 500, one of the first 500cc racing cars to be built. Small motor cycle-engined racing cars were not new. As early as 1925 the Jappic appeared at Brooklands powered by a 350cc JAP engine (J.A.P. stood for J.A.Prestwich the manufacturers of the engine and not, as one recent historian remarked *"...a Japanese engine."*). Nine years later another 350 using a Blackburn engine also appeared but these were built to attack class J records. There are also vague records - which the writer has not been able to confirm - that just before the war a twin-cylinder Scott-engined car was built in Glasgow as a dirt-track racer. It was water-cooled and the car was rear-engined.

Colin Strang's appearance at Bo'ness made some of the Scots interested in this type of racing. Roy Clarkson, a dentist from Falkirk, who was a real character, had a seat in Strang's car and immediately ordered an Iota. Shortly after this he moved to England and established a practice where he had his NHS patients in one surgery and his private clients in another where he also practiced hypnotism ! Roy also bought a Ferrari (195 Touring Coupe Chassis 0123S) in which he competed in the Tulip Rally with fellow Scot, and Autosport founder/editor Gregor Grant. Roy hated the car as it was so unreliable and sold it. He liked the Touring of Milan coupe body, however, and had it copied and put on a Triumph TR2-engined Morgan sports car. This *"Forgan"* or *"Morrari"* was later bought by Scots rallying enthusiast Sandy Forrest.

Another to embrace 500cc racing was Lord David Strathcarron. Though born in London, he was a Macpherson from Newtonmore and was always a bit of a lad in a racing car. Even today he occasionally rides up to the House of Lords on his BMW motor cycle and was seen inspecting an old Marwyn at Goodwood a couple of years ago. He tells the story of taking his brand new Marwyn 500 to Thruxton, long before it became a motor racing circuit, and having a monumental accident with it. *"We had fitted 19 inch wheels to the car so the centre of gravity left a lot to be desired. I came into this corner and the next thing the car looped the loop; luckily I was thrown on to the wet grass. Of course I was not wearing a helmet at the time but after that we fitted 15 inch wheels and thankfully never had that problem again."*

David Murray, later to found Ecurie Ecosse, was active immediately after the was and raced this 4CL Maserati originally owned by Johnny Wakefield.

Pat Prosser was one of the first Scots to race Coopers in 500cc Formula 3. He then took on the Scottish agency for Cooper and advertised his wares for the 1949 racing season.

Perhaps the most enterprising Scottish driver was Pat Prosser whose family business distributed Morris cars in Glasgow. Not only did he buy a Cooper but arranged with John and Charles Cooper that he would be Cooper's agent in Scotland. By 1949 he was advertising the cars and offering 500cc models for £575 and 1,000cc cars for £775. It was little wonder, then, that Bellshill garage man and motorcycle engineer Joe Potts Jnr. bought one as did Glasgow businessman Comish Hunter. Of the three, Hunter was probably the most successful. Later, when Joe Potts built his own 500cc car, Hunter became his first customer.

During the 1949 motor racing season David Murray, Edinburgh accountant, bought a Maserati 4CL from Reg Parnell's Scuderia Ambrosiana and had his first major race with it at the Easter Monday Goodwood meeting run by the BARC. He ran in the Easter Handicap race won by Parnell in his new Maserati 4CLT/48. David Murray finished fifth. He then went on to Jersey for the International Jersey Road Race and against all the leading continental drivers, he finished tenth.

In 1951, David Murray had changed his 4CL Maserati for a 4CLT/48 model that he bought from his old friend Reg Parnell. The photo was taken during practice for the 1951 German GP where he crashed heavily and retired from racing: however he did race twice more after he had formed Ecurie Ecosse.

Back in Scotland, people were still trying to create interest in motor racing. Lothian Car Club in Edinburgh sounded out the town council of St Andrews in Fife. Their idea was to hold a race meeting on the wide sands that run alongside golfing's famous Old Course. The date was Saturday July 30 1949 and Lothian set about trying to find entrants.

Scottish Sporting Car Club held its Bo'ness hill climb in June, as usual, and Denis Poore created a sensation with his ex-Hans Reusch Alfa Romeo grand prix car, setting a new record of 33.9 seconds for the half mile course. It also saw the first visit to Scotland by 19-year old Stirling Moss with an 1100cc Cooper. Stirling was actually the first person at that meeting to break Bob Gerard's hill record of 36.3, recorded in an ERA the previous year, but faster cars came up behind him until Poore dominated the meeting with his remarkable time. Fastest Scot was David Murray with the original R1A ERA and was the only Scot to break 40 seconds. The car was actually owned by David Hampshire who shared the driving with Murray. David Murray also shared ERA R12B when it, too, was owned by David Hampshire.

The big news in 1949, however, was the inauguration of Rest and Be Thankful hill climb by the Royal Scottish Automobile Club. At over a mile long and with some steep gradients it was the longest hill climb in Britain and became a major event in the British Hill Climb Championship. Denis Poore was clearly out to make it a Scottish double but was foiled by the legendary Raymond Mays driving ERA R4D who set the initial course record in 1 minute 8.6secs.

Racing on the sands of St Andrews was not new as it had been tried prior to the second world war. However, Lothian Car Club revived the event in 1949 where young Ron Flockhart had success with his MG TC.

The first class at that event was for racing cars of 500ccs with four entrants, all Scots. Joe Potts was quickest with a one second advantage over Pat Prosser and Comish Hunter all of them in Coopers. The fourth competitor was D Y Henderson in an MHM, a special built by John Scott Moncrief and based around a Marwyn 500.

The outright fastest of the Scots was the ebullient Mirrlees Chassels with his Special who proved to be quicker than Ken Hutchinson in his Alfa Romeo. The meeting was a tremendous success as it offered the thousands of spectators probably the best viewing conditions for any speed event in Britain: and what's more it was free !

After a lot of speculation, Lothian Car Club were finally able to organise their Sand race meeting on the West Sands at St Andrews. Some competitors were a bit cautious about racing their cars on sand normally covered by salt water but the club went ahead. They even managed to rope in the Scottish Daily Mail to present a 100 guinea trophy for the winner of the main event of the day, the 30 mile handicap race. Thanks to the Daily Mail one of the star attractions at the event was the appearance of film star Richard Attenborough, at the height of his fame as a dashing young actor.

St Andrews sands again, with Edinburgh motor trader John Brown winning his heat with his Riley Special.

The Lothian Car Club organisation was stretched to the limit and turned out to be chaotic. Few, if any, of the officials had any experience and had not asked clubs like Scottish Sporting Car Club to help; so, all told, the event was a bit of a fiasco. Coupled with the organisational problems, the sea began to recapture its beach and the track had to be modified towards the end of the afternoon. As the final event was the main race of the day you can imagine the frustration and angst involved. Added to this, despite the fact the organisers ran the sprint events before the handicap events, they did not modify the handicaps they had set on practice times. Any "sporting" competitor of those days would tell you that you always slightly stroked the car in practice to get a good handicap, particularly when you knew your handicap would not be changed despite your performance in the scratch events.

The winner of the 30 lap main handicap race was Gillie Tyrer with his streamlined Frazer Nash BMW. This was one of the BMW team cars in the 1940 Mille Miglia which had originally been ordered by the Aldington Brothers, the BMW distributors, but had been marooned in Germany at the outbreak of war. The car was eventually delivered to the Aldingtons after the war ended. Today it has been restored to its 1940 BMW factory trim and is in the BMW museum in Munich.

The opening event was a sprint for 1100cc racing cars and was won by Comish Hunter's Cooper JAP ahead of Moncrief's MHM and Edinburgh motor dealer John Brown in a very fast Riley Special. Brown was later to win the class on the second runs. He also won the 1500cc class ahead of a young ex-soldier engineer called Ron Flockhart who was airing his MGTC. It was Flockhart's first racing event. Gillie Tyrer in the FN BMW won the unlimited sprint class with John Brown again second.

Ron Flockhart demonstrated his future promise by winning the handicap race with the MG and the John Brown Trophy. In the 30 lap final, however, Gillie Tyrer was on scratch. Ron Flockhart at one stage held the lead but Tyrer was driving as fast as he could on a sand track that was already breaking up badly and took a well merited win. Gillie received the big Daily Mail Trophy only to lose it when there was a protest to the RAC as a result of which the race was declared null and void. Despite all this, Lothian Car Club applied for a date in 1950 to repeat the exercise.

If nothing else, the St Andrews affair helped focus more attention on the need to find a true motor racing circuit in Scotland. The Scottish Sporting Car Club, which probably had more experience than any, joined forces with A K Stevenson of the Royal Scottish Automobile Club in an approach to the

Earl of Dalhousie for the use of Easthaven aerodrome near Carnoustie in Angus. Everything seemed to be going smoothly and a date had been put on the calendar for 1950 but the Earl of Dalhousie suddenly collapsed and died and that put an end to the whole project.

The newly formed Scottish Motor Racing Club had discussions with Edinburgh City Council to use the huge promenade between Granton and Cramond as a sprint venue. This would have been sensational had it come off, as this promenade features long curves, rather than being a straight line sprint such as at Brighton. The project moved to the Lord Provost's Committee but nothing was ever heard of it again.

SMRC was also involved in the plan to use the little airport at Grangemouth, not far from Bo'ness, and even booked a date in the 1950 calendar. As time went on, however, doubts began to form as to whether anything would come of this. The local council and the Air Ministry were still negotiating when the time came for SMRC to pull the plug on the whole venture; at least as far as the 1950 season was concerned.

As we shall see, it is ironic that of all the clubs in Scotland that became involved with motor racing, the aptly named Scottish Motor Racing Club was the least successful in obtaining circuits until the mid-1960s and Ingliston. Today SMRC is Scotland's major motor racing club.

On July 2 1950 Lothian Car Club returned to St Andrews for their second sand race meeting. Though the sun shone on the morning of the event the organisers kept telephoning the nearby RAF base at Leuchars for an update. Clouds began to form, blotting out the sun but Leuchars kept insisting that it would be ok and so it proved even though the rest of Fife suffered a downpour.

As was the case the previous year, there were a series of sprints followed by handicap races and the organisers, along with the Scottish Daily Mail had as their special guest, Jean Kent one of Britain's leading film stars of the 1950s. Again there were problems. There was a public address system but few of the many spectators could hear what was going on. It was clear that the sprints were not as good as the actual handicap races and Lothian planned to drop these sprints the following year. There were two main handicap races, one of ten miles and the other of 30. In the former Ron Flockhart managed to beat his

In 1950 Ron Flockhart was to go back to St Andrews and win his race. His prize was presented by Jean Kent, one of Britain's leading film stars of the time.

handicap and win the race. In the 30 lap handicap Gillie Tyrer, who had "won" the previous year, was out-handicapped and could only finish in third place. The winner was Border farmer Alec Calder driving a Brooklands Riley. Alec later married Mattie Clark, Jim Clark's eldest sister.

August 25 1950 was an important date for motor sport enthusiasts in Britain for that was the date on which the first issue of a new weekly motoring magazine, devoted entirely to motor sport, hit the news stands: Autosport. The enthusiast behind it was a former cartoonist on the Bulletin newspaper in Glasgow called Gregor Grant. He had persuaded industrialist and racing driver Denis Poore, amongst others, to provide the financial backing. Needless to say there was a Scottish column right from the start, the original correspondent going by the name of Bodach (The Gaelic for "cantankerous old man!"). As they published his picture at the head of the page, everyone in Scotland knew it was Alex Bruce, who was at the time probably the only Scot covering motor sport and his name appeared everywhere. Whereas Alex could never be totally cantankerous he occasionally had his moments.

Meanwhile a group of enthusiasts were quietly working away at a plan to start motor racing in Scotland on a proper circuit and their dream came true later that year.

Alec Calder, the Border farmer, was very successful driving his Brooklands Riley. He wears the winners garlands from a race in Ireland. His Brooklands Riley was sold to Innes Ireland.

This first motor race meeting was run on October 7 1950. It took place at one of those little relief airfields the British Government built in the Borders of Scotland in preparation for war. It was called Winfield and skirted of one of the small roads that interlace the Borders around the towns of Duns and Chirnside. Ironically another airfield was built only a few miles away at Charterhall and it too was to be called into service as a racing circuit – indeed it lasted as a circuit longer than did Winfield.

The meeting was organised by the Berwick and District Motor Club, Lothian Car Club and the Hawick and Border Motor Club and it was a brave bunch of drivers who turned out for this first race meeting. Virtually nobody in Scotland had any experience of running a motor race and there were a number of people roped in from south of the border to give advice. As can be imagined, there was also a remarkable selection of cars from road cars to specials and proper racing cars. Reg Parnell, a great friend of David Murray, was persuaded by Murray, and his fellow Merchiston Motors sidekick Wilkie Wilkinson, to come north and bring his 4CLT Maserati. Murray already owned Reg's ex-Johnny Wakefield Maserati 4CL and Murray and Wilkinson also part-owned ERA R1A, the original ERA, so all three cars were pressed into service at the meeting.

The honour of winning the very first race at Winfield went to the local Ford dealer from Chirnside, Jock McBain. It was perhaps appropriate that Jock should win the race as he had been one of the driving forces at Berwick and District Motor Club that secured the two-year lease on Winfield from the Royal Air Force.

Driving his little MG, Jock won the sports car race up to 1200ccs, followed home by Kirkcaldy butcher Tom Christie, in an HRG with Border farmer Alec Calder third, in a Brooklands Riley. Alec was later to sell the Riley to the son of a Dumfriesshire veterinary surgeon, Robert McGregor Innes Ireland.

Only five cars made it to the line for the 500cc racing car class and one of them was Comish Hunter driving the JP 500, the first production racing car ever built in Scotland. Hunter's car was actually the second chassis built, the first was fitted with a Vincent HRD 1100cc engine by the car's manufacturer, Joe Potts. The main opposition to them came from Sassenach Bobby Leapingwell with his Cooper. It was obvious after practice that nobody was going to get near the flying Hunter. Pat Prosser made it a Scots 1-2 by finishing second nine seconds ahead of Leapingwell and ahead of John Moncrieff's special the MHM. The only other competitor, David Swan from Duns, retired on the opening lap in his older Cooper.

It is quite surprising how many drivers who were to become well known in British racing took part in that inaugural meeting. For example, Gillie Tyrer won two races with his 328 BMW, beating Bob Dickson from Carlisle who was running a Healey. Bob was later to become a staunch supporter of Aston Martins and competed in a number of International races. In the same race was another young Scottish driver called Jimmy Stewart with a Healey Silverstone.

The main racing car race was dominated by Reg Parnell, who won by nearly ten seconds from David Murray in the older 4CL Maserati, with Wilkie Wilkinson third in the ERA. In fourth place was Edinburgh motor dealer John Brown with a Riley special which he shortly afterwards sold and bought an HWM sports car with cycle wings. Joe Potts driving his own Vincent-engined JP was fifth. The honour of holding the first lap record at Winfield went to Reg Parnell in 1:28.5 or 81.86 mph. The sports car lap record was taken by Gillie Tyrer in the BMW in 1:31.8.

After the successful running of this event, a meeting was held to discuss plans for 1951 and it was agreed that two race meetings should be held, one in July and one in October. Scotland's active participation in motor racing history had begun.

The start of the first official motor race to take place in Scotland. It was in October 1950 at Winfield and a mixed bag of sports cars took off with Ewart McCartney's Singer in the foreground.

During 1950 additional support for motor racing in Scotland came in the House of Lords from Lord Weir. Lord Weir made the point that county authorities should allow roads under their jurisdiction to be available for three days in the year for motor racing. He opened his remarks by saying *"For some time I have studied with considerable interest the development of road racing all over the world. It seems to me it gives opportunities in three directions. The first is in the field of scientific design, the second is an appeal and an opportunity to youth and adventurer, and the third is that wonderful thing - British prestige. My suggestion is quite definitely, but entirely personal, that legislation should permit, through a single clause Act of Parliament, that one or two county authorities in Scotland should be given powers to close enough roads to give a circuit for three days of the*

Two great rivals in the Winfield days were John Brown - now with one of the ex-works HWMs and Gillie Tyrer with the streamlined BMW that had run in the 1940 Mille Miglia.

year". This Lord Weir was the son of the man whose company had built the Weir-Darracqs back in 1904 that started Scotland's flirtation with motor racing.

As far as motor racing was concerned, all eyes were focused on Winfield and the three organising clubs applied for, and had been granted, a National permit for the meeting in July. Naturally, all the local Scots were looking forward to competing against good Southern competition.

It therefore came a surprise when the clubs suddenly went up-market and set a race programme of three single-seater races, for Formula 1,2 and 3 and two races for Production Cars under and over 1500ccs. There was uproar as there were but a handful of cars in Scotland that would qualify for any of the races under the regulations. There was much muttering about handing over the meeting to the English competitors. At this, a fair amount of lobbying took place and in late April the organising clubs announced that they were going to drop the two Production car events and replace them with races for up to and over 1500cc sports cars which would allow a raft of Scottish cars and specials to compete. Honour was satisfied and the palace revolt was over.

Meanwhile, Scottish Motor Racing Club made a tentative approach to Kirkcaldy Town Council to hold a race meeting at Beveridge Park in the centre of town. It was rebuffed, but the Council clearly were interested as they asked the club to bring up the matter at a later date. Poor SMRC had been trying so hard to find a racing venue. They had looked at the Kings Park, beside Holyrood Palace, the Queen's home in Scotland, but had been unsuccessful in that venture also. They had also looked at possible circuits at Ballado Bridge and on the foreshore at Cramond, just outside Edinburgh, but again hit stony ground.

It is easy to imagine SMRC's problems if you consider the general situation in the country at the time. Despite being six years after the end of the war there was still heavy rationing and austerity and a pursuit such as

motor racing was probably deemed politically incorrect; particularly when SMRC were seeking to create a road circuit on public land as opposed to modifying an old airfield in private ownership. In a sense they were deliberately taking the hard option in order to create something that was a cut above a flat airfield circuit.

Their perseverance was rewarded in September when Kirkcaldy Town Council finally agreed to let the club run a race meeting at Beveridge Park in the spring of 1952. At the same time SMRC held a special meeting at Joe Potts' garage in Bellshill where all owners of 500cc Formula III cars were invited. As a result of this, SMRC became the organising body for 500s in Scotland.

On July 21 1951 the second race meeting was held at Winfield. Compared to nine months earlier, the facilities had slightly improved and now there was even a public address system so the spectators had more of a clue as to what was going on. The trouble was that the racing at this meeting was nothing to write home about.

For a start, many of the spectators came to see the great British white hope in grand prix racing, the BRM, in action but the cars were withdrawn before the meeting. Then the RAC gave a permit to the Gamston circuit on the same day and most of the southern competitors decided to stay at home. There was a big fuss about this because, for example, half the competitors in the Libre event simply did not turn up. One race official was quoted as saying *"...this is surely one certain way of alienating the public, without whose support motor racing could not pay its way"*

At least the weather stayed dry and there was a huge crowd of 40,000 to see five hours of racing that afternoon. In the Formula II race only seven of the thirteen entrants started, including local favourites Ron Flockhart with his JP-Vincent and Edinburgh motor dealer John Brown who had bought one of the very early factory HWMs. As it turned out, once more, nobody could catch Gillie Tyrer's BMW. John Brown entertained the crowd with some spectacular driving in the HWM but just could not catch the more experienced Tyrer.

In the Formula III race the young Peter Collins arrived with a JBS and though Jackie Reece originally led in a Cooper the JBSs of Curly Dryden and Collins soon swept past, only for Dryden to break a camshaft drive and retire.

As only nine of the original nineteen entrants for the Formula Libre race turned up, John Brown offered his HWM to Reg Parnell to race in the Libre event but Parnell broke a drive shaft on the line and did not even start. Archie Butterworth had his AJB special in the race but the class act was Philip Fotheringham-Parker with a Maserati 4CL. For the spectators the only thing to cheer about was David Murray taking the lead in his Maserati 4CLT chased by Irishman Joe Kelly in a grand prix Alta. Then Kelly retired after losing two gears. David Murray seemed safely in the lead, in what was turning out to be an utterly boring race, but had fuel feed problems and retired so Fotheringham-Parker ran out the winner. To give some idea how pathetic the field was, Gillie Tyrer finished second in his BMW and Ian Stewart third in his Jaguar XK120. What made the event even more disappointing was that it was the first event in Scotland to carry a National racing permit.

A great enthusiast and promoter of Coopers in Scotland, Pat Prosser, on the line at Beveridge Park, Kirkcaldy. Behind him on the grid is Ninian Sanderson in his earlier "Yellow Peril" Cooper.

Meanwhile, over on the West of Scotland, everyone was gearing up for the first race meeting at the Turnberry airstrip near Turnberry Hotel in Ayrshire.

It took place on Saturday September 1 1951 organised by Scottish Sporting Car Club with backing from the Scottish Daily Express newspaper. It was the third airfield circuit to be used for motor racing with both Winfield in the Borders and Crimond in Aberdeenshire predating Turnberry. Indeed from having no motor racing whatsoever Scotland suddenly appeared to have more race meetings than it could shake a stick at.

SSCC were clearly keen to underline that this was the first race meeting in the populous west of Scotland and the programme notes rather pompously announced "...an auspicious occasion for introducing to a West of Scotland spectatorate a galaxy of talented native drivers who, in a programme of 5 and 10-lap races pregnant with possibilities for exciting sport, will be afforded ample opportunity for displaying their prowess and for gaining more of that experience which is so essential to success in the wider fields of National and International rivalry".

Turnberry was one of the least imaginative circuits in Britain. But then, unlike other circuits, it consisted mainly of one main runway and very little else. The result was a circuit 1.6 miles long with few features save a long main straight followed by a right hand hook corner wide enough to let the competitors who arrived too fast to drift wide and still stay on the track.

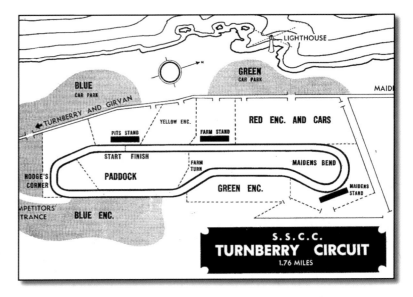

The layout of the Turnberry Circuit close to the seashore at Turnberry.

As this was essentially a club meeting, all the local drivers took part in as many races as possible So we found the rising 500cc racing star Ninian Sanderson running in the saloon car race with a Vauxhall and John Melvin with a Sunbeam Talbot in one race and his H.R.G. in another. The biggest entry was in the unlimited sports car race with no fewer than eleven Jaguar XK120s. The most interesting car in this race was, however, the Alfa Romeo 2900B driven by Ian Cunninghham. This car was owned by Major Edward Thompson, President of the Ben Shipping Line and a man who would become an important, if anonymous, backer of Ecurie Ecosse. The car had originally come to England for the Alfa Romeo stand at the 1938 London Motor Show with the strict instructions from Milan that it was not to be sold. However, it was sold off the stand and came into the hands of Hugh Hunter, a great enthusiast for racing Alfa Romeos. The following year, following correspondence in the press about the fastest road car in Britain, it was arranged that Hunter's Alfa Romeo and a Delahaye would be timed round Brooklands to finally settle the discussion. The Alfa Romeo proved to be quicker. Later the car was sold to Anthony Crook who raced in the post war years with Frazer Nashes and was to be the founder Chairman of the Bristol Car Company that still exists today. When Crook owned the car it was maintained by a young Scottish mechanic called John Romanes who was later to figure largely in the development of motor racing in Scotland in the 1960s.

When the Alfa Romeo was raced at Turnberry, Major Thompson had owned it for less than a year and it was resplendent in its Touring of Milan coachwork with long sweeping wings and running boards. Major Thompson, who had a thing about cycle-wing sports cars, was later to take a hack saw to its beautiful Italian bodywork leaving it totally denuded with rough and ready cycle wings and it stayed that way until it was sold in 1970.

The start of the sports car race at Turnberry with Ian Stewart in his Jaguar XK120 getting away quickly.

On Saturday October 13 1951 the final race meeting of the Scottish season took place at Winfield and at the time we were not to know that it would be the last meeting held on the circuit. The July meeting had attracted around 40,000 spectators underlining the fact that there was clearly a following for motor racing in Scotland.

To the organiser's relief there was a much better entry for this meeting than for the July meeting and, what is more, most of the entrants actually turned up. It is interesting to note that when asked what he thought about Winfield the great Reg Parnell said *"It is every bit as fast as Silverstone. I like the friendly organisation."* David Murray took the same theme : *"...Winfield to my mind is much better than Silverstone."* Gillie Tyrer who was a bit more down to earth spoke for many when he said *"It's a good circuit but it is bumpy".*

This October Winfield meeting saw the largest number of Scottish-built JP 500s ever entered for any race meeting with no fewer than eight of them to be driven by Bob Dickson, David Blane, Joe Potts, Ian Sutherland, Comish Hunter, Bill Smith, Cliff Carter and David Swan. A new name appeared in the Vintage car class, Keith Schellenberg, with a supercharged Austin Seven and he was to become a stalwart in Scottish motor racing from then until the 1990s.

The main racing car race was split into Libre cars and Formula II cars with seven ERAs lined up against Reg Parnell in the Thinwall Special Ferrari and Irishmen Joe Kelly (Alta) and Bobby Baird (Maserati). In the Formula 2 class Ron Flockhart raced his Vincent-engined JP against fellow Scots Billy Skelly with his Lea Francis special and David Murray in the ex-Peter Whitehead short wheelbase Ferrari V12. There were also three works HWMs for George Abecassis, Duncan Hamilton and Stirling Moss and so the huge crowd this time got their money's worth.

This race was over 50 miles. Nobody could touch Reg Parnell in the Thinwall Special Ferrari and it was no surprise when he set a new lap record for the course in 1minute 21 seconds. Behind him were the battling ERAs of Bob Gerard, Ken Wharton and Graham Whitehead. Gerard was soon out with a broken half shaft. In the Formula II category the three HWMs finished first second and third with Moss, Abecassis and Hamilton in that order.

It was interesting that at the dinner after the meeting Reg Parnell particularly praised the driving of Ian Stewart. Stewart's driving had not escaped the notice of Stirling Moss who spoke to Lofty England of Jaguar and Stewart was nominated to Jaguar's Le Mans team for the 1952 season.

That this was to be the last race meeting held at Winfield was certainly not envisaged because the programme encouraged spectators to watch out for an International race meeting at the circuit on July 19th 1952.

The reason behind the abandonment of Winfield centred around improvements the organising clubs wanted to make to the track. They had taken aboard criticisms by the leading drivers that it was too rough and bumpy so they looked into the cost of evening out and resurfacing the circuit with tarmac. The RAC had also indicated they might actually get an International permit for 1952 on the understanding that they attended to the track.

Before they went ahead with these improvements, however, they were hit by a bombshell. They were told by the Royal Air Force and the landowner, that they could fix the track, if they wanted, but there would be no guarantee of tenancy. To make a substantial investment on a circuit where they could not guarantee its future was out of the question. So the Berwick, Hawick and Lothian Car Clubs withdrew from organising any further racing events at Winfield. After this, Winfield was used for the odd sprint and rally stage: later still it was used by Colin Chapman to land his plane when coming to visit Jim Clark.

Scotland's only international grand prix driver was David Murray, an Edinburgh chartered accountant who owned some pubs in Edinburgh's High Street, and Merchiston Mews, a small garage in a quaint cobbled mews in the Bruntsfield district of Edinburgh. He had first seen motor racing at Brooklands before the war. In a moment of reflection later in his life he opined *"...isn't it sad that when you are young and most active you don't have the money to go motor racing but when you can afford it you are probably too old."* Certainly he was close to 40 when he started competing in an MG. Murray then raced and owned the first ERA built, R1A, and later a Maserati 4CL and a 4CLT. It was in the latter Maserati he had a serious crash in the 1951 German Grand Prix at the Nurburgring and "retired" from motor racing. Though he always quoted this as his last race he raced in at least two other events for his Ecurie Ecosse team after the Nurburgring accident.

Murray had brought to Scotland one of the best known racing mechanics of the time, Wilkie Wilkinson, and offered him a directorship in Merchiston Mews where he was soon ministering to all the local drivers who wanted more performance from their sports cars. One of these was a young student farmer called Ian Stewart who first had an SS100 Jaguar he had bought from another Scot, Noel Bean, and later one of the first Jaguar XK120s.

Meanwhile another Edinburgh driver, Ron Flockhart, bought Murray's ERA R1A with his friend Alastair Birrell and they called themselves Alba Union from the old name for Scotland. So this team was up and running before Ecurie Ecosse or Border Reivers came on the scene.

David Murray had the idea that, if he was not racing himself, he had the people around him to set up a team to race Internationally. He had taken delivery of the first Jaguar XK120 into Edinburgh but for some reason he left it in Jaguar dealer Rossleigh's service department in Annandale Street. Murray's car arrived about six weeks before young Ian Stewart took delivery of the second XK120 in Edinburgh and so they had two cars to form a team. However, at this juncture it would appear that Jenny Murray put her foot down. By all accounts David Murray sold his car, almost unused, to Edinburgh haulage contractor Bill Dobson who had been racing a 328 BMW.
Certainly Merchiston Motors advertised the 328 for sale and it can be assumed it was taken in part exchange against the Jaguar.

In the autumn of 1951, Stewart and Ron Flockhart were invited to David Murray's accountancy office in Rutland Square where Murray outlined his plans for a team to be called Ecurie Ecosse. He had already had talks with Reg Tanner the competitions manager for Esso who in turn had offered Murray a sum in the region of £5,000 if a team of three identical cars could be put together for sports car racing. The obvious car was the Jaguar XK120.

Stewart already had his and Murray's car was now with Bill Dobson so the idea was to persuade Ron Flockhart to sell his ERA and buy a Jaguar XK120. It later transpired that Flockhart had not only refused to sell the ERA and buy a Jaguar but was to go on to buy R4D the most famous ERA of all and one which brought him to the fore in British motor racing. As Ian Stewart remarked of Flockhart's refusal to sell his ERA and replace it with an XK120 *"...you don't give a Bentley owner a Vauxhall and expect him to enthuse."*

Over the winter of 1951, and with Winfield now unavailable, a meeting was called to form the Winfield Joint Committee. It was a group controlled by

Scottish motor racing 1950s style. Sir James Scott Douglas (right) displays his portly figure to Harry Slack who, with his friends Ian Hopper and Jimmy Gibbon decided to challenge Ecurie Ecosse with their own spoof team, Ecurie Ossity. Note the question mark as a team badge.

stalwarts of the Lothian Car Club led by two well-known Edinburgh lawyers, John Dick Peddie and Dan Mackay. I remember the latter very well for, at the tender age of 17 and a trainee reporter with the Edinburgh Evening Dispatch, I was occasionally allowed to attend the Sherrif Court for some of the smaller trials and was able to watch Dan McKay in action first hand. Dan had a huge reputation in Edinburgh at the time. It was said around the High Steet bars that if you ever murdered anyone Dan was your best bet to get you off. He was formidable in a courtroom and just as formidable outside of it. He would strut around and control affairs at Charterhall with a rod of iron. Though he could cut you down to size as quick as look at you, he was, in fact, a very kind and generous man. John Dick Peddie was more restrained, guarded and the soul of discretion. He too had a very generous side to him. I remember having to cover the first motor race meeting held at Charterhall in April 1952 and being stuck without transport to get there. Dick Peddie immediately offered a lift to and from the circuit in his brand new Bristol 401. He was David Murray's lawyer and maintained his interest and participation in motor sport right into the Ingliston era of the 1960s and '70s.

Meanwhile up in Aberdeenshire a new star was being born. Jock Lawrence from Cullen who raced this very early Cooper-MG.

The Winfield Joint Committee brought together not only representatives from the original Winfield triumverate, Lothian, Hawick and Berwick and District motor clubs but Aberdeen and District Motor Club, Kirkcaldy and District Motor Club and the MG Car Club led by that arch-enthuaist Douglas Mickel. Of these, only Lothian Car Club had a financial stakeholding in the WJC (£100), all the other shares being taken up by individuals with John Dick Peddie the largest single shareholder having invested £382 followed by local Borders notable, Lt Col Stanley Gallon TD with £227. Because the racing was taking place in the Borders, a few of the shareholders came from the North East of England with Jack Lawson, a wholesale confectioner from Newcastle, with £163 the largest. Jack Lawson was later to become the backer of young Jimmy Blumer as a racing driver who in turn went on to race for Team Lotus in sports cars.

A few miles from the Winfield airstrip was another much larger airfield called Charterhall. It had been built in the early part of the war and was not so much an operational station as a relief air strip with a main runway measuring a mile in length. There were also a couple of perimeter roads, of which the southern side was to provide the linking section of circuit. To the north were a couple of hangers and that was about all.

The whole concept of Charterhall, as with many similar airstrips on the Eastern coast of Great Britain, was to provide space for a war plane in difficulties flying across the North Sea, to land on mainland Britain. As we were to see with similar strips in Lincolnshire and the south, these became real lifelines to pilots with crippled planes during the war. Charterhall, being to the north, was out of the firing line, so to speak, and was rarely ever used. There was a story I have never been able to confirm, that five Spitfires diverted to Charterhall managed to get down but the runway was so rough only three ever took off again! The Charterhall airfield straddled two farms, one owned by Major Trotter and the other by a Mr Macdonald. An arrangement was hammered out whereby Major Trotter received £100 for every National or International race meeting held on the circuit and £25 for a club meeting. MacDonald on the other hand received £100 per annum as less of his land was on the track and spectator area. With such an arrangement WJC embarked on their first full season in 1952.

Three of the best known Scottish racing drivers, Ron Flockhart, Ian Stewart and Alastair Birrell, came up with the plan of competing in the Monte Carlo Rally in January 1952. It was Ron Flockhart's idea and to ensure he had an entry in the event he talked to A K Stevenson at the RSAC and told him that it would be a team of racing drivers and so could he put a word in for them. They were accepted with a factory loaned Ford V8 Pilot even thought the original plan had been to run a brand new Jaguar Mark VII. The Pilot was taken to Merchiston Mews where Wilkie Wilkinson tuned the engine and tweaked up the suspension. As Ron had spent time in the Italian mountains in winter during the war, he knew that the best bit of de-ditching gear would be a huge 15 cwt block and tackle and *"...a good ten fathoms of 1 1/2 inch rope"*. They certainly did not win but they finished.

On March 1 1952 Ecurie Ecosse officially came into being when the three privately owned Jaguar XK120s of Ian Stewart, Bill Dobson and Sir James Scott Douglas were handed over to Wilkie Wilkinson at Merchiston Motors so that they could be prepared and stored prior to race meetings.

For their first entry, Ecurie Ecosse ran just one car at Goodwood at the end of March. Bill Dobson was the driver and he was beaten into second place in the over 3 litre sports car race by Oscar Moore's unique HWM-Jaguar.

The following weekend was the inaugural meeting at Charterhall. As this was a new circuit the RAC rules required that the first meeting be a closed event with no spectators. For Ecurie Ecosse this was fortuitous as the feature race was a three-hour team handicap race. For this the full team of three Ecurie Ecosse Jaguar XK120s were run.

For a start they were clearly over handicapped and did not finish in the first three. The winning team was the oddly named "Ecurie Ossity", a team made up of Ian Hopper and Jimmy Gibbon with their Specials and Harry Havelock Slack with his Healey Elliot saloon. They dreamed up the name as a spoof to wind-up Ecurie Ecosse and arrived at the circuit with patches on their overalls showing a simple question mark. Amusingly, Harry Havelock Slack's grandson, Lance Gauld, races today, fifty years later, under his grandfather's team name of "Ecurie Ossity".

In addition to their Jaguars, Ecurie Ecosse raced this rare short wheelbase Ferrari Formula 2 car. The usual driver was Bill Dobson, seen here at Castle Coombe, who had a lot of success with the car.

With the sudden surge of interest in motor racing in Scotland, the real problem was lack of cars. Many of the cars being raced were either road cars hastily modified to race or old racing cars from pre-war days. Ron Flockhart and Alastair Birrell bought ERA R1A, the first ERA, from David Hampshire shortly after the Winfield race meeting the previous year. Ron's successful JP-Vincent, which had won the Ulster Trophy, was sold to

Beveridge Park in Kirkcaldy was a challenging circuit made more so by ebullient drivers like Charlie Headland who lost control of his Kieft on this downhill corner...
(Bill Henderson)

...ending up in a Rhododendron bush with the car on top of him. He was not injured. Note that the "parkie" had failed to pick up the empty beer bottles from the night before!
(Bill Henderson)

Belfastman Marshall Watson. Many years later Marshall's son John would win the British Grand Prix for McLaren.

Flockhart only raced this ERA four times. His most significant race was in the Ulster Trophy when he was lying third and then ran out of fuel. Flockhart had been in discussion with Raymond Mays, of ERA and BRM fame, and bought Mays' most famous ERA, R4D. He raced it for the first time in the 1952 British Grand Prix finishing fifth.

Flockhart sold the car at the end of the 1953 season for £1500 to Peter Bell for Ken Wharton to race. The other half of Alba Union, Alastair Birrell, continued to race R1A and took it all over Britain for Formula Libre events. He had two good wins at Snetterton in 1952 and 1954 and then, due to pressure of business, retired from racing in April 1955. It is interesting that he advertised the car for sale at just £400 and it was bought by Bill Moss.

Ninian Sanderson and Pat Prosser - the Cooper agent for Scotland - bought new Mark VI Coopers with Francis Beart-tuned Norton engines and both Joe Potts and Comish Hunter had new JPs also with Norton engines. Hunter's previous JAP-engined JP was bought by David Blane and Glaswegian Alex McGlashen was also JAP powered but with Ninian Sanderson's older Cooper chassis.

With the help of Major Thompson, David Murray of Ecurie Ecosse ordered two new single seater racing cars for the team. The first was a Mark 1 Cooper Bristol (CB/6/52) to be raced by Jimmy Stewart and Jock Lawrence in particular. To make the car easily recognisable, David Murray had a white cross of St Andrew painted on the wire mesh grille. It was painted in Ecurie Ecosse blue with the saltire badges on the side. The other car was a Connaught Formula 2 car, chassis A6, fitted with the familiar Lea Frances engine. This was also finished in blue and was initially raced by Ian Stewart. Another new single seater was ordered by Motherwell enthusiast Billy Skelly, one of only three Formula 2 Frazer Nash cars built.

Billy Skelly had studied car design and engineering at Coventry Technical College where he became friendly with a man who became Britain's greatest motor sport all-rounder of the day, Ken Wharton.

Ken had a small garage in Smethwick. He was the first professional racing driver Billy Skelly had met and young Skelly hung on his every word. At this time Billy had developed his own Lea Francis special with the help of Albert Ludgate the Chief Engineer of Lea Francis and it was a good

Crimond: Peter Bolton's Cooper-Jaguar lines up in the paddock ahead of a young Michael Salmon with his Jaguar XK120M. Though a Jerseyman, Salmon spent a number of years in Scotland during his early racing career. He was later to drive a variety of Jaguars and a factory Ford GT40. (Edwin Whyte)

little car. However, one day when talking about racing in Ken Wharton's house, Ken asked Billy what he thought about the Frazer Nash Le Mans Replica Donald Pitt had raced in the Ulster Trophy event. Pitt had taken this normal sports car, removed the cycle wings and stripped it down to make it eligible as a racing car. Billy remarked that Pitt's car had certainly been quick and had passed him on the straight as though he had been standing still. Ken then turned and said *"Can you imagine if that car was stripped and squashed into a single-seater body where it would be? It's got to have some potential."*

Wharton then had a word with his regular backer, Peter Bell and they both spoke to the Aldington Brothers who owned Frazer-Nash. The result was the Formula 2 Frazer-Nash. Billy's father had once driven Billy's Lea Francis Special and been horrified at the lack of brakes. He also had a dislike of Coopers as he had seen the wishbones break on them but this Frazer-Nash was a well-engineered F2 car and he suggested that they buy one.

As it turned out, only three Formula 2 Frazer Nashes were ever built, the first for Ken Wharton, the second for Billy Skelly and the third for Irishman Dickie Odlum. Billy was due to take delivery of his Nash in time for the Daily Express International meeting at Silverstone in April but the car could not be finished in time. It is interesting to note here that Billy Skelly took a great interest in the design of the car and decided he wanted to reduce the wheelbase of his F2 car by three inches from 8ft to 7ft 9ins. Many years later Billy was to admit this had not been a good move as he always suffered from horrendous wheelspin coming out of slow corners and he put it down to the shorter wheelbase. Skelly also changed the back axle of his car so he could use Girling brakes and never had any problems with brakes after that. The next thing was the engine. Always on the lookout for the extra edge, Billy had a word with fellow racing driver Basil de Mattos, who worked for Laystall Engineering. Laystall's boss, Bob Spikins, had been killed at Chimay in his Le Mans Replica and apparently the engine was very special, producing around 140 b.h.p. The Aldington's still had the engine in their stores and they sold it to Billy for his Formula 2 car. Thus equipped, Billy was ready to move into the big time. His first race with the car was at the first race meeting to be held at Charterhall in April 1952.

At that race meeting Billy found out how difficult it was to drive a racing car with the gearchange between his legs and he fluffed the start. He then realised that by changing the back axle he could not fit a limited slip differential. This was a big mistake and he suffered wheelspin on the tight corners. However, he had a good race and found that he was actually quicker than Ecurie Ecosse chief mechanic Wilkie Wilkinson who was taking a busman's holiday at this meeting, driving the Ecurie Ecosse Cooper-Bristol Formula 2 car.

Later that year, at Turnberry, Skelly was well placed on the grid for the Formula 2 racing, being right behind Denis Poore's Connaught. The start was a disaster. *"I remember seeing Denis having trouble on the line and as the flag dropped he stalled the engine. Unfortunately when you let the clutch in on the Nash it just took off. The next thing I knew I was up in the air and looking down into the cockpit of Denis' car. He didn't put his hand up and I didn't realise he had stalled because the Connaught actually moved about three feet thanks to the pre-selector gearbox. Fortunately the Nash had 16 inch wheels and the Connaught 15 inch ones so I mounted his car and when I landed I nearly hit Ninian Sanderson in the Ecurie Ecosse Cooper Bristol. I managed to continue but was black-flagged after one lap. I continued for another lap in case they changed their minds but was forced to come in. They let me out again but I found later the chassis was an inch and a half out on one side. I heard through Lea Francis that when the Dennis Poore's Connaught was taken back to the factory in Send they found I had knocked the de Dion back axle almost into the cockpit wrecking the car completely."*

One of the biggest International meetings held in Scotland was at Turnberry. where BRM turned up with two of their noisy V16 cars for Reg Parnell and Ken Wharton. As they manoeuvre on to the grid Ron Flockhart is at ease in his ERA R4D. On the far side of the front row is Mike Hawthorn with the Thinwall Special Ferrari and behind Hawthorn is John Barber's Cooper-Bristol.

When his father took seriously ill, Billy Skelly had to give up racing to run the family business, Skellys of Motherwell, and the Frazer Nash languished for some time before being sold to another Charterhall regular Phil Walton who took the body off and fitted a Fibreglass sports car body. The car led a chequered life, at one time being discovered as a wreck in Paris, but today it has been converted into a regular Le Mans Replica Frazer Nash and is owned by Jim Trigwell.

Of all the Scots racing at this time, the most talented and ambitious was Ian Stewart who had just finished college as a farmer and was working with his father, one of Scotland's leading cattle breeders well respected around the world. The name Stewart of Millhills was a guarantee of quality and he helped stock some of the largest cattle farms in Argentina.

Thanks to Stirling Moss, who had seen Stewart race at Turnberry in his Jaguar XK120, Ian's name had been brought to the attention of Lofty England the Competitions manager of Jaguar. As a result, Stewart was offered a place in the Jaguar team at Le Mans in 1952 partnering Peter Whithead. Unfortunately for him, Jaguar that year decided to build a low drag body on the C type with a tiny radiator grille. This led to the Jaguars having overheating problems and they all retired. However, Jaguar planned to put their C type on to the market as an over-the-shelf sports racing car. They gave the factory drivers the first chance to buy them and Ian Stewart bought Chassis No 006. To do this he privately had words with his father's accountant who suggested Ian take out hire purchase on the car so that his father would not need to know that his son had bought a racing car.

Unfortunately for Ian, his father found out and was shocked, not just that his son had bought a racing car, but that he had taken out hire purchase on it. At this Mr Stewart drove to Edinburgh, confronted David Murray of Ecurie Ecosse and virtually ordered Murray to buy the car to save the family from the disgrace of having a son who had taken hire purchase out on a racing car!

Ian, through Ecurie Ecosse, entered his C type Jaguar for the Jersey Road Race of 1952 run over an interesting road circuit on the Channel Isle. It was all very last minute as his car was only completed a few days before the race and Ian had to use the drive from Coventry to Jersey as the running-in period!

For Stewart it was a dream race and he won outright against strong opposition from the Aston Martin factory team and Ken Wharton in his fast Frazer Nash.

The Wakefield Trophy was held at the Curragh circuit in Eire as a handicap event and Duncan Hamilton with his C type Jaguar was expected to win but crashed on the second lap. With a reasonably generous handicap of a lap plus 30 seconds it was Sir James Scott Douglas in the Ecurie Ecosse Jaguar XK120 who led from his team mate Ian Stewart with the much quicker C type Jaguar. With three laps to go, the portly Scott Douglas still led but Ian Stewart had moved to 32 seconds adrift. A lap later and this was down to 21 seconds and at the start of the last lap Stewart had moved to just 10 seconds behind the XK120 and so, barring incidents, it would be Ian Stewart who would win. A mile from the line he stormed past Scott Douglas giving him a wave as he went by, to win his second most important race. Some weeks later Bill Dobson, deputising for Ian Stewart, who had a cold, won the second September Handicap at Goodwood beating Michael Head's C type Jaguar. This was Dobson's last major win as he retired from motor racing shortly afterwards. As for Michael Head, we were to hear much more about his young son Patrick. Many years later thanks to his successful partnership with Frank Williams and the Williams grand prix team, Patrick Head became famous.

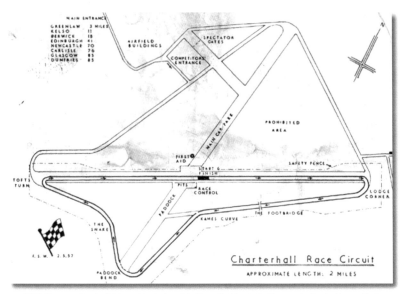

With its one mile straight, and hairpins at both ends, Charterhall was a test not of speed but brakes. The notorious and fast left hand kink at Kames Curve is where the only fatal accidents in Scottish motor racing have taken place. The circuit was 2 miles long and even by 1964 and the last race meeting the lap record was over 92 m.p.h.

Chapter 5
Racing in the Park

Scottish Motor Racing Club continued to work tirelessly to find a racing circuit of their own. As mentioned earlier, they had joined forces with the Royal Scottish Automobile Club and the Kirkcaldy and District Motor Club to organise a meeting in Kirkcaldy's Beveridge Park. The local authority relented and was praised for its pioneering spirit in allowing a public park to be closed and for a race meeting to be held on the narrow park roads. These, on the whole, were well surfaced and there was a tremendous turnout of spectators who were extremely well behaved and stayed behind the tapes that marked the spectator area from the track. All the spectators were kept on the inside of the track and so could roam from corner to corner.

A typical race at Beveridge Park in Kirkcaldy. Even though the races were restricted to 500cc Formula 3 cars they could only run five cars at a time and the chance of overtaking was minimal. Ninian Sanderson, left front row on pole.

Most of the park benches had been removed for safety and the odd straw bale was put in place to protect the trees, or the drivers depending on your point of view. As can be seen in one of the photos, the "parkies", however, had not cleared up the waste bins where the Saturday night locals had deposited their empty beer bottles.

Quite rightly the races were all for small 500cc Formula III cars. In view of the narrowness of the track the races were run in heats of five cars with the

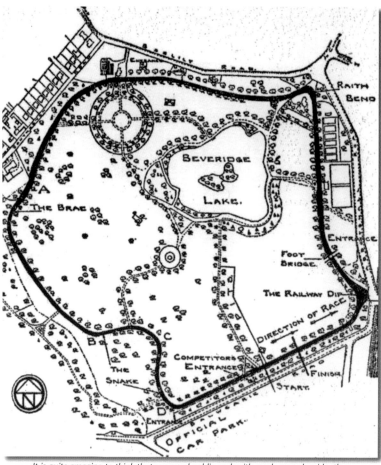

It is quite amazing to think that a normal public park with roads scarcely wider than 20 feet would be used for motor racing, but the Scottish Motor Racing Club ran two race meetings on the Beveridge Park Circuit in Kirkcaldy.

leading two moving on to the final. One of the young drivers taking part was Tommy Dickson with the world's oldest Cooper 500 but he did not last long as his car broke its exhaust.

SMRC had printed 20,000 tickets for the meeting and every single one of them was sold yet there were still queues lined up waiting to get in!

John Melvin bought this Frazer-Nash Le Mans Replica off the London Motor Show stand and had a lot of success with it.

One of Scotland's early specials, the Chassels Secial built around Frazer-Nash and Bentley parts and raced by the ebullient Dr Mirlees Chassels from Glasgow.

The star at this meeting was Charlie Headland from England with his Kieft. He set the outright lap record at just over 61.72 mph, not bad for a run round a park. However, during one of the heats in the second race, Charlie lost his brakes at about 90 mph on a downhill section and rolled the Keift into a large clump of rhododendron bushes. The Scottish hero, Ninian Sanderson, wrecked his engine in the first race but managed to replace it and won the second race.

Ninian Sanderson again, this time racing his new Erskine Staride F3 car at Beveridge Park. Note the unprotected park bench in the background, just one of the many hazards.

All the talk after the race meeting was whether this was a truly viable racing circuit. After all, to run each race as a series of heats for five cars leading up to a final, was hardly satisfactory. Added to this it was almost impossible to pass, as future grand prix driver Cliff Allison found out at the meeting. Cliff was reprimanded for allegedly baulking another competitor when the truth of the matter was that it was difficult, if not dangerous, to even try to pass. What was more important, however, was the reaction of Kirkcaldy Town Council which was overjoyed at the number of spectators and hinted that they may widen the roads through the park by ten feet but this never actually happened.

This was followed by a small race meeting at Turnberry where Bill Dobson won his first race with David Murray's short wheelbase Ferrari. He set a new outright lap record for the circuit thanks to improvements that had been made during the winter. At this race meeting David Murray had a long chat with Joe Potts and they talked about the possibility of building a sports racing car that would be run by Ecurie Ecosse. However Potts explained that all his JP 500s had been made in his spare time, and he was not geared up to the kind of production schedule that would have been demanded of a sports racing car so nothing more was heard of the scheme.

One of the leading figures surrounding the Winfield Joint Committee was John Dick Peddie, the Edinburgh lawyer.

In May, Ninian Sanderson, with his father Bob and loyal friend Alex McGlashan, set off with their converted bus as a transporter, for the Luxembourg Grand Prix. It was a pretty bold effort on Sanderson's part and he took a strong fifth place in the first heat behind all the leading 500cc stars.

Another interesting Frazer-Nash was this Formula 2 car bought by Billy Skelly and seen in the wet at Turnberry. This was one of only three built as single seaters. Today the car has been converted and now runs as a Le Mans replica.

For the final, Ninian was on the third row of the grid with Stirling Moss in his Kieft-Norton just ahead of him and drivers like Les Leston and Peter Collins behind him. When lying in seventh place, and with Stirling Moss now behind him, Ninian retired when his carburettor float chamber fell off.

On the same weekend, the Aberdeen and District Motor Club ran a meeting at Crimond where John Melvin ran his Frazer Nash Le Mans Replica for the first time, finishing second behind Jack Walton's Nash, and just ahead of Jimmy Stewart's Healey Silverstone.

Then came the May Charterhall meeting, the first open to the general public. It did not attract a large crowd but it was notable in having a new young British racing driver making his debut at the circuit: Mike Hawthorn. Hawthorn had been entered in the racing car event with his Cooper-Bristol and in the sports car events with Len Potter's beautiful cream Frazer Nash. In the sports car race Hawthorn was vanquished by Jack Walton in another Frazer Nash.
In the Formula Libre event nobody could touch Hawthorn who raced in a short sleeved shirt that billowed up around his neck exposing his bare midriff! Dennis Poore with the big Alfa Romeo was second. Afterwards Hawthorn was asked what he felt about the circuit and he complained it was very bumpy but apart from that thought it was as good as any in the country – a diplomatic statement.

At the end of May, everyone trekked to Crimond for the Aberdeen and District Motor Club meeting and over 20,000 spectators turned up to see the event. Bearing in mind the difficulty of reaching Aberdeen on the road system in the early 1950s the visitors were always welcomed with open arms and it was probably the most friendly and accommodating of all the Scottish circuits of the time.

This meeting brought to the fore a local driver called Jock Lawrence who had acquired an early Cooper-MG and he easily won the under 1500cc sports car race. In the bigger capacity class, the three Ecurie Ecosse Jaguar XK120s were roundly defeated by Jack Walton's Frazer Nash and in the main race Bill Dobson's Ferrari was soon out with an oil pump problem that dogged that car all season. Alastair Birrell was driving the Alba Union ERA R1A and had the misfortune to hit a dog in practice. In order to make the car driveable the shock absorbers were screwed up as tightly as possible and Alastair felt his way round in the opening stages. As the opposition

Perhaps Bernie Ecclestone would not approve, but this converted double decker bus held the timekeepers and sundry officials at Charterhall events. Others were perched on Jock McBain's tower and the clerk of the course and starter stood on the sidelines.

retired in front of him it was a surprised Alastair Birrell who crossed the line as winner of the race.

Another competitor at that meeting was the legendary Joe Little from Aberdeen who not only raced a Jaguar XK120 but bought a supercharged Alta.

Joe originally hailed from Grimsby but he arrived in Aberdeen just after the war and set up a very successful fish business in Torry, Aberdeenshire. In Grimsby he had been a friend of the Bloomer family who owned a large garage (one of the daughters, Shirley Bloomer, was a successful athlete who married Chris Brasher.) and through the Bloomers he was able to buy the Alta that had once been owned by George Abecassis. It was one of just three supercharged Alta F1 cars built. The Alta used to be transported to the circuits on the back of an open-top fish lorry amongst the fish boxes so it permanently stank of fish. However, the car suffered from severe wheel wobble at high speed and it was not long before it was sold.

There was a second race meeting at Crimond and the weather was bad with heavy rain sweeping in from the sea. By this time Ian Stewart had his C type Jaguar and he easily won the unlimited sports car race. Again Jock

Lawrence dominated the small sports car event with the Cooper-MG. As it turned out, the best race of the day was for 500cc racers and one of the leading British drivers, Don Parker, brought his Keift all the way from the south of England to take part. It was the day that Ninian Sanderson marked himself as a man to watch in the future. He harried Parker all the way and forced him to make a mistake, letting Sanderson through to win.

Ninian Sanderson was given his first big chance in the next race when David Murray let him drive the new Ecurie Ecosse Cooper-Bristol in the Libre event. Ron Flockhart took the lead with his D type ERA but lost his brakes tangled with the oil drums on the outside of the circuit. Ian Stewart held second in the Jaguar C type with Sanderson third until Flockhart recovered to get past Sanderson again. When Ian Stewart's back axle broke, Flockhart took over the lead and won the race.

It is interesting to note that the Aberdeen club paid travelling expenses to every competitor on a mileage basis. This was a very generous move and confirmed, once more, the generosity of the Aberdonians as opposed to their music hall reputation for meanness. At the end of the year Aberdeen gained another racing driver in the shape of an incomer from Jersey, Michael Salmon.

The downhill back straight at Charterhall showing the rickety bridge over the track. Ron Flockhart is at the wheel of a factory Connaught on this approach to Kames Curve.

Michael, who was to race Jaguars and factory Ford GT 40s, arrived at Rossleigh Ltd., the Aberdeen Jaguar dealers, as a kind of private trainee. As a fellow apprentice, Edmund Whyte describes *"...he was not a member of the staff but wore overalls, talked very posh and thoroughly entertained the customers. His duty was to ' learn the trade'."*

At the time, Michael had a heavy old Lea Francis sports car. He entered the Lea Francis for his first Bo'ness hill climb but the scrutineer, the irascible Alex Reid from Glasgow, took exception to Michael's seemingly arrogant manner and came up with an excuse that stopped him from competing. However, after his 21st birthday, Michael arrived back in Aberdeen with a new sand-coloured Jaguar XK120M and his first win with the car was back at Bo'ness. From there he moved to Rossleighs in Edinburgh where he was in his element and immediately started competing in all the Edinburgh University Motor Club events and at Charterhall. The first time the writer met Jim Clark was at a driving test meeting at Drem outside Edinburgh where Michael Salmon was at his best. There had been heavy snow and on

An early encounter at Charterhall saw John Coombs, pushing at the rear, with his crippled Cooper 500 that lost a wheel in a battle with Stirling Moss on Coombs' right at Charterhall. Pushing at the front is John Cooper himself.

one of the tests Michael went through the finish line at high speed and out of control, the Jaguar spraying fountains of snow in all directions.

The 1952 season came to an end with an ambitious International meeting organised by the Winfield Joint Committee and featuring Reg Parnell and Ken Wharton with two of the factory BRM grand prix cars and the 1950 world motor racing champion, Dr Guiseppe Farina at the wheel of Tony Vandervell's Thinwall Special Ferrari. This meeting was sponsored by the Daily Record. The Record clearly wanted to try and upstage their great rivals the Daily Express, who had sponsored the International event at Turnberry sometime earlier. This was one of the most memorable race meetings in the early days of Scottish racing as it not only saw some close racing but some turn ups for the books.

For example, in the race for 500cc racing cars Stirling Moss and John Coombs were much quicker than the opposition in practice. As John Coombs recalls *"After practice Stirling told me that as we were the quickest drivers, and as he was normally the quicker off the line, we would make sure it was a good race. I was having none of that and actually beat Stirling away from the start and led into the first corner. We had a real battle and I was still leading 21 laps into the race when a back wheel came off my Cooper at Kames Curve. Poor Stirling was so close behind he had to swerve on to the grass which let Eric Brandon into the lead and he went on to win the race."*

Whenever he could, Archie Scott Brown came back and raced a Charterhall. In this photo Archie, in the works Lister-Bristol, is harrying Ninian Sanderson in the ex-Ecurie Ecosse C type Jaguar.

For Scots the telling race was for sports cars where Stirling Moss rolled out to the grid with the latest C-type Jaguar boasting Dunlop's new disc brakes. This car was entered by journalist Tommy Wisdom but was in fact a factory car. His main opposition was to come from Ian Stewart in the Ecurie Ecosse C type Jaguar but this was a customer car with drum brakes so Stewart was at a distinct disadvantage. However, both were upstaged by Glaswegian Jimmy Neilson with his standard Jaguar XK120 who got a flying start and led through the first corner. On the back straight first Moss then Stewart swept past and Stewart's momentum through Kames Curve saw him outbrake Moss into Paddock bend an take the lead. This brought the crowd to their feet and from then to the end Stewart built up his lead by a second a lap and won easily. Stewart modestly put down his victory to a superior choice of gear ratios but there is no doubt it was one of Stewart's most impressive drives.

In the main race for the Daily Record International Trophy the BRMs and Farina in the big Thinwall Special were slow to get away. Bob Gerard in

Stirling Moss was a regular visitor to Charterhall in a variety of cars. This G type ERA with its Bristol engine was never a success. Behind on the right is Bobby Baird's Ferrari 500 F2 car and on the left Alan Brown's Cooper Bristol

the aged ERA and Peter Walker in his Cooper-ERA were first into Lodge corner. Farina came next but he was overtaken by Wharton's BRM only to be retaken by the Italian. Meanwhile Reg Parnell retired the other BRM with back axle trouble. Farina then caught Gerard on the sixth lap setting up fastest lap at over 85 mph. Four laps later Farina trundled to a halt at Kames Curve with his back axle broken. Meanwhile, to the embarrassment of the BRM supporters, Ken Wharton was struggling to catch and pass Bob Gerard in the 17-year old ERA. Eventually he made it only to spin on the exit to Paddock Bend leaving Gerard to roll across the line a happy victor. Frenchman Louis Rosier finished third in his big 4.5 litre Ferrari.

Late in the year, at Scottish Sporting Car Club's AGM, there was a relatively poor turnout, which was a pity as the club Chairman, John Stenhouse was about to drop a bombshell about the Turnberry races. He stood up and announced that there would be no further race meetings at the Ayrshire circuit to which the public could be admitted. He was quick to add that

Drivers came from far and near to Charterhall. For example Frenchman Louis Rosier was a frequent visitor, in this case with his early 250F Maserati

Another visitor was Prince Bira with his Maserati 4CLT powered by a 4.5 litre O.S.C.A. 12 cylinder engine.

rumours, which had circulated about arguments between the club, the circuit owners, Runways Ltd, and their main sponsor, the Scottish Daily Express, were totally unfounded.

What happened was that Runways Ltd had been paid a visit by the local Ayrshire assessor who intimated that if the company wished to promote motor racing with the paying public there would be a heavy increase in the assessment and that the Club would have to guarantee this assessment indefinitely, no matter what it might be.

Bolton again, being lapped by Archie Scott Brown's Lister-Bristol at Charterhall.

Stenhouse went on to explain that the club had incurred a considerable loss on their racing venture during 1952 as they had spent over £2,000 on track improvements during the winter of 1951 on the understanding that this would be steadily amortised through income from future meetings.

Furthermore, Runways Ltd had waived their claim for the rental of the circuit to the club. To give some idea of the cost of running meetings, their 1952 National event, which attracted the BRMs, had cost a total of £11,000

Lined up for practice are Peter Bolton (Cooper Jaguar) and Jimmy Gibson's Rover Special.

to put on. Faced with the fact that the actual spectator areas could not be increased in size there would be no additional income from the gate money.

In the circumstances, the club had no option but to drop the whole idea of running races at Turnberry even though there was a chance the assessor would be more lenient if the club ran two private meetings for club members only.

Douglas Mickel a leading light in motor sport and a member of SSCC congratulated the Board on their prudence in coming to this decision and so Scottish Sporting Car Clubs toe-dipping exercise into motor racing came to an end for the time being.

Over the winter of 1952 Winfield Joint Committee had done some work on Charterhall partially raising the road level on the outside of two of the bends so giving a slightly banked effect. This, in turn, helped improve the drainage of the track that had always been a problem.

A typical Formula Libre front row grid at Charterhall in 1953 with, left to right, Frank Curtis (HWM), Jimmy Stewart (Cooper Bristol), Bobby baird (Ferrari 500), Ken Wharton (Cooper Bristol) and Ian Stewart (Connaught)

A rare car for historians to ponder over. Archie Craig and his wife Betty working on this Cooper-MG. The car was the original Cliff Davis "barchetta" but fitted with a Falcon Fibreglass body shell after the original aluminium body had disintegrated. Today the car carries a replica of its original "barchetta" body.

The original programme for the 1953 Scottish motor racing season was to have seen two race meetings at Turnberry, five race meetings at Charterhall, two race meetings at Crimond, two race meetings at a new circuit at Crail in Fife and one race meeting in Beveridge Park. It was an ambitious programme and it was no surprise when the two Scottish Motor Racing Club meetings at Crail were cancelled as the circuit was not available for racing.

What happened was that Scottish Motor Racing Club had approached the Admiralty regarding the de-commissioning of the little airport at Crail on the East Coast of Scotland. It is a pretty little village and the airfield had been kept in good condition with a superb road surface. The Club were getting along well with the plans and were sufficiently confident to request dates for two race meetings in 1953. However, in January of that year they received notification from the Admiralty that they would not be permitted to run any race meetings on the circuit as arrangements had been made to loan the airfield to the St Andrews University Air Squadron as their main base. As we have seen, the Club had also made overtures to Dunfermline town council to organise a race meeting solely for 500cc racing cars round the town's Beveridge Park and they were to hold a final one on that circuit in 1953.

Le Mans start at Charterhall with Neil Brown sprinting towards his Triumph TR2. Amongst the cars in the background tail of the original Cliff Davis Cooper-MG can be seen.

Already some Scots were planning to go wider afield. Ninian Sanderson and his pal Alex McGlashan aimed to take their Cooper to four meetings

in France during the year. Ninian Sanderson decided to change his Cooper for one of the new Erskine Starides, designed and built by Mike Erskine. He ran the car for the first time in the Daily Express Trophy meeting at Silverstone in June. Also two of Scotland's Jaguar XK120 stalwarts, Peter Kenneth and Jim Neilson traded in their cars for Frazer-Nash Le Mans replicas. The Kenneth car had been raced by Roy Salvadori, who survived a near-fatal crash in it at Silverstone. It is interesting that this car resides once more in Scotland, in Andrew Fletcher's collection. The Jimmy Neilson car was formerly owned by TASO Mathieson and ironically it, too, came back to Scotland in the 1990s when it was bought by John Romanes, who was to feature in the development of the Ingliston circuit.

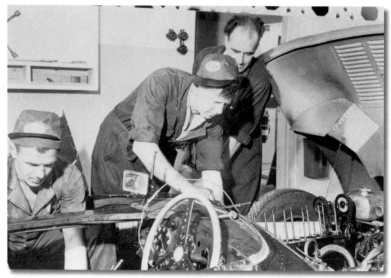

In Edinburgh the Ecurie Ecosse mechanics were building up a reputation with C and D type Jaguars. Ron Gaudion, Stan Sproat and Sandy Arthur do the work.

The opening race meeting of the 1953 season was a club event at Charterhall and there was not a particularly large entry.

Alex McGlashan, who had always raced in the shadow of his pal Ninian Sanderson, won the 500cc Formula III race ahead of a young driver from Newcastle called Keith Hall who was later to become a factory driver for Lotus and won the index of performance at Le Mans for them. Perhaps the surprise of the meeting was Jimmy Neilson's driving of the Frazer Nash. He split the Ecurie Ecosse C type Jaguars, finishing third behind Ian and Jimmy Stewart and ahead of Ninian Sanderson. Jock McBain in the ex-Eric-Brandon Cooper Bristol, running under the Border Reivers banner, ran the race of his career and might have won but he tipped a valve and retired, leaving Ron Flockhart the ultimate winner with his D-type ERA.

Scottish Motor Racing Club were back at Beveridge Park for their third meeting and the entry was better than ever with a number of leading drivers from the South taking part. The star driver at the meeting was a certain Ken Tyrrell with his Cooper, who easily won the first heat. In the final, however, he was beaten into second place by Ninian Sanderson. He made amends in the second race when Ken won ahead of Charlie Headland with his Kieft who, this time, kept the car on the tarmac.

Sadly this was to be the final race meeting at the pretty park. The road was no wider and it was noticeable at this meeting that more people ended up hitting trees and so SMRC wisely withdrew from racing on the circuit any further.

Ian Stewart's first Scottish race with his C type Jaguar chassis 006

As we have seen, two of Scotland's most promising young drivers, Jimmy Stewart and Ninian Sanderson, were fortunate in having fathers who were one hundred percent behind their racing. As a result both Bob Stewart and Bob Sanderson sat down with David Murray to see whether their sons could join the Ecurie Ecosse team. David Murray, a savvy accountant had his head screwed on straight. He pointed out that despite the fact the team had used Jaguar XK120s during 1952, Ian Stewart, who was a factory driver, had been allowed to buy one of the first C type Jaguars and had already shown how competitive it was. Murray explained that he would like to have the team run with identical Jaguar C-types in 1953. So, should Stewart and Sanderson consider buying C-type Jaguars for their sons the way would then be clear for them to join the team. Bill Dobson had retired from racing as his father wanted him back into the family contracting business full time and Jamie Scott Douglas had agreed to change his Jaguar XK120 for a C-type. He had already ordered one through Delacroix the French Jaguar distributors in Paris.

The new Ecurie Ecosse Connaught at Charterhall with Ian Stewart at the wheel.
Bob Gerard (ERA) alongside.

After thinking it over, both fathers decided to buy C-type Jaguars which were ordered through the Edinburgh Jaguar distributors Rossleigh Ltd. Jimmy Stewart's car (XKC 041) was the first to be completed on March 24 1953 and a week later XKC 042 was ready for Ninian Sanderson. This latter car had originally been destined for Argentina but there were customs difficulties and Jaguar switched the order to Ecurie Ecosse. The Jamie Scott Douglas car, (XKC 046) was finished a few weeks later and it too was

Alex McGlashan, left, bought Sanserson's Erskine Staride F3 car to replace his Cooper 500.

brought to Edinburgh. All three cars were prepared by Wilkie Wilkinson and his team at Merchiston Mews and all three cars, plus Ian Stewart's older car, were painted in Ecurie Ecosse flag metallic blue. It is worth mentioning here that this colour was conceived by Ian Stewart when recovering from an accident on his way to Turnberry in 1952 when he put his Jaguar XK120 through a hedge. He also drew the original design for the Ecurie Ecosse badge with the shield and St Andrew's Cross plus a little stick man. The stick man was dropped for the badges put on the side of the racing cars but remained on the small lapel badges and car badges produced by David Murray.

The May race meeting at Charterhall saw a last minute entry by Aston Martin Ltd of Reg Parnell in the new Aston Martin DB3S. This was the first time a DB3S ever raced and Parnell was faced by the full Ecurie Ecosse team of D type Jaguars. There were two other Aston Martins in the race, the heavy DB3s of Australian Tony Gaze and Bob Dickson from Carlisle. Ian Stewart in the Ecosse C-type was the early leader but a plug lead came adrift. Parnell swept into the lead and not even Ninian Sanderson with team mate Jimmy Stewart behind him, could challenge him so the DB3S registered its first win first time out.

The Saltire was a Scots-built sports racing car originally fitted with a Lea Francis engine but Syd Ritchie bought it and with the help of Bryan Wingfield fitted a Jaguar engine. It never handled well, such as here, sliding at Charterhall, and Ritchie was subsequently killed driving the car.

One of the newcomers racing in Scotland was Gordon Porteous who bought the ex-Percy Crabbe Tojeiro-Bristol. He also ran the car at Bo'ness Hill Climb.

Things at Charterhall then took a strange turn. Towards the end of 1953 the Winfield Joint Committee announced they were looking for support with a view to forming a limited company with authorised capital of £30,000 to finance the Winfield Joint Committee Ltd and, in turn, the racing at Charterhall. Clearly, all was not well with the WJC even though they were still led by the ebullient Dan Mackay who always oozed confidence.

Stirling Moss again, this time congratulating Reg parnell on his win in the sports car race at Charterhall in 1953. This was the first ever race for an Aston Martin DB3S that was being developed for an assault on Le Mans that year.

It was generally felt that by running such a big International event at the end of 1953, they had spent so much on attracting star names they had put themselves into financial difficulties.

There followed a deathly silence and the rumours began to grow that Charterhall was finished: WJC could not finance it any more. The proposed limited company was not formed until a year later.

Another group of enthusiasts got together to discuss this situation and proposed the setting up of another independent company to take over the entire assets and pay off the creditors of the WJC but still leave sufficient working capital to continue to run races. The modest sum they had in mind was £7,000. This received a favourable response and those behind the scheme estimated that they could not only raise this capital but also sufficient to continue to promote racing for five years. The group were also at pains to point out to potential investors that, at the end of the day, there would be little chance of showing a profit and a definite risk the capital invested might be lost.

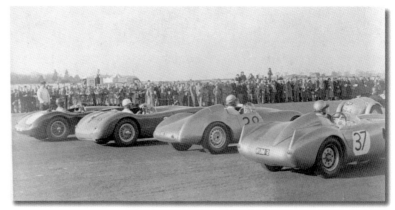

Charterhall Line up in 1954 with, left to right, Danny Margulies (Jaguar C type 038), John Lawrence in the ex-Ecurie Ecosse C type Jaguar (053), Peter Bolton in Jack Walton's Cooper-Jaguar and Jack Walton in his special bodied sports Cooper-Bristol.

Then the Winfield Joint Committee - who had the franchise from the Trotter family, the main landowners involved at Charterhall - announced they were now in a position to continue to promote race meetings at the circuit. This led to the disbanding of the private group.

The general feeling at the time was that the WJC were not coming clean in explaining the actual financial situation that led to this crisis. Also, why did the WJC estimate that £30,000 was needed but an independent group felt £7,000 would be sufficient? With the benefit of hindsight we could conclude that a figure somewhere between the two would probably have been more realistic all round. However, the real doubts, as far as the competitors were concerned, centred around the fact that the Winfield Joint Committee was a group of representatives from a number of Scottish motor clubs including Aberdeen and District MC, Scottish Sporting Car Club, MG Car Club, Lothian Car Club and Hawick and District Motor Club. There had always been parochial rivalry between the clubs, each wanting to contribute their tuppence-worth for the sake of saving face.

A few months later Winfield Joint Committee announced they had advised the RAC they were prepared to give up their International race meeting, planned for October 1954, and run, instead, a National race meeting in September. This allowed the BARC to upgrade the Aintree 200 meeting at the new Aintree circuit to International status.

Charlie Graham was a Scot with an engineering bent. He produced this unique de-Dion back axle on his Cooper 500 but the car never performed well.

Charlie Graham, from Glasgow, who bought one of Stirling Moss's lightweight Cooper 500s, came up with his own modifications. His Cooper Special appeared at Charterhall with a new stressed skin alloy body and de-Dion rear suspension. To my knowledge this was the only Cooper 500 to be fitted with a de-Dion back axle. The workmanship was superb but neither car nor driver was particularly successful.

Having moved up to Ecurie Ecosse, Ninian Sanderson sold his Mark VI Cooper 500 to Aberdonian Peter Gordon and that other 500cc stalwart, Alex McGlashan, sold his car to Borderer David Swan after which McGlashan retired from racing. Peter Gordon, however, displayed his youthful enthusiasm with some spectacular driving.

As far as motor sport is concerned the Royal Scottish Automobile Club are the RAC's representative in Scotland and at the end of each year they hosted a meeting in their Blythswood Square headquarters attended by

all the Scottish clubs to hammer out the competition programme for the following year. The meeting to plan for the 1954 season was held in the autumn of 1953. Winfield Joint Committee attended and in addition to asking for their usual dates they announced that they wished to hold an International race meeting once more at Charterhall.

The RAC - who are only allowed to designate a fixed number of meetings in Britain with International status - turned down the request but it illustrated that the WJC had had a successful, if low-key, 1953 season and had managed to iron out their financial problems of a year before. There was a line of opinion which dictated that as WJC had made a profit on their National race meeting, they would be unwise to press further for an International event when the most they could expect was a handful of minor foreign drivers who would be unlikely to attract a greater crowd.

For some strange reason, a meeting was held in London on November 1 1954 where members of the Winfield Joint Committee discussed the situation of their involvement in running motor racing at Charterhall. They reported they were now free from debt but again recommended that a limited liability company be formed called Winfield Joint Committee Ltd to take over all the assets and the promotion of motor racing. A committee was formed, of those interested parties present, to plan the formation of the company and the members included Jack Lawson, Jock McBain from Chirnside, John Dick Peddie, the Edinburgh lawyer, Charles Mauritzen from Edinburgh and A Riddel Innes from Hawick. Dan McKay was appointed interim secretary and, in time, the limited company was formed so freeing WJC of its almost impossible role of achieving accord with a consortium of motor clubs, all with their own agendas, involved in the running of Charterhall.

By 1957 Ecurie Ecosse were at the height of their fame. Here in the Mews the old Albion bus is loaded up with XKD504 on the ramp. On the right is sister car XKD561 with David Murray's service director, David Abbot looking on.

By 1955 motor sport in Scotland was beginning to attract its own exclusive support. Unlike in the early years after the war, the general public's interest and fascination for motor sport was being eroded by such things as television and greater personal mobility. This meant that families could go further afield and were being attracted to other pursuits. It was becoming clear that motor sport was only going to be supported and financed by the real dyed-in-the-wool enthusiasts.

As a result of this, some of the hill climbs began to suffer from a lack of spectators. This was particularly the case at Bo'ness hill climb and Scottish Sporting Car Club, which had originally started hill climbs on the site in the 1930s, began to have second thoughts about organising the climb when precious few entrants were forthcoming. On the other side of the country the Royal Scottish Automobile Club were faced with much the same financial constraint with their Rest and Be Thankful hill climb. Apart from two relatively small controlled spectator areas at the start and finish, people could climb down the hillside from the main road and spectate happily for nothing. Even then costs of running motor sport events were beginning to rise but there was a general feeling that if those two hill climbs were to stop then a very important nursery for new racing talent would be lost.

The only good news was that after two years of no activity the Aberdeen and District Motor Club had obtained a new two-year lease on the Crimond circuit and planned to run three race meetings in 1955.

The British Empire Trophy race of 1955 was an important event in the history of Scottish motor racing because it gave Archie Scott Brown his first major victory.

The great Ecurie Ecosse breakthrough was winning Le Mans in 1956 with Ron Flockhart and Ninian Sanderson, centre. On the right are David Murray and Wilkie Wilkinson

Archie was the son of a well known Paisley garage proprietor who had gone to Cambridge and ended up as a sales representative for Dobbies Four Square tobacco; a well known brand at the time. Because of a birth defect, which meant he had only a vestigial arm, the RAC had initially refused him a racing licence even though he had shown his brilliance in sprint meetings down south. Eventually they arranged a special medical board and he was given a full International racing licence for the 1955 season. Archie was a great character and brilliant racing driver who went on to race Connaughts in grand prix racing. Sadly he was killed in a racing accident at Spa in 1958 when driving one of Brian Lister's Lister-Jaguars and, though his accident could have happened to anyone, it created more stringent regulations regarding driver disabilities and the issuing of licences.

However, the British Empire Trophy races at Oulton Park in 1955 demonstrated what Archie could do and he won the Trophy driving a factory Lister-Bristol.

The Scottish racing season opened on April 16 on the cold and bleak wastes of Charterhall. One of the race winners that day was Peter Jackson with the ex-Cliff Davis Cooper-MG. This car was to have a number of links to Scotland after this. It was first bought by a Glasgow hairdresser who decided the Ferrari-style barchetta body was in too bad a shape and replaced it with a Falcon glass fibre body shell. In turn, the car was sold to Edinburgh enthusiast Archie Craig who completely rebuilt the car and ran it successfully. It was then sold to a relative of the classical traveller and diarist James Boswell, before finally being rebuilt in its original "Cliff Davis" style.

The Heath-Robinson nature of Charterhall race organisation continued in the race for 500cc Formula 3 cars where the cars were given not one but two warm-up laps. As they came round the second time, the starter, C M Mauritzen, a former 500cc racer himself, dropped the flag so everyone had a flying start. Tommy Dickson in his Erskine Staride and Johnny Higham in his Cooper, who were running at the back, were still gently turning into the main straight when Stuart Lewis Evans (Cooper) and Don Parker (Kieft) were already racing into the first bend a mile away! Ninian Sanderson had ordered a new Martin Special but it was not ready so he reverted to his Erskine Staride. He found the Staride a bit of a handful and spun twice during the race so letting Keith Hall finish in third place with the Border Reivers Cooper-Norton. When the Martin was delivered Ninian sold his Erskine Staride to John Bain a young Kilmarnock lawyer who was later killed at Charterhall driving a Le Mans Replica Frazer-Nash.

At this meeting, Ninian Sanderson was also racing the ex-Ecurie Ecosse C-type Jaguar now owned by J K Hunter as there were no Ecurie Ecosse entries. In the main sports car race Ninian was outfoxed by the wily Archie Scott Brown, who had won the British Empire Trophy at Oulton Park the previous week driving the same Lister-Bristol.

Up at Crimond the following weekend the rain pelted down but it didn't dampen everyone's enthusiasm. The meeting as a whole, however, was not a great success with a lot of non-starters which must have dampened a lot of the tremendous enthusiasm from the loyal band of Aberdeen members. At the meeting there was a handicap saloon car race won by Peter Gordon's Austin A90 with Jock Lawrence driving a highly modified Standard 8 saloon in second place. Peter Gordon was to become something of a character in

Ron Flockhart occasionally raced this Austin Healey 100S in Scotland and was to crash it on the Mille Miglia.

Scottish motor racing and in addition to the ex-Ninian Sanderson Cooper 500 he was racing at the time, he raced a Lotus Eleven and eventually wound up working in a lock-up alongside Ecurie Ecosse in Merchiston Mews.

Much as expected, Scottish Sporting Car Club cancelled their Bo'ness hill climb when they received only 40 entries. They held a meeting and asked Bo'ness town council for a guarantee against loss but this was denied. Typically, as soon as there was a hint of a problem, the club was flooded with entries including two Ecurie Ecosse D type Jaguars. But it was too late, the event was cancelled ,as was the other fixture in September, so Bo'ness dropped from the calendar.

The last truly big International race meeting at Charterhall took place in August 1955 with a host of leading drivers. One interesting entry was from an Australian called Jack Brabham with a central seat Cooper.He promptly put the car on the front row of the grid alongside Bob Gerard in the Stirling Moss Maserati 250F, Horace Gould in his 250F, Leslie Marr with a streamlined Connaught and John Young with another Connaught. Forty years later, when talking about this meeting with Brabham, Jack remarked. *"When I drove up for the event I couldn't find the circuit so I stopped at the nearby village (Greenlaw) and asked a policeman who gave me instructions. Thank God he pointed down the road I should take as I couldn't understand a bloody word he said !"*

Adding to the International element was Frenchman Louis Rosier with a 250F Maserati and his 750 Monza Ferrari. He had previously raced at Charterhall with a Ferrari 375 F1 car. Another Frenchman practiced on the Friday but crashed his Lotus VI on his way from the track to Broomdykes, where he was staying. He was Gerard "Jabby" Crombac – later to become a close confidante of both Jim Clark and Colin Chapman. The three Australians who formed the Kangaroo Stable of Aston Martin DB3S' were also there with David Mackay, Tony Gaze and Tommy Sulman.

As there was no commercial sponsorship of racing cars back in those days, all the leading teams and drivers relied on financial support from fuel and tyre companies. When Charterhall could not persuade the fuel companies to bring their transporters to the meeting a number of interesting entries were withdrawn including Colin Chapman, who withdrew the Lotus 11s he entered for himself and Peter Jopp and John Coombs' Lotus-Connaught. There was an amusing incident before the start of the small capacity sports car race. It was a Le Mans start with the drivers on one side of the road and the cars lined up alongside the pits. Starter John Dick Peddie remonstrated with Ian Scott Watson for not wearing a crash helmet only to be informed that as he was racing a saloon car in the event - his DKW - he didn't need one. That ruling was later to be changed by the RAC so that all saloon car racers had to wear crash helmets.

The sports car race at this meeting was well supported for, in addition to three Aston Martin DB3S' Ecurie Ecosse fielded D type Jaguars for Irishman Desmond Titterington and Ninian Sanderston. Archie Scott Brown and Noel Cunningham Reid had Lister-Bristols, Jock Lawrence, Bill Smith and Rosemary Vickers with C-type Jaguars and Louis Rosier his Ferrari 750 Monza. Desmond won the race from Rosier and Scott Brown. Bill Smith was a young Scot who lived in Lincoln. His father had bought an ex-Ecurie Ecosse C-type Jaguar - the car Duncan Hamilton had used to win Le Mans in 1953 - and Bill was a real driving talent. David Murray was to give him a drive in an Ecosse D-type at Crimond and then promptly signed him up for the 1956 Ecurie Ecosse team. Lofty England at Jaguar was also interested in signing him but, a month later, Smith, driving a Connaught sports car, was killed at the Tourist Trophy race at Dundrod so nipping a great talent in the bud.

In August, the Berwick and District Motor Club held a sprint meeting at Winfield notable in having an interesting young newcomer called James Clark Junior winning the unlimited saloon car class with his Sunbeam Talbot. Jim had been competing in sprints and rallies all season with the car and had co-driven with his cousin Billy Potts in the International Scottish Rally with an Austin Healey 100.

Up in Stonehaven, Fred Stephen, who was gathering entries for the Crimond meeting, was suffering in the same way Scottish Sporting Car Club had suffered, with lack of entries. The Aberdeen club were still prepared to run the meeting but at least one of the races, the 500cc Formula III event, was dropped from the programme as there were fewer than ten entries. In the end it was a good meeting. Ninian Sanderson won both the sports and the racing car events with the Ecosse D-type and officially broke Jock Lawrence's outright lap record for the circuit. Bill Smith took two third places in his first D-type drive but Jock Lawrence was the star of the meeting in the C type. As a result of this, and the tragedy that was to befall Bill Smith, Jock Lawrence was officially drafted into the Ecurie Ecosse team for 1956.

The closing race meeting at Charterhall in 1955 was a very low-key affair though one interesting visitor was John Ogier with his Jaguar XK120. The ebullient John was to go on to be the financial backer of John Tojeiro and was responsible for ordering the first Tojeiro-Jaguar. Ogier and David Murray of Ecurie Ecosse were to become close friends and the first Tojeiro-Jaguar raced by Ecurie Ecosse was actually loaned to them for the entire season free of charge by Ogier. Later Ecosse bought their own cars.

Crimond was an important racing circuit for Jim Clark as it was the first one on which he raced. He raced the Border Reivers D type Jaguar there in 1958 for the last time.

As we have seen, ever since 1950 there had been various groups interested in finding new venues for motor racing and one of the most promising, and yet unlikely, concepts was to use the narrow road round Hollyrood Park in Edinburgh, next to the Queen's official residence in Scotland, Hollyrood Palace. The man behind this latest project was an enthusiast who had become Secretary of the Lothian Car Club, Bert Weller. Bert was the eternal optimist and thought big if, at times, with a blindness towards practicality. He had not been the first to look at Hollyrood but at least he attempted to take things further. The circuit would have been spectacular but even the most willing enthusiast, with an eye to the way in which motor racing was beginning to develop in 1955, would have seen that this plan was always going to be a non-starter.

Firstly, the road circled Edinburgh's famous Arthur's Seat, an extinct volcano, and its nickname "the radical road" was no joke. It climbed quite steeply from what would have been the obvious start and paddock area on a twisting road with solid rock on one side and an equally solid wall on the other. In places the road would have been pushed to reach the 30-foot width that was the minimum standard for a new circuit at that time. It certainly would have been spectacular on the upper reaches with the hill side making a natural grandstand but then came the twisting downhill section at the back of Arthur's Seat. It would be a brave person who even attempted to overtake at this point. To make things more difficult, the fastest stretch would have been a long sweeping downhill into a fast right hander on to the main straight again. Quite how far the venture went, and with whom Bert discussed the plan, I do not know, but when the Le Mans Disaster took place in June 1955 any thought of progressing with the idea was quickly dropped. It was certainly a bold concept and would have been a Scottish Nurburgring.

Talking of safety, the RAC announced new rules regarding circuit safety, which, in today's climate, sound positively quaint and rather obvious. For example, they ruled that if there was no protection in front of spectators they had to be at least 1000 feet from the edge of the circuit, also that pits should be segregated from the circuit with what we now call a pit lane. However, they softened this ruling by adding *"...failing more permanent arrangements, a line on the roadway would be accepted as a method of demarcation."* It was also ruled that competitors would be required to complete a lap of the circuit after the race had finished as there had been some nasty accidents caused by drivers crossing the finishing line and braking hard before turning into the pits.

By now Alastair Birrell had long since sold ERA R1A and replaced it with the Ecurie Ecosse Cooper-Bristol. This led to some confusion during the season as Border Reivers had been running the ex-Eric Brandon Cooper-Bristol for Jimmy Somervail, which was then sold. When he was unable to drive his ex-Ecosse car, Birrell occasionally loaned it to Jimmy Somervail hence the confusion between Border Reivers and the two cars. There was even more confusion later in the life of the Ecosse car. It was almost destroyed in an accident and rebuilt by Bill Wilks as a sports car, using the running gear. Wilks later bought the Aston-Butterworth F2 car, which had a Cooper chassis, and eventually the chassis of the Bill Aston car and running gear from the Ecosse car were put together again. The car is still racing today in historic events as the Ecurie Ecosse Cooper Bristol.

Tommy Dickson occasionally switched Lotus 11s with Jimmy Mackay such as here at the test meeting held at Edzell in Aberdeenshire.

Chapter 6
Border Motor Racing Club

Over the winter of 1955/56 the ebullient Jock McBain, Chairman of Border Reivers racing team and Chirnside Ford dealer, felt the Winfield Joint Committee had a stranglehold on racing at Charterhall. He felt that being a Border circuit , Borderers should have a bit more say in its organisation. He talked this over with a young farmer called Ian Scott Watson, and originally asked him if he would form a supporters club, presumably for Border Reivers. Eventually they decided they would create a new motor club, to be registered with the RAC, that would only organise motor racing and speed events. One of the reasons for McBain's angst was that he had been the man who canvassed entries for the big National and International meetings at Charterhall and felt he was being blamed by the directors of the WJC for the financial losses and was slowly being edged out.

The only World Champion ever to race in Scotland after he had won the Championship: Dr Guiseppe Farina with the Thinwall Special Ferrari.

Scott Watson came up with the name Border Motor Racing Club and, as Jock McBain was a member of the British Racing Drivers Club, he loaned Scott Watson the constitution and rules of the BRDC which were incorporated into the first draft constitution for BMRC. Because motor-cycle racing was strong in Scotland BMRC was open to both car and motor cycle enthusiasts and the subscription was set at two pounds two shillings or £2.10p for the car people and £1.05p for motor cycle racers.

All of this was decided at a gathering of interested parties at the Rum Puncheon restaurant in Berwick upon Tweed, owned and run by the Stoddart brothers who were regular competitors on the Monte Carlo Rally. It took place on February 15 1956 and from those present an interim committee was formed with Jock McBain as Chairman, Ian Scott Watson as Secretary and a local bank manager, Bill Martin, as treasurer. Amongst the committee selected were Jim McCaig - a sports car driver from Prestonpans and no relation to Hugh McCaig who was to enter the scene many years later - and two north of England representatives, Charlie Fairbairn and motor cycle man Les Stockill. Scott Watson was asked to approach David Murray of Ecurie Ecosse to become President but Murray declined. Jock McBain contacted his old friend Reg Parnell and he agreed to become the first President of BMRC.

By now Ian Scott Watson was in his element. He was ready to joust with the Winfield Joint Committee to try and secure a BMRC race date at Charterhall for the 1956 season. He wrote letters to both Dan McKay and Charles

John Brown from Edinburgh was one of the first Scots to buy a contemporary racing car. His 1950 HWM-Alta was one of three works cars raced that year. He later sold the car to Ray Fielding.

Mauritzen, a local Borderer and Chairman of the Winfield Joint Committee Ltd, to ask for a date. Almost by return he received a typical Dan McKay letter *"...We thought it must be made clear to your members that you have nothing whatever to do with the running of events at Charterhall. While your club is to get certain concessions, it must not be misunderstood by the other supporters of motorsport throughout the country.*

"We shall be obliged, therefore, if you will refrain from issuing to your members statements which suggest that your club and the Company are closely associated. I do not want to enter into a correspondence with regard to this matter....", He did concede, however, that the new BMRC members would be allowed a 50% discount on tickets to Charterhall meetings.

In his original letter Scott Watson had asked for a race meeting in July 1956 and a few days later Dan McKay poured cold water on this idea pointing out that, if given a date, the Club would not only have to pay a further £25 to Major Trotter but the RAC charges would be added and warned it would cost the club close on £200 to run such a meeting. As a compromise he suggested that Border Motor Racing Club could be allowed 40 minutes at the June 30th race meeting to run a single race of their own.

Unfazed, Scott Watson decided to set out on a pilgrimage to find his own circuit venue. He wrote to the Duke of Northumberland, who was a prominent landowner in the area, but was told that RAF Acklington was still in occupation and full use, that part of the Boulmer airfield was now a public road, and that Eshott didn't belong to him and he didn't know the state of affairs as far as that one was concerned. Scott Watson also searched everywhere in Scotland and found East Fortune airstrip but was refused use of this because it was close to a sanatorium. The other promising airfield on the outskirts of Edinburgh was Kirknewton that had been a US air force base. However, the Air Ministry said "no" and proceeded to cover the field with radar masts.

Eventually he found a small airfield at Brunton, Beadnell and set too organising a High Speed Reliability Trial. This meant he got round the tight motor racing regulations but at least had something to offer the members. The plan was to run this opening event in 1956 and then have another High Speed Reliability event and a relay race in 1957.

Brunton Beadnell in the North East of England, was potentially perfect for both sprints and races because it was asphalt-surfaced rather than bitmac and stood up to the sometimes wild east coast weather. It had been a Fleet Air Arm airfield and was not completed until 1943. If you are travelling by rail to Scotland on the East coast line you can still see the remains of Brunton Beadnell.

This event was run with a complicated handicap system created by Scott Watson and around forty club members took part. Amongst the saloon cars was James Clark Junior with Scott Watson's DKW Sonderklasse

A windy day at Cromond with Ian Scott Watson, left, and the author with Jim Clark and the Border Reivers Porsche 1600S in the background. He also drove the Jaguar D type on that day.

WINFIELD JOINT COMMITTEE LTD.

B.M.R.C. Members' Race Meeting

CHARTERHALL AIRFIELD

Saturday, 5th October, 1957

For Official Use Only

Car No. 11

Recd. £ 1 : 10 :

Ack. ....

F.I. sent .....-1 OCT 1957

ENTRY FORM

TO I. SCOTT WATSON, HARELAW L'MOOR, GREEN LAW, BEFORE 30th SEPTEMBER, 1957

NAME OF ENTRANT ....James Clark Junr........ MEMBERSHIP No. ....

ADDRESS ....Edington Mains, Duns, Berwickshire....

PHONE NO. Chirnside 221

Class A—Production Saloon Cars
Class B—Production Sports Cars
Class C—Sports Cars
Class D—Racing Cars

Entry per Class 15/-.

Enclosed ....

Class(es)	Make of Car and Model	c.c.	Year	Reg. Number
B	~~D.K.W. 3-6~~ Porsche	~~896~~ 1582	1957	CSH 750
A	Sunbeam	2267	1955	BSH 510

MODIFICATIONS

Engine .... Type of Cylinder Head .... Exhaust System ....

Number of Carbs. .... Make of Carbs. .... Compression Ratio ....

Transmission and Suspension ....

Gear Ratios .... Final Drive.............. Tyre Size ....

Any additional Modifications ....

(Please state make of modified parts)

"I have read the Supplementary Regulations issued for this meeting and agree to be bound by them and by the General Competition Rules of the Royal Automobile Club. In consideration of the acceptance of this entry or of my being permitted to take part in this meeting I agree to save harmless and keep indemnified the Winfield Joint Committee Ltd., the Royal Automobile Club and their respective officials, servants, representatives, and agents from and against all actions, claims, costs, expenses and demands in respect of death, injury, loss of or damage to the person or property of myself, my driver(s), passenger(s), or mechanic(s) (as the case may be) howsoever caused arising out of or in connection with this entry or my taking part in this meeting and notwithstanding that the same may have been contributed to or occasioned by the negligence of the said bodies, their officials, servants, representatives or agents."

"I declare that to the best of my belief the driver(s) possess(es) the standard of competence necessary for an event of the type to which this entry relates and that the car entered is suitable and roadworthy for the event having regard to the course and the speeds which will be reached."

"I understand that should I at the time of this event be suffering from any disability whether permanent, temporary or otherwise which is likely to affect prejudicially my normal control of my automobile. I may not take part unless I have declared such disability to the R.A.C., who have, following such declaration, issued a licence which permits me to do so."

"I undertake that at the time of the event to which this entry relates I shall be in possession of a certificate of medical fitness made within the preceding twelve months."

SIGNATURE OF ENTRANT ....J. Clark Junr........ DATE ....25/9/57....

" Any indemnity and/or declaration as prescribed by the paragraphs above which is signed by a person under the age of 21 years shall be countersigned by that person's parent or guardian, whose full names and address shall be given."

SIGNATURE OF PARENT/GUARDIAN ....

Jim Clark's entry form for the BMRC members meeting in 1957. As Ian Scott Watson had just sold his DKW, Jim changed the entry form to Scott Watson's Porsche 1600S. The other car was Clark's personal Sunbeam Talbot that he ran in the saloon car race. Note that he signed his name "James Clark Jnr."

and Jim ran his own Sunbeam Talbot in the sports car class. The local Border Reivers entered Jimmy Somervail in their Lotus 11 Climax in one sports car race and Edinburgh driver Alastair Birrell in the same car in the other sports car race. The furthest travelled drivers were Nick Newall with his XK140 Jaguar and Ronnie Miller with Pat Melville's Vauxhall 30/98 from Glasgow. Ronnie, who was chief executive of the huge Motherwell Bridge company, later bought a Lister-Jaguar in kit form from Brian Lister and had it built by Wilkie Wilkinson at Merchiston Mews. This car had a slightly different body to most of the other Listers and still appears at historic racing events in the hands of its present owner, David Ham. The Brunton course measured 2.2 miles and the fastest times were set up by Sommervail and Birrell with the Lotus and Peter Jackson with his Cooper-Climax at an average speed of 86 mph. Thanks to Scott Watson's unique handicap formula an awful lot of drivers were credited with the same time and so as a measure of individual performance it was pretty ineffectual. It is fair to say that by the following February, and a committee meeting in Berwick, Scott Watson had cobbled together some reasonable results for the event and it seems that almost everyone got a prize of some sort.

One of the minutes of the subsequent committee meeting read *"..A financial statement prepared by the treasurer showed that the event had left about £4 to go towards the purchase of awards!"* Sadly it was also reported that a letter from the tenant of Brunton had advised the club that he had cancelled permission for the club to use the track, again, on the instructions of his landlord, the Duke of Northumberland, who had received a complaint from a local resident. What happened was that by agreement with the Duke, any profit from the meeting was to be given to the British Empire Cancer Campaign. However, half way through the meeting the police arrived on the site and told the organisers that the meeting had to stop because they had received a complaint from the Hon. H G O Bridgeman DSO who owned about a quarter of an acre of the site. He told the police that when he originally handed over his part of the land to the Ministry of Defence it was on condition that it could only ever be used for agriculture once it had been de-commissioned. He also happened to be Chairman of the Lords Day Observance Society and as it was a Sunday this added fuel to his argument. The police, who obviously had sympathy for the event, agreed to turn a blind eye so they could finish the meeting. That was the end of Brunton.

THE BORDER REIVERS

offer for sale (subject to their still being available) two of their meticulously maintained 1958 team cars (started 51 events, finished 50, 1 puncture!)

D-TYPE JAGUAR—Many spares, including set road wheels, 3 alternative axle ratios, spare axle complete, reconditioned clutch, brake caliper, quick-lift jacks, etc. One of the fastest Jaguars in the Country.

Offers over £1500.

TRIUMPH TR3 (Nov. 1957) — Overdrive, wire wheels, disc brakes, Koni shock-absorbers, hard-top hood, tonneau, third seat, radio. Never raced, but fastest TR ever up Rest-and-be-Thankful. Cost £1250 new. £900 o.n.o.

All enquiries to :

IAN SCOTT WATSON, Harelaw L'Moor, Greenlaw, Berwickshire. (Tel. Westruther 218).

The advertisement that appeared at the end of 1958 when the Reivers D type and Jim Clark's own Triumph TR3 were put up for sale, The price is enough to make a modern historic racer weep.

At the same BMRC committee meeting, Jim Clark was appointed Assistant Secretary of the club. What this really meant was unwittingly revealed by Scott Watson in a letter to Noreen Garvie the secretary of the Aberdeen and District Motor Club a couple of months later when he wrote *"Jimmy Clark is now my assistant secretary and its quite a help when it comes to addressing envelopes"*

In the build-up to the 1956 season a number of interesting cars arrived in Scotland. One was the CSM-Ford. It was bought for Colin Kirkcaldie whose father was a Glasgow businessman. This car was the prototype of what was to become the first Elva. Mike Chapman had built the car for Frank Nichols and he was so pleased with it he and his mechanic Mac Witts built an improved version which they called the Elva.

In addition to the Border Reivers Lotus Eleven, another appeared with its new owner, a young car salesman called Tommy Dickson. The car he bought was one of the first Lotus Elevens to come to Scotland through Lewis Fraser in Perth who had become the Scottish Lotus distributor. Tommy had long since disposed of his old Cooper Mk IV and had sufficient accidents with his Erskine Staride to make him feel a switch to sports cars would be a good idea; and so it proved to be.

Meanwhile Lewis Fraser, who was the Ford distributor in Perth, had considerable success with a Mark VI Lotus powered by a Ford Consul engine. When he decided to buy one of the new Lotus Elevens and sold the original Lotus-Consul to Jimmy Mackay from Scrabster. Now Mackay had a competitive car and this was to prove very successful.

Jimmy Mackay from Scrabster sweeps round the outside of Johnny Higham's similar Lotus Eleven. Mackay was one of Scotland's most successful Lotus sports car drivers.

All the excitement and anticipation was dulled at the first race meeting of the year at Charterhall when John Bain, driving his Frazer Nash Le Mans Replica, arrived at the notorious Kames Curve too fast and ran on to the grass. He tried to turn the Nash back too quickly and the car dug in and rolled, killing the driver. Ted Evans also ran off the road avoiding Bain's car. It was the first fatality at Charterhall and the first fatality at any Scottish motor race meeting.

At the same meeting, Brian Naylor brought his brand new Maserati 150S and recorded two wins. Brian had previously raced in Scotland with his Cooper-MG but he soon took the engine out of the Maserati and put it into his own Lotus-based JBW chassis.

In the main sports car race, Ecurie Ecosse entered three of their D type Jaguars for Ninian Sanderson, Jock Lawrence and Peter Hughes. Hughes, who lived in Glasgow, had previously raced the fearsome ex-Brian Lister Tojeiro-JAP and was a close friend of David Murray. He drove well and finished second to Ninian Sanderson and ahead of Jock Lawrence. In the unlimited racing car race, Sanderson gave up his seat in the D type to Ron Flockhart who won with Hughes again in second place and Lawrence third. One of the ex-Ecurie Ecosse C type Jaguars was also running in the race driven by Keith Hall who was now a factory Lotus driver. At the same race meeting Bobby McIntyre the Scottish motor cycle champion, had two superb wins with Joe Potts-prepared 250cc and 500cc Nortons.

Douglas Mickel and Ernie Herrald of the MG Car Club had been searching for a sprint venue and found one at an old army camp near Hawick. Like Beveridge Park, it was small and the road width varied from 13 - 20 ft! However, as only one car would be running at a time it was felt sufficient. It was a great success and a date was set for the following year. Tommy Dickson, John Romanes and Jim Clark all took part; Clark in Ian Scott Watson's Porsche 1600S

The June 16 meeting at Crimond was an important one as far as the future of Scottish motor sport was concerned. The Aberdeen Club had organised a handicap saloon car race for which there was a first prize of two-dozen bottles of whisky. Ian Scott Watson entered his DKW Sonderklasse - a three cylinder two-stroke that was particularly quick- and when he saw the club had a small entry for the sports car race he suggested his "mechanic", Jim Clark, should run the DKW in that event. Clark had harboured ideas about racing but his father and mother were very much against it. Scott Watson pointed out that as they were miles away from the Borders he could run in the sports car race - which he would not win anyway - and nobody would be any the wiser. The whole plan backfired, as far as Scott Watson was concerned, as sports car practice came first on the

programme and Clark duly set up a time in the DKW. When the saloon cars went out to practice, so allowing the handicappers to work out relevant handicaps, Scott Watson could not match Clark's times. He was hauled up before the Stewards and accused of driving slowly to get a better handicap. He was able to explain that he was driving as fast as he could but that Jim Clark - who had never raced a car before - was better than he was. As it turned out they gave Scott Watson an impossible handicap and Clark finished his first race at the back of the field in the DKW. Little were we to know the consequences of this illicit drive on that June afternoon. It transpired some of Jim Clark's farming relatives were spectators at the meeting and by the time he got back home his father and mother already knew he had raced!

The race meeting also saw the debut of a number of new cars. One was the Hammond-Gordon Special built by Gerald Hammond and Peter Gordon. It was Ford-powered and was nothing to write home about. However the Saltire, built by Ronnie Miller and Pat Melville with the help of Wilkie Wilkinson of Ecurie Ecosse, was a much more professional job, powered by a Lea-Francis engine. A couple of months later, Pat Melville blew up the Lea Francis engine and Wilkie Wilkinson persuaded the pair to invest in a Jaguar engine.

Another new car was Brian Naylor's Lotus-Maserati. He had put the 1.5 litre Maserati engine into a Lotus II chassis and was the star performer winning two races and finishing second in another two, including the racing car event. The handicap saloon car race prize of a couple of cases of scotch whisky went to the cheerful Glasgow competitor Pat Melville driving his Light Fifteen Citroen and those of us who knew Pat would agree it could not have gone to a more appropriate competitor!

Ecurie Ecosse were going from strength to strength and Lofty England, Jaguar's competitions manager, was always willing to support David Murray. When the Belgian racing team Ecurie Francorchamps was unable to take up one of their entries for Le Mans Lofty quickly wrote to the Automobile Club de L'Ouest and suggested they might like to invite Ecurie Ecosse to take part with one of their D-type Jaguars. In those days you had to be invited to compete at Le Mans.

Lofty pointed out that the team would put on a good show and so David Murray received the offer to enter one car for the 1956 race. The car he chose to enter was XKD 501 that carried the Edinburgh registration number MWS 301. This car had been supplied new to Ecurie Ecosse in May 1955. In March 1956 the car had been heavily damaged at Snetterton by Wilkie Wilkinson during a testing session. Then Ron Flockhart took a second and a first place at Goodwood before the car was set aside to be specially prepared for Le Mans.

When Innes Ireland drove the Ecurie Ecosse Tojeiro-Jaguar at Charterhall in 1957 against Jim Clark and Ron Flockhart he got into some difficulty at the end of the straight, spinning off on the gravel...

...the marshals helped Ireland remove an oil can jammed under the car and he continued in the race.

For Ecurie Ecosse this was something of a challenge. For a start, it was their first 24-hour race and they realised they would have to get a large team together to cover things like timekeeping, lap scoring, and signalling at Mulsanne, so David started to look around. He had already decided the drivers would be Ron Flockhart and Ninian Sanderson. Ninian immediately suggested that two of his favourite drinking pals should be roped in to help out. One of them was Willie Lawrence, son of one of Glasgow's biggest housebuilders, and a real character. Willie had bought a Cooper-Norton to race and hill climb but his driving style bordered on the suicidal so he quickly retired from racing. The other pal was S Livingstone (Livvy) Neil whose family business was in wholesale fishmongering. The antics of Lawrence, Sanderson and Neil at Le Mans in 1956 was a testament to political incorrectness. They created mayhem, including filching the BBC's passes from the organisers so that Willie and Livvy could be free to roam anywhere.

The year 1956 was the first time the pit signallers had been banished to the far side of the circuit, immediately after Mulsanne Corner. This was part of the safety effort after the previous year's horrendous accident at Le Mans. David Murray chose Sandy Arthur, the team's truckie, to organise the signalling out there and Murray also suggested that Willie Lawrence and Livvy Neil should be sent with him to keep them as far away from the pits, and the team, as possible. Another member of the team was Peter Hughes who had raced for them at Charterhall a few weeks before. Peter's job was timekeeping alongside Jenny Murray.

The Le Mans race that year was wet and slippery and yet Ninian Sanderson was confident that if they "kept the heid" they would be in there for a good placing. Ninian was so hyped up about the race he never slept the whole night of the race and when not at the wheel was in the pits checking out how they were doing. Ron Flockhart kept notes during the race and they are quite enlightening. For example he noted that the Aston Martins were quicker through the Esses, Tertre Rouge, Indianapolis and Mulsanne corners, which he put down to them having better brakes than the Jaguar. In fact it was more likely because the Astons were slightly lighter.

For once the factory Ferrari's were not in the hunt and early on it was obviously going to be a battle between the Ecurie Ecosse D type Jaguar and the strong Stirling Moss/Peter Collins Aston Martin DB3S. The fact that the lone Ecosse car managed to hold on to the lead to the end and win the Le Mans 24 Hours created something of a sensation at the time.

The Moss Aston Martin finished second just ten miles behind the Ecosse D type and David Murray could not believe his good fortune. He was grateful to Jaguar for all their help and support and wrote to William Lyons, the owner of Jaguar, *"...now that I have re-surfaced after being drowned with congratulations I should like you to know that it is quite impossible for me to thank you adequately for all the assistance I have received from the members of your firm. I am so glad that we were able to pull it off not only for Jaguar but for Britain"*. Jaguar team manager Lofty England replied *"...as you no doubt realise, we consider a win by a private owner in a major event of more value than winning ourselves."*

Only one incident marred the Ecurie Ecosse victory. Driving back from Le Mans in his Porsche 1600 Peter Hughes, probably tired and distracted, collided with a car near Lockerbie in the south of Scotland and was killed.

The Winfield Joint Committee was having a pretty poor season, their early race meeting at Charterhall saw few spectators turn up and the August meeting was almost washed out completely. The paddock was inches deep in water. The organisers contacted Edinburgh fire brigade but they refused to send a couple of fire engines the forty miles from Edinburgh to

For a race at Monza against the Indianapolis cars, Ecurie Ecosse built this single seater Lister-Jaguar.

the Borders to empty water from a race circuit. By contacting some local farmers they did manage to find two petrol-driven pumps and then set to work. To keep everyone amused Keith Schellenberg nipped into the Border Reivers transporter, changed into running gear and proceeded to lap the circuit in his running shoes - he explained *"...rugby season starts this week old boy!"* After his eight-mile trot he returned to the paddock to be greeted by blaring car horns for a noble effort. Then the Winfield Joint Committee announced that the event would become a sprint with the competitors starting at Kames Curve and going in the opposite direction slightly uphill and then left handed on to the main straight. The motor cyclists and side car riders proceeded to do this. Then the WJC changed their mind and decided the track was fit for racing and so practice started at quarter to four in the afternoon! The race meeting itself immediately followed. The star driver was Highlander Jimmy Mackay who romped home in the second race in the Lotus VI-Consul ahead of Lewis Bramley's more modern Lotus II. Jimmy also won the handicap race. The racing finished at 7.45 pm.

Towards the end of the season the fledgling BMRC ran a sprint at Winfield where Jock McBain and Jimmy Somervail shared the Border Reivers Lotus 11 to finish first and second. Young Jim Clark entered for four classes, two with Scott Watson's DKW and two with his own Sunbeam Talbot and ran out winner in all four saloon classes!

The Suez crisis of 1956 led to a spell of petrol rationing and naturally it affected motor sport in Scotland, but only to a slight extent as the winter period saw very little action anyway.

By April 1957, however, things had eased and the British Empire Trophy was again held at Oulton Park. It proved to be a successful event for Scots with Archie Scott Brown winning the main race in the factory Lister-Jaguar. Ron Flockhart won one of the heats with John Coombs' Lotus II and Tommy Dickson took a tremendous second place in the first heat with his Lotus Eleven behind Graham Hill's factory car. Tommy was always affected by his eyesight and I was witness to his comment to mechanic Hugh Shannon as he arrived back in the paddock after the race *"Who was that guy in front of me ?"* he asked. As anyone knows, Graham Hill's London Rowing Club crash helmet was easy to recognise but Tommy could not quite focus on this. To give some idea of Tommy's performance he headed Peter Ashdown, Innes Ireland and David Piper all in similar Lotus Elevens. Tommy at one stage led the race but lost two gears and finally his clutch and still finished second.

During 1957 both Jock McBain and Col. Stan Gallon managed to extract from the Winfield Joint Committee one race date at Charterhall per annum

The first and only Edzell race meeting saw Colin Murray race Brian Naylor's JBW-Maserati sports car.

for Border Motor Racing Club, on the understanding that there would be no spectators. If the truth be told, there was never any great love between WJC and BMRC.

In 1960 Border Reivers ran their Aston Martin DBR1 at Le Mans with Jim Clark and Roy Salvadori at the wheel. They finished third overall and won the Motor Trophy which was presented at a dinner in Berwick on Tweed.

The success of Ecurie Ecosse at Le Mans led Ian Scott Watson and some of his farmer friends into forming a new motor racing team called Ecurie Agricole. Initially all the members were farmers with an odd collection of cars. For example there was Scott Watson, now with a Porsche 1600 Super to replace the DKW, Jim Clark with his Sunbeam-Talbot, Oswald Brewis with a Triumph TR and later a Jaguar XK140, Bill Potts (Austin Healey) and Perthshire farmer Ronnie Dalglish (Triumph TR2). The writer was approached to be team manager but as I had no farming experience I had to go to Auchterarder in Perthshire where Ronnie Dalglish provided me with one of his tractors and a set of triple grass cutters. I was instructed to mow the pitch of the Auchterarder Cricket Club as a kind of initiation test to allow me to take on the job of team manager. When Ecurie Agricole entered no fewer than five cars for the subsequent Charterhall meeting we had the satisfaction of entering more cars than Ecurie Ecosse!

In June 1957 Ecurie Ecosse returned to Le Mans but this time with two entries. On this occasion David Murray decided to split the Ron Flockhart and Ninian Sanderson pairing bringing Ivor Bueb in to share one of their ex-factory long nose D type Jaguars with Ron Flockhart and Jock Lawrence shared another ex-factory long nose with Ninian Sanderson.

Unlike in 1956, most people felt the D type Jaguar was getting a bit long in the tooth and that the new Ferraris, Maseratis and Aston Martins would battle it out between themselves. Both Ferrari and Maserati had four factory cars each, the latter with two 4.5 litre V8s boasting far more power than the Jaguars. Despite this, Duncan Hamilton set up the quickest time on the Mulsanne straight of 178 mph with a D type. For the Italians the race was

The first truly modern grand prix car to come to Scotland was this Emeryson Climax that was bought by Eric Liddell. The photo was taken in practice before the car caught fire and was burned out.

a disaster. The two big Maseratis were out within three hours and the two leading Ferraris were also out early so that the Jaguars were once more in a strong position early in the race. Ron Flockhart and Ivor Bueb were soon in the lead in the Ecosse car and were to hold this lead to the end. To make David Murray's day even more complete the Sanderson/Lawrence car moved into second place and so for the second year running, Ecurie Ecosse won Le Mans. Indeed five Jaguar D types finished in the first six positions, the only interloper being the Stuart Lewis Evans/Martino Severi Ferrari.

There is no doubt this was one of the greatest moments in the history of Ecurie Ecosse and many years later David Murray told me he let this second win go to his head. Certainly, David was so convinced about the D-type's suitability for Le Mans he continued to enter them for the next three years. He was the last entrant ever to race a D-type Jaguar at Le Mans when he ran a 3 litre car in the 1960 event for Ron Flockhart and Bruce Halford. Sadly the new 3-litre engine failed and the car was retired.

Meanwhile, back in Scotland in 1957, the Winfield Joint Committee ran one of their most successful race meetings with a crowd to rival the last International event they held back in 1954. By now Jack Lawson from Newcastle had realised Jimmy Blumer's potential and had bought a Cooper-Climax for him to race. Charterhall was also beginning to attract a number of Irish competitors to boost entries. One of them was Malcolm Templeton, a staunch Lotus supporter. In the up to 1200cc sports car race Tommy Dickson in his Lotus II was the winner with Blumer second and Templeton's Lotus II third. The medium-sized sports car race was won by Frank Elliot with the ex-Jack Sears Lister-Bristol. This car is now back in Scotland and raced in historic events by Barry Wood.

John Ogier returned to Scotland and entered his new Tojeiro-Jaguar but could not start as he had totally demolished his shock absorbers and their mountings on the bumpy Rest and Be Thankful hill climb the previous day. A number of other hill climb competitors took part: Tony Marsh ran his

Formula II Cooper Climax and won the racing car event outright. However this race meeting truly pulled the curtain down on the old 500cc Formula III which had been a mainstay in offering inexpensive single seater racing in Scotland. There were only seven entrants of which three were non-starters and only two finished: Peter Procter and Andrew Goodfellow with their Coopers. If the truth be told, it was a pretty miserable meeting all round and must have given Winfield Joint Committee a few headaches wondering what to do to get competitors and, more importantly, spectators to the future events.

A couple of new young Scots also took part in that Charterhall meeting. Eric Liddell, who was better known as a speedway rider at the time, bought an aged Cooper 500 and ran the car for the first time. Eric was to go on to race a variety of cars including a Lola Junior and later he bought one of the F1 Emerysons. In the 1960s Eric was a regular racer in various cars including a Ford GT 40 and Lola and Ferraris. The other newcomer was Andrew Goodfellow in a rather decrepit Cooper 500 and he became a Scottish racing stalwart with a variety of cars, usually Coopers.

On July 27 1957, following the Ecurie Ecosse triumph at Le Mans, the Ecurie Ecosse Association was formed in Edinburgh. The man responsible for thinking up the idea was Edinburgh advertising man Bill Woolward. He gathered a number of like minded enthusiasts from around Scotland led by Lord Bruce - now the Earl of Elgin and Kincardine. Amongst them was John Stenhouse, whose family insurance business was one of the largest in Scotland and Harry Ballantyne, who had an iron foundry in Bo'ness. The Association was formed specifically to help raise money for Ecurie Ecosse and it was a tremendous success, the club having over 1,000 members at one stage. I remember at the time writing that it was a bit late in the day to be starting this as David Murray could have done with such support a year earlier when he was almost forced to call a halt to Ecurie Ecosse. Luckily the accessory manufacturers sustained the team and allowed them the chance to have their great success at Le Mans.

Jackie Stewart on the start line at Charterhall with the Marcos. Note the casual style. In the foreground is Iain Fraser's Cooper Mini.

I also went on to remark that we were in a situation in Scotland where our racing circuits were virtually rotting away and there were no signs of any major support coming along to develop the circuits to create more opportunities for potential future Scottish drivers.

Shortly after this, and other comments. I received a letter from John Hugenholtz, circuit manager of Zandvoort, who had become a noted circuit designer. He confirmed that he had been in touch with Lord Bruce about the possibility of designing a circuit on Bruce's Broomhall estate in Fife. He further offered to come to Scotland and look at any possible sites. Seven years later Hugenholtz, again with Lord Bruce, was involved in the Polkemmet circuit project of which there will be more later.

The Crimond race meeting, that took place the weekend after the dismal Charterhall event, saw nearly 15,000 spectators at the circuit. There is no doubt that Crimond could really pull in the enthusiastic crowds whereas Charterhall's audience was much more fickle. At that meeting there were only 37 cars but it did not seem to matter. Tommy Dickson had three wins in a brand new Lotus-Climax that had only been delivered a few days earlier. Tommy had sold his previous Lotus Eleven to a school friend of Jim Clark, Andy Walker. Ever quick to grab a promotional opportunity, David Murray arrived at the circuit with the D type Jaguar that finished second at Le Mans and gave it to local hero Jock Lawrence to demonstrate to the crowd: also to hand out membership forms for the new Ecurie Ecosse Association!

The Association was also at the Charterhall race meeting two weeks later but this time with its own tent. The only sad note was that David Murray, who had sent the transporter and the Le Mans winning D type Jaguar along with Ron Flockhart and Ninian Sanderson to do some demonstration laps, was stopped at the gates and forced to pay admission to the circuit. The same was true in the paddock where some officious soul decided that Ron Flockhart would not be allowed in. Luckily this was noticed and face was saved but it was this kind of treatment that was creating a rod for the Winfield Joint Committee's back.

Winfield Joint Committee also finally relented and let Border Motor Racing Club run a race meeting for their own members. The secretary, Ian Scott Watson, decided that, as it was a club event, every race should be on handicap and the poor soul spent the short time between practice and

the races with his slide rule trying to balance out the performances. He also put up the BMRC Trophy. The leading drivers in the first four races would automatically go into a handicap final and the winner would get the trophy.

As he was not racing, Scott Watson gave his Porsche 1600 Super to Jim Clark, who up to then had only had the odd outing with his Sunbeam Talbot. This race proved to us all that Jim Clark was certainly someone to look out for. In his heat he had a lot of trouble with the brakes, one minute with none and the next minute with them locking up. Despite this he finished third behind the Austin Healey 100S' of Jimmy Blumer and Ted Evans and qualified for the final. Clark was also entered for the handicap touring car race with his Sunbeam Talbot and won it easily on the road but due to his handicap he finished second overall to a Morris Minor!

When it came to the final, the heavens opened and the rain poured down. Scratch man was Jimmy Blumer in a Cooper-Climax and though he won the race on the road, Jim Clark in the Porsche drove as though the roads were dry and finished only half a lap behind the flying Blumer. Clark, however, was the only driver in the race to actually beat his handicap and so he emerged the first winner of the Border Motor Racing Club Trophy. There were a few ironic remarks about favouritism by Scott Watson but anyone who watched the race saw that in Jim Clark, Scotland had produced a class act.

John Hugenholtz, holding spectacles, visited Charterhall when planning the Polkemmet circuit in 1964. He was shown the circuit by Jackie Stewart, second from the left, standing at the notorious Kames Curve. Centre right is Border Motor Racing Club committee member, Bill Hume.

Towards the end of 1957 Ian Scott Watson thought up the concept of the Scottish Clubs Speed Trophy which would be presented to the driver who scored the highest number of wins over a raft of speed events, race meetings, hill climbs and sprints, organised by a group of Scottish Clubs. Originally it was to have a model of a D type Jaguar mounted on a plinth and Tony Belm, a well-known model maker and father of sports car driver Ray Belm, was approached for a quote to make the Trophy. The cost appeared a bit too high so Scott Watson compromised by ordering a basic model of a Lotus XI from Belms company, having it silver plated and made into a trophy. It went missing some years ago and was the first major trophy won by Jim Clark.

Amongst the Scots buying new racing cars for the 1958 season was Norman Barclay who invested in a Formula 2 Cooper. Barclay, whose family business was involved in the Scots whisky trade, was something of an adventurer. He was constantly getting himself into hot water such as when he decided to promote water ski-ing - at that time in its early development in Scotland.

OFFICIAL PROGRAMME, 1/6d.

SCOTTISH MOTOR RACING CLUB

MEMBERS

MEETING

INCORPORATING THE
BORDER MOTOR
RACING CLUB

Sunday,
4th October, 1964

CHARTERHALL

BY COURTESY OF THE WINFIELD JOINT COMMITTEE LTD.

The programme cover for the final racemeeting held at Charterhall
in October 1964. Fittingly, Jim Clark was on the cover.

He left his office beside the River Clyde in the centre of Glasgow and, with bowler hat and briefcase, proceeded to water ski all the way to his home in Helensburgh. Neither the police nor the Clyde Water Board was very impressed by this and Norman was arrested as "an unauthorised pleasure craft." When the case came up in court, Norman was at his impish best and the small fine that resulted was, in his opinion, worth all the hassle. His mother, Florence Barclay, had already been an enthusiastic rally driver on the International Scottish Rally and Norman simply followed in her footsteps. He and the equally quixotic Keith Schellenberg bought an ERA together (R14B, the ex-Johnny Wakefield car). Norman tried it out at Oulton Park, went off the road and decided he didn't want to drive it again so sold out his half share to Schellenberg for £325! Barclay was to go on to be a member of the British Olympic Bobsleigh team under Schellenberg. His

racing came to an end after a daft midnight water-ski jumping accident in which he almost lost an arm! Another of Barclay's friends, Gordon Porteous from Kirkintilloch, also took up racing with a Tojeiro-Bristol but like Barclay, his bravery far exceeded his ability and he did not stay long in racing.

Border Reivers were about to be reborn as a serious International team. Jock McBain decided they needed to buy a racing car that would extend the talents of his young farming client Jim Clark to whom he had sold the odd Ferguson tractor. The original plan was that Clark would share the car with regular team driver, Jimmy Somervail. Even Ian Scott Watson held out hope of racing this car but an initial test session at Charterhall soon settled the issue. Jim Clark took to the big D-type like a duck to water. Ian Scott Watson tried the car but suffered from poor vision at the high speeds and the gentlemanly Jimmy Somervail conceded that Clark was undoubtedly the quicker driver and he virtually stood down from racing the D-type.

The Reivers D-type Jaguar was originally built in 1955 and was chassis XKD 517. It had been sold by Henly's to Alex McMillan and Gillie Tyrer, both of whom had raced at Charterhall, but they sold it in 1956 to the Murkett Brothers who were Jaguar dealers in Huntingdon for one of the Murketts to race. However the car scared him and Murketts roped in Henry Taylor to race the car successfully for the rest of the 1957 season. Jim Clark was to race it in twenty events in 1958 and managed to rack up 12 wins before the car was sold to Alan Ensoll who converted it into an XKSS. Today the car is owned by well-known historic racer Nigel Corner.

Tommy Dickson, who had been successful with his Lotus Eleven, now decided to upgrade to a Lotus XV Twin Cam. The car arrived in Perth in kit form and Tommy's trusty mechanic, Hugh Shannon, got down to building it. The car initially proved to be a real dog, first the suspension collaped and then all sorts of minor ailments cropped up before it began to run well around mid-season. Indeed Jimmy Clark in later years said that at the end of the 1958 season the toughest opposition to his D-type Jaguar came from Dickson in the Lotus 15.

The first Charterhall meeting of the 1958 season provided much the same field as the last meeting of 1957. However, Jim Clark made his first racing appearance at the circuit with the Border Reivers D-type Jaguar. He was still getting used to the car and could not catch Tommy Dickson's Lotus XV. At the time Dickson was the king of Charterhall. Another newcomer was Bryan Wingfield with a Riley 9. Brian built one or two specials and helped Syd Ritchie with his cars. He later joined Ford Motor Company and built some of the best and earliest Jaguar D-type replicas.

In the main sports car race Jim Clark had further D-type opposition in the shape of world bicycle racing champion Reg Harris in another D-type. Harris was certainly a tryer and spun the car a number of times; as far as I am aware he never actually drove the car again. Mind you, Jim Clark also spun the Reivers D-type at this meeting and it was left to Jimmy Somervail to record Border Reivers' first victory with their D-type Jaguar.

During the season Scottish Sporting Car Club managed to persuade the owners of the Heathfield airstrip, close to Prestwick International Airport, to give permission to run a sprint meeting. The course was roughly triangular and measured just over a mile to the lap. This meeting saw the debut of the Pat Melville/Ronnie Miller Lister-Jaguar and Pat took it to a class win ahead of the Austin-Healey 100Ss of Ted Evans and Bill Thompson. The fastest time of the day was set up by Norman Barclay with his Formula 2 Cooper.

At the September Charterhall meeting the crowd were given their first chance to see a real Ecurie Ecosse versus Border Reivers battle. David Murray entered Ron Flockhart in a Jaguar D-type and gave Innes Ireland his first chance to race the team's new Tojeiro-Jaguar. Lined up against them was Jim Clark in the white Border Reivers D type and Tommy Dickson with his Lotus XV. It is quite interesting how many Lotus IIs were now finding their way into Scotland and, as we were to see, these cars rarely left Scotland being bought, sold and handed down from one enthusiast to the next making it difficult, today, to trace the individual histories of most of them.

In the main sports car race it was Innes Ireland who shot off into the lead with Jim Clark in second place and Ron Flockhart third. Tom Candlish, another Scot, borrowed Alan Ensoll's C type Jaguar (XKC 052) and managed to hold on to fourth place but was quite a way behind the

battling threesome at the front, all of whom broke the sports car lap record during the course of this race. Both of the Ecosse cars had 3.8 litre engines whilst Clark had a 3.4 plus a set of very old and worn Dunlop tyres. Innes Ireland eventually won the race and Flockhart managed to get past Clark's sliding D-type to take second. David Murray was smiling broadly.

All three were out again in the Formula Libre event where there was only one single seater, Norman Barclay's Cooper Climax. Once more, Ireland sped off from the start closely followed by Jim Clark. On the second lap Innes hit the notorious bump at the start finish line and managed to knock the gear lever of the Tojeiro into neutral. Ecosse chief mechanic Wilkie Wilkinson visibly winced as the engine revs rose but Innes managed to whip it back into gear. This let Ron Flockhart catch up - Flockhart having passed Clark - and both Ecosse cars arrived at the braking point for Lodge Corner side by side. Innes was on the outside and got on to the marbles. He shot across the grass with a marker barrel jammed under the front wheel but managed to get going again and finished well down the field.

Innes Ireland had also brought the Rupert Robinson Lotus 11 he normally raced and expected to have an easy win in the up to 1500cc sports car race. However, he did not reckon on Keith Hall, another factory Lotus driver, in his own Lotus 11. The two of them were never more than feet apart for the whole of the race until Hall blew a gasket and had to pull off the road. Jimmy Mackay from the far north of Scotland was again well placed and in such competition Jimmy was absolutely brilliant.

At the Border Motor Racing Club dinner dance in Berwick at the end of the year, A K Stevenson presented the Scottish Clubs Speed Trophy to Jim Clark for his consistent performances in Scottish speed events during 1958. Clark was also given an unique trophy presented to him by Border Reivers. On a black plinth was mounted a model of each of the three cars Jim used to win the Speed championship, the white D-type Jaguar, his white Triumph TR2 and the white Porsche 1600S. The following week Border Reivers offered the D-type Jaguar for sale at £1500!

The car was bought by northern enthusiast Alan Ensoll who converted it to XKSS specification and used it as a road car. Many years later the car ended up in the hands of Willie Tuckett who bought it from under the nose of Henry Taylor, who had raced the car just prior to the Reivers. Taylor then had a replica of the car built by Bryan Wingfield. Towards the end of 2001 the famous Reivers D-type Jaguar, TKF9, was sold to Nigel Corner.

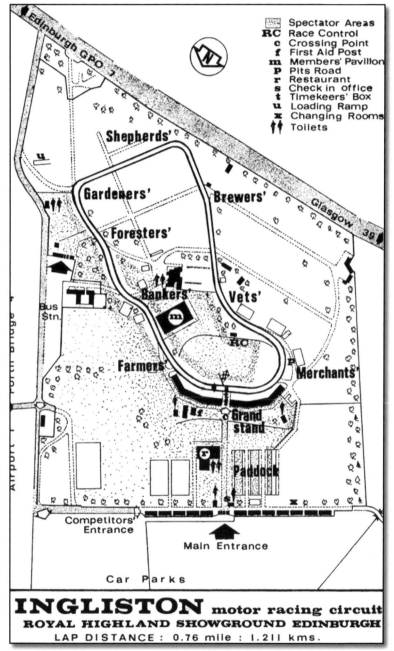

The original track layout for Ingliston that was used for the first two seasons. It was later extended.

The first practice day at Ingliston saw Ecurie Ecosse produce their hybrid Ecosse-Climax, a single seater built up from the remains of the Cooper-Monaco crashed by Jackie Stewart at Oulton Park. The driver was Bill Stein and he was to set the first lap record of the circuit at the opening official race meeting.

The new Lotus Elite was attracting a lot of attention and Ian Scott Watson had the idea of replacing his Porsche with an Elite. Towards this end he sold his Porsche 1600S to Jim Clark and, with Clark, attended a practice session Colin Chapman had organised at Brands Hatch before the end of the year.

Jim Clark had visited Brands as a boy to watch the racing but had never actually driven on the circuit. He tried the prototype Lotus Elite and Chapman immediately saw the potential in this newcomer. As Lotus were also testing their new Formula 2 car, Chapman suggested Clark have a drive in it. Jimmy duly set off and put in some fast laps. Chapman remarked to Scott Watson that Clark drove well but couldn't remember seeing him race at Brands before. At this, Scott Watson pointed out that Jim had never actually raced on the track before that day: Chapman went white and immediately had Clark flagged in. Graham Hill continued to test the Formula 2 car until a wheel came off. Seeing this, Clark turned to Scott Watson and said he wouldn't drive that thing again. This rather scuppered the secondary plan, which was for Border Reivers to replace the D-Type Jaguar with a Formula 2 Lotus!

The car Scott Watson eventually bought was a pre-production Elite that had the bad habit of having various nuts and screws fall out of it, even as you drove along the road. It was immediately entered for the Boxing Day Brands Hatch race meeting where Colin Chapman and Mike Costin had entered factory Lotus Elites. I remember Jim Clark telling the story of how he had gone to the gents toilets at Brands Hatch prior to the race only to hear Chapman and Costin in the next cubicles decide which of them was going to come first and which second : they were that confident. This got right up Clark's nose and he determined to show them a thing or two. As we now know, Clark not only battled into the lead, ahead of Chapman and Costin but might have won the race had he not met a spinning Austin Healey Sprite on the last lap allowing Chapman to nip ahead and win. Now Chapman was seriously interested in Clark.

The opening of the Ingliston circuit in April 1964. The leading lights behind the development were driven round the circuit by A K Stevenson in a veteran Albion car. Beside Stevenson on the front seat is Jim Clark with Ian Scott Watson behind him. John Romanes is hidden behind Stevenson's cap and in the trilby hat is Jimmy Lyon.

The 1959 season opened to some good news. Aberdeen and District Motor Club, which had been advised that they would no longer have the use of the Crimond circuit for racing, had searched all over the North-East of Scotland for an alternative circuit. They were lucky when they had the chance to try out Edzell in Aberdeenshire. This was another former airfield and looked like it would be very quick indeed. Permission was given for a race meeting by the Royal Air Force and the land-owner David Carnegie.

The winner of the first King Hussein Trophy was Peter Gethin with his Formula 3 Brabham. King Hussein handed over the trophy to Gethin whilst Ian Scott Watson and various bodyguards look on.

All of a sudden there was more interest and enthusiasm for motor racing in Scotland thanks to Ecurie Ecosse and now Jim Clark. Lothian Car Club made their own arrangements to bring Bo'ness back on to the hill climb scene and in turn it meant that Scots buying racing cars had probably two new venues on which to use them.

The 1959 season also saw the arrival on the racing scene of someone who was to become one of Scotland's great motor racing characters, Jock Russell. Jock was a member of the Russell of Bathgate contracting business and he and his friend George Clark bought Austin A35 saloons to go motor racing. The two of them experimented with four Amal carburettors, which was never a success, but at least it got them started. Jock was to have a chequered career, ending up with his own Formula 5000 car based on the McRae 5000 he raced in the 1980s.

Border Reivers were on the lookout to find a replacement for the D-Type Jaguar and managed to persuade Bill Moss to sell them the "flat-iron" Lister-Jaguar raced by Bruce Halford in 1958. For the British Empire Trophy at Oulton Park that year the car had been loaned to Archie Scott Brown to race, when his normal Lister broke down, and so the car came with a good racing history. Clark and Scott Watson travelled to the South of England to collect it and the plan was that Jim Clark would drive the car back to Scotland on the road using Jock McBain's set of trade plates. Jim found the cockpit tight for space but once he took off his shoes he was able to drive the car all the way back to Scotland in his socks! Meanwhile, Reivers had lost one of their mechanics, Fred Ross, who moved to Lotus Engineering and then on to California where he opened his own shop. He drove successfully over there winning the Mirror Glaze Trophy at Riverside driving a Cooper Bobtail.

Ecurie Ecosse were also modifying their equipe and sold one of their D-type Jaguars to Jaguar enthusiast Michael Salmon and Hill Climb drivers Agnes and Gray Mickel sold their AC Aceca-Bristol and replaced it with an Aston Martin DB3S once raced by Ken Wharton. Tommy Dickson also got his first big break when he was asked to drive a factory Elva sports car at Goodwood but later was snapped up by Colin Chapman for the factory Lotus team.

In the Spring a number of racing cars and racing motor cycles were invited by Aberdeen and District Motor Club to go and see the new Edzell circuit. Located 50 miles north of Perth and south west of Aberdeen. It had two major advantages over Charterhall, an absolutely smooth racing surface and a lap length of three miles. The approach to the first corner was slightly downhill followed by a long straight and flat out left hand kink. Towards the end of the lap was a 1-mile straight with a chicane in the middle to slow the cars down.

Though Ecurie Ecosse did not attend, Wilkie Wilkinson came along to look after the Ronnie Miller/Pat Melville Lister-Jaguar - which incidentally was fitted with a Jaguar 2.4 litre engine rather than a 3.4 or 3.8. Wilkie was able to take the wheel of the car and try the circuit for himself and was very impressed. Every one of the Lotus 11s that ran was outperformed by Jim Clark in the Border Reivers Lotus Elite save Jimmy Mackay's Lotus 11 which was really flying. Though no official times were taken, the quickest cars were lapping at an average speed of over 90 mph; and this was just a test day. There were still doubts as to whether the circuit could be used because there was a rumour the US Marines were going to take it over as a possible base for mountain training in the Highlands. It was technically still an active airfield on the Air Ministry list.

As they had not heard anything further, the Aberdeen club held their one and only race meeting at Edzell on June 20 1959. There was a good crowd estimated at between 10,000 and 15,000 despite the fact that facilities were limited. The new circuit attracted a number of drivers from South of the Border including Colin Murray at the wheel of Brian Naylor's JBW-Maserati, Stan Hart - son of one of the most famous speedway riders of the day, Ollie Hart - with a Formula 2 Cooper and Bill Allan with a Formula 2 Lotus. The track proved to be more difficult than most airfield circuits as some of the bends on the far side were off-camber and there were a number of spins. At the end of the meeting the 19-year old Hart set the fastest lap at an average speed of 95.6 mph. He might have been challenged by Bill Allen racing the Curtis Smith Racing Team Formula 2 Lotus 12 but the Lotus expired during practice. Jimmy Mackay was entered by Tommy Dickson and won not only the small sports car race from John Romanes' Lotus 11 but also the Unlimited sports car race ahead of Colin Murray in the JBW-Maserati and Ronnie Miller's Lister-Jaguar.

The doubtful honour of being the first person to crash in a race at Ingliston went to Jimmy Veitch who crashed his Lotus Elite at the Esses, 200 metres from the start of the first race.

We all left satisfied that Edzell would be a great circuit, as far as the drivers were concerned, but the thing which dogged all circuits back in those days was lack of trackside facilities. Viewed in today's context it is doubtful if anyone would visit a circuit with very few toilet facilities or elevated positions where the crowd could properly see the racing. However, a sudden silence fell upon the whole project broken only by the news that the United States Air Force were going to take over the facility. Once more our hopes of having an additional motor racing circuit were dashed, for Edzell was never again used for racing. It is interesting, however, that some thirty three years later, in 2002, there was talk of investigating Edzell once more as a potential racing circuit.

It was a tough blow for Aberdeen and District Motor Club as they had been tireless in their efforts to bring and maintain motor racing in the north-east. After the collapse of Edzell they used a small circuit at Fordoun for karts and then mainly turned their attention to their Fintray hill climb which became a British Hill Climb Championship venue for many years.

Early in the year, Border Reivers had been given an entry for the 1959 Le Mans 24 hour race with their Lotus Elite and the original second driver was to be Tommy Dickson. The problem was that Scott Watson did not want to use his pre-production car as it was not exactly in Le Mans trim. He ordered a new car from Colin Chapman to be ready for Le Mans. As it turned out, Colin hadn't even started on the car when the crunch came. Colin's answer was to purloin a competition Elite that had just been completed and was due to be delivered to regular Frazer-Nash driver Dickie Stoop. The car was re-directed to Scott Watson. I believe that until the day he died Dickie did not realise the delay in the delivery of his Lotus Elite was because it had been plucked from the competition department and given to Border Reivers!

This initial Reivers trip to Le Mans, with a purely amateur support team. The old Reivers Bedford Duple bus was pressed into service and used as a transporter- cum-caravan. Tommy Dickson did not make the trip and his place was taken by Sir John Whitmore. Amongst the other Scots at Le Mans that year were Innes Ireland sharing an Ecurie Ecosse D-type Jaguar with Masten Gregory, Ron Flockhart and Jock Lawrence in the Ecurie Ecosse Tojeiro-Jaguar and Ninian Sanderson in a factory Triumph TR.

In first practice on the Wednesday both Jim Clark and John Whitmore found the clutch would not stand up to the loading they were giving it and so a proper racing clutch was fitted overnight before the second days practice. The famous Le Mans start, where the drivers stood on the other side of the track opposite their cars and then ran to them, was still in operation in 1959. As a result, we were to see something that was to be repeated many times later in similar Le Mans starts. When the flag came down Stirling Moss with his Aston Martin and Jim Clark with the Lotus Elite were the fastest two cars away, only Clark was way down the field and was immediately faced with all the traffic. There were three Lotus Elites in the race with the Reivers car quicker than the Peter Lumsden/Peter Riley car and well ahead of the French-entered Vidille/Malle car that was aiming for the index of performance prize where speed and fuel consumption counted.

On the eighth lap Clark came into the pits with the car misfiring. They found, to their dismay, the starter motor had jammed at the start and the battery was almost flat. Thirteen minutes later Clark set off again. Between then and the first driver change Clark had moved from 52nd place after the pit-stop to 39th at the change. Then John Whitmore pulled the car up to 26th place when again it would not restart just as dusk was falling. The entire starter motor had to be removed and repaired, dropping the car back again. In the early morning one of the clips on the distributor cap had stretched and it took eleven minutes to find this and repair it. Then they realised they had to remove and repair the starter motor again, as the rules did not allow you to replace it. By now the factory Lotus cars had retired so Willie Griffiths and Stan Elsworth of Team Lotus mucked in. In the end the Clark/Whitmore car finished in 10th place overall, an amazing effort bearing in mind the problems they had, but they lost the class win to the Lumsden/Riley Elite. As for the other Scots, Ninian Sanderson had rotten luck when his Triumph TR3S holed its radiator with one hour to go and both the Flockhart/Lawrence Tojeiro-Jaguar and Innes Ireland/Masten Gregory Tojeiro retired with blown engines.

The June event at Charterhall was a disaster with rain so heavy it was reported that a haystack had been seen slowly drifting down the track towards Kames Curve! All the entrants turned up but as the morning went on it became obvious there would be no racing so the event was postponed until October.

The skeletal wooden frames for the Royal Highland Show buildings proved to be an initial obstacle. Here Sowden's Bentley demolishes one of them in the Vintage race at the first meeting.

The weather conditions were much better for the next Charterhall event. Jim Clark was not present for this race as Border Reivers had entered him with the Lotus Elite in the GT race at Zandvoort in Holland. As the Lister-Jaguar had been left back in the Borders, Jock McBain decided to offer the car to Sir John Whitmore to race after his sterling efforts at Le Mans. John was able to have some practice the day before the meeting and promptly spun the Lister a couple of times as he was not used to the power of the Jaguar engine.

The following day, however, he had a tremendous battle in the racing car event with Lewis Bramley's Lotus and, despite being hit by the Lotus, Whitmore continued and won the race. When he returned from Zandvoort Jim Clark was furious that Whitmore had been given "his" car to drive, particularly when the car now had a dent in the door where Bramley had hit it. The Charterhall meeting also emphasised the fact that there were fewer Scots taking part and there was still a dearth of good racing machinery north of the Border. The Ronnie Miller Lister was clearly uncompetitive and young Syd Ritchie, who was one of the real dyed-in-the-wool enthusiasts, found his Jaguar-powered Special, the Saltire, a bit of a handful. The dearth of competitors was illustrated at the final race meeting of the year when there were only 67 entries for the BMRC meeting at Charterhall.

However there was some glimmer of hope as the first information on a new inexpensive single-seater formula called Formula Junior was beginning to leak out. This small capacity class seemed to offer good racing at a reasonable price. It was felt this might also regenerate some of the other classes in Scotland that were beginning to flag.

Around this time Jimmy Mackay was contemplating retirement from racing as he had blown the engine in his two-year old Lotus 11. Hugh Shannon,

a works study officer at the Royal Navy establishment in Perth, had been working with Tommy Dickson and preparing his engines. Seeing Jimmy Mackay's plight he told him *"Leave your car with me and I'll look after it."* This completely transformed Jimmy Mackay's performances and he and Hugh Shannon made a great team. It also meant that Mackay could leave his Lotus at Perth to be prepared so saving him the long tow from Thurso. Two years later the Mackay/Shannon partnership recorded sixteen wins out of seventeen starts. This led to the Shannon-Climax as Hugh completely redesigned the rear suspension of the Lotus and the car was still winning a number of years later when it should have been totally outclassed.

It is difficult to imagine the long drives Jimmy Mackay embarked upon going, for example, from Scrabster to Brands Hatch. Eric Liddell remembers one occasion when Jimmy arrived at Brands with Tommy Dickson in Tommy's plane. At scrutineering Jimmy found he had forgotten his medical card and so was sent to the doctor for a quick check up. When asked why he had forgotten his card he said *"...I drove the fish lorry doon frae Scrabster early this morning and in the rush to get to Perth to meet up with Tommy, I forgot it."* When it came to the eye test Jimmy had difficulty reading the top letter but the doctor took pity on him, signed him off and the bold Mackay went out to race. He was to become something of a star and a legend at Brands and his class lap record there in the Shannon-Climax stayed on the record books for years.

For Ecurie Ecosse the season ended badly when Masten Gregory crashed the teams new Tojeiro-Jaguar at the Goodwood Tourist Trophy race. This was the one and only occasion Jim Clark raced for Ecurie Ecosse and he shared the car with Gregory. Prior to that race meeting, Jim Clark had always held Gregory in awe since he first raced against him in the Border Reivers D-type Jaguar at Spa in Belgium. Spa had been Clark's first ever Continental race and racing a D-type on that frightening circuit for the first time provided a new dimension for him. He had been lapped by the eventual winner, who was Masten Gregory in the Ecurie Ecosse Lister-Jaguar, and I remember him telling me shortly afterwards how he just could not believe anyone could drive as fast as Masten. This impression lasted throughout the 58 season and now, at the end of 1959, he was invited to share a car with Gregory.

Up to that time Jim Clark had slightly held David Murray at arms length. Clark felt that both with the D-type Jaguar and the Lister Jaguar he had more than proved he was worthy of a place with Ecurie Ecosse but the offer had never come. Clark remembered things like that! However, when David Murray eventually asked him to drive with Gregory he could not resist the chance to race for the team. In practice he was surprised to find himself quite close to Gregory's times but the car handled like a beast. Jim explained that on the fast uphill off-camber Madgwick corner the whole body would rise up on tip-toe and yet when he braked heavily for the chicane it would plunge down and almost scrape the ground. In a situation like that Clark was the quicker to adjust and before long he was lapping faster than Gregory and felt content he had proved to himself he was the quicker driver.

Chapter 7
The 1960s Revolution.

Formula Junior got off to a promising start at Brands Hatch in December 1959. Jim Clark was offered the chance to race a single seater for the first time when Graham Warner entered him with the Gemini Junior. However, of greater significance, was the entry of a Lotus 18 by Colin Chapman. This was to be the car that changed future design in Formula Junior from front engine to rear engine. In order to compete in this new class, the fledgling Cosworth company prepared their own Formula Junior engine based on the Ford 105E engine but by December 1959 they had only completed two of them. One was destined for the Lotus and the other for the Gemini. However, after Alan Stacey had engine trouble with his Cosworth engine in the Lotus, the second engine was taken back from Gemini and given to Lotus so the Lotus 18 could start. As a result Jim Clark's Gemini was fitted with an Austin engine, as were all the Coopers.

During Ingliston's second season King Hussein of Jordan, a great racing enthusiast, visited the circuit and gave Scottish Motor Racing Club a superb trophy, still presented every year. Seated from left to right are Doris Romanes, wife of the Chairman of Scotcircuits Ltd., Princess Muna of Jordan, His Royal Highness King Hussein of Jordan and John Romanes.

It looked like the first Formula Junior car to come to Scotland would be bought by the Hillhead Automobile Company in Glasgow. This garage was started by Glasgow enthusiast, Hutton Shields and Douglas Weir: grandson of "Darracq" Lord Weir. The previous year they had engaged a young sailing enthusiast called Bill Mackay as a salesman. Bill had only just passed his driving test and had been so deeply immersed in yachting he didn't know anything about motor racing. When Hutton Shields took an Austin Healey 100S as a trade-in on a deal he suggested to Bill that he use it in sprints and races. Mackay was therefore pushed into motor racing somewhat against his will. He began to race cars in the manner he sailed yachts, with a bravado which bordered on insanity. Urged on by the publicity, the plan was to buy a Formula Junior Lola for Mackay to drive in 1960. As it turned out they bought a Lola sports car instead and it was with this that Mackay raced in 1960 before being called up by Ecurie Ecosse.

Having seen what Jim Clark could do with a Lotus Elite, Jock Russell decided to buy one, running it for the first time at Bo'ness Hill Climb. On his first run he came into the Courtyard on full opposite lock in one direction and then full opposite lock in the other. David Boshier-Jones, the British Hill Climb Champion, saw this take place and remarked *"Does he always drive like that?"* Later he was overheard describing Jock's driving to his mechanic

with the remark *"I don't know how these fellows do it !"*. Jock, too, branched out and was to buy Tomy Dickson's Lotus XV when Dickson signed up to race the new Ecurie Ecosse Cooper Monaco.

The Bertram brothers in Edinburgh decided to sell their ex-Keith Hall Lotus Eleven and invested in a brand new Mk IV Lola sports car. Then another new entrant came along in the shape of Barry Filer from Glasgow. Barry is an easy-going guy who bought an AC-Bristol and had it prepared at Dumbuck Garage near Dumbarton. Dumbuck was the home of the Stewart family and the youngest son, Jackie, had started on the petrol pumps as part of his apprenticeship. As a great motor racing enthusiast, Barry roped Jackie in to help him with the AC-Bristol. Barry chose Jimmy McInnes, who had done a fair bit of rallying and sprinting in a variety of cars, as the driver. My favourite recollection of the period was the occasion at Rest and Be Thankful hill climb when Barry, Jackie and Jimmy were standing together at the start line watching the various cars set off up the hill. McInnes turned to Jackie and said "Jackie, go and warm the car up !" to which young Stewart scuttled down the paddock, got into the AC Bristol and brought it to the start line. Little was Jimmy, or the rest of us for that matter, to realise what would become of Jackie Stewart only a few years later.

The first Formula Junior to come to Scotland was the Lotus 18 built up by John Romanes. John was a confirmed supporter of Colin Chapman even though the kit of bits that came from Cheshunt rarely built up into a racing car without a lot of mechanical ingenuity. The Romanes Lotus 18 was one of the earliest cars sold, chassis no 7, and he was to come second to Tim

The Mini Cooper was designed for Ingliston so it was no surprise when hordes of them turned out for the early race meetings at the circuit. They were at their best on the sweep up through the Esses.

Ingliston's Caravan Corner was always a tricky one. At one of the earliest meetings Tommy Reid (11) spun his Brabham In front of Willie Forbes' Lotus and Bill Stein in the Ecosse-Climax single seater. Meanwhile Malcolm Templeton takes his Lotus round the outside.

Parnell at Aintree during 1960 and seventh at the big Silverstone Formula Junior race supporting the British Grand Prix.

During the 1960 season, an Ayrshire garage owner called Bill Seaton, who was a bit of a whiz with Renault Dauphines, began work on his own Dauphine-powered Formula Junior car. The Seaton-Renault, however, was never a competitive starter.

To add more excitement in Scotland, David Murray finally decided that his ageing Jaguars were perhaps over the hill and though Ron Flockhart tried to persuade him to buy a Lotus 19 sports car he actually bought a Cooper-Monaco for Tommy Dickson to drive. Tommy was to go on to record six wins out of seven races. The seventh race, incidentally, was the sports car race alongside the British Grand Prix when Tommy's main opposition was none other than Ron Flockhart in the John Coombs Cooper Monaco. Before the race I said to Tommy *"Now see and beat Ron."* To which Tommy just smiled and said *"Oh I don't think I'll be able to do that. Have you not noticed that when John Coombs gets his hands on a car it always seems to go faster than anyone elses. I think he's got the fastest Cilmax engine available in that Cooper."* Tommy in fact led the race ahead of Flockhart until the gear lever came out from its roots.

Talking of Ecurie Ecosse, David Murray still had two D-type Jaguars. He gave Bill Mackay a drive at Silverstone and as he didn't do anything silly he was clearly going to be given other chances. Another young Scot, Bill Turnbull, who had raced a Lotus VI and was now sales manager at David Murray's small showroom in Edinburgh, was also given a test for Ecurie Ecosse along with Eric Liddell.

Border Reivers, meanwhile, had sold their Lister-Jaguar to Gordon Lee. Thanks to Jock McBain's friendship with Reg Parnell, now Team Manager for Aston Martin, a deal was hatched whereby Border Reivers would buy the Moss/Salvadori DBR1 that caught fire and almost burned out in the pits at the 1959 Goodwood TT. This was a really good car. Clark took to it like a duck to water and was to finish in third place overall at Le Mans sharing it with Roy Salvadori. Clark raced the car once or twice at Charterhall.

During the winter of 1959 Jim Clark was invited to go to Goodwood to test for the Aston Martin grand prix team. Aston Martin had planned to race two DBR4 Grand Prix cars in the 1960 season and had already signed Roy Salvadori. Now they were looking for a second driver. Reg Parnell had paid close attention to Clark and was the first major Team Manager to recognise his possible talent in Formula One. Jimmy duly drove the car at Goodwood and was impressed with it. What was more important was that Reg Parnell was impressed and signed Jimmy to race for the team. Sadly Clark never raced the car as Aston Martin cut back on their racing programme. When Colin Chapman found his driver John Surtees was unavailable for the Dutch Grand Prix in 1960 he asked Reg if Jim Could drive a Lotus 18 in the race : the rest is history.

Scotcircults Chairman John Romanes still found time to race his Lotus Formula Junior in the early seasons.

In Scotland racing took something of an upturn in 1960 with many more cars and the fledgling Scottish Television decided to make the first live outside broadcast of motor racing in Scotland at the July Charterhall race meeting.

As I had been appointed motoring correspondent for Scottish Television, I was clearly, and eagerly, in the running to do the commentary. However, they decided they needed an experienced hand as the main commentator - as I found out many years later from a leaked internal memo. They brought a relative newcomer from the South called Murray Walker to be the lead commentator whilst I filled in as the "colour" man. As can be imagined it was a laugh from start to finish.

The arrival of Formula Ford in Scotland brought along a crop of new drivers including George Franchitti whose sons Dario and Marino were to become more famous as racing drivers thirty years later.

For a start STV were not used to outside broadcasts away from the confines of football stadia. Their idea of a commentary position at Charterhall was to build scaffolding in the middle of the paddock with an open top, a table, two small black and white TV monitors and then dotted the cameras around the circuit. They forgot one thing. They had built this huge edifice in such a way that the sun was behind us shining into the monitors and it was almost impossible to make out who was who. Murray was as enthusiastic as usual and started off the first race in great form but once the cars left the start line he was commentating on blobs. On lap two, still talking, he turned, shrugged his shoulders and improvised. Meanwhile I was not even looking at the monitors but trying to follow the race. I obviously never saw the broadcast result but it must have been horrendous. However, Tyne Tees Television was sufficiently impressed to come to an arrangement with STV to repeat the programme later that week.

There was an amusing follow up to this affair. During the telecast I had made some interviews with people like David Murray of Ecurie Ecosse and then noticed there was an American racing in the event ; something rare in Scotland. The driver had a Turner sports car with an Alexander-tuned Austin engine and so I interviewed this 'token American'. Twenty-five years later I happened to telephone an American for some information about a Ferrari he owned and we arranged to meet. I remarked that I was looking forward to meeting him. He startled me by saying *"But we have already met...at Charterhall when I raced my Turner and you interviewed me for Scottish Television."* The young American concerned was Peter Sachs, a member of the Goldman Sachs dynasty and today one of America's leading car collectors and historic racers.

The number one Mini Cooper driver in Scotland in the mid-1960s was Bill Borrowmon who also played a part in starting the racing career of Tom Walkinshaw.

During the 1960 season Barry Filer was obviously enjoying the idea of running the AC Bristol and so ordered one of Jem Marsh's new Marcos kit cars and had it built to race. He sold the AC and his Porsche 1600 and bought an Aston Martin DB4GT lightweight. He took both the Marcos and Aston Martin to Oulton Park for a test session and took with him Scotland's leading motorcycle racer Bob McIntyre and Barry's young "mechanic", Jackie Stewart. The result of this test day ensured that Jackie Stewart would be the driver of the Marcos in 1961. This was going to be a problem for Jackie. His mother had made it perfectly clear that after what she had gone through with his older brother Jimmy, racing for Ecurie Ecosse and Jaguar, she did not plan for her second son to become a

Andrew Fletcher – whose grandfather was Scotland's first true racing driver – was an early competitor at Ingliston with his Formula 3 Brabham. He went on to race Chevrons in the European Sports Car championship.

racing driver. It called for a rather transparent plan. When Jackie appeared at Charterhall in 1961 for his first race he was entered as A N Other. His mother did not find out about his racing but both Jackie and Jimmy had a feeling she knew all the time. As for Bobby McIntyre, he drove well at Oulton but was clearly committed to his factory Honda contract. He left the door open for a future test in a racing car. It was reported that Henry Taylor was going to buy a Lotus 18 for McIntyre to race but McIntyre was killed in a motor-cycle Grand Prix not long afterwards.

In 1960 Jim Clark, by now relishing his new role as a grand prix driver with Lotus, realised he would not be able to race on his home circuit of Charterhall on many more occasions. He persuaded Colin Chapman to let him bring the factory Lotus 18 Formula Junior he was racing at Oulton Park the day before to the final meeting of the season at Charterhall . He had won the Junior race at Oulton but at Charterhall the crown wheel and pinion broke and he retired from the race. Mike Warren, Jim's mechanic on that occasion, remarked that it was the first time the crown wheel had broken on Jim's Junior all season. It was the last car he ever raced in Scotland. (Pedants may argue that Jim was to "race" an electric milk float at Ingliston some years later but I have ignored that.)

It was at this last meeting we saw the potential of Jock Russell as a racing driver. He and Adam Wylie had bought Tommy Dickson's Lotus XV and Jock proved to be a hard man to beat: a fact Jim Clark admitted when Russell stormed past him on the back straight : mind you Clark was in a Formula Junior car so not even he could compete against a 1500cc Climax engined Lotus XV. Jim Clark also took the opportunity, on what was to be his last racing visit, to drive the Border Reivers' Aston Martin DBR1. He won one race and was beaten by Tommy Dickson in the Ecurie Ecosse Cooper Monaco in another. Jackie Stewart - who had raced earlier in the season as A N Other – came out of the closet and raced under his own name and whereas the Marcos was not as fast as the Lotus Elites he had a win in the GT race with Barry Filers Aston Martin DB4GT.

One of Scotland's most promising drivers in the 1960s and a great friend of Jock Russell, was Adam Wyllie, who raced this Brabham at Ingliston. He was later killed in the Leinster Trophy Race in Ireland but is remembered each year by Scottish Motor Racing Club with the Adam Wyllie Memorial Trophy.

That final race meeting of the season closed on a sad note when, for the second time in the history of Scottish motor racing, a driver was killed at the track. In the race for Sports cars Syd Ritchie, driving the now 3.4 litre Jaguar-engined Saltire, went wide going into the fast left hander at Kames Curve. The inside wheel appeared to have hooked the edge of the tarmac which ripped the front suspension off the car. It subsequently rolled killing Syd instantly. Syd was the typical enthusiast who had run a number of Specials in sprints, hill climbs and races. It put a real damper on the meeting. A number of drivers had serious misgivings about Kames Curve that was approached at high speed on a slight downhill which then called for heavy braking to get round the following tight Paddock bend.

Not long afterwards we were congratulating Innes Ireland for giving Team Lotus their first grand prix victory in the US Grand Prix at Riverside.

At the annual dinner of the Ecurie Ecosse Association David Murray stood up as usual and laid down his plans for the 1961 season. At the end of 1960 there had been a rift between David and his partner in Merchiston Motors, Wilkie Wilkinson. Wilkie was bitter about this in his autobiography and when he was offered the chance to move south and join the Owen Organisation as BRM's customer relations man, he jumped at it. During the Association Dinner the impression was given that Ecosse and BRM were now co-operating. There was much muttering that the team would move from Edinburgh to Bourne in Lincolnshire, but this was all hot air. There was never any plan for Ecosse to move and it helped smooth over the transition to an Ecurie Ecosse without Wilkie Wilkinson.

There was another surprise at the dinner when Murray announced that in 1961 they would be racing their Cooper Monaco and an Austin Healey Sprite. There was silence at this. A Sprite ? This was the team that had raced and won at Le Mans with D-type Jaguars, what were they doing with a little Sprite? As it turned out, the car was one of the factory Sprites sent to Sebring that year and it was going to be rebuilt with a slightly more streamlined nose. It was planned to race the Sprite prior to Le Mans. However, as often happens, there was a tremendous panic to get the car even prepared in time. It was also hinted that a second of those Sprites might be available to Ecurie Ecosse. As things turned out the whole Sprite project went no further than Le Mans.

During the winter of 1960/61 Bill Mackay and Jack Wober bought one of the Ecurie Ecosse D-type Jaguars that had raced at Le Mans in 1960 and was almost obsolete. This was the car with the ugly addition of a boot to satisfy the Le Mans regulations in 1960. They raced it occasionally during the year but it proved to be an expensive exercise. At the end of the year, Jack Wober, who had previously raced a Lotus VII, decided to drive it to London and sell the car. In these pre-speed limit days he claimed to have hit 165 mph on the Preston by-pass on the way down. (Note: the Motorway system had not yet been built and the Preston by-pass was the first completed section.)

Another Scot, Angus Clydesdale, bought a Lola sports car in kit form for racing down south and was quite successful with it. After racing the Lola, Angus bought a 250F Maserati (2526) which was the car used by Jean Behra for the factory. It had later been raced by Behra with a V12 engine in the Italian Grand Prix. On the death of his father, Angus became, and remains, the Duke of Hamilton.

There has always been a stream of drivers from Aberdeen in Scottish racing and Willie Forbes was one of them. Forbes first caught the eye with his Elva-BMW before switching to probably the most unsuitable car for racing at Ingliston, a Lola F5000.

Forbes had a number of problems with the Lola such as here, when the rear suspension broke.

Drivers from the North of England were great supporters of Scottish racing, none more so than Andy Barton from the Newcastle Area seen here in the middle of the front row with his Mini. He started with the Morris Minor and the Mini was followed by a number of single seaters, including his own Barton.

John Romanes, who had raced one of the first Lotus 18 Juniors, sold his car and took delivery of a Lotus 20 kit. John always liked to build his own cars and set to work to get the car ready for the new season.

1962 was also the year Graham Birrell started racing with an Austin A40 - the one with the squared-off Pininfarina bodywork. He was later to be joined by his younger brother Gerry Birrell driving the same car and some years later by third brother Ian Birrell who raced a Mini Cooper at Ingliston. Unfortunately, as Ian was a blender at Highland Distillers, the company took a dim view of one of their highly trained palates being out on a track racing so they banned him from doing any more races.

Work had started on the new Ecurie Ecosse Tojeiro Climax GT, the first of the mid-engined GT cars built in Britain that raced before the original Lola-Ford. Team mechanic Stan Sproat travelled to Tojeiro's workshops at Barkway and physically built the car before bringing it back to Merchiston Mews to be finished off.

To get everyone warmed up for the season, a practice day was held at Charterhall and it was interesting to see Jackie Stewart at the wheel of the family E-type Jaguar demonstrator "FSN 1". He was very quick but it so happened his older brother Jimmy was there - he had retired from racing

Richard Scott, another Aberdonian, with the ex-Willie Forbes Elva-BMW, Scott went on to race in the European Formula 2 Championship ond build his own F2 car, the Scott.

seven years before - and was .2 of a second quicker than Jackie in the same car! Another interesting car present was the very special Jensen 541 run by David and Douglas Bertram. They had thrown away the Jensen engine and replaced it with a full racing 3.8 litre Jaguar engine.

Highland Car Club, based in Inverness, now came into the picture having arranged to hold a sprint meeting in August that year at a small airfield circuit called Evanton in Ross-shire. This first event was low key with the emphasis on saloon and sports cars. In the saloon event the most interesting entry came from the Sutherland brothers from Thurso with a Supercharged Ford Classic! They also ran their Lotus Super Seven in the event.

The shortcomings of Charterhall as a racing circuit were obvious to everyone. It was not particularly interesting, it was rough, and the cars were getting faster and faster. Various people were still looking to find an alternative and during the early part of 1962 a group led by Lord Bruce discussed, with the Duke of Buccleugh, the possibility of building a circuit at Castlesteads Park within the walled estate of his family home, Dalkeith Palace.

When the Mini Cooper lost its lustre, the Hillman Imp became the car to have in Scotland, Logan Morrison bought one of the Fraser-Imps built by Alan Fraser that had won the British Saloon Car Championship. Logan's driving style was borrowed from his days as a factory rally driver for BMC In oll the main Internationol rallies.

The site certainly had a number of attractions. For a start there was superb access to the main roads around Dalkeith and the spectators would have all been housed on the inside of the track rather than the outside. The paddock would be situated on the outside with a footbridge over to the pits on the inside.

The track itself was planned to be 30 ft wide with a flexible bitumen surface to allow for any subsidence - as this area was criss crossed by derelict mining operations -and the banking on the inside of the track would be built up to provide superb spectator facilities.

I visited the site with Ian Scott Watson and Jim Clark. From the proposed start and finish line there was a downhill section with some fast swerves and then a dog-leg corner and a climb of 25 feet to a flat section with sweeping right and left bends. The track then ran uphill to a banked hairpin bend, very much like the Karussel at Nurburgring. Noel Bean, who was a director of Wimpey, the contracting company, was advising the syndicate on the physical construction - as he was to do on two other occasions - and

This is what brought the crowds to Ingliston, racing with no holds barred. Jim Dickson tries to squeeze Frank Gunn's Mini Cooper on to the grass at Caravan corner.

he estimated that building the track, including the earthworks and safety barriers, would cost around £45,000.

The only doubtful section of the track was near the start where it plunged down towards the River Esk. The ambitious plans came to nothing as there were various objections raised by the tenant farmers on the land and the whole affair was quietly dropped. Another site nearby at Carberry was briefly looked at but as the main house was used by the Church of Scotland it was also a non-starter.

The 1963 season was the tenth in the history of Charterhall and the Winfield Joint Committee presented long time resident scrutineers John Garden and David Stephen with commemorative stop-watches. Throughout the history of Scottish racing there have always had an interesting bunch of scrutineers. Of them all both John and David were the quiet persuasive types unlike some of the later ones like Alex Reid and Bill Cleland, who both believed in the principle that the best gamekeeper was a poacher at heart. Alex Reid was famous for his Specials. He had managed to evade scrutineers

Forever a showman, Jock Russell raced a number of cars in Scotland including this Lotus 43 which was the actual chassis (01) used by Jim Clark to win the 1966 US Grand Prix. As the car had been fitted with a flat 12 BRM engine Jock bought the car with no engine, which is why he fitted a Ford V8 engine to it and used it for Libre events,

A few kart races were held as support events at Ingliston and David Leslie – at the rear – cut his early racing teeth at the circuit in a kart.

many years before with one of his specials where the body was made of papier-mache smoothed out and painted to look like steel. Bill Cleland was a well-known rally driver who had an impish sense of humour and was later to become one of the leading lights in the development and running of Dealer Team Vauxhall. He originally forbade his son John to race so when John started out he had to do sprints and hill climbs. Later father relented and John Cleland raced for the first time at Ingliston a few years later in a Mini Cooper.

The 1963 season also saw the most travelled racing driver in Britain, Jimmy Mackay from Scrabster on the most northerly coast of Scotland, out with his Lotus II that had been modified by mechanic Hugh Shannon and fittted with a hard top to transform it into a GT car. When asked why, Jimmy pointedly remarked *"Because I can't afford £2,500 for a modern car."* Meanwhile, he still had the Shannon-Climax for sports car events.

It is remarkable that Jimmy Mackay was still racing the GT Lotus Eleven in 1965 - eight years after the original car had been built ! At the August Bank Holiday meeting at Brands that year only the Lotus Elans, driven by people like Mike Beckwith, Jackie Oliver and Roy Pike, were quicker than his old Lotus Eleven. Indeed his practice time at that meeting was the same as Jack Pearce's fast E-type Jaguar. In the race itself he broke the lap record for 1100cc GT cars by four seconds. *"This gave me great satisfaction and I felt sorry that I was soon to finish the game for good. However I knew that I was now on the wrong side of fifty and the next day would be my twenty sixth wedding anniversary."*

Gordon Stupple had this spectacular accident on the exit to Caravan Corner. Note the positioning of the spectators.

Much closer to Jimmy Mackay was the new airfield circuit at Evanton in Ross-Shire. The Highland Car Club were the organisers and they had negotiated with Novar Estates, who owned the land, to run the event. To get things going they ran a closed sprint on August 4 1962 with fifty entrants. A number of well-known competitors from around Scotland quickly joined the club and took part. Following this, the circuit was licenced for motor racing in 1963.

The two Mallock brothers, Richard, left and Ray, were regular early visitors to Ingliston where Richard Mallock became a regular winner with one of his father's Mallock Clubmans cars. On the right is Hugh McCaig who was to link up with Ray Mallock when the new Écurie Ecosse team was formed in 1984.

The Club was permitted to run just one event a year, in August, and so the first race meeting took place on Saturday August 31 1963. Despite the fact the event clashed with the Invergordon Highland Gathering around 3000 spectators turned up. The track was not at its best with dried up mud that caused a lot of problems with cars spinning. However, as the meeting progressed the times got faster and the lap record was set by Bill Stein with his Lotus 22 Formula 3 car at 79.2 mph. The fastest car on the track was Jock Russell's ex-Jim Clark Lotus F1 car now fitted with a Ford V8 engine.

Formula Libre provided a class where many Scots could buy relatively cheap racing cars that could not be raced elsewhere. One such was this Intercontinental Cooper bought by Andrew Goodfellow from Falkirk.

*Bill Dryden, when not driving for the Vauxhall Dealer Team,
raced single seaters like John Romanes' Brabham Formula 3.*

His rear suspension failed in the main race and Willie Forbes ran out the winner with a Lotus 22. The saloon car race was won by Mike White with Ian McDonald's Weber carburetted 3.8 Jaguar.

An interesting new car to arrive in Scotland was one of the Emeryson-Climax Formula 1 cars that had been bought by Eric Liddell. The Emeryson, designed by Paul Emery who had a chequered career in motor racing, was, by 1962, owned by an American, Hugh Powell. He raced the car with fellow American Tony Settember at the wheel. At the end of that year the Emeryson team was wound up and Powell developed a new grand prix car, the Scirocco-BRM for 1963. The two 1962 Emerysons were then sold, one of them going to Eric Liddell.

He proudly brought the car to Charterhall for the first meeting of the 1963 season and everyone was horrified when, during practice, the car caught fire. Eric was able to bring it to a halt and jumped out but then had to stand back and watch his investment go up in smoke. This was a great pity as it was one of the first contemporary Formula 1 cars to be bought for racing in Scotland.

*By the early 1970s mop-haired Tom Walkinshaw had moved south and
was racing in Formula 3 with a March with help from Ecurie Ecosse.*

The biggest Scottish motor racing story of 1963, however, was Jim Clark becoming Scotland's first world motor racing champion. Though Jim was a relatively patient and down to earth person he was thrown into the spotlight and from then until he died he rarely had a moment to reflect on his success. It also lit a beacon in Scotland and led to what I feel was a motor racing renaissance and a long list of successful Scottish racing drivers. Ask any of them, Tom Walkinshaw, Richard Scott, John Cleland, Allan McNish, David Coulthard or Dario Franchitti and Jim Clark's name always comes up.

By 1964 Border Motor Racing Club had over 1300 members and Scott Watson persuaded the committee they should seek an accommodation with the dormant Scottish Motor Racing Club whereby Border Motor Racing Club would take over the name and promote future events as SMRC. Whilst Border Motor Racing Club and Winfield Joint Committee had been running their race meetings, Scottish Motor Racing Club had lain dormant since the 500cc Formula Three races at Beveridge Park in Kirkcaldy. The directors of the Club paid company tax each year so as to keep title to the name and the three leading lights in SMRC were Willum Stewart, Edinburgh businessmen Tom Leggat and Geoff Waugh. They, by now, were also on the committee of Border Motor Racing Club and so the subject of merging BMRC with Scottish Motor Racing Club was a mere formality.

The long-time SMRC secretary was Edinburgh wool merchant Willum Stewart whose family busines, Stewart Brothers of Galashiels, was one of the biggest wool merchants in Scotland. When agreement was reached to merge the two clubs the name Border Motor Racing Club was dropped in favour of the more nationalistic Scottish Motor Racing Club. As a gesture of friendship and support, Willum Stewart was named its first chairman. From then SMRC has gone from strength to strength and indeed the club was

*Another Scot making good in England was Gerry Birrell who was
sponsored in Formula 3 by John Stanton, left, with a Lotus.*

Ingliston proved to be a second home to all the up and coming Irish drivers, including Kenny Acheson and John Watson. One of the most successful, however, was Patsy McGarrity who became Scottish Libre Champion.

deeply involved in ensuring that Scotland would continue to have motor racing.

Ecurie Ecosse had taken one of their Tojeiro Buicks and had it modified to hold a full-house Shelby Cobra Ford V8. At the time, Jackie Stewart was their number one driver having completed his first season with the team. However, it was clear David Murray was still not too sure about Jackie's natural talent for in May of 1964 he wrote a letter to Innes Ireland.

Dear Innes,

Some time ago, probably in a rash moment, you said to me that if ever you could help Ecurie Ecosse you would.

My request is for you to drive our Ford Cobra Tojeiro at Silverstone for the final testing.

As you know we have been working on this Tojeiro-chassisied car for some time now but only recently have we installed the Ford engine.

The only driver I have at call is Jackie Stewart who, in my opinion and in confidence, has not had enough experience to express an expert opinion and accordingly if you could help out I would be most grateful.

*Kindest regards
David Murray.*

As far as I am aware this test never took place and it was Jackie who did the testing. Two months after that letter was written Jackie raced the car in the support race to the 1964 British Grand Prix. At the end of grand prix practice Jim Clark persuaded Colin Chapman to let Jackie drive his Lotus grand prix car round the circuit. Colin made the arrangement with the officials who asked the marshals to stay at their posts for another fifteen minutes.

As the crowds drifted home, Jackie moved out on to the circuit to drive a grand prix car for the first time. He drove safely and sensibly but the car developed an engine problem and he came into the pits. Chapman had clearly seen the potential and later in the year it led to an amusing incident involving the writer.

At the time I was competing as a rally co-driver and was friendly with a young Italian called Cesare Fiorio whose father was Director of Public Relations for Lancia. Cesare was running the Lancia factory rally team. He rang in mid-summer and asked if I could find out whether Jim Clark, and this young Scottish driver Jackie Stewart, would be interested in driving Lancia Fulvia Zagatos in the 1965 Monte Carlo Rally. I told him that Jim was out of the question not only because of his Lotus contract but because the rally would clash with the South African Springbok series. I said I would ask Jackie. When I raised the subject with him he was very interested and as a result a provisional entry was made in Jackie Stewarts name. In late October I was advised that we would probably be needed in Monaco in early December to start reconnaissance, that we would be allowed two days "leave" for Christmas and then it was back to Monaco. This sounded all very exciting until Colin Chapman rang Jackie a few days later and asked him to drive a Formula 1 Lotus for Team Lotus in the Springbok. Needless to say the Monte Carlo Rally project was dropped and Jackie Stewart's first Formula 1 race was in a Lotus.

During the 1963 and 1964 seasons the Highland Car Club still ran their occasional race meetings at Evanton. It was the most northerly motor racing circuit in Britain. A restricted race meeting was organised for August but it did not work out too well as the circuit surface was breaking up.
That meeting brought together a good entry and despite the fact the racing was poor, there were 5000 spectators. The highlight of the meeting was a tremendous scrap between Graham Birrell in his Cortina GT and young Sandy McCracken with a Lotus Cortina. When Birrell ran wide McCracken took the lead but in a last minute lunge Birrell retook the lead on the last corner and won. In the next race Graham's younger brother Gerry Birrell drove the Cortina GT and again there was a battle that ended with McCracken punting Birrell's GT and eventually being black flagged. A lot of blame could be placed on the condition of the track and it was no surprise when Evanton was never used again.

Charterhall, had moved into what was to be its final season in 1964. At the beginning of the year all seemed serene but as the season progressed there were more and more hints that the circuits days were numbered.

One of the regular Charterhall visitors from the north of England was Phil Barak - who, 35 years later was still racing a 2 litre BDG-engined Lotus Elan. Phil had bought an interesting Cooper Monaco, the ex Roy-Salvadori car, fitted with a Ferrari four cylinder 750 Monza engine. This had been built by George Pitt in partnership with Brian Naylor, the engine being from Naylor's JBW-Ferrari sports car.

When it ran, the car was a flyer and on the Saturday before the first Charterhall meeting in 1964 Phil entered for a sports car race alongside the Aintree 200. Unfortunately his starter motor acted up and Mike Wilson, the Clerk of the Course at Aintree, would not let Phil start the race. He packed up his kit and drove to Charterhall for the racing the following day. "I knew the officials at Charterhall would let me start without a starter motor" Sadly for him the long Charterhall straight was too much and Phil suffered a major engine blow up with a con-rod coming through the side of the block. He was in no financial position to go to one of the acknowledged Ferrari experts to repair the engine. He took it to a friend of his in the Newcastle shipyards who was quite used to heavy engineering and he patched up the Ferrari block. Added to this, Phil used to have his car prepared by Jimmy Blumer's mechanic Jack Dowson. He tells of getting his Ferrari engine back from Jack plus a plastic washing up bowl with half the valve mechanism in

There were many variations on the theme of downforce in the 1970s. This was John Crossle's answer with two indiviual rear wings on the Crossle he ran for Brian Nelson.

it! When Phil asked why all these parts were left over Jack cheerily remarked that the engine would go just as well without them!

When the Cooper-Ferrari ran at that Charterhall meeting Phil was able to set a new outright lap record at over 91 mph. Talking about that visit recently Phil ruefully remarked. *"I thought I would end up as the outright lap record holder for all time but at the very last race meeting at the circuit Jackie Stewart took the Ecurie Ecosse Cooper Monaco Climax round in a quicker time and I was really pissed off about it".* Jackie Stewart's outright lap record at Charterhall was set at the September meeting at 92.07 mph and so this stands in the record books as the ultimate record : one wonders what the lap record at Charterhall would be with todays cars !

Two weeks later, on October 6 1964, the Border Motor Racing Club were hosts to the final race meeting. It was fitting, too, that at that last meeting Jimmy Mackay should win the sports car race with the Shannon-Climax which was by now of pensionable age. The fact that he managed to defeat more modern cars such as John Romanes' Lotus 23 proved that Jimmy was a match for anyone on any circuit.

The final race was the BMRC Handicap Trophy, a traditional event created by Ian Scott Watson back in 1957. The handicapper, on this occasion, Dr

Lewis Jamieson, worked out a complicated system that would balance an MG Midget with a Lotus 22. For this event Ian Scott Watson loaned his Lotus Elan to Anita Taylor, Trevor Taylor's sister, who had previously raced at Charterhall with a Ford Anglia. The handicapping system worked so well that the first four cars finished within 11 seconds of each other and it was Anita Taylor who won the event. Thus Anita Taylor became the last person ever to win a race at Charterhall.

During 1963 and 1964 more and more people were concerned about Charterhall continuing as a racing circuit. For a start the RAC were now more interested in circuit safety, even though nobody at the time had much of a clue what, exactly, to do. Everyone knew that not only was Charterhall very rough in places, with some cars even taking off on the hump on the main straight, but that Kames Curve, at the bottom of a slight hill on the back straight, was very dangerous. As we have recorded, John Bain had been killed on this corner in 1956 and Syd Ritchie was killed on the same spot when his Saltire spun and went through a fence on the inside of the corner. Now, in 1964, came the third fatality when Bill Carmichael's Lotus 7 crashed, also on Kames Curve. Now the RAC began to make serious noises and it became clear the circuit would not receive a licence for 1965. Incidentally these are the only fatal accidents in Scottish motor racing in Scotland in fifty-two years.

Chapter 8
The Ingliston and Knockhill Years.

Charterhall had served its purpose: it had virtually sustained motor racing in Scotland whilst other circuits had started up and closed down. It was far from perfect, the organisation was far from perfect, but at the time we really didn't know any better. Behind the scenes everyone was trying to find an alternative and now the pressure was really on. As explained in another chapter, Lord Bruce had led his team in a bid to build a circuit at Polkemmet between Edinburgh and Glasgow and had commissioned designs from both Ian Scott Watson and the famous Dutch designer John Hugenholtz, but nothing came of the development.

During the period of the Polkemmet project, Ian Scott Watson had been looking closely at the Royal Highland and Agricultural Society's permanent showground site on the old estate surrounding Ingliston House. This estate had first been sold and turned into a golf course. Then, when it became necessary to expand Edinburgh International Airport, part of the estate was chopped off and subsequently sold to the RHAS which had been searching for a permanent site for their Royal Agricultural Show. This large event was annually moved around Scotland from site to site but the sheer logistical problem of dragging things like a very solid looking grandstand all over Scotland was something of a financial disaster. A permanent site was the answer and Ingliston proved to be ideal.

Shortly after the Royal Highland and Agricultural Society bought the site and was planning the layout it was approached by A K Stevenson the Secretary of the Royal Scottish Automobile Club and David Murray of Ecurie Ecosse. They put forward the idea that when planning the permanent roads within the grounds, the RHAS should consider making these wide enough so that motor racing could be held on the ten months during the year when the site lay empty. The RHAS Committee at the time dismissed the idea and Stevenson and Murray went home empty handed.

In 1964, the Highland Society was having financial problems thanks to a huge overdraft. Ian Scott Watson, himself a farmer and life member of the Royal Highland and Agricultural Society, decided to go and speak to them again about modifying the site to make it into a motor racing circuit. When he arrived he was surprised to find that there was a kart meeting going on. A similar approach had been made by the East of Scotland Kart Club to use a small part of the little linking roads as a kart circuit and so they were actually the first to use Ingliston as a racing venue.

Encouraged by this, Scott Watson had a word with Jim Dickson the Master of Works to obtain a proper plan of the showground as what he and his colleagues had in mind might help the RHAS to reduce their overdraft. Dick Lemmon, the secretary of the RHAS, and the Chairman all expressed interest in the proposition and it was agreed that Scott Watson should come up with a plan and some proposals.

Scott Watson needed a reliable, feet on the ground, businessman and racing enthusiast to help put this over. He telephoned John Romanes, who had been racing various Lotuses for years, and they arranged to meet at the beautiful little seaside resort of Canty Bay. Between them they hammered out a form of contract which would be offered to both the Royal Highland and Agricultural Society and Scottish Motor Racing Club. The timing was also right as Jim Clark had become world motor racing champion at the end of 1963 and he was not only a farmer but also a member of the RHAS so there was a degree of reflected glory involved.

The original team involved in Ingliston consisted of Scott Watson and Romanes, with the tacit support of Jim Clark plus Jim Clark's Berwickshire lawyer Jimmy Lyon and accountant Chris Weir. They had various meetings with the RHAS and eventually got together to form a company to run the motor racing. At the initial meeting Scott Watson suggested it should be called the Scottish Racing Development Company Ltd, but it was felt to be too much of a mouthful and Romanes came up with the idea of shortening it to Scotcircuits Ltd.

One of the first modern grand prix cars at Ingliston was this Surtees raced by Graham Hamilton who, with his friend Gordon Dalzell, took on the franchise for Ingliston in the late 1970s.

The next problem was raising the money needed to make the necessary changes to the existing roads within the circuit by widening the ones that would be used for motor racing. For this the team had a generous player on the sidelines waiting to become involved. This was Eric Knight, Chairman of bankers Lombard North Central, and his Scottish director Gordon Skilton. They pledged to support the project and were in fact the largest shareholders in the original company, which had a total paid up share capital of £18,000. John Romanes invested £3,000, Scott Watson and Jimmy Lyon £2,000 each and Scottish club racing drivers, David Bertram, Ronnie Morrison and Jim Clark's brother in law, Alec Calder, invested £1,000 each; the rest was put up by Lombard North Central.

They were further aided by one of Scotland's great unsung enthusiasts, Noel Bean, who happened to be Technical Director of the giant Wimpey concern based in Edinburgh. Bean had raced and sprinted a Jaguar SS100 before selling it to young Ian Stewart, and had been involved in the Polkemmet development. Noel Bean and his works foreman, David Young, came up with an interesting offer. He explained that Wimpey were constantly experimenting with new types of road surface and if Scotcircuits were willing to let Wimpey use an experimental surface for the circuit they would make sure the price was right. Needless to say, this offer was taken up with alacrity and it is a testament to Wimpey's skill that, apart from occasional patching, the track surface laid down early in 1965 was basically the same surface as was used right up to the circuits closure in the mid-1990s. Ingliston also installed three band Armco barriers that were rare at the time as most circuits used only two-band Armco. The next problem was that as SMRC also had a motorcycle membership most of the Armco had to be removed and replaced with 80 tons of straw bales if a motor-cycle meeting were held. In fact very few motor-cycle meetings were ever run as the motor cyclists found the circuit too tight for them and also a bit dangerous.

With Formula Ford a constant and popular series in Scotland, it became the first step for many successful drivers, including Tom Brown with his Van Diemen who won more championships than anyone else.

The circuit, as originally used, was less than one mile to the lap using part of a newly designed perimeter road and a centre road. The main grandstand and start was on a short straight which curved up to a swooping set of esses followed by a kink and then the tight Caravan corner, a right hand corner leading into short back straight of about 150 yards then another right to take you back down towards the left and right into the grandstand area. This, then, was the original Ingliston circuit.

As can be imagined, there was a tremendous build up to the first meeting at Ingliston. Over the winter of 1964 a complete new section of roadway was built which formed the esses and what made this interesting was the slight elevation at this point. Indeed the esses were to become the trickiest section of the circuit. As is always the case, the work had not completely finished by the time Scottish Motor Racing Club held an open day for club members, with no spectators, in order to fulfil the RAC circuit licence requirements and get the marshals familiar with the layout.
Meanwhile, at Merchiston Mews, the home of Ecurie Ecosse, Stan Sproat, the chief mechanic, was in a hurry to finish off the Ecosse-Climax in time for the meeting. David Murray had decided that Ecurie Ecosse had to support the new track. As the remains of the Cooper Monaco that had been heavily crashed by Jackie Stewart at Oulton Park two years before, were still lying around, he suggested to Stan that it might make a good single seater.

To build the car, Stan incorporated the 2.5 litre Coventry Climax engine, a Cooper Jack Knight gearbox and the steering rack, front suspension uprights, clutch, rear hubs and bearings from the Monaco. Most of the rest of the remains went to the local scrappy.

This was a real Ingliston special and Bill Stein was called in to race it.

Bill Stein had started racing with a Lotus VII and then had some excellent results with a Lotus 23. Indeed he had been spotted as potential talent by David Murray at Oulton Park at the same meeting where Jackie Stewart wrecked the Cooper Monaco. Bill Stein raced the Ecosse single seater at both the closed meeting and the official opening meeting at Ingliston and had the honour of becoming the first ever lap record holder at the circuit.

Five years later, the car was sold at auction to an 9-year old American, Todd Peyton Jenkins, whose publisher father was staying at Gleneagles Hotel at the time of the auction. Many years later, when Todd grew up, the car was carefully rebuilt as a Cooper Monaco by former American racing driver Bob

Akin and is now back in Britain in the hands of arch-Ecurie Ecosse collector Dick Skipworth.

For the opening race meeting at Ingliston, the Royal Scottish Automobile Club brought along the 1905 Rolls Royce which had been bequeathed to them by Adam Macgregor Dick: it is the only three cylinder 1905 Rolls still in existence. This veteran, exactly sixty years old, was used to transport A K Stevenson, the RAC Steward at the meeting, and the directors of Scotcircuits Ltd, John Romanes, Jim Clark, Ian Scott Watson and Jimmy Lyon, round the track to open the circuit.

The first race was for the small capacity sports cars and was dominated by Lotus Elans. The quickest in practice was a young Glasgow driver Ronnie Martin and he led the race from start to finish. He was chased all the way by rally driver Andrew Cowan driving Ian Scott Watson's Lotus Elan and Eric Liddell in his Elan but Liddell lost it, coming out of Caravan Bend, shot across the wet grass and hit the wooden framework of one of the Highland Show standholders.

When only 17 years of age American Eddie Cheever was a regular visitor to Ingliston with the factory Modus F3 car before going on to race in Formula 1.

The compactness of Ingliston is emphasised in this helicopter photo of the start and finish area, Note the large 5,000 seater grandstand and the sweep up to the esses on the lower right of the photo.

This was initially a problem at Ingliston and part of the compromise between having a racing circuit that also doubled as the site of the Royal Highland and Agricultural Show. At that time most of the permanent show buildings were mere timber skeletons to which panels were added at the time of the show. In the Vintage Car event a Bentley went off on the outside of Caravan corner and knocked a whole row of those vertical wooden pillars, which saw the entire structure progressively collapse behind it. Some years later, when these old skeletons were removed, they were replaced by more solid buildings but by then they were all protected by crash barriers.

The honour of being the first person to crash at Ingliston fell to Jimmy Veitch who managed to put his ageing, and much modified Lotus Elite into the barriers just 200 yards from the start!

Probably the best performance at that opening meeting came from Andrew Fletcher with a Formula 3 Brabham. In his race with Adam Wyllie's Lotus 31, Fletcher was brilliant and got faster and faster. Indeed he came close to breaking the winner, Bill Stein's, lap record in the 2.5 litre Ecosse Climax.

The only faux-pas of the day came in the saloon car race when the stewards black-flagged Bill Borrowmans Mini Cooper by mistake and brought him into the pits. They should have black-flagged George Percival's Ford Anglia and Borrowman did not find the mistake very funny as he was the potential race winner.

A few weeks later, the second meeting took place. There was a bigger entry and the weather, for once, was dry. This meant that Bill Stein's outright lap record of 44.8 seconds (61 mph) was bound to be broken. The man who

Tommy Dickson was keen to promote his son Norman in racing and formed a two-car team of Formula Atlantics to race in Britain. Richard Scott was chosen as the second driver for the team.

did it was Willie Forbes from Aberdeen with his Elva-BMW who raised the lap record by more than 7 mph. Forbes was to become the dominant driver at Ingliston for the next two seasons.

The main race at that meeting was for the Guards Trophy and it provided a lot of excitement, particularly at Caravan bend on the opening lap when four cars went off nose-to-tail, including Tommy Reid, Bill Stein and Andrew Fletcher. This left Alan Rollinson clear with his Brabham. Ecurie Ecosse brought out their Tojeiro coupe and gave it to Andrew Cowan to drive into second place behind Forbes in the Elva.

Already the new circuit had attracted a large number of new Scottish racing drivers as well as drivers from Ireland and the north of England, so launching what could be called the second major era in Scottish motor racing history.

The Chevron B19 was popular and Laurence Jacobsen raced one after selling his Hillman Imp. His partnership with Robin Smith led to them briefly owning the Chevron company. Running behind Jacobsen in this photo is Stuart Lawson's Van Diemen FF2000.

The 1965 season at Ingliston proved extremely successful. Attendance in the first year averaged 12,000 per meeting and SMRC membership soared to over 3,000. Part reason for this success was a 5,000-seater grandstand alongside the start and finish, good toilet facilities for the time and, with the building of the timber-framed MacRobert Pavilion, you could also buy a

decent lunch and shelter from the rain. Already, Ian Scott Watson had plans to extend the circuit. Behind the main grandstand and paddock was a huge parking area, now used for Ingliston Market, and Scott Watson's idea was to extend the circuit outside the boundaries and into the car park.

This was ruled out but a compromise small loop gave the top straight an extension, albeit with a kink in the middle, leading to the tightest hairpin bend in motor racing. On the exit of this bend was a formidable oak tree which was removed many years later when the RAC safety inspector advised that it had to go. The return leg led into a smooth radius left-hander to rejoin the original small circuit. Ingliston continued with this layout from then onwards.

Today Nell Ginn is a prominent motor racing organiser but in the 1970s his father worked with Shell in Scotland and he started his racing career there. He later raced in the British Formula 3 Championship with sponsorship from Y-Fronts!

The year 1965 saw Jackie Stewart join Jim Clark in the grand prix world championship. Though it is often said that he moved straight into Formula 1, in fact Jackie had been courted by a number of teams for at least nine months before signing for BRM. The first person to suggest a drive was Tim Parnell who ran his own team in grand prix racing. This early recognition of his talent slightly fazed Stewart and he turned down the chance. Then came the moment mentioned earlier when Jim Clark arranged for him to try out Clark's Lotus-Climax at Brands Hatch at the end of practice for the British Grand Prix. A week before this, however, Stewart had been approached by Louis Stanley of BRM about joining BRM and somewhere in the wings was John Cooper who had also seen Stewart's talent and wanted him for the Cooper team. It was BRM that clinched the deal with an offer of £4000 to sign for the 1965 racing season and plenty of opportunity to test for the team. This is an element of Stewart which is rarely brought up, his absolute passion for testing to extract the last iota of performance and handling from a race car.

1965 was also the year Jim Clark finally broke the Indianapolis spell and became the first European driver to win the Indy 500 since Dario Resta thirty years before. This led to some amusing sidelights. For example he obviously won the pace car but as it was a Plymouth Sports Fury convertible, Ford Motor Company would have nothing of it and gave him a beautiful green Ford Galaxie instead. Amongst his other prizes was voucher for a $1,000 wardrobe from Dick's Mens Store in Indianapolis. As Jim said at the time *"...one of the conditions of the prize was I had to select about 20 ties*

Tom Brown again, hard pressed by Keith Wickham's similar Van Diemen at Caravan Corner with Brown going on to clinch yet another Formula Ford Championship. He was to win six Scottish Championships in his career.

but have you ever seen American ties?" He was also amused by an American newspaper comment *"...He flies back to Europe between qualifying runs for road car races or tea with the Queen or whatever else is on the schedule like shearing the sheep. Jim Clark can deliver a baby lamb as smoothly as he can deliver the goods at Indianapolis."*.

All of this was good for Scottish motor racing. Not only did we see a raft of young hopefuls taking up the sport at Ingliston but a new and younger audience which was to help Scotcircuits Ltd, become a successful company. This impetus was maintained for nearly fifteen years.

For the 1966 season they invested in concrete edging on all the corners at Ingliston because they were faced with a huge bill from the Royal Highland Society for repair to the grass where the drivers had been clipping the corners, not just by a few feet but the occasional yard! On the car front, Aberdonian Willie Forbes sold his Elva-BMW sports car to another up and coming Aberdonian, Richard Scott, and Forbes replaced it with a Lotus 35-BMW. New names included Bill Dryden - who was to become a Dealer Team Vauxhall driver - with Nick Cuthbert's competition Lotus Elan and it was this car which set Dryden on his way. Cuthbert was also keen to promote Eric Liddell's racing career and bought one of the dazzling new Ford GT40s for Liddell to race. This too set Liddell on his way to a successful career in sports and GT racing.

When 1100cc Saloons became all the rage in Scotland, the Hillman Imp soon out-powered and out handled the Mini Coopers. Ian Forrest was probably the most successful of the Imp drivers with a string of different Drambuie sponsored Imps over the years. He is leading Laurence Jacobsen in his Cuthbertson's Dairies Imp.

71

The last of the "Scottish Chevrons" was the B60 Sports 2000 that was run as a prototype by Laurence Jacobsen.

Andrew Cowan was perhaps best known as a rally driver but had driven Ian Scott Watson's Lotus Elan at Ingliston. He was a farming neighbour of Jim Clark and it was no surprise when Jim persuaded Colin Chapman to let Cowan race a Formula 3 Lotus at Goodwood. It was all very low key to the extent that Cowan was entered for the Chichester Cup as "A N Other". It was one of two drives offered by Chapman but Cowan stepped back and decided to concentrate on his rallying career and from then on only drove in club racing with Harry Ballantyne's Marcos-Volvo.

All this activity persuaded Scottish Television to suggest that they cover a few Ingliston meetings live as part of their "Scotsport" programme which looked good for the Scots who had just started to collect commercial sponsors. The opening meeting of the year, however, had everything, lots of non-starters following the Easter weekend races down South, and even snow. In the main race Bill Stein's dominance in the Libre events with the Ecosse-Climax single seater was threatened by Willie Forbes' Lotus-BMW. The winner of the Edinburgh Students Charities cup would be decided on the aggregate of two races and though Andrew Fletcher's Brabham was on pole for the first heat he had problems in both races and could only finish fourth overall. Forbes won the first heat but in drying conditions Bill Stein got past in the early

David Leslie became Scottish Formula Libre Champion driving the Hope-Scott Ralt beating Andy Barton's March seen following.

When Hugh McCaig took over the franchise for the Ingliston racing circuit, he still managed to race his Jaguar XK120 Cabriolet in historic events. The car had been raced many years before by its original owner, Bob Hamilton from Falkirk. Chasing McCaig is Willie Tuckett in the ex-Border Reivers D type Jaguar.

laps and opened up sufficient of a lead to ensure an overall win on aggregate. One Irish newcomer at that meeting was John Watson with a Brabham.

True to their word Scottish Television went live to Ingliston for the May race meeting. As it was wet and greasy there were plenty of spins and they were pleased with the response and vowed to televise the circuit again. Graham Birrell had already shown great promise with his Austin A30 and now the Perdal Anglia but his younger brother Gerry Birrell now came on the scene and he was to have a successful career in motor racing. On this occasion, however, he won his first race with a Singer Chamois prepared for the Singer Distributors in Glasgow by George Percival of Perdal and Tommy Dickson's old mechanic Hugh Shannon. Not to be outdone, Graham Birrell had two wins with George Percivals Perdal Anglia.

Ingliston's biggest ever crowd (14,000) came to the King Hussein Trophy race meeting in July attended by His Majesty King Hussein of Jordan. This created quite a stir at the circuit and throughout the meeting Hussein had half a dozen well-armed security men situated in the latticework underneath the main grandstand. As he was a great motor racing enthusiast, Hussein enjoyed his day out and there was a good entry. The main race for the trophy was won by Peter Gethin driving one of the Ron Harris Lotus Formula 2 cars with his team-mate, John Cardwell in second place. It might have been different had Jock Russell not blown his gearbox

in the Ford V8-engined Lotus F1 car. The engine of this car had come from the factory Lotus 30 which broke in two at Brands Hatch during a race. Peter Gethin also raced a Formula 3 Brabham and won the F3 race despite a monumental spin. For this meeting Graham Birrell's Perdal Anglia had been given independent suspension and a push-rod 1900cc engine and won first time out.

The Ecurie Ecosse racing effort was winding down but after converting one of their Tojeiro Coupes into a spyder they ran it with Bill Stein in the support race to the British Grand Prix. Stein had a horrific accident which ended his racing career. Shortly afterwards David Murray privately rented Ingliston and tested both Graham Birrell and Bill Dryden in the Ecosse-Climax and their new Ecosse-Imp. As it transpired they each ended up racing their respective cars for the rest of the season. Both were out for the August meeting sponsored by the Scottish Milk Marketing Board.

Once more there was a big turnout of spectators lured by the fact that Jim Clark was going to "race". This was the first time Clark had run on the track apart from being a passenger in a veteran car at the opening meeting. His last racing appearance in Scotland was back in 1960 with a Lotus Formula Junior. Clark came along to join in the fun and take part in a mock race using electric milk floats. There were around ten milk floats entered by various milk companies and farmers and Jim was loaned one to take part. The idea was that they would do one lap of the circuit stopping at various points to pick up a crate of empty milk bottles. Clark was resoundingly beaten!

That season the Scottish Formula Libre Champion was Alan Rollinson driving a Brabham and the only Scot who really gave him any trouble was Andrew Fletcher, also in a Brabham. Fletcher was later to turn to sports cars, usually Chevrons, and had a successful run in the European 2 litre sports car championship. Rollinson went on to race in Formula 5000 but missed out on the chance to get into Formula 1.

At the end of the season the bunch of Falkirk enthusiasts led by Tony Evangelisti, who called themselves Scuderia Centro Scot, bought a Formula II Lola to be shared by Evangelisti and his team mates Pat Callander and George Stuart. They were also to race a Chevron B8 until Evangelisti managed to park it on top of the banking at Silverstone so ending the short career of Scuderia Centro Scot.

At the Racing Car Show of 1966 a new formula called Formula Vee was launched and it was announced there would be a four race Championship for Formula Vees at Ingliston during the 1967 season. The first of these was in July and thirteen cars turned up, all of them from south of the Border. Three of the cars were entered for Scottish drivers. Andrew Cowan was given the factory Smithfield Vee to race, Dryden the factory Beach whilst Gerry Birrell - Graham's younger brother and a promising talent - was given an aged Dolling Vee. The star of the meeting was a Journalist called Nick Brittan who gave some racing tips to a young rally driver called Jennifer Nadin. Jenny later married Graham Birrell and as Jenny Nadin had a successful racing career as well as becoming a formidable administrator of the BTCC twenty years later. Despite the fact that Formula Vee racing was successful and Gerry Birrell in Wooler Engineerings factory car had won the National Championship, the National organiser, Nick Brittan, decided that there were no Scots willing to buy Formula Vees and so all future Scottish races were abandoned.

This announcement came in the same week that Scottish Motor Racing Club invited Dave Lazenby of Team Lotus to come to Scotland and talk about this new Formula Ford class which was about to be introduced in 1968. Unlike Formula Vee, Formula Ford was totally embraced by the Scots and it became the dominant single seater formula for the next thirty five years.

If there had been a prize for determination, Geordie Taylor from Aberdeenshire would have been a leading contender. He raced various Formula Fords for nearly twenty years, getting remarkable results. He eventually became Scottish Formula Ford Champion in the 1990s.

Everyone looked forward to this, as the 1967 motor racing season at Ingliston had been pretty dull and boring save for occasional visits from drivers in England. If things had continued this way in 1968 the portents for motor racing in Scotland were not good. But it didn't and Formula Ford brought new enthusiasm and opened the flood gates for new drivers.

When Ecurie Ecosse was reformed in 1984, Hugh McCaig bought this Chevron FF2000 from John Clark. It was raced initially by Willie Hourie from the Orkney Islands.

Formula Ford started quietly, but as the 1968 season progressed we began to see progress. One driver who began to really make his mark was Gerry Birrell with an old Lotus converted to Formula Ford specification. Birrell was a superb engineer. Formula Ford, however, eventually gave him his break when Wooler Engineering, which ran the factory Crossle Formula Ford, introduced him to John Crossle. Now Birrell was in his element and was responsible for making the Crossle one of the leading marques in Formula Ford. This was not overlooked by Ford Motor Company who were to sign Gerry Birrell to a contract which led him into a development role with Ford on cars like the Cologne Capri. Birrell moved to England and became a professional racing driver the following year. He was consistently good in Formula 2 even though he never raced with a truly competitive team until 1973 when he was in the factory Chevron team. Sadly he crashed heavily aa Rouen and was killed.

The other newcomer who was soon to make his mark was Tom Walkinshaw, a young market gardner who had raced at Ingliston with an MG Midget. He was one of those at the meeting who was inspired to invest in a brand new Lotus 51 Formula Ford and he was to become Scottish Formula Ford Champion the following year, 1968. However, the whole of the 1968 season was overshadowed by the death of Jim Clark at Hockenheim in April. As with racing drivers everywhere, nobody could believe that someone as talented and skilled as Clark could be killed in a racing car. As we were to find out later, Clark's Formula 2 Lotus almost certainly had had a puncture which caused it to slide off the road but this did not stop most racing drivers from wondering about the safety of racing when a driver of Jim Clark's calibre could be killed. Ironically it was his fellow Scot, Jackie Stewart, who had already started to do something about it with his bid to improve motor racing circuit safety. On the very day Clark was killed Jackie was at the Jarama circuit in Spain checking out the barriers. To the modern generation of drivers it might appear unthinkable that Stewart would be criticised for what he was doing but at the time Stewart was vilified in many motor racing circles. Indeed the leading motor racing journalist of the day, Denis Jenkinson of Motor Sport, was the leading critic of Stewart. In the following two years Stewart had even more reason to continue his struggle as many of his friends were killed in racing accidents. Today, who knows how many racing lives Jackie Stewart saved in his virtual one-man stand to promote motor racing safety. Few drivers before or since stuck their necks further out than Stewart did in those critical years.

The same year, 1968, there was a second upset as far as Scottish motor racing was concerned when David Murray, the founder and power behind Ecurie Ecosse, suddenly left Scotland for the Canary Islands. For some time it had been known that David, who owned a string of public houses in Edinburgh as well as Merchiston Motors, was in financial difficulties. He had spent a lot of his own money in the team as well as having substantial financial support from Major Edward Thompson the President of the BEN Shipping Line. Murray was now in serious financial trouble and as Spain had no extradition laws, he chose the Canary Islands. It was a very sad story as most of his friends could not believe that such a shrewd accountant could get into such difficulties. It was said to be unpaid debts to brewers or to the Inland Revenue but nothing ever came out and all his affairs were handled by his lawyer. Indeed only his lawyer knew his actual address in the Canary Islands.

The talented Bryce Wilson was helped in his early racing by Laurence Jacobsen, who ran him in this Formula Atlantic Chevron. He was a regular winner and eventually moved briefly into Formula 3.

Had David gone there to live on his money it would be understandable but, as it turned out, he went there on his own promising to send for his wife Jenny, who stayed in the flat in Edinburgh, until he was settled. David got a job serving behind a bar. One day his aged Mini was hit by a bus and he was taken to hospital with relatively minor injuries. However, in hospital he had a heart attack and died. It was one of the great tragedies in Scottish motor racing.

David Murray's disappearance left Ecurie Ecosse in a difficult position and with the help of a private group, Friends of Scotland, and the Ecurie Ecosse Association they muddled through the year. During the winter a number of private meetings took place so that in 1969 Ecurie Ecosse reformed themselves. Riley driver, and a leading light in the Ecurie Ecosse Association, Harry Ballantyne, took over the running of the team with the financial backing of the Ecurie Ecosse Association and the Friends of Scotland group.

Harry Ballantyne and his brother Eric were partners in an old established firm of ironfounders in Bo'ness. He originally ran a Bentley at Bo'ness in 1948 but then bought the Riley Sprite he used for racing, hill climbs and rallies. The car was the one originally raced before the war by Bob Gerard in the Tourist Trophy. Harry then bought a Marcos kit from Jem Marsh and built his own Marcos-Volvo that he raced himself and occasionally loaned to Andrew Cowan to race at Ingliston.

Ecurie Ecose bought the ex-Jochen Rindt Brabham BT23B for the European Formula 2 championship and Graham Birrell was chosen as the driver. Graham was a logical and safe choice for the car as he had a lot of experience. His only misfortune came at the fast Enna circuit in Sicily when he went off the road and crashed heavily. He ended up in the lake and had to be rescued by boat! As was always the case with David Murray, the car had been well insured and with the insurance money and the bits from the wreckage they were able to buy a new Brabham BT30 chassis for 1970.

Harry faced a difficult task when he took over the running of Ecurie Ecosse because money was very short and they lost around £1,000 in potential starting money when a couple of the rounds in the European Formula 2 championship were cancelled. Also, too late, he realised that if they had bought a Ford van and a trailer, rather than use the ageing and slow Ecurie Ecosse transporter, they could have saved about 50% of their fuel costs.
At the end of the 1969 racing season, Harry Ballantyne had to step down as Team Manager of Ecurie Ecosse and return to the family business but he had done a remarkable job with such meagre resources. He remained involved in the team in an advisory capacity.

Richard Scott from Aberdeen, who had been racing an Elva-BMW for a number of seasons, launched his 1969 campaign buying a Brabham Formula 3 car. He was not happy with it and during the season switched to a Chevron B15 but found the going even tougher in the British Formula 3 championship.

Just prior to the August race meeting at Ingliston, Denys Dobbie arrived back on the Scottish scene. Denys had been a great enthusiast and was the first secretary of the Ecurie Ecosse Association. He had bought Archie Craig's Bongazoo - a supercharged MG Special - intending to race it but had an accident at home and had to sell the car before even running it. When he passed his exams as a chartered accountant he did not fancy the low wages as an apprentice in Scotland so he joined a company in Vancouver and steadily made his pile. Eventually, he ended up in Nassau in the Bahamas with Peat Marwick. He had not forgotten motor racing and had raced a Formula Vee out there but hankered for a Lotus 62.

One of the most interesting Scottish projects was the development of the AMC Spirit for the European Touring Car Championship. Sadly it never turned a wheel in anger and later ended up in minor saloon events in England.

Caterham Car Sales found one for him but when it arrived in the Bahamas it was actually a race prepared Lotus 47 - the road version of the 62. In financial circles in those days one of the star companies in which to invest

Denys Dobbie, a Scot who had made his fortune in the Bahamas, returned not only to run Knockhill but to form DART with Graham Birrell driving their Chevron B16.

was Poseidon and Denys was an early investor. He shrewdly sold out his holdings before the company collapsed and decided to return to Scotland. In October 1969 he again contacted Caterham and bought a Chevron B8. Hearing about the B8, two Edinburgh brothers, Colin and Victor Brown, who were active members of MG Car Club and owners of one of Edinburgh's more up-market household furniture stores, approached Denys about entering Graham Birrell in the car to race at Ingliston with their company, C & J Brown Ltd, as sponsors.

By now Dobbie had in mind the idea of running his own team in International racing and formed DART (Dobbie Automobile Racing Team). He decided to order a brand new Chevron B16 for Graham Birrell to race and he (Dobbie), would race the B8. This idea was dropped after Denys had a monumental spin in front of the pits when testing at Oulton Park and Denys decided to retire from competition altogether and concentrate on running the team.

Meanwhile, Graham Birrell's brother Gerry had a good season in the European Formula Ford Championship. Driving his factory Crossle, he dominated the championship. As a result of this he was one of the group of FF drivers sent to Sebring for a "World Championship" race meeting.

In the 1969 Scottish Formula Ford Championship Gerry was not so successful, having been beaten by another Scot, Tom Walkinshaw from Prestonpans. Tom had shown great determination all season in a Hawke Formula Ford. Tom had been helped along in his championship win by the

fact that Gerry Birrell had to miss the last two race meetings of the season at Ingliston. However, Tom Walkinshaw was also marked as a coming man. Indeed Tom moved southwards shortly afterwards to take over the management of the Hawke Formula Ford team for the 1970 racing season.

Just one year after Jim Clark's tragic death at Hockenheim, Scotland was able to celebrate a second world champion in Jackie Stewart who took Ken Tyrrell's Matra-Cosworth to a convincing win in the championship, confirming that Jackie Stewart had truly fulfilled the promise he had shown just eight seasons before.

At the Scottish Motor Racing Club dinner that year there was a touching moment when Jim Clark's father, James Clark Senior, stood up and presented the Jim Clark Memorial Trophy to Jackie Stewart on his victory in the world motor racing championship. The inscription on the trophy, which was a silver crash helmet that had originally been presented to Jim Clark, read *"To a Scotsman for outstanding achievement in the field of motor sport"*. The following day Jackie was accorded a civic reception in his native town of Dumbarton.

There was a touch of nostalgia at the end of 1969 when, following David Murray's hasty departure the previous year, it was announced that Merchiston Motors Ltd would be leaving Merchiston Mews. The old Mews had served as their headquarters for over 17 years. The motor company was technically absorbed by Eastern Motor Company Ltd, which was run by John Brown, himself a former racing driver and old friend of David Murray. Though the company name continued to be listed on the letter heading it quietly and sadly disappeared from the mainstream.

For 1971 Denys Dobbie decided to make a serious effort in the European 2 Litre Chamionship series. The B16 and B8 were sold and Denys persuaded Dave Wilson from Chevron to leave the company and became team manager. John Miles and Graham Birrell were engaged as the drivers of two brand new Chevron B19s and there was some sponsorship from Burmah Oils - a division of Castrol.

They ran in the BOAC 1000kms at Brands Hatch and Miles and Birrell in the B19 romped home in the class to beat the new Lola T212 driven by Jo Bonnier and Peter Westbury. Incidentally, in the Group 5 class of this race another Scot, Andrew Fletcher, with Willie Tuckett as his co-driver, won in his B16 Chevron. At Salzburgring Graham Birrell was pushed into the barriers by a hustling Vic Elford in a Lola and broke his wrist. For Silverstone two weeks later Dobbie brought in Dutchman Toine Hezemans who beat Helmut Marko's Lola to win the class.

Later in the season Brian Hart built his own alloy block to take the new Cosworth BDA head and this engine appeared for the first time at

Ecurie Ecosse moved info Formula 2 racing early in 1970 with this ex-Jochen Rindt Formula 2 Brabham BT23C, driven by Graham Birrell.

Hockenheim in the DART B19 driven by John Miles. But it was all getting a bit too expensive and Denys Dobbie decided to scale down the European bit and concentrate on the RAC British Sports Car Championship which John Miles went on to win outright in the DART B19. There was a slight diversion when Denys asked Graham Hill to test one of his cars and there

When Patsy McGarrity was not winning races, his fellow Ulsterman, Tommy Reid, continued the success with his Brabham BT40.

was every chance Hill would race it at the 1971 August Bank Holiday meeting. However, they could not sort out the fuel and oil contracts as Hill was a Shell driver and the team had Castrol backing.

It was no surprise when, at the end of the 1971 season, Dobbie wound up the DART team but got himself involved with Derek Bennett of Chevron and Bob Faulkner in a project to build the pretty Chevron B16 into a road car. Dave Wilson, DART's team manager, moved back into the Chevron fold where he was to remain. The Chevron road car project fell on stony ground as Derek Bennett was not really interested in the complexities of building a road car and the team could not decide on their marketing plan. At one time a BMW engine was considered but this was going to be too expensive, then a Ford engine was discussed. In the end the whole project simply foundered. Later Dobbies name was mentioned with regard to GRD but this too was short lived.

Chapter 9
Quiet times and a Fife hillside.

The early 1970s continued with Ingliston as the sole racing venue. With relatively low key racing, a lack of incentive to buy racing cars and only one circuit, racing in Scotland was beginning to stagnate even though Jackie Stewart won his second World Championship in 1971. What was needed was a real jolt and it came from an unlikely source. Tom Kinnaird, a Fife potato farmer, had some derelict land in the lee of a hill called Knock Hill and decided to do his own thing and build a motor racing circuit. The land was not much use for farming and had carried an old mine railway that had long since disappeared. Tom, with the dogged determination that was part of his character, got out his bulldozer and started to carve out the basis of what is today's Knockhill racing circuit. He was in no rush, and from time to time we heard of his plans but, sadly, nobody paid much attention to him. As a truly independent individual he kept on ploughing and built a small track. Eventually he and entrepreneur Denys Dobbie got together which resulted in Dobbie leasing the track from Kinnaird and taking over the project. Denys was full of enthusiasm and aimed to launch Knockhill as a serious motor racing contender. He immediately got down to the task and his plan was to open the circuit for the 1975 racing season.

Whether it was something to do with Denys Dobbie's plans for developing Knockhill or not, there was a marked change in attitude in 1974 and people began to pay more attention. For a start the Formula Ford class literally exploded.

In early season testing at Ingliston, John Cleland, who had been very active in hill climbing, crashed his Chevron into the barriers which was a set-back for his first serious attempt in racing. Tom Walkinshaw confirmed he would be racing a Ford Capri in the British Touring Car Championship and Richard Scott decided to build his own Formula 2 car, the Scott.

As for Scottish racing that season, John Romanes had negotiated sponsorship from Rothmans for the opening meeting on April 14 and for a change we had warm weather. This meeting brought up a problem that occasionally arose at Ingliston. Scotcircuits Ltd were only allowed to start 16 cars in any race but there were 28 entries for the Formula Ford race! This, obviously, led to the running of two races for FFs which was becoming and was to remain, the most popular formula for young Scots. Stu Lawson emerged as the dominant driver in the Formula that year with Graham Hamilton driving well in the MacDonald Shand Van Diemen. Shand Carpets, was a carpet company in the south of Scotland run by Douglas Shand.

The sports car line-up for one of the first races ot Knockhill photographed from Tommy Dickson's helicopter.
On pole position Iain McLaren's Chevron B36 and on the left of the front row, Eric Liddell's Jensen-Healey.

One of the early Knockhill race meetings in 1975 featured a non-championship Formula 3 race. Leading the field through Duffus Dip is Belgian driver Patrick Neve with Swede Gunnar Nilsson in third place.

Another newcomer with a well-known name was having a harder time of it. Norman Dickson, son of Tommy Dickson who had raced for Team Lotus and Ecurie Ecosse, had started racing a Hillman Imp but moved into Formula Ford. He had two monumental accidents, writing off his original Crossle and later his new Van Diemen. He eventually won his first Formula Ford race at Ingliston and proved to be a much better driver than we initially imagined. Once he got into more powerful cars he had a satisfying few years in racing supported by his father's helicopter company and the family business, Dickson Motors in Perth. Campbell Graham also appeared at Ingliston with an F2 engine in his Chevron that had come out of one of Denys Dobbie's DART Chevrons. Iain McLaren turned up with a new Formula 2 car, one of the first independent cars designed by Ron Dennis, the Rondel, and though he was enthusiastic about it at first, he changed his mind when, late in the season, he rented Campbell Graham's Chevron.

In the opening meeting of the season the need to give more protection to the toilets on the kink of the back straight at Ingliston became obvious when Tony Charnell in his Lola made the mistake of selecting the wrong gear. Despite taking the bend in neutral he shot over the grass and almost into the toilets that were unoccupied at the time! Some time later Douglas Niven in his Boss Escort had the throttle jam wide open on the same bend.

Chris Amon was interviewed by Jimmy McInnes when he opened the Knockhill circuit in 1975, Denys Dobbie, who had made it all happen, is on the left in sun glosses.

The Capri flattened the barrier and spun round the back of the toilets injuring two spectators. That winter John Romanes announced that the toilets would be moved further back from the edge of the circuit!

Talking of Douglas Niven, he had approached a young Glasgow engineer, Dan Wright, to see if he could improve the handling of the Boss Escort. Dan was a great enthusiast and talented engineer who went on to become very successful and even develop his own supercharging system. Whilst still a student at University he was introduced to Irish driver Brian Nelson and Nelson's sponsor, Desmond Mack. As a result, he developed some interesting aerodynamic mods to the team's Crossle. Now, with the Escort, he developed an unique wing mounted under the car at the rear and the car ran successfully throughout the season. Dan was invited to Hethel to have a word with Colin Chapman but nothing came of the talks. After a successful engineering and designing career in England, Dan returned to Scotland and was involved in the rebuilding of the Albion name with a commercial vehicle components company

Amon prepares to set off on his inaugural lap at Knockhill.

Around mid-season Jock Russell despaired of trying to get spare parts for his McRae F5000 and decided to use it as the basis of his own car, the Russell, but it was not to race for some time. Also, behind the scenes in the paddock, chief scrutineer Bill Cleland (father of John) resigned and his place was taken by Iain Bennie who was was to hold the job for the next twenty years. Bill had taken some stick over the eligibility of Kleber tyres on the James Ross Hillman Avenger raced by Hugh Chalmers. Though Bill later admitted his mistake, he had clearly decided to step down which was a great pity as he was always good for a joke in the paddock. Bill Cleland came from the old school of scrutineers who knew every trick in the book.

Amongst the newcomers to Scottish racing in 1974 was George Franchitti with a Hawke Formula Ford and who, after a few seasons, retired from racing to help encourage his eldest son Dario with his karting whilst his younger son Marino watched from his pram. At the same time Tom Walkinshaw made a comeback to Ingliston winning with a Ford Capri.

The year 1975 marked the tenth anniversary of Ingliston and by now the prospect of Denys Dobbie's revamped Knockhill arriving on the scene was widely anticipated. One reason for this was that Scottish Motor Racing Club had a monopoly on Ingliston and no other clubs could run events there. The reason for this was fairly obvious as the Royal Highland and Agricultural Society limited the number of practice days and race meetings on the circuit to a total of 12, or six race meetings each with a practice day. This was not understood by some people, who were crying "cartel", and there was a bit of ill feeling in certain quarters. Knockhill's arrival, however, would give the many Scots now racing the chance of a few more races during the season as well as other clubs the chance to organise motor racing. As it turned out Scottish Sporting Car Club were to take on the job but eventually Scottish Motor Racing Club took over the running of Knockhill events also.

A shadow was cast over everything with a general melt-down of the economy that saw some sponsors pulling out of racing. This must also have concerned Denys Dobbie who was in the process of creating the new circuit. Tom Kinnaird's original work was very much a low-key affair but Dobbie approached Knockhill in a more ambitious way with a much wider circuit clearly aimed at future National or even International events. Ingliston's fortunes were boosted when John Romanes was given the opening round in the Tricentrol British Saloon Car Championship. At the same time, amidst speculation that Ingliston was closing, Romanes was able to confirm that Scotcircuits Ltd had obtained a ten-year contract to continue racing there plus a further ten-year option which would take the track to 1995.

Gunnar Nilsson in the March 753 was to go on to join Team Lotus before suffering cancer from which he died.

One of the regular competitors at Ingliston, who became very popular with the spectators, was Irishman Tommy Reid. He had first come to Scotland to race a Lotus 18 at Charterhall entered by his long time pal, Mick Mooney. He then became involved with John Crossle, the Irish designer, and drove the original Crossle sports car. Unfortunately he had the worst accident of his career driving the V8 Daimler-engined Crossle single seater. The lady doctor who attended him told him he would never walk again but twenty years later he was still racing, now in historic events. When convalescing from this accident he came up with the idea of forming T D Reid (Braids) Ltd as he had always been in the textile business. He made a great success of it which allowed him to continue racing a variety of cars

Allan McNish moved from karts into Formula Ford with support from Hugh McCaig. His David Leslie-run Van Diemen was the car to beat.

Also, unfased by the economic situation, Douglas Shand came to an agreement with Lord Elgin to use the name Ecurie Ecosse for their new team. This included a new 753 Formula 3 March for Graham Hamilton to race in specific F3 events and two Formula Fords, a Van Diemen and a Hawke for Gordon Dalzell and Stu Lawson. There was talk of a second March being bought for Stu Lawson to race but this never came about.

Also on the car front, Iain McLaren sold his Motul to fellow Scot John Barr who in turn sold his Lotus Atlantic car to Bob Rollo. To replace the Motul, McLaren was able to buy the works development Chevron BT31 sports car, the "Chocolate Drop" which Brian Redman had raced successfully. Campbell Graham's Chevron was sold to Edinburgh driver Andrew Jeffrey and the ex- DART Chevron sports car was bought by Keith Millar. All of this wheeling and dealing was a welcome change and an indication that things were once again moving in Scotland.

Despite the fact that visiting racing drivers from England used to pale after their first practice lap round Ingliston, and complain that it was too narrow and dangerous, it was in fact an inherently safe circuit. In nearly thirty years of racing on the tight little track there were very few accidents. The main reason for this, as the local Scots soon found out, was that you needed to be precise and conscious of the limits of the circuit otherwise your car would be badly damaged. Looking back on the entire period it would be naive to assume that a fatal accident could not have happened but it didn't and in that we were fortunate. Every year the RAC, usually in the shape of Derek Ongaro their safety expert, inspected everything with a fine tooth comb and I can remember no year when something was not slightly

The man to beat in Formula Ford in the late 1980s was Cameron Binnie with a Van Diemen, Binnie's family farm was only a mile or two from the Scottish border, so he was accepted as a Scot.

modified; such as the huge oak tree on the exit of the hairpin. In the early days of Ingliston Keith Schellenberg used to enter his huge Barnatto Hassan Bentley for the historic race and he was the only driver given a dispensation to leave the track, go round the oak tree on the grass, and then return to the track again!

Ingliston was a very safe circuit and the only fatality occurred, ironically, in a karting demonstration when one of the karts slid wide at Caravan bend and the tiny wheels hit the edging of the track tipping the kart over and into the steel barrier. Had Ingliston not started when it did, motor racing would have come to a complete stop in Scotland in 1965 and might never have developed to help produce all of the leading Scottish racing drivers of today.

When Formula Vauxhall Lotus was announced, Marlboro stepped in and set up the first professional team with Allan McNish and a young Finn named Mika Hakkinen. The press launch of the Marlboro team was held at Ingliston.

The most anticipated thing to happen in 1975 was the opening of the long-awaited Knockhill circuit. There had been a number of problems not least of which had been the weather which delayed the laying of the final road surface. It was a problem we have experienced ever since at Knockhill as the rain clouds have a bad habit of tripping on the top of Knock Hill and pouring their contents onto the track. As is normal with new circuits, the first event was held under a closed licence so only members of the organising club could compete. The weather was good and Denys Dobbie invited grand prix driver Chris Amon to open the circuit with his Amon grand prix car. However, by the end of 1974 Chris had abandoned the project after a number of testing accidents. He still honoured the invitation and arrived at the circuit with a Talon Formula 5000 car. In his demonstration laps to open the circuit he set an unofficial lap record of around 88 mph. Then, in the racing proper, Andrew Jeffrey with a Formula 3 March took the honour of setting the first ever official lap record at 88.20 mph and Knockhill was on its way.

One of the rounds in the Formula Vauxhall Lotus Championship was held at Knockhill where McNish emerged the winner ahead of Justin Bell, left, and promising, but underfinanced Scot, Andy Sim.

It was quite surprising, even at that opening meeting, to see how the regular Scottish drivers, used to the confines of Ingliston, coped with the much faster and more open Knockhill. Probably the greatest revelation was Norman Dickson. At the time, and after watching him with his March at that opening Knockhill meeting, I wrote *"...at Ingliston he always seemed to be in search of an accident whilst at Knockhill he was much more tidy and extremely quick"*. For me, however, the man of that opening meeting was Eric Liddell in the Jenscot Jensen-Healey and I suggested that a lot of drivers new to the circuit could do worse than just follow Eric round and duplicate his lines through the corners. Elsewhere, however, things were not so good. In the haste to complete the circuit, the sloping car parks were not adequately drained and a lot of the spectators found themselves churning around in the mud and not getting very far.

We had scarcely caught our breath from the first meeting than the first major meeting at Knockhill was upon us. This was a 2-litre sports car race and there was a good entry. Richard Scott made his return to Scottish racing with one of the Roger-Hire 2 litre Lola sports cars, rather than his normal Durex-sponsored Lola 5000. Jock Russell ran his Russell F5000 for the first time at this meeting but the car was far from right.

As a result of Richard Scott's switch, normal sports car specialist Iain McLaren had some real opposition with his Chevron. The third man on the front row of the grid was emerging sports car and Clubmans driver Sandy Watson who, in the 1990s, was still racing and won the European historic sports car class with his Chevron B8.

Scott got the jump at the flag with McLaren behind him. On the second to last lap McLaren was right on the Lola's tail and on the run up to the flag he feinted one way and then swept past to win one of the best races ever seen at Knockhill. McLaren's fastest lap of 52.4 seconds (88.56 mph) actually broke the outright circuit record. Despite the heavy rain there was a good crowd attending the first major public meeting at the circuit and as a result a few more got caught in the muddy car park.

Not content to rest on his laurels, Denys Dobbie decided to offer reasonable prize money for a full-blown 2 litre Sports Car race on the circuit and attracted a class entry. Unfortunately his sponsor, Shell, suddenly backed out and he was left to pay out the money from his own pocket. He changed the prize fund into one related to the number of spectators who turned up. As a result, he lost Richard Lloyd, John Hine and Richard Scott who felt this was not likely to compensate for the long trip. There was still a good entry with Richard Robarts in the British Caledonian Lola T294, Guy Edwards with the Lola T390, John Lepp with the factory March TS5 Hart and Martin Raymond in the Fisons Chevron B31. The surprise came in practice when Ian Grobb in the Sphere Drake Chevron B31 put himself on pole equalling Iain McLaren's lap record. Lepp was second fastest with Richard Mallock third in his incredible Mallock.

The Sunday race saw heavy clouds and equally heavy rain and though Autosport reported a crowd of only 1,000 spectators there were, in fact, 3,000. Martin Raymond won the first heat from Iain McLaren and Richard Mallock and in the second Iain McLaren was the winner. On aggregate McLaren ran out overall winner with Mallock second.

It could truthfully be said the impact of Knockhill that season was tremendous, and to cap it all, a non-championship Formula 3 race was organised for later in the season. Once more there was a superb entry with a number of drivers who were to go on to become successful in grand prix racing. On the surface Denys Dobbie's enthusiasm, and willingness to lash out money, was making Ingliston look like the poor relation but John Romanes, Chairman of Scotcircuits, was no fool and was saying nothing.

At stake for the Knockhill Formula 3 race was the Jim Clark Trophy and everyone was trying to find a car to take part. Andrew Jeffrey managed to get the Daily Record newspaper to stump up the money to rent Harry Gilbert's March 743. One Scot hoping to compete was Donald McLeod in the GRD but he was a non-starter as was Stephen South with the factory Ray. It became clear that the March chassis didn't suit the swoops at the back of the Knockhill circuit. Everyone had assumed that the two top March drivers, Gunnar Nilsson - later to drive for Lotus in Grand Prix racing and die prematurely of cancer - and Alex Ribiero - later to star in CART - were hung out to dry by the 18-year old American Eddie Cheever with his works Modus. His pole position of 52.4 in an F3 car equalled Iain McLaren's outright circuit record and this was only Cheevers third-ever Formula 3 race!

When asked how he would do in the race Eddie remarked "...Well, in my last two races my engine has let me down." It was a prophetic remark. As for impressions of the circuit future Indianapolis winner Danny Sullivan thought the track was too narrow and little Alex Ribiero said that in the steep dips he was so small he couldn't see where the track went ! Best placed Scot was Graham Hamilton in the McDonald Shand Ecurie Ecosse March on the third row of the grid ahead of Ribiero and behind Nilsson.

The opening lap was a disaster. Cheever out accelerated everyone down to the first corner. "...all of a sudden the engine just died on me and then picked up again." This was enough to set off a chain reaction right down the field. Hamilton got through on the inside of Cheever but Mike Tyrrell (March), Herve Regout (March), Rupert Keegan (March), Richard Hawkins (March) and Alex Ribiero all tried to go through a gap that would only take one

car and the result was mayhem with cars spinning in all directions. Out of all this came the Belgian driver Patrick Neve - later to drive a Brabham in Formula 1 - who took the works Safir into the lead from Danny Sullivan, Gunnar Nilsson, Ingo Hoffman, Graham Hamilton, Pierre Dieudonne and the fast recovering Alex Ribiero. So it was the little known Patrick Neve who won the race with the highest placed Scot, Graham Hamilton.

To complete a season with a lot of interesting new races and cars, and a new circuit to boot, Ingliston staged a race, sponsored by Shand Carpets, called the Shand Carpets 100 for 2 litre sports cars. Race promoter Paul Watson organised the event and there were some good cars with Martin Raymond in his Fisons-sponsored Chevron and Ian Grob who totalled his Chevron in practice when he hit the accelerator instead of the brake at the Ingliston esses.

It became obvious that the battle would be between Guy Edwards in the factory Lola and John Lepp in the factory 2 litre March with the March obviously better suited to the oversteering Lola.

Patrick Neve was a surprise winner in the Formula 3 race as he was driving the relatively unknown Safir.

Another visitor was BBC disc jockey Noel Edmonds who had been roped in to drive the SMT Vauxhall Magnum, sponsored by Chunky Chickens. Jennifer Birrell was out in another Magnum provided by Bill Montgomery. In the smaller saloon category the drivers, who had the edge at that time, were John Fyda and Ian Forrest with their Hillman Imps. A new driver appeared on the scene in the shape of Laurence Jacobsen who was not only to become very successful in Scotland and elsewhere, but was later to help young Bryce Wilson on his way. Jacobsen took a strong third place.

The main emphasis was on the sports cars and in the first heat John Lepp led in the March chased by Richard Scott in a rented Chevron B26. In turn Iain McLaren with his Chevron was pushing Guy Edwards hard who was having an exciting time keeping control of the Lola which seemed out of its depth on Ingliston. Another man up there chasing Richard Robarts' Lola was Richard Mallock in his Hart-powered Mallock. Some of the other competitors objected to having this "Clubmans car" in the race but Richard provided a lot of the fireworks. In the second heat John Lepp was again the winner and took the money.

Edward Labinjoh, whose father was a Ghanain surgeon in Edinburgh, had a brilliant win in Jack Fisher's Alfa Romeo ahead of Noel Edmonds and Jenny Birrell. In the production saloon class Hugh Chalmers was in great form

Mika Hakkinen furiously throws his glove into the cockpit of his FVL at Knockhill after flying off the road of the bottom of Duffus Dip.

with the James Ross Avenger, that had been developed by Sandy Cormack, in the special saloon class. He took the lead ahead of the local heroes Bill Dryden and Douglas Niven and ended up as the race winner.

To my mind 1975, despite the arrival of Knockhill, or perhaps because of it, was probably Ingliston's greatest season. It ended in spectacular fashion with a Formula Libre race that saw the return of Eddie Cheever in his factory Formula 3 Modus to compete against the Ingliston regulars. McDonald Shand sponsored Cheever in the event.

The Irish were over in strength with John Pollock, Patsy McGarrity and Bill Gowdy all taking part. Indeed this had become a regular feature of racing in Scotland since the 1950s. With the ferry service to Stranraer offering competitive rates, all the Scottish circuits benefited from an influx of Irish drivers. Of these Patsy McGarrity was probably the most successful but his success led to a near disaster for Scottish Motor Racing Club.

One season Patsy was overall winner of the Libre Championship and took back to Belfast the superb Jock McBain Trophy. This had been

presented to the club after Jock's death and was a solid silver plinth on which was mounted a silver and wood rimmed steering wheel. It is one of the Club's most spectacular trophies. However, Patsy, a catholic with a garage in the protestant part of Belfast, seemed to attract the local Irish bombers and he suffered at least three times from bombs blowing up in his garage. The reason, I was told, was that Patsy refused to pay protection money to the IRA and so they bombed his place. As he was a catholic the protestants also chose to bomb it! Patsy, one of the great characters in Irish motorsport, who came from a family of jockeys, used to laugh the whole thing off but the threat to his life, and that of his family, was no laughing matter. In one of the bombings the Jock McBain Trophy was blown up and seriously damaged. With the compensation he received from the British Government, Patsy had the trophy beautifully repaired and it is awarded every year at the SMRC Dinner.

Patsy, however, was in good form in this final race of the 1975 season at Ingliston. Eddie Cheever gave an indication of what was to come in future years by fighting his Formula 3 car through the field of Atlantics and F2 cars to take the lead, only to find that he was losing air from a rear tyre. The Modus started to wallow and McGarrity and Andy Barton piled on the pressure. Eventually, going into the final bend, McGarrity tapped Cheever's nearside rear tyre when going round the outside of him. The Modus slewed round and climbed up the back of McGarrity's Chevron almost reaching the cockpit. Andy Barton took advantage and shot through to cross the line just ahead of McGarrity's car with the Modus and Cheever perched across the engine compartment. It was a spectacular end to the season.

Norman Dickson struggled during his two seasons in Internationol Formula 2. Here, at Pau, he arrived late and failed to qualify.

Over the winter, Ian Forrest managed to secure sponsorship for his Imp from the Drambuie, the whisky liquor company, and they were to be his prime sponsor for a number of years. This was one of the few times a whisky company has been involved in sponsorship. The reason for this was that the Scotch Whisky Association had recommended their members did not get involved with sponsoring anything to do with motoring. This said, a number of companies did indulge in some modest sponsorship and of course Scottish Motor Racing Club themselves had received financial support from Hartley Whyte whose grandfather founded Whyte & Mackay Scotch whisky.

For the 1976 season Norman Dickson persuaded his father to field a two-car team in the British Formula Atlantic Championship. A Formula Atlantic Modus chassis was ordered. The original plan was that if Andrew Jeffrey could find sponsorship, a second Modus would be raced by Andrew. Eventually sponsorship for Norman Dickson's car came from British Caledonian Airways, and Fife and Kinross Car Auctions sponsored a second car for the experienced Richard Scott. Part way through the 1976 season, however, the cars were upgraded to full Formula 2 specification and they switched to the European Formula 5000 championship. The long-term plan was to move, in 1977, into the European Formula 2 Championship or else move into the even more competitive Formula 3 championship. Towards this end, they signed up with Colin Bennett to prepare the cars for them and Bennett became become team manager during their exploits.

From the start, Richard Scott was the quicker of the two as this was a steep learning curve for Norman Dickson. At one time Scott held a good 7th place in the European Championship against F5000 cars. When they

brought the cars back to Ingliston they had a field day with Norman breaking the outright lap record three times and Richard Scott four times in a fifteen lap race! The previous record had stood for three years to Irishman Tommy Reid with a Brabham BT40.

That Ingliston meeting - held in July 1976 - saw one of the largest crowds ever, 16,500, thanks to John Romanes having secured a visit by the BBC Radio 1 Road Show with Dave Lee Travis broadcasting live from the circuit that afternoon. Though a fair percentage of the crowd were young fans of the radio show, the racing was so good that they came back and Ingliston benefited greatly from the visit. To help things along Radio 1 DJ Noel Edmonds was at the height of his fame and he raced an Opel Commodore in the saloon car event.

In the small GT event John Kirk (Davrian Mk5) and Kenny Allen (Clan Crusader) repeated their 1-2 result from the previous meeting. Kenny Allen was one of the most tenacious and successful Scottish club drivers who, up to then, had concentrated mainly on sprints and hill climbs. However he proved to be an even better circuit driver and when he changed to Clubmans cars he and John Fyda were to become the dominant drivers in that class.

The most competitive class was still the small 1000cc saloon car class. One reason for this was a Scottish love for the Hillman Imp - built just outside Glasgow. This lightweight Coventry Climax-based engine coupled to some lightening of the body panels made the Imp the car to have once the all-conquering Mini was on the shelf. At the time the leading drivers were Ian Forrest, Laurence Jacobsen, John Fyda and Hugh Chalmers.

For the 1977 season John Romanes had, as usual, lined up a host of sponsors for both events and championships so Ingliston was doing well. In the Scottish Touring Car Championship the title seemed destined for English visitor Jim Evans with his AET Skoda that was, in effect, a Chevron B19 with a light glass fibre Skoda-like bodywork. However, he wrote the car off at Croft when handsomely leading the Scottish Championship and in the end the surprising winner was Jimmy Pinkerton's Mini Cooper from Walter Robertson's 2 litre Ford Escort BDG.

The season also saw the return of Scottish Sporting Car Club as organisers of a race meeting. This time it was Knockhill and the last time had been Turnberry almost exactly twenty-five years before. Norman Dickson was out to set a new lap record with the Gleneagles Helicopters March-BMW but was foiled by the weather. The existing lap record at Knockhill had been set the previous year by Australian Larry Perkins with a Formula Atlantic Sana which later came into the hands of Andy Barton and was raced in

As Knockhill developed, a series of races for historic cars proved popular but the cars were a mixed bog. Tom Mcwhirter in his Tojeiro-Jaguar leads a motley field.

Scotland. Another man out for a lap record was relative newcomer David Leslie who, at the time, held the kart lap record for Knockhill. Now he was back with his Royale RP24 Formula Ford. Though Leslie won two races he didn't manage to break the record. At the end of the season he won the Ron Flockhart Trophy as the most promising new Scottish driver.

If anything, this race meeting finally established Knockhill as the circuit of the future in Scotland. All of a sudden drivers realised they had wide open spaces to play with and from then on entry levels were maintained at the Fife circuit where they had fluctuated in the previous two years.

At the September Ingliston meeting Mick Hill arrived with his Ford DFV-engined Volkswagen Beetle and blew everyone into the weeds. It was therefore no surprise when Douglas Niven, Jim Clark's farming cousin, bought the car to race in Scotland.

1977 also saw the introduction of a class for 2 litre sports cars as a number of them had arrived in Scotland. To make sure there were enough entrants the class was open to the new FF2000 cars. This, in a sense, made history as Scottish Motor Racing Club were given a special dispensation to run closed wheel cars with open-wheelers: something which had previously

been banned. The championship was sponsored by Insurance brokers Dalgleish Baillie which also sponsored the Chevron B26, uprated to B31 specification, raced by David Philp. This Chevron had originally been owned by Iain McLaren.

In the end Philp, by his consistency, won the championship ahead of Laurence Jacobsen's Chevron B23. The only FF 2000 of note was Stuart Lawson's Hawke DL16 but fifth equal place with Jim Baird's Chevron B23 was the highest he could manage. Stuart had better luck in the Edinburgh Flying Services Formula Ford championship where he won in his Hawke DL19 ahead of George Franchitti's older Hawke DL15.

What made the 1977 season so special was that it brought out another whole new group of young drivers who were to go on to be successful not only at Ingliston but futher afield. For example there was Cameron Binnie and Roy Low, both of whom were to become Scottish champions, and George Macmillan and Bernie Hunter who went on to bigger things with Formula Atlantic. What they were not to know was that Scotland's kart champion Tom Brown had decided to take up car racing and planned to buy a Formula Ford. Tom was to go on to become a six-time Scottish Formula Ford champion.

Amongst the rare historic racing cars to come to Scotland was "Old No.8", the first factory Jaguar racing car, a heavily modified SS100 model raced ond hill climbed before the war and then raced regularly by Campbell McLaren the Scottish Jaguar enthusiast.

At the end of the 1977 season Laurence Jacobsen, who had promoted the talent of teenager Bryce Wilson by providing him with his Chervron Atlantic/Libre car, decided to see how his protégé would fare in a proper Formula 3 race against some of the leading British drivers. Accordingly, he got in touch with Roger Heavens, who had just won the European Formula 3 Championship with Jan Lammers. He negotiated a rental deal for Bryce to drive the Lammers Ralt RT1 at the BARC Plastic Padding Race day at Thruxton, a non-championship event. Jacobsen's sponsor, Leslie Cuthbertson, willingly agreed to provide the backing. The white car was hastily decked out in orange Rosetta Fruit Juices stickers and Bryce was ready to go. In first practice there was slight mist over the circuit and Bryce came in to complain he had difficulty seeing the corners. At this Jacobsen pointed out that he still had his tinted visor on his helmet and once this was removed Bryce went a lot faster! Amongst his competitors were the Dave-Price Racing Unipart March-Dolomite 783s driven by Tiff Needell and New Zealander Brett Riley, Dutchman Huub Rothengarter in the Alan Docking Ralt RT1, Eddie Jordan with the Marlboro Team Tiga Ralt RT1 and Derek Warwick with the Warwick Trailers Ralt RT1. At this time Eddie Jordan was beginning to plan his future and was about to run his own team.

Once the weather cleared Bryce put himself on the third row on the grid, sixth fastest, which created something of a sensation as nobody at Thruxton had ever heard of this 18-year old Scot. When the flag came down Derek Warwick literally disappeared into the distance but Bryce had a flyer of a start, nipped through on the inside of Brett Reilly's Ralt-Dolomite and headed for the esses right behind Tiff Needell who was second fastest. They both went for the corner. Tiff Needell naturally felt the corner was his but Bryce was never one to back off and so the cars touched and both spun off on to the grass. Whereas Needell stayed off, Bryce got back on the track at the very back of the field and drove probably the greatest motor race of his life. He sliced his way up through the field to finish fourth having tried to pass third place man, John Bright, at least three times on the last lap. The reaction to this was quite astonishing. Eddie Jordan asked me for all the information on Bryce and hinted that he might have a place for him in his new team because, as he explained, "... he passed me like a f..... bullet". Tiff Needell, on the other hand, was less complimentary and wrote a scathing letter in the following week's Autosport criticising inexperienced drivers!

At the same Thruxton race meeting David Leslie was given the chance to race a Formula Ford 2000 for the first time in the non-championship race. He drove brilliantly to finish second and secured himself a drive for the following season.

Norman Dickson also progressed. He had considered buying a Hesketh Formula 1 car but Guy Edwards bought the car from under him and instead bought the Marc Surer Formula 2 March 772P factory car for the 1978 season. There then followed a bit of confusion as Norman did a deal with Tom Walkinshaw to race a TWR-backed BMW in touring cars and sold the March to Walkinshaw. Walkinshaw then sold the March to Aberdonian Jimmy Jack. The next thing we knew, the Dickson/Walkinshaw deal was all off and Norman rushed off and was able to buy the other factory March 772P, the Bruno Giacomelli car, to race in 1978.

Another interesting project came on the Scottish horizon: AMC Racing.

To say this was a convoluted story would be to simplify matters. Having been personally involved in the project from the start it makes an interesting case-history into the sometimes frustrating evolution of a motor racing team.

It all began with a telephone call from David MacDonald who, though born in Worthing, Sussex, had a strong Scottish ancestry on Loch Fyne-

side. His father was an engineer in the Royal Engineers and a great uncle was secretary of state for Scotland, who in his spare time built a steam yacht and a steam car.

David was brought up at St Catherines, near Strachur, won a scholarship to Fettes College and wanted to become an aeronautical engineer. Eventually he joined James Jack Advertising in Glasgow and then became marketing Manager for the Motherwell Bridge company - owned by Ronnie Miller whose name has already appeared in this story with his Lister-Jaguar. MacDonald's jack-in-the-box career continued in Holland with a marketing consultancy and in 1973 became loosely involved with Graham Hill and his Embassy Racing team. In conversation he told me he had also joined Chris Amon and John Dalton with the Amon-Dalton project to build an F5000 car. He also claimed to have designed and built a mid-engined GT road car to be built in Ireland and backed by Hertz!

By 1978 MacDonald had moved to the City of London and became "an expert on acquisitions and mergers".

When David moved to the North of England he formed Brompton Engine Developments, with former Dealer Team Vauxhall engine man Pete Hennigan. The company specialised in race and rally car preparation. Thus equipped, he approached American Motors in the United States with a two-year plan to race two American Motors AMX Spirits in the European Touring Car Championship in 1979. The new AMX Spirit compact was an interesting car and appeared to have a lot of potential. The deal he negotiated was that AMC in the United States would pay the cost of development and provide cars and bits. The long-term plan was to develop an AMX Spirit four-wheel drive rally car. At the same time he was trying to interest American Motors in acquiring AC Cars and was even talking about such a joint venture leading to the purchase of Lamborghini!

When the approached came to assist him, he confirmed he had sponsorship from Kismet-Dynaflex, that he hoped to have Derek Bell, and American Brett Lunger, as drivers, that an Irish advertising agency was going to raise additional money and he had big plans for supporting American Motors dealers in Europe. He also planned to get involved with a pharmaceutical company to use the team and drivers for studies into stress management. This would be followed up with sales incentives and sales contests for doctors. It was ambitious to the point of being ludicrous.

When Knockhill held a non-championship Formula 3 race In the late 1980s, a number of Scots drivers rented cars. One of them was Jim McGaughay who had cut his teeth in saloon car racing.

The cars were AMXs with 5-litre Trans-Am based V8s producing 495 bhp and prepared by Traco. Two engines were bought from Roger Penske and the first car was air-freighted to Britain on January 8 1979.

The first job, apart from getting Mike Taylor Developments in Northallerton to prepare the bodyshell and chassis for racing, was to get FIA papers. This was duly completed by American Motors through the FIA's branch in Washington D.C.

On June 1 1979 the AMX Spirit with a 5 litre engine, four speed Borg Warner T-10 gearbox and dry sump lubrication was duly homologated. David had hoped to have the car running at Croft by February but this was way too optimistic. Then there was the matter of the drivers. Originally MacDonald had Jeff Allam, Tony Dron and Brett Lunger involved.

Brett Lunger was an interesting choice. As an heir to one of the branches of the Du Pont family, he had begun racing with a Corvette in 1965 going on to race the Caldwell-Chevrolet in the Can Am series. He was very much the gifted and enthusiastic amateur driver and then joined the Marines in Vietnam before returning to racing in the Can-Am in 1971. Lunger went on to race in 32 grand prix races for Hesketh Racing, Surtees and March. He then formed his own team, Liggett Group B&S fabrications, using McLarens. Sponsorship was from the Chesterfield cigarette group of Liggett & Myers. His last GP was the US GP East 1978 with an Ensign.

Iain Forrest, who had dominated the 1000cc saloon classes in the 1970s, was still racing in 2000 but this time in the hotly competitive Ford Fiesta class where he was recently joined by his son Sandy. Today Iain Forrest is one of the Knockhill managers.

Six months had now passed since that US GP race so perhaps Brett was drawn into the team because of his strong links with corporate big hitters who might help in raising sponsorship. In February, Macdonald offered Lunger a drive in the ETC and Lunger confirmed his interest on February 20 1979. However, being a professional racing driver who had been down this road many times, set down certain provisos, namely, that he should have a minimum income guaranteed against prize money and a percentage of the gross revenues from any sponsorship he should bring to the team. Finally, on March 13 Lunger confirmed he would drive the AMX Spirit at Brands Hatch in the ETC round on April 29 1979 - five weeks later. He agreed to waive his normal driver retainer *"for this one event"* but there was no chance the car would be completed by that time. In fact engine builders

Traco were having trouble with piston ring failures at high power outputs but on one occasion they managed to show 495 bhp before the rings failed. The launch was put off until the Jarama round.

By early May, Brett Lunger was beginning to lose patience. In a letter to MacDonald he opened *"Credibility. That, in a single word, is the factor which will determine the nature of any business dealings under taken by you and me in the future."*

By July, things were no further forward even though the first car was almost complete. I wrote to MacDonald to say that *"...this whole affair has turned out to be one of the most amateurish pieces of organisation I have ever come across and it disappoints me greatly that I have wasted the past six mnths on what is obviously a rather futile motor racing venture."*

A short time later John Bluth of AM's International Sales Promotion department in USA requested a breakdown of costs to finish off the first car. It came to $9,000 which would pay Mike Taylor, who had outstanding bills to pay for the work he had done, and purchase the necessary equipment, tyres, testing etc. Brett Lunger, meanwhile, was in touch with American Motors to try and rescue the project.

David MacDonald's latest plan was that Lunger, along with Scots Bill Dryden and Douglas Niven, would be the drivers. David MacDonald owned the engines. But eventually MacDonald formally signed over the cars and equipment to Brett Lunger. Immediately, Lunger explored the possibility of going for the 1980 European Touring Car Championship as the 1979 season was now almost at an end. From then on the whole project steadily dissolved. The AMC-Spirits never did race in the European Touring Car Championship but that first car was completed and a few years later was unsuccessfully raced in Britain. The whole AMC project was one that has been repeated many times in motor racing: a case of enthusiasm running miles ahead of practicality and ability.

As for David MacDonald, some years later he appeared briefly in a BBC Television Programme in which the industrialist Sir John Harvey Jones acted as a company doctor visiting companies and making helpful suggestions. One of the companies he visited was the Norton motor-cycle company where David MacDonald appeared as chief executive!

Motor racing in Scotland was, on one hand, continuing successfully at Ingliston but at Knockhill there were some problems. Though Denys Dobbie had the lease to develop and run the circuit, the farmer who owned the land and started it all, Tom Kinnaird, was landed with a £6,000 rates bill. As a result he planned to close the circuit as a commercial venture and simply allow the kart drivers to race in the paddock area. There was much discussion that ultimately resulted in the circuit and land being sold, first to local motor cycle racer Alan Duffus, and then to the present owner Derek Butcher.

Meanwhile, at Ingliston one season seemed to be melding into the next. There were a few newcomers on the scene but generally the racing was once more falling into something of a rut. The highlights in 1978 were, however, Norman Dickson's dominance in the Libre events with his March that saw him win the Glasgow Herald Libre championship. He had a fright during the season, however, when Jimmy Jack loaned Eddie Cheever his March and Cheever and Dickson had a great battle between themselves. The dominance of saloon car racing, however, was the main difference from the past, and certainly the saloon car classes were filled with some great cars and great racing. Douglas Niven won the Championship with his V8 engined VW Beetle but there were a lot of people chasing him hard, Bill Dryden's Firenza, Walter Robertson's BMW F2-engined Ford Escort and the like. In the separate production saloon class, Graham Birrell took his Opel to victory and in Formula Ford, Cameron Binnie was Champion.

The 1978 season did provide one crucial turning point in Scottish motor racing. At the end of the year John Romanes, who had run Ingliston for thirteen seasons, decided to slow down. He had talks with Formula Ford racers Graham Hamilton and Gordon Dalzell which resulted in them taking a seat on the board of Scotcircuits Ltd. Shortly afterwards, they were offered, and took up, the other main shareholding in Scotcircuits Ltd held by John and Doris Romanes and Alec Calder.

Hamilton and Dalzell certainly set out to change the whole racing scene at Ingliston with some progressive ideas about championships and sponsorships. In this they were initially successful but as time went by the promotion of big events, calling for equally large outlays in sponsorship and support money, became a financial strain. For everyone in Scotland the important thing was that Ingliston was now in new hands and concern surrounding Knockhill's future appeared to be drifting away.

Robin Smith bought the first 3-litre Grand Prix car to race in Scotland during the winter of 1978: an Ensign N174 (Chassis MN02) that had been raced by Chris Amon and Dutchman Roelef Wunderlink. Prior to this, Jock Russell owned the ex-Jim Clark US GP -winning Lotus but it did not have its original BRM flat 16-cylinder engine. Also, to add spice to the Formula Libre events, Russell Paterson bought a March 743, George McMillan the Chevron Atlantic car raced by Bernie Hunter, and Bob Rollo sold his March to Stuart Robb. The biggest threat to the single seaters came with Iain McLaren's decision to sell his Chevron sports car and purchase a Chevron Formula 2 car.

Over the winter of 1978, a plan was discussed between Norman Dickson and Laurence Jacobsen for Bryce Wilson to race Dickson's March in a team that would be managed by Laurence Jacobsen but the deal fell through. Clearly Bryce had shown immense talent and thanks to Jacobsen's friendship with Austrian racing car builder and engineer Dr Joseph Erlich, a deal looked like being cut. Dr Erlich ran his Erlich team from a base in Milton Keynes on a small budget but he was a great enthusiast. The previous year he had run New Zealander Brett Riley and, before that, Jody Scheckter had raced the Erlich so he was a seasoned campaigner. It was arranged that Bryce Wilson would be his works driver for the 1979 season for the Vandervell British Formula 3 Championship in the Erlich RP4 with a Toyota Novamotor engine. Bryce was also to be entered for the Monaco and Monza Formula 3 events. For Bryce it was the chance of a lifetime. Despite the fact the Erlich was not going to win the championship, Wilson was going to be racing against the best drivers and such talent as he had would surely be recognised. As Jacobsen still had the Chevron, now fitted with an Atlantic engine, Bryce would also do some smaller British events with sponsorship from Leslie Cuthbertson's Rosetta Fruit juices.

Meanwhile, Ingliston opened with some good racing and Tom Brown, now with a Van Diemen, was beginning to show his considerable potential. Another driver to be noticed at the time was Keith Lawrence whose father Willie Lawrence had been Ninian Sanderson's great friend and buddy. Willie, thankfully, had a short racing career with a Cooper 500 way back in the 1950s as he was a pretty wild driver and wisely stopped racing before he hurt himself. Keith, on the other hand, was much quieter and more disciplined than his father but only raced for around three seasons before retiring. Jimmy Robertson from Cardenden had moved up in the saloon class with a Ford powered Skoda which he crashed heavily at Croft but repaired in time for the first Ingliston. Another super saloon was Walter Robertson's DFVW, a Volkswagen fitted with a full house 3 litre Ford Cosworth DFV with which he had a lot of success.

Norman Dickson took a fourth in the Oulton Park round of the Aurora Libre Championship driving his new March 792 and won the F2/F.Atlantic race at Brands Hatch the following day. However, Bryce Wilson's promising racing career came to a sudden end.

He ran in the first round of the F3 Championship at Snetterton and had a bad practice time, ending well down the grid. On the opening lap he was sensational in the Erlich and passed at least seven cars, but on the main straight he came level with Mike Thackwell. Their wheels touched and both went off the road at high speed. Bryce then packed his bags, left Milton Keynes and came back to his girl friend in Scotland and announced he was going to the outer Isles to become a fisherman. It was a disasterous decision after all the effort Laurence Jacobsen and others like Dr Erlich, had put into getting him into Formula 3. Many years later Bryce, a much older and wiser man, realised it was the biggest mistake he ever made. Though he came back into racing in the 1990s and was successful in various minor classes, he missed out. It was a story that sadly underlined a truism. You can have all the talent in the world but if you do not have a degree of self discipline and a respect for the work others do to help, you will not get very far in motor racing.

Tom Walkinshaw returned to Ingliston, ten years after he left to go south, bringing his Pentax sponsored Mazda RX7 with an impressive set up that indicated the lad had made good. He only demonstrated the car at this Pentax sponsored meeting but it was good to see Tom back where he started out in racing.

Iain McLaren bought a McLaren M26 grand prix car but the original engine was a dog. He replaced it with a better engine and set a new outright lap record at Croft before bringing it to Ingliston to race. Meanwhile, we were still waiting to see the first Formula 1 Grand Prix car race at Ingliston. Robin Smith had brought the Ensign to an early meeting but was a non-starter and he and Richard Jones traded it for a Surtees.

Robin, with Tony Charnell, had success with their Chevron B36 at Le Mans winning the Gp6 class. They won the Motor Trophy for the highest placed British finisher. The last time the Motor Trophy was won by a Scottish team was when Jim Clark and Roy Salvadori in the Border Reivers' Aston Martin DBR1 finished third. This led to a plan to build a very special Chevron with a Cosworth DFV engine to compete at Le Mans in 1980. Scots aerodynamicist Dan Wright, who had designed special wings for Brian Nelson's Crossle and a unique low rear wing for Doug Niven's Ford Escort, was interested in designing the aerodynamics on the car. A boatbuilding company in Dumfries, which specialised in glass fibre construction, was going to build the body but nothing came of it as the team did not raise the £25,000 sponsorship necessary for the effort.

Graham Hamilton and Gordon Dalzell threw themselves into promoting Ingliston and persuaded Barrett Homes to sponsor a meeting with a feature Formula Atlantic race so that Barretts could run their own sponsored Argo driven by Rick Gorne. Amongst the competitors was Scot Jim Crawford who was racing at Ingliston for the first time. Jim was to go on to race grand prix for Lotus and then in America in Indy cars including the Indianapolis 500. At this meeting Robin Smith raced the Surtees TS19 but took things easy, leaving Norman Dickson to win the Libre event with the March 792.

In the feature race for the Barratts trophy, Jim Crawford was literally uncatchable in the Chevron B42. Local Scot Andrew Jeffrey was slow out of the box with his B49 and it was Derek Daly in the ex ICI Chevron who was up there. As for Barratt's own driver, Rick Gorne, he was lying third when he lost it at the top of the esses, the Argo ending up hitting a solid oak tree.

Ironically the oak tree is the symbol of Barratt Homes and company owner Laurie Barratt, a spectator at the meeting, was not amused.

There was another Scottish highlight at the August race meeting when Jackie Stewart was persuaded to come to Scotland and demonstrate his Tyrrell 003. As the car had been in the Glasgow Transport Museum for some time Jackie asked Robin Smith to collect it and do the necessary work to prepare it. Everything went fine until it came to the tyres. As the car had last raced around eight years before, the tyres were like rocks but none of the suppliers could come up with ones of the right size. At this, Jackie, a consultant to Goodyear at the time, put on pressure and lo and behold a set of fresh tyres arrived. They proved to be sports car tyres and slightly too large but Jackie put on a great show and after doing a number of laps round Ingliston, he proceeded to do doughnuts all the way round the track to great applause. He explained afterwards he wanted to make sure he didn't have to demonstrate the car again and the best way was to destroy the tyres! Jackie's sons Mark and Paul were there to watch, they being the actual owners of the car. When Jackie was presented with the car at his retirement dinner in the Savoy Hotel in London he gave it to Mark and Paul as a gift and they are still the owners of the car to this day.

The last time Jackie Stewart demonstrated a racing car in Scotland was at Ingliston when he brought his Tyrrell 003 out of retirement in Glasgow Transport Museum. The car had to be fitted with enormous Goodyear sports car tyres as the proper Goodyears could not be found.

Also present when Jackie Stewart demonstrated the Tyrrell, were the car's owners, Mark and Paul Stewart. They had been given the car by Jackie shortly after he retired from grand prix racing.

As mentioned earlier, throughout the 1970s and 1980s one of the most competitive classes in Scottish motor racing was for 1,000cc saloons with Hillman Imps in various forms generally dominating the class. It was a pity that many of the drivers who excelled in this class rarely had the chance to develop further in other categories. The majority of them were club drivers through and through and the chance of securing sufficient sponsorship to move into other categories just did not exist. For example, in earlier days Laurence Jacobsen, John Fyda and Iain Forrest started out racing Imps with Forrest literally dominating the class for many years. Then you had other drivers like Ricky Gauld and Jimmy Jack from Aberdeen, Eric Paterson, Jim McGaughay and even Norman Dickson who were all weaned on Imps in the 1,000cc class.

The 1980s were to usher what could be termed another new era in Scottish motor racing. For a start, Ingliston appeared to be revitalised and Knockhill was in line to come back strongly on the scene. What is more, the next wave of Scottish racing drivers to go on to bigger things was about to break, mainly thanks to the tremendous enthusiasm of Hugh McCaig who was to help youngsters like Allan McNish and David Coulthard on to the first step in the ladder.

The eighties opened with a few changes in Scottish motor racing. In Edinburgh, the British Leyland dealership, Hope Scott, had been running Andrew Jeffrey in a Formula Atlantic Chevron. Kyle Laidlaw, who ran Hope Scott, dropped Andrew in favour of a Scot who now lived in Carlisle, David Leslie. David had been successful in Formula Ford and Ford 2000 and for the 1980 season Hope Scott bought a new Ralt for Leslie to use in the Hitachi Formula Atlantic championship. It was the first big break for David, who had actually been pushing for three years to get into Formula 3, without success. Around the same time David Duffield, another promising Scot, was also given a chance to move up the ladder when an old karting friend of his called Hugh McCaig bought a Ralt RT1 for David to race under McCaig's Caledon Coal Company banner. Prior to this Hugh had helped David with his Formula Ford racing through another of his companies, Hubert Mitchell Ltd.

George Franchitti, who had been racing in Formula Ford, moved into the Formula Libre ranks with the ex-Teddy Yip/ Rupert Keegan March 792 that had been rebuilt by Robin Smith. Norman Dickson had also moved up and had bought one of the ex-works Lotus 78' Grand Prix cars for the Aurora championship and after a second place at Oulton Park he brought it to Ingliston. Before the season was out, however, Norman had retired from motor racing to concentrate of the family motor trade businesses.

Another boost for motor racing in Scotland was the announcement by Tom Brown of a racing school at Knockhill. Tom used his Van Diemen RF78 and a Ford RS2000 in the initial stages and at the same time bought a new Van Diemen RF80 to race during the 1980 season. Tom was former 250cc Superkart champion and also had two stock-block Yamaha engined superkarts in his school stable.

At the opening meeting of the season, David Leslie won the Formula Libre race in the Hope Scott Ralt RT4 with regular competitor, Andy Barton, in second place. Both of them lowered the circuit lap record in this race. David Duffield took a sensible fifth place with the Caledon Coal Ralt. The 1,000cc saloon class also saw some fresh faces in Harvey Gillanders and Bob Leckie with their Imps and both of them were to go on to race single seaters.

In May 1980 Laurence Jacobsen and Robin Smith bought the assets of Chevron cars - see Scottish Racing Cars section - and set to work trucking mountains of spares from Bolton to Scotland to commence work on a Sports 2000.

John Milne lines up for a handicap race at Charterhall.
Race winner Jim Clark is in the white porsche.

Ecurie Ecosse chief mechanic Wilkie Wilkinson gives one of the teams D-type Jaguars a check over before being put in the transporter for Spa.

Clubs all over Scotland were on the lookout for new venues and Douglas Mickel of MG Car Club managed to get permission to use an old army camp at Stobbs, near Hawick, for a sprint meeting. Lined up waiting to go out on to the track are Bill Turnbull (Lotus 6) Jim McCaig - no relation to Hugh - with his FMC Special, Jim Clark's Porsche and Ninian Paterson's MGA. Patersons son, Russell, raced a number of cars at Ingliston twenty years later. On the right is MG club Chairman Ernie Herrald.

Charterhall 1957: Norman Barclay with his Formula II Cooper lines up alongside newcomer Jim Clark with the Border Reivers D type Jaguar.

A real mixed bag of cars lined up for the start of this race at Charterhall around 1956 with Ted Evans in his Austin Healey 100S on pole position. Talking to him in the yellow trousers is Julian Sutton whose black Austin Healey 100M is in the middle of the second row. Also on the front row is Jimmy Blumer (Austin Healey 100S), David Bertram (Triumph TR2) and Ronnie Morrison (Triumph TR2). In the foreground with the ex-Ecurie Ecosse Jaguar C type is Tom Candlish. The car nose on the left is the Cooper-Jaguar of Peter Bolton.

Tommy Dickson had many successes with the Ecurie Ecosse Cooper Monaco and when he retired from racing the car was taken over by newcomer Jackie Stewart.

A rare colour photo of day to day work at Merchiston Mews. The Ecurie Ecosse Tojeiro-Buick is being prepared in one of the lock ups that made up the Ecurie Ecosse facility.

One of Jim Clark's school friends, Andy Walker, bought an ageing Lotus Eleven and had no luck at Crimond in his first race, the car retiring.

Jim Clark's first visit to Crimond with the Reivers D type Jaguar saw him on pole position alongside his great rival Jimmy Mackay (Lotus Eleven). Car 18 on the second row is the rare Tojeiro-Bristol raced by Gordon Porteous.

At the 1960 Boxing Day Brands Hatch meeting Jim Clark lost a wheel on the way up to Druids Bend but was able to park the Border Reivers Lotus Elite on the grass.

In his first season of grand prix racing in 1965 Jackie Stewart, right, strides along beside the BRM in which he was to finish in fifth place at the British Grand Prix.

Care for a cup of tea? Jim Clark takes time out from British GP practice in 1964 to offer the writer a cup of tea. Peter Arundel is on the left of the picture and Colin Chapman has his back to the camera. Chief mechanic Jim Endruweit, right foreground, works on the car.

Stuart Lawson (March), foreground, moved up from Formula Ford into Libre where he had a number of battles with David Duffield in the Caledon Coal sponsored Ralt.

It was perhaps appropriate that for his last season of motor racing in Scotland Iain McLaren should choose to buy a McLaren M23 from his friend Ron Dennis from whom he had earlier bought a Rondel Formula 2 car.

One of two Americans racing at the first Knockhill F3 race in 1975 was Danny Sullivan with his Modus. Sullivan went on to win the Indianapolis 500 and raced in Formula 1 with Tyrrell.

The other American at the 1975 Formula 3 race at Knockhill also had a career at Indianapolis and in grand prix racing. That year, however, at only 17, Eddie Cheever was merely starting out with the works Modus.

The notorious Duffus Dip has claimed many victims. At the Formula 3 race in the 1980's it is about to claim the fast-starting Damon Hill who managed to squeeze into the corner first ahead of team mate Martin Donnelly only to brake heavily and fly off into the earth banking.

Irishman Martin Donnelly won the race from Gary Dunn whose father, John Dunn, ran Swindon Racing Engines. In the background is Knock Hill after which the circuit was named.

When Ecurie Ecosse returned to International racing in 1984 they ran their Ecosse-Ford at Monza and Le Mans. Here, at Brands Hatch, Ray Mallock led the race until he had brake failure and the car was destroyed.

After Mick Hill brought his remarkable VW Beetle-Chevrolet to race at Ingliston, Douglas Niven, Jim Clark's cousin, bought the car and raced it successfully for a few seasons. The car is seen entering the notorious esses at Ingliston with Niven at the wheel.

The Clubmans class was a favourite in Scotland as it provided fast racing with affordable cars. One of the kings of clubmans was John Fyda seen here with his immaculate Vision.

Andy Barton moved from saloon cars into libre cars and this AC ME3000GT with which he won a number of races. At this time modified GT cars were all the rage.

Innes Ireland and friend appear bemused at the American piper - nicknamed Popeye - who serenaded him before the 1984 Daytona 24 Hour Race where he was racing this Porsche 924 Carrera. It was his last major International race.

Le Mans 1987, Ray Mallock leaves the pits for the last time during the race in one of the two Ecosse-Fords entered for the race that year. Hugh McCaig is hidden amongst the people on the right.

Derek Butcher, in addition to owning and running Knockhill still occasionally found time to race. His Cosworth-RS was a familiar sight on his home track.

Despite the fact that Mika Hakkinen took pole position for the first ever Formula Vauxhall Lotus race - at Thruxton - it was Allan McNish in the other red and white Marlboro car, starting from the second row, who had the honour of winning the first race in the series.

At the end of the 1994 grand prix season the entire Williams team was lined up for a photograph with drivers Damon Hill and David Coulthard at the front. (Photo Williams.)

Jackie Stewart explains his ambitious plans for the New Ingliston circuit when the project was launched. Unfortunately local government and special interest groups saw to it that planning permission was refused so ending Scotland's last major chance to build a modern circuit for the twenty first century.

Already there are number of young Scots climbing the motor sport ladder. One of the most successful is Ryan Sharp who, at the time of writing, is leading the Renault V6 Championship. Perhaps he is a star of the future.

Dario Franchitti's first race in Formula Vauxhall Junior was at Thruxton.

Johnny Dumfries had a hectic season with John Player Lotus in Formula 1 where he was always in the shadow of team-mate Ayrton Senna. Johnny scrutinizes his lap time at Silverstone in the British Grand Prix.

John Cleland was a permanent fixture in the Vauxhall team and won the BTCC for them.

When driving for Paul Stewart Racing Dario Franchitti ran well in the Macau Grand Prix in 1994.

Ecurie Ecosse, in the shape of Hugh McCaig had an involvement with Proteus Racing when two Aston Martin AMR's were run with backing from Aston Martin. At Donington Park both cars ran well up the field in the early stages.

Allan McNish has tested for many grand prix teams including Jordan where he did some of the initial testing of the Peugeot grand prix engine.

David Coulthard had a successful run with McLaren-Mercedes which included second place in the World Drivers Championship.

In recent years Peter Dumbreck has been one of the most successful British drivers in the DTM, German Touring Car Championship. In 2004 he was lead driver for the Opel team, right, where he took the battle to the mighty Mercedes squad.

(Photo Courtesy Opel Motorsport)

At the time, there were a mere handful of Sports 2000s in Scotland, and in order to have a race they were given a class in the Clubmans race. Sports 2000, like FF 2000, never really developed in Scotland or attracted visitors from England and they were both to fluctuate throughout the 1980s only to virtually disappear by the end of the decade.

Once more the nature of motor racing in Scotland made it difficult for any of the new formulae - except the universal Formula Ford - from developing to any great degree. Since then we have seen other examples of this for the plain and simple reason that there is not a large enough competitor base to embrace a new formula with sufficient cars to make up a race. It is a problem that has dogged Scottish motor racing almost since the beginning and with tighter economic times ahead it is a problem unlikely to change.

There was a frisson of excitement when it was announced, in May 1980, that motor cycle racer Barry Sheene would be taking part in the BMW Counties Championship race at Ingliston. A variety of well-known National racing drivers took part in the series and Ingliston was included, to give support to the Scottish dealers. What made this special was that Barry Sheene was at the height of his fame as a motor-cycle racer and this would be his first-ever car race. In addition, he was still recovering from having the tip of one of his fingers removed after a motor-cycle racing accident!

We were treated to an example of Barry Sheene's superb racecraft on this appearance at Ingliston. As anyone who has raced at Ingliston will know, it was a very tight circuit where you had to judge all the corners perfectly. Most of the drivers in the BMW Counties Championship event were, like Sheene, newcomers to the circuit and were almost baying to get out on to the track for official practice as pole position would be crucial. When the barrier went up they tore out in a mass, save for Barry Sheene who held back and let the last car get half way round the circuit before he set out, giving himself a perfectly clear track. It was a shrewd move as Sheene set up fastest time and was on pole position. In the race he got a lightning start and won outright.

As he was not registered for the Championship he scored no points. It was just as well, for in the race there was an incident and Sheene was called up before the stewards. Much to everyone's embarrassment, when asked for his licence, he produced his International motor-cycle racing licence as he didn't have a valid RAC car racing licence! The matter was quietly forgotten by all concerned.

Graham Hamilton and Gordon Dalzell managed to secure a round of the Hitachi Formula Atlantic Championship for Ingliston and though there was a good entry, many of the top drivers stayed in England. Out in the Erlich was Ian Flux and he threw the car round Ingliston on this, his first visit, to be second fastest to David Leslie's Ralt RT4. It was David Leslie who won the race and this season was to help him go on to bigger things in the future.

Later that season, Walter Robertson took the DFVW to Donington for the support race to the Formula 2 event. Much to his surprise, the German grand prix driver Manfred Winkelhock took a great interest in this funny Volkswagen with the Cosworth DFV. Walter, being Walter, offered Manfred a drive in the car and he took it round Donington for a lap and came in to complain that he couldn't see the tops of the wings of the car. Walter borrowed a cushion from Norman Dickson and, thus padded, Winkelhock set off once more. As Walter remarked "within about six laps he was down to 12.9's and I had been doing 14's." Walter then walked out to the circuit to watch how Winkelhock was doing it and was amazed that Manfred was selecting fifth gear at the 200 metre marker only to brake heavily at

the 100 metre marker! Eventually Winkelhok got down to 12.1. At the next Donington meeting, Walter decided to steel himself and do what Winkelhock was doing and managed to get down to his personal best of 12.0. Winkelhock was to go on to race in Formula 1 with the ATS team and was killed in a Porsche at Mosport in Canada in 1985.

By now, Ingliston was becoming more popular with organisers of Championships in the south as the prices for running races at the major circuits were beginning to rise steeply. At the end of the 1980 season three Scots racing stalwarts, Mike Shakespeare, Sandy Watson and Alastair Mackintosh all put up sponsorship money from their companies to sponsor a major race for Clubmans Register cars and the entry list saw all the leading Clubmans drivers in Britain taking part. As the new Scottish-based Chevron company had just finished their first B52 Sports 2000 car, it made its debut in the same Clubmans race as there was no other suitable class for it. In the race, Ayrshireman Andy Smith was the winner with his Mallock passing Paul Gibson's works Mallock M22 just before the end. The season also closed with Tom Brown as Formula Ford Champion and David Leslie in the Hope-Scott Ralt as Formula Libre Champion. However, in this last round David Duffield, in Hugh McCaig's Caledon Coal sponsored Ralt, ran Leslie close and was clearly going to be worth watching in 1981. To help him on his way, McCaig bought the Hope Scott Ralt RT4 for Duffield and sold the RT1.

The 1980s were also marked by a slowing down of the economy. Suddenly everyone was struggling to find cash to race. This, in turn, had its effect on racing at Ingliston and Knockhill.

At Ingliston, Hamilton and Dalzell continued to spend money attracting a variety of rounds in Championships and even brought singer David Essex to the circuit to add some pizzazz. The 1981 season provided some pretty good racing with David Duffield just losing the Formula Libre Championship by one point to Andy Barton. In the saloon car class Jim McGaughay's Renault Turbo super saloon provided Walter Robertson's V8 engined Skoda with a lot of opposition.

In Formula Ford, the race for the championship was now between Tom Brown and Roy Low and that year another newcomer joined the ranks, Stewart Roden, later to become one of the leading Formula Ford drivers in Scotland. Later still he raced in the Ferrari Challenge. Roden became an entrant himself in 2003 with a race-prepared Ferrari 360 Modena.

The 1981 season ended tragically with an accident to kart driver Granville Grubb. It was in a kart demonstration at Ingliston. His kart slid wide at Caravan Corner and was tipped into the barrier. Granville subsequently died in hospital. Granville was a former Scottish kart champion and had come on the demonstration run at the suggestion of his friends Sandy Taylor and Sandy Dalgarno who also demonstrated their karts. This was the only fatal accident ever recorded in the thirty year history of Ingliston race circuit and ironic that it should happen in a demonstration rather than in a race. It was also ironic that Ingliston initially came into being as a kart track.

In January 1982 Scottish motor racing was hit with another bombshell. James Davidson, Chief Executive of the Royal Highland and Agricultural Society which owned Ingliston, attended a meeting of the RHAS in Aberdeen and was quoted in the Aberdeen Press & Journal as saying that motor racing at Ingliston might be threatened because alleged loans by Scotcircuits Ltd, had not been paid. Scotcircuits Ltd held the concession to promote motor racing at Ingliston and were responsible for all the sponsorship, prize money, insurance and the like. For this Scotcircuits paid a set fee each year, plus a percentage of the gate money to the Highland Society.

Graham Hamilton, Chairman of Scotcircuits, gave assurances that everything was in order and the RHAS were still keen to lease the circuit for motor racing as it added income to their coffers when their Showground was not utilised for the Royal Highland Agricultural Show.

The whole affair was cleared up and Hugh McCaig gave financial support to Scotcircuits Ltd during the 1982 motor racing season. Recalling this time Hugh, with a twinkle in his eye, remarked *"...I wanted David Duffield in our Caledon Coal Ralt to win the Formula Libre Championship and he couldn't have done it if there was no racing at the circuit."*

This incident, however, was to have long term effects, not only on Scottish Motor Racing Club, which became more concerned with the running of the races, but with Scotcircuits Ltd., who were having difficulty raising sponsorship for the various Championships and race meetings.

The 1982 motor racing season at Ingliston was poor and attendances dropped. Many of the races saw the same old faces and the same old results. During the season there had been one or two interesting developments. A young driver from Orkney, Willie Hourie, began to make a name for himself driving a Crossle 32F: his trips to Ingliston being even longer than those taken by Jimmy Mackay from Scrabster thirty years before.

John Clark took time off from developing his BMW dealership in Aberdeen to race a Chevron B52 Sports 2000 but had a patchy season. He was later to take up historic racing in the mid-1990s and today is one of the leading drivers in the field.

The season also saw the rise of Ron Cumming who had been racing a Fiat with a Ford engine but switched to a much modified Lotus Esprit and was now challenging Jim McGaughay's Renault Turbo Ford which had been dominating the special saloon class all season. George Coghill, also from the north, was beginning to make his mark with the Norfrost Esprit. In Formula Ford, Geordie Taylor, who always seemed to have outdated equipment and raced on a shoestring, was again showing promise and despite the lack of the latest equipment he was to win many races and the Formula Ford Championship. He was still racing and winning in Formula Ford in 2003!

At the the end of the season there was again speculation about the future of Ingliston as Scotcircuits had clearly had another bad year. Hugh McCaig was helping to subsidise the racing even more and the point arrived when something drastic would have to happen.

In November 1982 Hugh McCaig took over Scotcircuits Ltd, and recruited Graham Gauld and Walter Robertson to join him in the venture. Eventually, a new company was formed, Ingliston Race Circuit Ltd. McCaig's enthusiasm, when sparked, can be infectious and he set about the task with great gusto. Both Ingliston and Knockhill were duly visited by the RAC to check on safety and the modifications at Ingliston were undertaken by McCaig with more substantial and higher barriers and additional Armco elsewhere. At the same time, dialogue was started with Scottish Sporting Car Club to bring together Ingliston and Knockhill by including four meetings at Knockhill into the Ingliston Championships so making them truly Scottish Championships.

Chapter 10
The Changing Decade: Ingliston and Knockhill

The new team at Ingliston was heartened by an opening meeting with a crowd of over 5,000 for the Marlboro Challenge event. In the Formula Libre race the favourite, David Duffield in a Ralt, was pushed down to third in the early stages by George MacMillan who in former years had raced in Formula Ford. MacMillan was a press on driver who was never at home in Formula Ford and was to have a successful few seasons with the Ralt before retiring to continue with his garage business in North Berwick. Duffield, however, got the bit between his teeth to take the lead. Then, when pulling away, not only broke the outright circuit record but became the first driver to lap Ingliston at an average speed of over 85 mph; a considerable feat as anyone who has visited the circuit will tell you. Sadly for him, there had existed an offer of £10,000 to the first person to average over 85 mph round Ingliston but the offer had been withdrawn some years before.

An innovation at this meeting was a class for purely stock road saloons. The rules were simple, the car had to be taxed and insured, run on normal road tyres and be driven to the circuit. To give the race a boost Hugh McCaig entered his road Audi Quattro and doyen of the special saloon class, Douglas Niven, entered his farm Ford Capri. There were only six competitors and they included one of the most impecunious of Scottish drivers, Eddie Beerman, who ran his Ford Cortina without a windscreen - it was not laminated! What with McCaig using the Quattro's four wheel drive to run along the grass and pass Niven on the inside, and Ayrshire garage man Jimmy Fleming running his ex-Stig Blomquist rally Toyota on knobbly rally tyres, the spectacle was enough to keep the frozen spectators in their places to the end. It was to herald a series of road saloon car events in Scotland but as time wore on the regulations were changed to allow a little more leeway.

Another Scot to start a racing season in England was advertising man Vic Covey who took part in the National Metro Challenge. His car was prepared by Roger Dowson racing and support from Canon Systems Division. Vic had a successful season and even ran at Nurburgring with success. Campbell McLaren also took part in the series with his Metro but business kept him

It is hard to imagine how Scotland would have survived without Formula Ford and, as this recent photograph shows, it is still a healthy class for young Scots getting started in racing.

The next Scot to receive help from David Leslie senior was David Coulthard. Coulthard with his Reynard gets a helping hand from Leslie on the start line at Ingliston.

from competing in all the rounds. Another driver competing in National championship rounds was Anthony Reid who drove the Argo Ford 2000 run by another Scot, John Kirkpatrick.

The pre-season discussions regarding true Scottish championships paid off for at the first meeting of the joint venture, at Knockhill, the entry list was bulging. From then until the closing down of Ingliston in the 1990s all Scottish racing championships were run with rounds at both Ingliston and Knockhill. Also, later, Scottish Sporting Car Club pulled out of the organisation leaving it to the highly efficient Scottish Motor Racing Club.

Whilst all this was going on Hugh McCaig, Walter Robertson and Graham Gauld were embroiled in another idea, the re-formation of Ecurie Ecosse, Scotland's most successful motor racing team. Ecosse had last raced in 1971 and the Ecurie Ecosse Association, which had run the team in its last two seasons, had all but been disbanded. The Earl of Elgin, President of the Ecurie Ecosse Association and Friends of Scotland, held title to the team. When Elgin heard of the long term plans Hugh McCaig had in mind he had no hesitation in passing the Ecurie Ecosse title to the new group. Initially,

the plans were modest. As John Clark had bought a Royale Sports 2000 he had a virtually brand new Chevron B52/54 available and this was purchased and painted in Ecurie Ecosse colours. A young Formula Ford driver called Willie Hourie was nominated as the driver of the Chevron and the team was officially launched at the July Ingliston race meeting. A number of former Ecurie Ecosse drivers came along to see the fun, including Jimmy Stewart and Desmond Titterington.

The Sports 2000 was not Hugh McCaig's ultimate aim. He wanted to see Ecurie Ecosse back at Le Mans and towards that end he started thinking about the 1984 event. At that time, the World Sports Car Championship was due to be changed to have two classes from 1984, Group C1 for the big turbocharged Porsches and Group C2 for cars of smaller capacity, weight etc. This was the class McCaig had in mind. At the time there was nothing that could be bought off the shelf and so McCaig recruited Ray Mallock. Between them they found what appeared to be the ideal car, a De Cadenet sports car that had run in the 1979 Le Mans driven by Alain de Cadenet and Francois Migault. The car had been sold to Dorset Racing and ran in the 1981 Le Mans race driven by Martin Birrane, Viv Candy and Nick Faure. The car, which was an open prototype, was up for sale complete with its Ford Cosworth DFV engine and this was bought to be converted into a Group C2 car. The work was done by Ray Mallock Racing which had been involved with the development of the Aston Martin Nimrods. As a result, Ray had access to the Nimrod drawings so it was no surprise when the rebodied de Cadenet appeared looking like a scaled-down Nimrod. It was renamed an Ecosse-Ford and prepared for Le Mans. Much of the car was rebuilt and lightened using a honeycomb construction and the tub was narrowed by seven inches resulting in a very compact car.

Scottish built racing cars are few and far between and Bishopbriggs fireman Graham Millar arrived at Knockhill with his Rotor JT1, a self-built space-frame Formula Ford. Imagine Graham's surprise when he received a telephone call from none other than Ron Tauranac of Brabham complimenting him on the design and finish of the car. (See the Appendix on Scottish Racing Cars at the end of the book.)

By the end of the 1983 motor racing season, a new face appeared in a racing car, Derek Butcher. Derek had been a successful motor-cycle racer for over 9 years and originally worked in the security alarm business. He bought a Lotus Caterham Seven and in his first race at Ingliston not only led the whole way but set a new class lap record and was clearly promising. Derek was later to play an even greater part in Scottish motor racing when he took over Knockhill and has run the circuit to this day. Another visitor to Ingliston that year was a young Argentinean racing car designer called Sergio Rinland. He had designed the PRS Formula Ford car and was invited to Scotland by Lance Gauld to help him prepare his PRS. Rinland was the enthusiast's enthusiast and it was no surprise when he went on to design grand prix cars from the Williams to the successful 2002 Sauber.

Throughout the year, Derek Butcher had been in negotiation with farmer Tom Kinnaird about the purchase of the whole of Knockhill including the land. Up to that time the circuit had been leased to Denys Dobbie and Alan Duffus. Derek realised that in order to expand the circuit he needed the freedom and flexibility to develop it as he wished. In order to do this he sold his security alarm business to Honeywell PLC. Derek had founded his business from scratch with just £400 and by the time he sold out he had over 2000 clients, 23 engineers and admin staff. It is interesting that by 2003 he had developed Knockhill to such an extent that it now has 37 full time staff and many more part time staff. Butcher's purchase of the entire facility has clearly paid off as he has steadily developed driving schools and corporate days so that today the motor racing activities represent less than half of the turnover.

In April 1984 the "new" Ecosse-Ford Group C2 car was taken to Silverstone for a brief check-over before it was brought to Ingliston to be demonstrated for the first time before a home crowd. At the time, the three nominated drivers for the car in the world championship events were Ray Mallock, David Duffield and Walter Robertson but this line up was to change before the season was out. Firstly, Walter Robertson discovered that his licence did not allow him to race at Silverstone and despite a lot of rushing back and forwards to the RAC Walter was sidelined and there was no way he could qualify for a full International sports car licence in the time. As a result, he never actually raced the car.

At the April meeting Hugh McCaig revealed his latest car for the production road car class, a Vauxhall Chevette and persuaded six-time British Rally Champion Jimmy McRae to race the car. It all happened on a flight from Edinburgh to London when McCaig was introduced to McRae and they got on like a house on fire. Needless to say McCaig offered Jimmy the Chevette to make his racing debut and Jimmy accepted. Nobody told Jimmy about race technique and he amazed the spectators with his sideways power slides through the kink on the main straight.

Throughout this entire 1980s period special saloons and clubmans cars continued to be popular in Scotland and a number of interesting cars took part. Apart from the American V8-engined cars like Douglas Niven's Boss Escort both Jim McGaughay and Ron Cumming came up with their own specials, McGaughay clothing his Toleman Formula Atlantic car with a Lancia Delta Turbo body. Ron Cumming had a highly modified Lotus Esprit and Eric Munnoch appeared with a Sunbeam Stiletto powered by a Rover V8 engine. Ian Forrest still continued to dominate the 1,000cc class with his Drambuie-sponsored Hillman Imp.

Ecurie Ecosse's first race on the Continent for thirteen years took place at Monza. Ray Mallock and David Duffield were joined by the experienced Mike Wilds. It was the first round of the World Sports Car Championship and the Ecosse car finished a creditable eighth overall and second in the Group C2 class to a Lola-Mazda. The team protested that on one of the pit stops the Lola had not had its engine switched off, but the protest was thrown out. At scrutineering there had been a question about the pedal box on the car and whether it conformed to the rules and this was to create all sorts of problems as the season progressed.

Behind the scenes Ingliston Race Circuit Ltd, had come to an arrangement with Scottish Motor Racing Club whereby the club would receive a percentage of the gate receipts and this was to continue so that today SMRC has a substantial bank balance that is now being used to promote and create new events and championships.

After retiring with a seized gearbox at the Silverstone 1000kms event, the Ecosse Team went to Le Mans full of high hopes. However their problems began at scrutineering when the dispute about the pedal box came up again and the scrutineers refused to pass the car. The original Ecurie Ecosse team had a similar scrutineering problem at Le Mans many years before with their Cooper Monaco so it was par for the course. Where the fault lay was that the cubic area in the pedal box was legal but the dimensions did not fully conform. It became stalemate in the scrutineering bay until someone came up with the FIA ruling about drivers being able to get out of the car within five seconds. It was agreed that if Mike Wilds, fully kitted up and with belts on, could get out of the car within the allotted time the car would be allowed to start. This pantomime in the main park at Le Mans created quite an audience and when Mike managed it, the car was given its all important scrutineering ticket. However, the team was told that unless the pedal box was changed, the car would not be allowed to run in any of the other rounds of the World Championship.

In practice for Le Mans, Mike Wilds lapped the circuit 11 seconds below the existing class lap record and hopes were high. Unfortunately, a small washer in the fuel pump broke up and the car retired.

The team realised it would be impossible to modify the pedal box on the Ecosse and so it was withdrawn from the Championship. The car made one more appearance at the support race to the British Grand Prix at Brands Hatch where Ray Mallock and David Leslie were to drive it. Mallock drove brilliantly to take the lead but on the way up to Druids Bend the rear brakes failed and Mallock ploughed into the safety bank at high speed. The car was totally destroyed. Eventually what was left of the bent tub was kept by Hugh McCaig and it was agreed a completely new car, but with the same shape, should be designed and built for the 1985 season.

The first big Historic Race took place in Scotland at Ingliston in 1984 with a huge field of cars that had to be whittled down as Ingliston could only start 18 cars in any race. The winner was veteran grand prix driver Bruce Halford with the Lotus 16 he had originally raced over twenty years before. John Harper was second with the recreation of the single seater Lister-Jaguar Ecurie Ecosse built for the Race of Two Worlds back in 1958.

Ingliston was having a good season with good crowds and motor racing was beginning to look up again.

As the year ended, Tom Brown was again winner of the Formula Ford Championship of Scotland and to this day he remains the winner of the most Formula Ford titles. Had he raced more often down south and abandoned the Scottish series he might have progressed in other fields as he had great talent. Unfortunately that talent was never fully realised. It was passed on to his son, Ian Brown, who, like his father, has had considerable success but has always been dogged by lack of substantial sponsorship.

This matter of sponsorship has been a perennial problem for the majority of Scottish racing drivers. Whereas many young drivers south of the Border seemed to have an easier time raising commercial sponsorship Scotland has a different business discipline and is much more hidebound and backward in promotional terms. It would be hard to name any Scottish company that has seriously invested in motor racing and young Scottish talent, as part of its marketing mix. The most obvious area of sponsorship was the Scotch Whisky companies but the Scotch Whisky Association, early on, encouraged their members not to put sponsorship into motorised sport for fear of a drink and driving backlash. Indeed one of the few people to have whisky sponsorship - and that in a very minor way - was Jackie Stewart who received some sponsorship from Stanley P Morrison Ltd, the whisky brokers and owners of Bowmore distillery on the Isle of Islay. Ian Forrest also received considerable backing for a number of years from Drambuie the Scots whisky liqueur and David Duffield from Old Court Scotch whisky but we are speaking about peanuts. Most other sports in Scotland had an easier time raising sponsorship money than motor racing.

Had Scottish business embraced motor racing more enthusiastically, and marketed it properly, we might well have seen some of the other successful Scots going further up the tree. As it was they were to remain in Club, or if they were lucky, National racing.

At the end of 1984 the main prizes for the most promising Scottish drivers went to Hugh Chalmers for his exploits in saloon car racing and Formula Ford drivers Stewart Roden and Harvey Gillanders. Chalmers, a practicing Doctor, was restricted in his racing programme but was to destined go on to race with Laurence Jacobsen in one of the DFV engined Ecosse cars and later still in International historic Formula Junior races with a Lotus. Stewart Roden continued to race in Scotland but eventually, in the late 1990s, was able to compete in the Ferrari Challenge events and planned to run his own Ferrari 360 Modena GT at Le Mans in 2004. Harvey Gillanders moved to England and raced a number of times but never truly progressed.

By early 1985 the new Ecosse Group C2 car was taking shape and just to be sure it conformed to FIA's rules, Frenchman Alain Bertaut, a member of the commission, was invited to check it out and gave it the ok. Enough parts were built for three cars though Ecosse planned to build only two of them. An American driver approached the team about buying the third car and using a Buick V8 motor but nothing came of the plan. The team had a middling 1985 season with sponsorship from the Bovis group. They had bad luck at Le Mans when leading the Group C2 class by miles, David Leslie having broken the class lap record.

The team, however, maintained faith with David Murray's traditions of racing in Scotland and ran David Leslie in the car at Ingliston where, despite torrential rain, he controlled the race from the front.

The first real downturn for Ingliston came shortly after the Bradford football disaster where a grandstand burned down causing considerable loss of life. Every local authority in the land was urged to inspect all grandstands and when the Edinburgh District Council officials came to Ingliston they ordered changes to be made to the main stand and the removal of the secondary stand at the back of the circuit. Sadly, some of the spectators blamed Ingliston Race Circuits Ltd for the closing of the two ends of the main stand rather than the local authority. After discussions with the Royal

Unofficial outright lap record holder at Knockhill - the lap was established in a demonstration and not a race - was the ebullient Ron Cumming who raced this Arrows grand prix car all over Britain. Indeed his unofficial record was only broken in 2002 when a young Japanese called Takuma Sato set up the current official lap record during a round in the British Formula 3 Championship.

Highland and Agricultural Society it was the circuit promoters who paid for the nececessary modifications to be made. A few years later the stand was removed altogether. It was the final blow and marked the serious decline of Ingliston as a racing circuit.

Ecurie Ecosse finished off the season by winning the Group C2 class at Brands Hatch and finishing sixth overall behind three factory Rothmans Porsches and two factory Lancia-Turbos. Out of six starts that season the Ecosse had won its class at Silverstone, Hockenheim and Brands Hatch and might have won the class at Spa but for the fact that Mike Wilds was eased off the road by Martin Brundle's TWR Jaguar. By way of celebration, the Ecosse-Ford was successfully raced at the final Ingliston meeting of the season with Ray Mallock at the wheel.

It was not until the following May that Ecurie Ecosse announced their 1986 plans, the reason being that Ray Mallock and Hugh McCaig had been in consultation with Austin-Rover about using a suitably modified Metro 6R4 V6 engine in their Group C2 Ecosse. One of the reasons for the delay was that the engine was proving unreliable in the factory Metros running in the British Rally Championship. It kept throwing its Pirelli belts and there were doubts about its reliability, particularly in long distance events. This was solved by the new Ecurie Ecosse designer Max Boxtrom with the help of Uniroyal in Dumfries. The Uniroyal factory had originally been used by Arrol-Johnston to build their cars. To modify the engine, Ecosse went to their regular engine man, John Dunn at Swindon Racing engines and John managed to extract 410 bhp from the Metro engine. What with the new and lighter engine and a new tub modified to hold the V6 the 1986 Ecosse-Rover- as it was called for marketing reasons - was 70 kilos lighter than the 1985 car.

The plan was to race the 1985 Ecosse-DFL alongside the Metro-engined car and as the first Metro engine only had a few hours running before practice at Silverstone, the Ford-engined car was there in case of trouble. As it turned out, Ray Mallock qualified the Rover engined car faster than the previous year's time with the DFL and so he and Mike Wilds chose to run the Ecosse-Rover. At one stage in the race the car was three laps ahead of its nearest challenger but then came the misfire and the car retired. At Le Mans the team had bad luck when Mike Wilds "lost" the car on some oil dropped in Jo Gartner's fatal crash in his Porsche. Though Wilds tapped the barrier everything would have been fine had he not been hit by Jochen Mass in the factory Porsche who had also spun. The Ecosse car managed to struggle back to the pits and was repaired only for David Leslie to suffer a tyre blow-out at over 200 mph on the Mulsanne Straight causing more damage. He eventually got the crippled car back to the pits again but the team were disqualified. The Ford-engined car had been rented out to three American privateers, John Hotchkis, Andy Petery and Les Delano and they soldiered on to finish and score a single point in the championship which was to be crucial later in the year. The team went on to win its class in a number of the other rounds so that by the final round at Mount Fuji stood poised to become Group C2 champions provided they could beat the Spice-Ford. When Ecosse won the class and became Champions it fulfilled Hugh McCaig's dreams for Ecurie Ecosse. He and the team had restored the Ecurie Ecosse reputation as one of the most successful private teams motor racing teams in the world.

Scottish Motor Racing Club viewed the dwindling entries in the Formula Libre class, that had always been a mainstay in Scottish racing, and began to think about dropping it. However, Ron Cumming arrived that year with a Formula 2 March so guaranteeing a reprieve but the opposition mainly consisted of the Mallocks from the Clubmans class and the Formula Ford 2000s. The FF 2000 class had really taken over from Formula Libre with FF2000 Reynards driven by such contenders as Tom Brown, Stewart

Roden and Stephen Robertson so the Libre category's days were clearly numbered.

The normal pattern of the Ingliston season was broken up that year due to Edinburgh hosting the Commonwealth Games. Ingliston was one of the boxing venues; quite appropriate if you think of some of the metal to metal jousts that had taken place over the years on the racing circuit. This meant Knockhill was able to fill the gap. Some drivers were still not keen on Knockhill after the confines of Ingliston but anyone with an eye to the future could see that the Fife circuit held greater potential for development.

Though Formula Ford was the usual starting point for young talent, another entry level class was for Ford Fiesta Challenge cars. At the end of that National Series a large number of them were brought to Scotland. Ross Mickel from Edinburgh started out in the class and moved on to Legends.

By now Harvey Gillanders was the man to beat in Formula Ford but he was being challenged by prominent Scottish karter, Andy Sim. Andy had done some racing on a shoestring at Ingliston but then moved south to work as a mechanic with Reynard. Now he was back in Scotland with a Reynard FF1600 and was challenging for the championship against some former champions like Cameron Binnie. Eventually Binnie became Champion with Sim in second place. Alas Andy Sim was later to suffer the same fate as many others and just could not raise the sponsorship to continue in racing.

Though press publicity for motor racing in Scotland was also dwindling, Scottish Television agreed to slot the September race meeting into their live Scotsport programme and this gave an added boost to the competitors who were having difficulty with their sponsors. The racing was good and there were hopes that STV would repeat this the following year, but they never did.

The club nature of motor racing in Scotland, and the almost complete lack of local sponsorship, was again underlined by the introduction of classes for Ford Fiestas that had previously raced in the National championship. At the same time the 1000cc special saloon class was declining fast due to the increasing cost of preparing some of the sophisticated Imps with their special racing engines. As expected, the specific Formula Libre class had virtually been dropped and any car that turned up would be raced with the growing field of Formula Ford 2000s. The two leading FF2000 drivers going into the season were multiple Formula Ford Champion Tom Brown and Stewart Roden who had managed to secure valuable sponsorship from the ANC parcel servce. One of the most promising newcomers to the class was Stuart Gray

Every decade brings a crop of new Scots in racing and Susie Stoddart is now making a name for herself in Formula Renault and was a McLaren Autosport nominee in 2003. Before Susie, Sacha Pearl and Gillian Butcher had both moved South to race.

who had also managed to secure sponsorship from housebuilders Mactaggart & Mickel. Douglas Mickel, Chairman of M & M was the secretary of the MG Car Club. He and his son Bruce Mickel - the present chief executive of the company - have been long time supporters of motor sport in Scotland.

The Ingliston circuit received a boost from the RAC when SMRC were allowed to race 18 cars rather than the 16, a rule which had applied since 1964. By way of explanation, the RAC imposes a ratio of starters in any race to the overall lap length of the circuit. With just over a mile to the lap, Ingliston was allocated the lowest number of starters of any circuit in Britain. Due to the work Ingliston Race Circuits Ltd had done regarding safety provisions, and the circuit safety record, the number was increased by two.

At Knockhill Derek Butcher got down to some serious work on his circuit, carving out larger car parks including one cut into the slope above the braking area for the hairpin in the style of Brands Hatch. Now spectators could park there and watch the racing from the comfort of their cars. Scottish Motor Racing Club threw their entire weight into supporting Knockhill and this was to be the key to the future success of the circuit.

Ecurie Ecosse received a huge boost for 1987 with substantial sponsorship from the post office's Swiftair air delivery service. This meant the cars had to be repainted crimson. As Rover were no longer supplying engines, the team reverted to Ford Cosworth DFLs, once more prepared by John Dunn's Swindon Racing Engines. Belgian driver Marc Duez was brought into the team on a semi-permanent basis and it was decided to pair David Leslie with Ray Mallock and Mike Wilds with Duez. However, as Duez had some other contracted events, it meant he could not race in every event in the world championship and so a number of guest drivers drove for Ecurie Ecosse including Johnny Dumfries and Win Percy. Once again, Ecurie Ecosse planned to compete in the Scottish events this time with an Opel Manta 400 in the road saloon classes. With Swiftair sponsorship for the main team, the Opel was liveried in identical fashion and Walter Robertson was nominated as the driver.

The 1987 season also saw the debut of Scotland's latest driver, Allan McNish. Though only seventeen, he had been a multiple champion in karts since he was eleven. His father Bert McNish bought a new Van Diemen FF and entrusted the organisation and running of the car to David Leslie senior. Some years before, Bert, through his garage Crossflags Motors in Dumfries, had sponsored young David Leslie in Formula Ford and so it was an appropriate arrangement. As it turned out old David Leslie was to become a very important stepping stone for a number of future drivers including David Coulthard and Dario Franchitti who were to start their racing careers with him.

Allan McNish turned up at the first race meeting of the 1987 season at Ingliston. To the surprise of everyone, except Hugh McCaig of Ecurie Ecosse who had helped sponsor Allan's karting and now racing car career, McNish was fourth fastest in practice just behind reining Formula Ford champion Cameron Binnie. Ahead of them were Harvey Gillanders and Colin Harper but both Binnie and McNish soon got past Harper, and then McNish started to harry Cameron Binnie. It was all too much, and when McNish's Van Diemen snapped sideways on the entry to Caravan corner he careered into the barriers and collected all four corners. Obviously McNish was distraught but it was later established that something on the car had broken as McNish was running on his own at the time.

The following month McNish was back in Scotland racing at Knockhill where he was out sprinted by Roy Low in his Crossle 62F but McNish hung on and eventually passed Low to record his first-ever motor racing win. He also ran in the main Formula Ford race and impressed by taking second place to Cameron Binnie.

Another young Scot racing in the British Formula Ford Championship was Paul Stewart, Jackie's elder son and he, Allan McNish, and occasionally Gordon Wilson, another Scot, raced against each other that season. Gordon Wilson was something of a smoking gun who would appear with a Formula Ford and either win or take all the wheels off it. His great friend, and fellow Formula Ford driver, Roy Low, was instrumental in helping him in his early days and in the 1987 British championship he drove the best race of his life with a rented Swift, finishing third in the Birmingham Superprix Formula Ford event on the streets of Birmingham.

Despite the fact the grids, the drivers, and, to be honest, the results, tended to remain the same during 1987, motor racing in Scotland was still very healthy with plenty of drivers. However, the steadily changing social patterns of the 1980s, where husbands began to share the family weekend chores, resulted in a perceptible tailing off as far as spectators were concerned. This, coupled with a decline in the support given by the sports editors of the main Scottish newspapers for Scottish motor racing events, was beginning to generate some concern both at Ingliston and Knockhill.

Hugh McCaig's enthusiasm for racing saw him consider using one of his open cast coal mine sites near Falkirk for a club racing circuit. As the site had been closed it was due to be landscaped, but the idea was not taken any further.

In 1990 the New Ingliston circuit was proposed to be built on a green field site 300 metres from the existing circuit bordering the Edinburgh Airport access road on the eastern side. Behind the project were Jackie Stewart and McGregor Holdings PLC one of whose directors, Roddy Paterson, was a club racer at Ingliston with his Lotus Elan. The whole saga of New Ingliston is told in a separate appendix at the end of the book concerning phantom circuits. It was a classic case history of luddite thinking from the left-leaning Edinburgh District Council and Lothian Regional Council linked to the desires of some special interest groups.

Ironically it was not to be the last attempt at a new green-field circuit. The next, and so far, final attempt was actually led by a Scottish district council! It is sufficient at this juncture to record that despite all the work put into the project throughout 1990 the rug was pulled out of it in the mid 1990s

At the end of 1990 David Leslie joined his father and formed David Leslie Racing. As we have seen "old" David had already gained a reputation by running both Allan McNish and David Coulthard in their formative years and now young David was joining him to run a two-car Formula Vauxhall Junior team in 1991 with another new young Scots driver at the wheel, Dario Franchitti.

Scotland also celebrated another Scottish champion when Heather Baillie became British Truck Racing Champion.

By 1991 Scottish Race Promotions Ltd, decided that Ingliston's days were numbered. The RAC safety requirements were becoming stricter to impose on a circuit with limits to spectator access, and the Royal Highland and Agricultural Society were showing signs of being tired of the race meetings with the uprooting and setting down of the barriers before and after each Highland Show. The financial burden for the barrier removal and replacement was carried by Scottish Race Promotions Ltd (Formerly Ingliston Race Circuit Ltd) who were also faced with a heavy bill from the Highland Society for the damage caused to the verges of the track by drivers going over the kerbs. All these costs were making it impossible to make even a meagre profit on a race meeting. By that time the promoters needed a minimum of 120 competitors for a meeting to even wash its face and sponsorship had been increasingly difficult to obtain since the removal of both grandstands. These had been a great attraction and comfort for spectators. Also, changes to the Health and Safety rules put this responsibility in the hands of local authorities. When Ingliston was visited by Health and Safety they came up with a number of recommendations that further restricted public access to the paddock in case someone was injured. Former multiple Formula Ford champion Tom Brown expressed an interest in taking over the lease of the showground for motor racing. By the end of the 1991 season the handover was complete and Ingliston went into 1992 under new management.

Derek Butcher was working hard on Knockhill and steadily investing in the kind of changes necessary to substantially improve the facilities surrounding the track. With the freedom to invest and expand, Knockhill was in a position to develop this way. Scotland was still attracting a handful of Irish competitors, mainly in the Formula Ford classes, but not as many as had been the case in the 1970s when there was more of a partnership between Scottish Motor Racing Club and the 500 Club of Northern Ireland.

As for Scottish drivers, the most promising newcomer was Alex Jack, whose grandfather was his greatest supporter and helped to raise a meagre amount of money for Alex to race with a Swift in Formula Ford. He went on to win the First Time Racing/Auto Windscreens award that carried a sponsored drive in the Brands Hatch winter series. Alex was to go on to win the Formula First Championship but it led to nothing as there was no budget to continue. As was the case with most other promising young Scots, like Jason Yeomans and Andy Sim, the problem was making the step into serious racing south of the Border where talent can be more readily spotted. For the most part Scottish motor racing is dominated by the club driver with no great opportunity, no matter what his aspirations, to move up the ladder.

One man who was moving up that ladder, however, was Allan McNish who was on a testing contract with McLaren in Formula 1 but was also trying to wrestle with the Lola F3000 car for the DAMS team. By 1991 it was clear that the Reynard chassis was superior to the Lola but McNish was as dogged and determined as always. Half way through the season he remarked. *"It's really going to be tough because Christian (Fittipaldi) is going to be hard to catch now but I want to stick with the Lola. It would be easy to give up and just switch to a Reynard but I honestly feel the potential is there and we just need to sort out the problem."* It wasn't and they didn't and he ended a miserable season with few new prospects.

By now we had another promising newcomer in David Coulthard. A fellow competitor of Allan McNish in karting, David was supported by his father, Duncan Coulthard, and moved into Formula Ford. Once more the Leslies ran the team and David Leslie's cool and calm preparation made it easier for Coulthard to rise fast up the ranks in the British Formula Ford Championship. As with Allan McNish, we were now seeing the development of Scottish drivers who went straight to England, to race at the highest level they could afford, in order to be seen by those that matter.

David was to go on to join Paul Stewart Racing in Formula Vauxhall Junior, Formula 3 and Formula 3000 before getting a break in the Williams grand prix team.

Despite the fact he retired from racing in 1984, David Duffield still held the outright lap record at Knockhill with the Ralt but it tumbled during the season, not to another Formula car, but to a kart. Knockhill hosted a round of the FIA World Kart championship and Dutchman, Perry Grondstra broke the outright lap record for the circuit!

In August the home Scots had a chance to see how Dario Franchitti was getting on with a round of the British Formula Vauxhall Junior championship at Ingliston. Dario was there with David Cuff, his team-mate, in the David Leslie Racing combo, and another Scottish team was run by John Kirkpatrick. One of John's two drivers was later to make a name for himself in British touring car racing, James Thompson. In the Junior race the winner was Mexican Freddy Van Bueren with Cuff second and Dario third. In the main Formula Vauxhall Lotus race most of the field got below Eugene O'Brien's existing FVL lap record and in the race itself Kelvin Burt in John Village's car was the winner from Scott Lakin and Piers Hunniset. The only Scot in the race was Scott Ramsay who rented a car and found it quite a step up from Formula Ford. Scots girl Sacha Pearl also ran in the Junior race.

On the home front, the Formula Ford races saw Louis Di Resta and Jim Forsyth coming to the fore and seriously challenging regular winner Cameron Binnie. In order to encourage the Scottish Formula Ford group to race more competitively in the south, Bernard Buss of Scottish Motor Racing Club and David Duffield organised a team of Scots to go to the Formula Ford Festival at Brands. Many had previously raced there as individuals but this time the Club put up the money for a marquee at Brands so the Scots had somewhere to go between races and it proved a successful venture. Two articulated trucks left Scotland with the Formula Fords of Jim Forsyth, Colin Low, Stuart Thorburn,Thomas Irvine,Campbell Chisholm, Geordie Taylor, Cameron Binnie, Tommy Pearson and Lance Gauld. The other Scots, who travelled independently, included Joe McKeand, Scott Ramsay, Derek Butcher and Louis di Resta.The most successful was Geordie Taylor who won the pre-85 race for the second year running.

At the end of the year the traditional Macau Grand Prix took place in the tiny Portuguese colony tacked on to the South of China - now part of China itself since the Portuguese hand-over. This is one of the toughest circuits in the world with no room to make mistakes. It has a hairpin bend followed by a downhill section where it would be foolish to overtake and along the front it has one of the true heartstopping flat out 150 mph Lisboa bend.

It has always been said that the winner of the Monaco Formula 3 race is destined for a great future but this is very much a myth. It is to Macau you must look for the future champions; win Macau and you are going

places. Take for example some of the previous winners up to 1991, Michael Schumacher, Ayrton Senna, Riccardo Patrese and Maurizio Gugelmin.

On this occasion, 1991, David Coulthard was visiting for the first time with the Paul Stewart Racing Ralt-Mugen RT5 and was second fastest on the grid to Rikard Rydell's Tom's Toyota. His team-mate, and boss, Paul Stewart, was on the sixth row.

Towards the end of the opening lap of the first heat, Coulthard managed to outbrake Rydell and take the lead. It was such a fine move David thought he had actually touched the Swede's car. In the second heat he and the Spaniard Jordi Gene battled for the lead and though Gene passed him towards the end, David kept close enough to ensure that he would win the event outright on aggregate over the two heats. Paul Stewart finished tenth.

Derek Butcher kept up the pressure for rounds in National Championships and was rewarded with a real feather in his cap, a round in the British Touring Car Championship in 1992. He was to hold on to his place on the BTCC calendar for the next ten years. Scottish Motor Racing Club planned ten race meetings for the 1992 season with six at Knockhill and four at Ingliston.

During 1991 yet another plan to develop a motor racing circuit in Scotland began to emerge but this time from Lanarkshire District Council who were keen to develop a tourist facility beside the M8 Motorway at Forrestburn, almost exactly half way between Glasgow and Edinburgh. The site can be seen on the northen side of the Motorway in the area between the two large television masts for Scottish Television and the BBC. Central to this area is a small reservoir and the original concept was to build a hill climb on the northern shore of this reservoir as phase one and eventually a full motor racing circuit as phase two. The development is described in the separate chapter on Phantom Racing Circuits. The discussions and plans linked to a private development company were developed over the next five years until the whole house of cards toppled and we were left little or nothing to show for what was an interesting development.

Season 1992 was a turning point in Scottish motor racing and saw the final demise of Ingliston as a circuit. Tom Brown threw his heart and soul into running racing at the circuit but everything was against him. The weather in the early part of the year saw crowd figures down and entries few. Then, after the break for the Highland Show, the circuit was not ready with many of the barriers still lying beside the track. Some of the SMRC officials and drivers set too and helped get the barriers set up in time for practice to start. It was a sad situation and one that was not to improve so it was no surprise when Ingliston quietly faded from the scene. Derek Butcher's Knockhill then took over the role as Scotland's major circuit and it has continued this way for the past twelve years.

After his terrible 1991 season in Formula 3000, when his Lola was simply uncompetitive and where his relationship with his French team broke down, Allan McNish appeared to be in the doldrums until an unlikely hand came from Ron Dennis of McLaren for whom he was test driver. Dennis put up the money for Allan to run his own Reynard in the 1992 Championship but then the real tragedy struck.

First, he was involved in a high speed accident at Donington when a team helper was killed and then he contracted a virus which not only laid him low but no one in the medical profession could define. As a result his F3000 season fizzled out and he became yesterday's man. If anyone needed any reminding of how tough motor racing can be they just need to look at

McNish's career at that time. After a tremendous start in 3000 in 1990 he began running backwards due more to equipment than ability.

Meanwhile Paul Stewart Racing took advantage of an F3000 testing session at Le Mans in March. As their second new Reynard 92D chassis had not arrived they rented one of the 91D Reynards from Il Barone Rampante Racing. Paul Stewart had already already driven their first 92D car and had it at Le Mans whilst the rented car was given to David Coulthard to drive. This car had a Mugen engine and Coulthard set up fastest time with Paul in third equal place. Rubens Barrichello was fifth fastest in Il Barone Rampante's new 92D Reynard so Coulthard was happy with his first proper test against the other competitors he would face. This season demonstrated that Coulthard could race comfortably in the bigger class but it was to be another season before he began to shine. Coulthard was selected by Tom Walkinshaw to race a Jaguar XJ220C at Le Mans and came away with a GT Class win but they were later disqualified for having an exhaust system that did not conform. David Leslie also drove a TWR XJ220C but his car retired in the race.

Another Scot in line for a Championship was John Cleland in the British Touring Car Championship. John has always been one of the most determined drivers and after dabbling with sports cars he became Scotland's greatest touring car driver. In 1992, he was on the verge of winning but was faced with the BMW's of Tim Harvey and Steve Soper at Silverstone. What happened in the race created considerable controversy

with Cleland and Soper clashing and letting Tim Harvey romp home as the new Champion.

Though everyone expected Allan McNish to be Scotland's next contracted grand prix driver it was, in fact, his friend David Coulthard who stepped up to take the vacant space in the Williams team when Ayrton Senna was killed at Imola. As test driver for the team he was in line for the drive but probably would have preferred if his elevation had not been because of Senna's death. However, he impressed in that first season and when dropped by Williams was quickly signed up by McLaren where he will stay until the end of 2004.

In 1995 there had been hints that Jackie Stewart was up to something and all was revealed in January 1996 when a five-year agreement was signed between Jackie Stewart and Ford for a research and development programme that would result in the building of the Stewart grand prix car. Typically, Jackie was not rushing into things and during 1996 he gathered together his design team and linked up with Ford's Advanced Vehicle Technology Division firstly to develop the electronics package. What this deal meant was that Stewart had some of the most advanced technological support in the development of his car. Work went on all year and the SF1 (Stewart-Ford) was launched on December 10 1996 with Brazilian Rubens Barrichello and Dane, Jan Magnussen named as drivers. Barrichello started his grand prix career with Jordan in 1993 and stayed with the team until the end of the 1996 season when he switched to Stewart Racing. Magnussen

Today, the Scots to watch for the future ore the two Ryans, Dalziel and Sharp. Dalziel took the USA route and has been a leading contender in Indy Lights whilst Ryan Sharp, here, has been successful in Renault V6.

had raced in Formula 3 with Paul Stewart Racing in 1993 and then won the British F3 Championship with the team the following year. During both 1995 and 1996 he had been a test driver with McLaren-Mercedes and made his F1 debut in the Pacific GP in 1995. He then raced sports cars and Indycars before signing with Stewart in October 1996.

By the end of the 1990s Scottish motor racing was beginning to look tired and though Knockhill was host to the British Touring Car Championship for a number of years, it was dropped from the National series for a season but has been brought back again. However, a new trend has begun to take off. To understand what happened we must take a broader view of motor racing in Great Britain.

Octagon took over the group that held rights to Brands Hatch, Snetterton, Oulton Park and Mallory Park : the bastions of Club motor racing. As the European arm of a giant American sports conglomerate, the new owners tended to look closely at the bottom line. Past benign attitudes towards club motor racing linked to low rental costs, were reviewed upwards. For some of the smaller clubs this meant they could not longer run the kind of programme they preferred to run. In turn the multitude of Championships for everything from Formula Renault to TVR Tuscans and Unlimited Saloons were faced with a problem. Venues for rounds in these less popular championships became scarce: but then there was Knockhill.

Thanks to some heavy lobbying by Scottish Motor Racing Club and Derek Butcher's team at Knockhill, a raft of championships began to have rounds in Scotland. In a sense, the wheel of motor racing fortune had come full circle. Remember the beginnings in the 1950s. With few circuits around, many of the southern drivers lugged their cars all the way up the old road system from England to places like Charterhall, Turnberry and even Crimond in Aberdeenshire. Now, with fewer circuit dates available and an infinitely better road system, the penny suddenly dropped that Scotland was perhaps not so far away after all.

Today, Scotland hosts rounds of most of the national championships including Formula 3 - something that never happened even thirty years ago. The fact they are taking place in Scotland has provided a boost to Scottish racing. This has been underlined by a new crop of young drivers like Ryan Dalzell, Ryan Sharp and Paul di Resta. Ryan Sharp has shown great promise and now has Jackie Stewart in his corner helping to smooth the way. Born in Aberdeen Ryan demonstrated the old adage that you have to go out on a limb and sometimes risk everything. The crunch came during the 2003 season when he opted to compete in the German Formula Renault Championship and won it outright. He then had his first experience of the Renault V6 engined cars at Monza before the season's end. It will be interesting to see what happens to him particularly as he was nominated for a McLaren Autosport award. Ryan Dalzell has done the same thing and has been racing successfully in the United States. But the latest newcomer to show real pace is teenager Paul di Resta. Paul looks set to go the distance what with the backing of his father Louis and his uncles, Dario and Marino Franchitti. Back in the 1980s Louis di Resta always looked promising in Formula Ford but he was developing his various businesses and could not devote the time needed to lift him out of Scottish racing but clearly he wants to see his son take up the challenge.

Louis' greatest drive was one wet day at Ingliston when he beat the up and coming Richard Dean. Today Louis is throwing his efforts into young Paul who has already been Junior karting champion.

Away from single seaters, there are a number of other Scots who have come forward in other disciplines. Peter Dumbreck, for example, was successful in Formula Nippon in Japan and smoothly moved into GT racing

clinching a drive with the Mercedes Benz team at Le Mans and then with Mercedes in the German Touring Car Championship. In 2003 he moved to Opel and was the only driver to compete with the championship winning Mercedes team. Robin Liddell is another driver who, helped by his father Eric, moved into racing in England and today is also carving a name for himself in GT racing with Porsche and Ferrari. Barry Sime has raced in a number of classes but came good in the 2003 British Porsche Cup and looks like moving further up the ladder. Then there is Nathan Kinch. His father, Larry Kinch, has a successful oil servicing business and has been in the position to give Nathan's talent its head. At the time of writing he has built himself a niche in the European GT Championship sharing the factory Lister-Storm with Jamie Campbell-Walter- himself a Scot. So Scots can still boast of a serious presence in motor racing.

As for racing in Scotland, if you take away the rounds of National Championships, you find Scottish motor racing is much the same as it has always been. The majority of drivers have real jobs to go to on Monday morning and they race for the fun of it. They all have ambitions, of course, but are realistic enough to appreciate that ambition and opportunity do not always go hand in hand. For the best part of ten years there has been a successful championship for Ford Fiestas but they are beginning to get a bit long in the tooth. Then there are the Legends, those tiny and ridiculously fast single seaters clothed in American style saloon bodywork.

This latter has become a healthy Scottish Championship to the extent that six of the leading Scottish drivers made the trip to the USA for the World Legend Finals held at Sears Point in November 2003.

Despite the fact there were over 160 competitors, mostly from the United States, the Scots came back with a barrowload of trophies including two World Championships. John Higgins, who is a Scot and won the British Championship, won the Professional Championship and was backed up by Ross Mickel who finished second and Jamie Clark fourth. Derek Pierce won the Semi-Pro World Championship and in the Masters World Championship Colin Noble took second place with Jamie Clarke's father, Jim, fourth.

Then there is Susie Stoddart, born and brought up in Oban, who, in 2003 became the first girl to be nominated for the final of the McLaren Autosport awards. When she was 8 her father took her to Knockhill where she tried karting and she was hooked. She was nominated for the McLaren Award following a promising season in Formula Renault. So no matter what the class, major or minor, Scots can still go abroad and be successful.

The first season of the Scottish Mini Cooper Challenge Series in 2003 proved to be a headache with close racing and the odd wrangle behind the scenes with Aly McKeever running out the first Champion, thanks partly to help from Bryce Wilson.

So motor racing in Scotland continues to attract new drivers but for many years it has been well understood that if you want to go to the very top, and have the latent ability, you have to move South and be seen around the regular venues where the talent scouts are watching.

Scotland was late into the motor racing game but it was sustained by enthusiastic people who never lost the will to encourage young talent. As mentioned earlier, this is not a view embraced by Scottish business which has more or less totally ignored the promotional appeal of motor racing. Were that penny ever to drop, who knows what would happen. Despite the financial limitations, Scotland has much to be proud of in motor racing. Indeed, at the risk of being hung drawn and quartered, it is my opinion that motor racing has brought more international sporting fame and acclaim to Scotland than football and rugby put together. But then perhaps I have a bias.

Chapter 11
Scottish Racing Drivers and People

It would obviously be impossible to name and describe every Scotsman who ever raced a car; even if one wanted to. Probably over three thousand Scots have, at one time or another, taken out an RAC competitions licence and raced at one of the various circuits in Scotland and around the world. What I have tried to do here is give pen pictures of some who have particularly come to notice in National and International events, as well as people who were notable in the development of racing in Scotland.

MARGARET ALLAN

In the 1930s one or two Scots, by virtue of living in England, took part in racing at Brooklands, but not many. One of the least known, and perhaps the most colourful, was a girl of 22 called Margaret Mabel Gladys Allan who was born on July 26 1909 into the family that ran the Allan Royal Mail Shipping Line in Perth. Her father was also the principal shareholder in a small company which came out with the unique idea of running a Clyde-based paddle steamer that was teetotal! At that time Clyde Steamers had a reputation for being floating pubs and would disgorge their wavering passengers on little coastal towns the length and breadth of the Clyde. The temperance ship was not a successful venture.

Margaret had a fine education at Bedales and was an enthusiastic equestrian competitor but in 1929 she bought a second hand Riley 9 and so began her interest in cars. In 1932, when she owned a two litre supercharged Lagonda, she had a hankering to do the Monte Carlo Rally but her car was not exactly suitable. However, a friend of hers, Eve Staniland, offered her the chance to co-drive on the Monte in Eve's car. After this she was persuaded to enter her Lagonda in a Novices handicap race at Brooklands.

The sprightly Margaret not only led the race but was a lap and a half in the lead when she blew the engine. At the same meeting Christopher Jennings, who was to go on to become Editor of Motor magazine, also blew up his Riley. They met and later married.

In 1933 and 1934 she won three Junior Long Handicaps at Brooklands in a 4.5 litre Bentley and was invited to join a private team of ladies driving supercharged MG Magnettes. She was then invited by Cecil Kimber of MG to join the first all-female MG factory team driving 850cc MGs. They were called the "Dancing Daughters" and in 1935 Margaret Allan was entered for Le Mans. The Dancing Daughters team was managed by land speed record holder Captain George Eyston.

The three MGPAs finished in 24th, 25th and 26th places with Margaret Allan and her co-driver Colleen Eaton finishing 26th.

Her racing career advanced in virtual leaps and bounds. In 1935 she won at Brooklands in Dudley Folland's Frazer-Nash and the following season Richard Marker, one of the great Bentley enthusiasts, entered her at Brooklands in the famous "Mother Gun" 6.5 litre Bentley. This huge car was very difficult to drive on the bumpy Brooklands track, where it spent a lot of time bouncing through the air, yet Margaret won the Whitsun Long Handicap event averaging over 115 mph. Her fastest lap of 122.37 mph meant she earned the coveted Brooklands 120 mph badge.

When she married Christopher Jennings, she virtually stopped racing and when war started she was recruited to the famous intelligence headquarters at Bletchley Park where she worked in the Italian naval subsection. She spent the War in counter intelligence. After the War she was appointed motoring correspondent of Vogue magazine and was made an honorary member of the British Racing Drivers Club. She still maintained her enthusiasm for cars and on one occasion Autocar magazine had the brilliant idea of asking her to road test three high-powered sports cars in the Welsh hills. On the test she left the normal staff testers behind, despite the fact she was over 80 years of age at the time.

BILL BINNIE

In present-day International historic racing, the name Bill Binnie will be familiar to you as the quick driver of various Maserati and Ferrari cars. Bill was born in Glasgow but when he was very young his parents took him to the United States where he developed a successful business. For the past six or seven years he has raced a Maserati 8CM and a Maserati 3000S sports car.

BOB BIRRELL

Bob Birrell is probably an unfamiliar name to most racing enthusiasts. In the 1950s he was brought into the sport by his schoolboy enthusiasm and became a flag marshal at Charterhall. Born in Dunfermline in 1946 he joined the army in 1965 as an officer cadet and retired thirty-two years later as a Lieutenant Colonel.

Nearly all his racing took place in the Army. When posted to Northern Ireland in 1968, he first raced a Radbourne Fiat Abarth at Kirkistown and Bishopscourt. The following year he bought one of Johnny Walker's Imp-engined single-seaters and won a race at Mondello with Edmund Irvine - Eddie's father - in second place.

This part came to an end in 1970 when he was posted to Singapore. He talked his way into a sponsored season in a Hawke DL2A Formula Ford and won a number of races in the Far East. Back in England in 1972 he again went for a Hawke, a DL2B, which he bought from Graham Cuthbert in Dundee. Then followed cars like a Super Vee and a March 813. When the money ran out he was offered a drive in Fred Boothby's Jaguar XK140 and has stuck with historic racing cars ever since.

Today Bob is head of the British Army Motoring Association and is on a variety of historic racing committees. He has his own Brabham BT6 Formula Junior which he ran at Monaco in 2002 and shares the ownership and driving of a Lotus 23. His ambition is to race on 100 different circuits before he retires: so far he has raced on 62!

GERRY BIRRELL

Gerry Birrell was a product of the early Ingliston school of motor racing. He had been involved in racing helping his brother Graham with the development of an Austin A40 Farina that launched Graham into motor racing. His first race was at Charterhall in 1961 just two weeks after he obtained his driving licence. His brother Graham let him borrow his Austin A40 - which also served as Graham's daily transport - but entered him in the GT race. Gerry's only comment about his first race was "Well, I wasn't quite last!"

Gerry Birrell was poised for a superb win at Thruxton with his F2 Chevron in 1973 when Mike Beuttler tried this kamikaze move which ended in tears for both.

good third place at Mallory Park in the car. Early in the race he took the lead and then panicked "...there was nobody to follow ". He also modified the car to Series 2 spec and fitted a de-Dion back axle.

When he joined Claud Hamilton Motors, the Singer distributors, he got down to racing a Singer Chamois and eventually "Clauds" ran a team of three Chamois in the saloon car races at Ingliston with Graham and Gerry Birrell and Eric Liddell as the drivers. He went on to modify one of the Chamois with a full house Coventry Climax racing engine and won the Scottish Speed Championship. In 1967 he even took part in the International Scottish Rally finishing 12th overall, highest placed Scot. This led to him being entered for the RAC rally in a factory Hillman Imp alongside Rosemary Smith and Andrew Cowan but that year the RAC was cancelled due to an outbreak of foot and mouth disease. From then on motor racing was Gerry Birrell's game. He was clearly good and moved to the South of England for the 1967 racing season to join Wooler Engineering building Formula Vees. He was their works driver in the British National Championship and won fourteen races to become champion.

For 1968 Wooler moved into Formula Ford and had a partnership with Irish racing car builder John Crossle. This gave Gerry's inventive mind its head and he and Crossle had a very successful relationship.

At the end of 1969 he reached a crossroads. His skill as an inventive engineer led to a number of good job offers in the motor trade and he had

Gerry was born on July 30 1944 and was one of three Birrell brothers. Gerry served his apprenticeship with the Glasgow Renault dealers Wylie & Lochhead and became very friendly with Hugh Shannon who fettled for Tommy Dickson. When brother Graham bought a Lotus Eleven in 1962 little brother Gerry was allowed to have the occasional drive and took a

Gerry Birrell's performances in the Sports Motors Brabham BT40 led to his factory drive with Chevron for the 1973 season.

just married Margaret. But the racing bug had bitten and he decided to turn professional for the 1970 racing season.

John Stanton took him on to race his Formula 3 Brabham-Holbay. Amongst his successes he won the French Championship Formula 3 race at the inaugural meeting at Paul Ricard, the Guards Trophy Formula 3 race at Brands Hatch and the European Cup race at Thruxton. He had chosen to do a number of races on the Continent to learn the circuits and at the end of the season L'Equipe, the French sporting newspaper, rated Gerry Birrell the most successful Formula 3 driver of 1970.

That same year he drove Andrew Mylius' Chevron-based 2-litre Gropa in the BOAC 1000km sports car race winning the class. Sports Motors in Manchester also gave him a couple of drives in their Formula 2 car.

The first was at Hockenheim in their Brabham BT30 and, despite being only his first race in Formula 2, he qualified ahead of his brother Graham who was driving the Ecurie Ecosse Brabham BT30. After 11 laps Gerry was lying in fourth place behind Peter Westbury, Emerson Fittipaldi and Vittorio Brambilla but spun when Brambilla braked heavily in front of him. Then the engine broke a valve spring. The second race, at Imola, was actually run under the Team Brabham name and Gerry lined up on the grid alongside Francois Cevert in the works Tecno. In the first heat he finished 12th and in the second heat 10th but overall he was given 8th place.

For the 1971 season, John Stanton bought a Lotus 69 (69-71-3) and right away Gerry was on the pace. At Mallory Park he put himself on the front row of the grid alongside Ronnie Peterson (March 712M) and Henri Pescarolo (March 712M). He finished second in both heats to Pescarolo and so was second overall.

In 1972, however, he moved to the Sports Motors team with a new March 722 and again he had some great results, bearing in mind the opposition included Niki Lauda, John Surtees and Jody Scheckter. By now he was also heavily involved with Ford Motor Company and did some of the development work on the Cologne Ford Capris in which he was also successful. He raced the car at Le Mans.

Then came the fateful 1973 season. He was signed by the factory Chevron team to drive a B25 (B25-73-09) replacing John Lepp for the Hockenheim Formula 2 race. He ran in a number of Formula 2 events in the factory team that year. At the Rouen event he suffered a puncture that threw the car into the barriers and he was killed. It was said at the time the mounting for the barrier at that point had not been set in concrete. When Gerry hit the barrier it rode up over the nose of the car.

Gerry's greatest attribute was a cool technical brain and, apart from his racing performances, he contributed a lot to motor racing development. For example, it was he who persuaded the Avon tyre company to develop their cross ply tyre for Formula Ford as opposed to the radials everyone else used. To prove the point Gerry won the European Formula Ford title driving a Crossle. John Crossle had great respect for Birrell, as did the legendary Walter Hayes who became Vice-President of Ford Motor Company. Shortly after Gerry was killed he told the writer that the loss of Gerry had a greater effect of Ford Motor Company than that of Jim Clark. By this he was not trying to downgrade Clark but to emphasise the enormous amount of testing and development work done by Gerry for the Ford competitions department. When he was signed up to Ford by the legendary Stuart Turner, to help push forward their Cologne Capri project, Turner remarked "When we brought Gerry into Ford saloons we needed someone who was level headed, technical and not a prima donna. There was also an element of winding up Cologne about it." Later, after Gerry had been killed, Turner added : "I suspect the reason he didn't get into a good team was that he

was too nice a person and too loyal to friends. A sad comment on our sport, perhaps. I certainly lobbied Ken (Tyrrell) hard on Gerry's behalf. Gerry is one of the few (drivers) I remember so well that if he walked in now, I'd say where the hell have you been and carry on exactly where we left off."

GRAHAM BIRRELL

Graham Birrell is the better known of the Birrell brothers, not only for his racing but his 1960s motor accessory shop in Glasgow that became the regular haunt of all the racing drivers in the west of Scotland. He started out modestly with an Austin Farina A40 but graduated to a Lotus Eleven before being chosen by Glasgow Ford dealers Wylies to drive a Ford Escort in the saloon car classes at Ingliston. Graham Birrell was extremely successful with the car and was Scottish saloon car champion. He was then chosen by David Murray to race the team's new Ecosse-Imp single-seater at Ingliston in April 1967. He was given Chassis No 2 but was to race both chassis during the 1967 and 68 seasons. It was not a particularly successful car as it needed more power than the Imp engine could give. At one Mallory Park race he and his brother Gerry ran both Ecosse-Imps, the first time both brothers raced identical cars.

For the 1969 racing season, however, with Harry Ballantyne running the Ecurie Ecosse team, Graham was chosen as their main driver and raced the ex- Jochen Rindt Brabham BT23C. He had some good top ten positions in the European Championship, notably at Zolder, Hockenheim and Monza where he finished in 6th place on each occasion.

In the 1970 season a new Brabham BT30 was bought and Graham raced it at Nurburgring but Ecurie Ecosse were in the financial doldrums and the team was to be wound up the following season. Graham continued to compete and was the cornerstone of Denys Dobbie's DART racing team with Chevron B8 and B19 sports cars. Today Graham is retired from racing and runs a successful agency business.

BERNARD BUSS

Though a man of Kent, Bernard Buss has been instrumental in developing motor racing in Scotland for the past thirty years. He originally came north to join Ian Scott Watson in the Celtic Homes housebuilding business but in more recent years has been a director of Fleming Homes in Duns. Bernard bubbles with enthusiasm but never lets it run away with him. As a director of Scottish Motor Racing Club he has provided a balancing influence and can take credit for many of the successful developments at Scottish Motor Racing Club to make it probably the most financially secure motor club in Scotland. His skill in negotiation has seen him introduce new classes and encourage more and more rounds of British Championships to take place in Scotland. His wife Margaret was for some years the Club Secretary and in 2003 Bernard began to wind down his general involvement in the club but has been the guiding light in the Mini Cooper Challenge series.

JOHNNY BUTE (DUMFRIES)

Better known as Johnny Dumfries, he was born in Rothesay, Isle of Bute on April 26 1958. His father was the 6th Marquis of Bute, one of the oldest Scottish families that had considerable holdings of land in Scotland, England and particularly Wales. The family seat is Mount Stuart on the Island of Bute just off the Clyde coast.

This privileged background did not help Johnny when he first had the idea of racing. He came into racing the hard way.

He had been inspired to race by his cousin, Charlie Crichton-Stuart who used to visit Mount Stuart during the days Charlie was racing in Formula 3 and enthralled the younster. Johnny had learned to drive at an early age with a battered Mini Moke so he and Charlie used to have a lot of fun on the moors and tracks around Mount Stuart.

Johnny Dumfries' highlight came when he drive a factory John Player Lotus in Grand Prix racing alongside Ayrton Senna.

"At that time I had a passion for driving and at that age had no thoughts of ever becoming a racing driver. By the time I began to race I was living on my own and working with a company selling automotive tools to mechanics.

"When I left school I had lots of different jobs, I worked on building sites and did painting and decorating but wanted to be self-employed so that I could go racing. The guys I worked with were racing 100 National karts and that is how I started. It was all so much simpler then. All we wanted was to work during the week to earn some money and go racing at the weekends.

"In 1978, thanks to my cousin Charlie, I was working with Frank Williams. The story goes that I drove the truck but in fact, as I didn't have an HGV licence, I was actually his van driver - an even lower form of life. I was then promoted to being a 'gofer' and was going to all the races. I wanted to be a mechanic and spoke to Frank about it and he told me I wasn't going to be a mechanic on his team unless I had been properly trained so I became a driver instead.

"My first racing car was a 1978 Crossle 32F Formula Ford and ironically my first race meeting was at Croft which was nearly as far as driving back up to Scotland. That year, 1981, was my learning year and I did the Dunlop Star of Tomorrow series. I didn't win anything but had quite a few accidents, actually.

"For 1982 Paul Gerrish and I did a deal with Bert Ray who supplied the chassis and we ran as the factory Ray team. We had a reasonable season. I won two races and sort of made a name for myself.

"For 1983 I managed to find an Italian sponsor, Luigi Graziano, who wanted to start his own Formula 3 team. He bought Dave Price's Team BP Ralt RT3 from the previous year for the British Formula 3 championship and the team manager was another ex F3 man, Dave Morgan, who had successfully run Lola's Formula Ford team. Dave was a great influence on my career. He had a great approach and I remember early on a cold wet test day at Silverstone we were sitting in the transporter discussing the handling and set-up. Dave had a very scholastic approach to things and an avuncular attitude to me as a young driver and we hit it off immediately. He turned, looked at me seriously and said ' now listen, what this year is about is Martin Brundle and Ayrton Senna, just forget about anybody else because they don't matter'. That remark really sharpened my focus on how you should prioritise your approach to racing. At the end of 1983 David Price offered me a drive in his BP team car for the last round of the European F3 Championship at Donington. Though I had a scrape

and didn't finish I think it was enough for Dave to persuade Les Thacker of BP that I should join the team for the 1984 season when he planned to run just one car."

As the records show, Johnny Dumfries became Marlboro British Formula 3 Champion in 1984 and almost won the European Championship so he was now on a high. Once again his cousin, Charlie Crichton-Stuart came into the picture.

Charlie had a telephone call from John Hogan, the competitions manager for Marlboro. Apparently Hogan and Ferrari's team boss at the time, Marco Piccinini, had discussed the possibility of signing Johnny on a testing contract to Ferrari. *"This was staggering news to me"*, admits Johnny.

"At that time I realised the way things were stacking up I had a serious career in front of me and that is how I looked at it. Obviously, any contact with Ferrari was the kind of thing I couldn't possibly pass up. I started having discussions with Piccinini in London. At that age I was quite unsure as to the way the land lay. Looking back on it now, I was quite naive and it was almost too good to be true. It was a slightly surreal situation for me and there were other confusing elements. Ferrari were not the only people showing an interest in me.

Peter Warr at Lotus had given me a full day's private testing at Donington Park and Peter told me to stay in touch. They knew Ayrton Senna would be staying with them but were not quite sure if Elio de Angelis would be staying. The other person who was interested, and for whom I tested, was Bernie Ecclestone who owned Brabham at the time. Bernie sent me down to Kyalami in South Africa to do three day's testing with their regular drivers Nelson Piquet and Teo Fabi and Bernie was talking about signing me on a testing contract for 1985. I had no Formula 3000 options so it was a confusing period. Bernie then offered me, in addition to the testing contract, a place with Onyx racing in Formula 3000 but in the end I went for the Ferrari deal. In retrospect, I should have gone for Brabham!"

As it turned out Mike Earle at Onyx offered Dumfries a drive in Formula 3000 in 1985 but he only ran four races before the money ran out.

After Johnny had decided on Ferrari he had to go down to Maranello where he met the legendary Brenda Vernor who literally took Johnny under her wing.

"She is a great character with a tremendous sense of humour and I found everybody there was shit scared of her except the old Man.

"When they fired Rene Arnoux at the beginning of 1985 Brenda went completely ballistic, marching up and down the corridor screaming her head off in Italian and everybody was running for cover. The rationale given to me was that Ferrari were developing their four cylinder turbo engine and my programme was to develop this engine.

"In the early part of the year I spent a lot of time in Maranello and started to learn Italian but it never really got off the ground because the regulations changed and Ferrari shelved the project. I was left with no great results in Formula 3000 and not enough experience in testing to be considered to replace Arnoux so Ferrari chose Stefan Johansson. I was offered a drive with a works Lola 3000 team run by Frenchman Monnier but we were using an Indy chassis and it was hopeless. It was a very odd year for me and potentially it could have been damaging for my career. Luckily for me Lotus maintained an interest in me and that is where I ended up."

This move to Lotus was not quite as simple as that. Renault, who provided engines for Lotus, had taken their own team out of Formula 1 and it appeared clear that Ayrton Senna's partner in the 1986 season would be former Renault driver, Derek Warwick. Everything appeared right as sponsors, John Player, wanted to have a British driver but there was one problem - Ayrton Senna. At the time it was reported there was a line in Senna's contract indicating that Senna was not to be overtaken by his team-mate in races. (Shades of Michael Schumacher in the 2000s). This did not suit Warwick and it was also rumoured that Senna wanted another Brazilian in the team - Mauricio Gugelmin being in the frame - but in the end it was Johnny Dumfries who got the drive.

He explains the situation thus :
"The whole thing made it a bit difficult for me. The British motor racing press were firmly behind Derek Warwick. Senna clearly had his contract and the story got about that he had vetoed Warwick. Now I couldn't put my hand on my heart and say this was true but, for whatever reason, Lotus chose not to sign Derek Warwick. Maybe it suited their interests to have a newcomer to F1 who wasn't too demanding and they could give Senna undivided number one treatment. It may eventually have been a strategic decision rather than a contractural one with Senna.

"It was in my contract with Lotus that Ayrton had preference over the T-car and if I was in a position to finish in front of him and he needed to get past that is the way it had to be. It was all written out in my contract. I had an example of this at Monaco where I was given the car with the experimental six-speed gearbox that was simply not reliable and kept breaking. I shunted the car in practice so in the second practice session I went out in the repaired car but had gear selection problems. I had to wait quite a long time to get into the T-car until Senna had set his time and I ended up not qualifying. It was just one of those things."

Dumfries had only one season in Formula 1 with Lotus. "They told me they were letting me go at the German Grand Prix as Honda were going to be the Lotus engine supplier in 1987 and Honda wanted a Japanese driver.
"I didn't have a sponsor for 1987 so ended up without a drive. That is when I went into GT and Sports cars as a freelance driver on one-off contracts. I drove for Hugh McCaig's Ecurie Ecosse team, with Rob Dyson in the USA, Peter Sauber's Kouros-Mercedes team at Le Mans, Richard Lloyd Racing at Brands Hatch and Tom Walkinshaw in the Jaguars."

In 1988 Dumfries won Le Mans for Tom Walkinshaw with Jan Lammers and Andy Wallace as his partners. "....then Tom gave me the bullet as I think

I had had too many accidents for his liking. Although we won Le Mans I had made a few silly mistakes so I started to talk to Toyota. They were keen to come into the World Championship as they had a very powerful engine. Actually it wasn't a bad little car with a four-cylinder turbo engine and I will never forget the first European race we did in 1989. I think I finished up on pole position and they cranked the boost up for qualifying. I was used to Formula 1 power, because in 1986 when I was with Lotus we had phenomenal qualifying power, but this Toyota, I am telling you,was highly impressive ; it was like a rocket. The trouble was we had appalling reliability and fuel consumption so we had some promising results but were a million miles away from winning world championship 1000 km races.

"My last race was a classic piece of bad judgement. I left Toyota at the end of 1990 and had no contract for 1991. We were in recession, my father was terminally ill with cancer and I didn't have a job but of course, like all racing drivers, I was desperate to get out and into a car. Courage in France offered me a drive at Le Mans and that car was appalling. It was a very bad last race, it was a low point."

Two years later John Crichton-Stuart, the sixth Marquis of Bute died of cancer and Johnny Dumfries became the seventh Marquis. A few years later he changed his name to Johnny Bute and put the same determination he put into his motor racing into the huge task of managing the Bute family holdings. He opened Mount Stuart to the public and in 2002 launched the Mount Stuart Classic with a display of grand prix and sports cars provided by his many friends in racing.

HUGH CHALMERS

Hugh Chalmers might have made a career of motor racing but as a doctor, he confined his racing in the early years to the odd event at Ingliston and Knockhill, driving a variety of cars. He raced the James Ross Hillman Avenger occasionally and then ran his own Davrian and a Sunbeam Talbot Lotus before being roped in to race the Ecurie Ecosse Vauxhall in Scottish events.

When Laurence Jacobsen bought the ex-Ecurie Ecosse Ecosse-Ford DFL he asked Hugh Chalmers to partner him in the British GpC Championship. He also raced in the British Thundersaloons championship with an Ecurie Ecosse Opel Manta.

Eventually, shortly before retiring as a doctor, he took up historic racing off his own bat and raced various Formula Juniors ending up with a Lotus 22. He also raced the Ecosse Tojeiro-Buick at the Goodwood Revival race meetings.

JIM CLARK

What can one say about Jim Clark that has not already been written, mulled over, and written again?

Like Jackie Stewart, he has been the subject of a number of books and so for a detailed description of the careers of Jim and Jackie I would refer you to these biographies.

However, there is no doubt Jim Clark was the finest racing driver of his particular generation. To many people he personified the ideal racing driver. He was well educated - even though he

Jim Clark's enthusiasm for motor racing saw him try any car that he found interesting. This rare photograph shows Jim at the wheel of Ralph Watson's famous Lycoming Special at the Teretonga circuit in the early 1960s. (Photo Ralph Watson archives.) Clark is giving Watson the thumbs up sign to show he is enjoying himself : Jackie Stewart, who was present on the same day refused to drive the car as he felt it was totally unsafe.

left school quite young to settle down to the life of a farmer - and had a natural relaxed charm and honesty which endeared him to anyone who ever met him.

His destiny was farming as he was the only son of James and Helen Clark, who had four daughters before the birth of Jim; his father had two farms, Kerchesters and Edington Mains. After leaving school Jim took over Edington Mains. Any ambitions of owning a fast sports car were quashed by his father who offered him a pedestrian Rover but Jim managed to persuade him to buy a Sunbeam-Talbot instead, which looked a little more sporting. He was soon rallying with the Berwickshire Young Farmers Club and Berwick and District Motor Club where he was befriended by Ian Scott Watson whose enthusiasm was mildly infectious. Scott Watson at the time had a thing about DKW cars and raced a front wheel drive DKW Sonderklasse that he offered to Clark to race for the first time at Crimond.

When Scott Watson bought an early Porsche 1600 Super Jim Clark ran this in hill climbs and sprints and won the very first BMRC Trophy handicap event at Charterhall, his first race win.

The amateur racing team Border Reivers, was reformed and a D type Jaguar, formerly raced by Henry Taylor, was bought for Jim Clark and Jimmy Sommervail to race. Sommervail acknowledged the fact that young

Even Colin Chapman was forced to admit that the original Lotus 40 was not his best design but Jim Clark was one of the few drivers able to make it competitive such as here at the Oulton Park Tourist Trophy race.

Clark had great potential and retired from racing so that Clark could race the car exclusively. He came to the notice of everyone by finishing eighth in his first International sports car race at Spa in 1958. Towards the end of that year, Scott Watson bought one of the early Lotus Elites and Reivers were interested in buying the new Lotus F2. They attended a test day at Brands Hatch where a number of drivers were given tests alongside factory driver Graham Hill. Clark was quick but when a wheel fell off the F2 car with Graham Hill at the wheel, Clark vetoed the plan.

At the Boxing Day Brands Hatch meeting later that year, Clark in the private Lotus Elite faced Colin Chapman and Mike Costin in the works cars and proceeded to lead the race until he had to avoid a spinning Sprite, letting Chapman through to win. Chapman recalled the situation *"I managed to get a good start in the race and I remember thinking that this was it. Then Jimmy came past me in his Elite and I thought: good God what's happening here....so I offered Jimmy a ride. Again he said he was not taking racing seriously as he was having a certain amount of parental discouragement and it was not until a year after that I managed to get him to drive for me; even then it was only on a casual basis. To me, though, getting Jimmy to drive on a casual basis was better than having some other racing driver on a permanent basis."*

In 1959 Reivers changed the Jaguar D-type for a Lister-Jaguar and Clark continued to go on winning. He competed in his first Le Mans that year in the Border Reivers Lotus Elite - this time a new car prepared by Lotus - and was winning the class easily until a starter motor gave trouble. He still finished tenth overall and second in the class. At the Boxing Day Brands Hatch meeting at the end of the year Clark had his first race in a single seater, a Gemini Formula Junior car with an Austin engine. Alongside him on the grid was Alan Stacey in the brand new factory Lotus 18 Junior, as yet unpainted and it was a car to play an important part in his future.

Jim Clark had come to the notice of Reg Parnell, team manager of Aston Martin. They had produced a new grand prix car and at Goodwood in February 1960 they held a testing session with Jim Clark and John Surtees. Prior to a second test at Goodwood, Clark had whispered to Mike Costin at Lotus that this was going to take place and mysteriously a Lotus 18 Junior car turned up whilst Clark was testing the Aston. Chapman naturally asked Parnell if Clark could try the Lotus 18 and so the plot to lure Clark to Lotus had begun. Though Clark actually signed to race the Aston Martin in Grand Prix racing in 1960, the signs were that there would be no car for him to race and Aston were to pull out of Formula 1 after the British GP that year. Clark, who had been persuaded to drive for Lotus in F2 and F Junior that season, was on hand when Colin Chapman could not secure the services of John Surtees for the Dutch GP. Surtees had a conflicting motor cycle grand prix that day so Clark was immediately drafted into the team and from then on he was a Lotus driver. In that race, his first Grand Prix, Clark was up to fifth place when the gearbox broke.

The last time Jim Clark raced a car in Scotland was at the Charterhall meeting at the end of the 1960 racing season when he brought the works Lotus 18 Formula Junior. He nips inside Charlie Harrison's TVR at Lodge Corner.

To give a further indication of how good Clark was, even at this stage of his career, he had gone to Monaco for the first time for the Monaco Formula Junior race with the factory Lotus 18 and lapped the circuit nearly 10 seconds below the existing lap record set up by Michael May in a Stanguellini the previous year. Clark's time in the Formula Junior would have qualified him for the Monaco GP two years before!

A third place at Le Mans, sharing the Border Reivers Aston Martin DBR1 with Roy Salvadori, showed he had not lost his skill as a sports car driver and only Lotus' problems with the Lotus 23 were to stop Clark doing even better at Le Mans.

The only time Jim Clark "raced" at Ingliston was in a "race" sponsored by the Scottish Milk Market-ing board where a group of local milkmen raced their electric milk floats round the track stopping at places around the circuit where they had to pick up a crate of milk bottles. Clark thoroughly enjoyed himself and George Pirie's milk float must now be worth a fortune!

By 1963, his third season in Formula 1, he was world champion and had made his debut at Indianapolis finishing second as a rookie: there is no doubt Indianapolis politics stopped him from being the winner that year. (The leader, Parnelli Jones, was leaking oil causing at least two cars to crash, yet he was not disqualified.) Jim was so angry at this he demanded Chapman enter him for the next round of the Indycar championship on a small one mile oval at Milwaukee where he faced the same drivers as at Indianapolis. Here he not only broke the lap record on almost every lap but lapped everyone in the field, save second place man A J Foyt. He admitted that he could have passed Foyt but felt by sitting right behind him to the end of the race he had made his point clear; that he could beat all the Indianapolis drivers, given a fair chance.

Two years later, in 1965, Clark not only won the grand prix world championship again but also won the Indianapolis 500.

That Clark would have won more grand prix championships is almost certain for in 1968 with the Lotus 49 and a Cosworth engine, he would have been unbeatable. However, Clark agreed to race a Formula 2 Lotus at Hockenheim in 1968 and in miserable conditions. He was running in eighth place, and suffered a slow puncture in a rear tyre. At that time knowledge was limited as to the dynamics of racing tyres which were getting bigger and wider. The tyre suddenly lost all pressure and the car slid sideways across the wet grass into a tree, killing Clark instantly. Today, thanks to measures taken after the Clark accident, the tyre would have been bolted to the rim and there would be barriers to bounce off. In that respect modern grand prix drivers are great deal safer than the drivers in Clark's era.

In the final judgement Jim Clark will be remembered not only for his uncanny skill, speed and tactics but for his versatility. He could drive and race anything and win. He was fascinated by interesting racing cars. Within three laps of stepping into a 1930s supercharged ERA owned by fellow Scot the Honourable Patrick Lindsay, Clark was quicker than the owner. In 1966 he competed in the FIA World Championship RAC Rally in a Lotus Cortina at a time when the Scandinavians were winning everything. He managed to put himself in amongst them and reached sixth place before clipping a rock on the Loch Ard special stage; with a battered and repaired car he continued until the sheer bad handling saw him retire later in the night. Jim Clark was a driver of stellar quality and ranks alongside other champions of other ages like Ascari, Fangio, Stewart, Fittipaldi, Senna and Schumacher.

JOHN CLARK

Born in Edinburgh, John Clark started out in the motor accessory business but clearly had a mission to be in business on his own. Today he has built up a group of garages based in and around Aberdeen and has been able to indulge in his new interest and passion for historic racing.

In the 1980s he bought one of the first Chevron Sports 2000s which he sold to Hugh McCaig as the foundation of the new Ecurie Ecosse team and from time to time raced BMW saloons before devoting more time to historic events.

His favourite cars are his Cooper Bobtail and Cooper 1.5 litre Formula 1 car with which he has had considerable success. With the Bobtail he won the Sports Car event at the Nurburgring in 2002 with Alasdair McCaig.

JOHN CLELAND

John Cleland has been wrapped up in motor sport all of his life. His father, Bill Cleland, was an active member of Lanarkshire Car Club and later Coltness Car Club, and rallied his Mark 1 Ford Zodiac with the kind of abandon his son was to adopt when he came to race cars.

Young John was destined to take over the flourishing garage business he and Bill had created and so was despatched to Coventry to serve an apprenticeship with Standard-Triumph. Whilst there he ran in a number of rallies and driving test events with his modest Triumph Herald before returning to Scotland and the family business. His first event in Scotland was in 1972 at an autocross in a Mini. This led to sprints and hill climbs with various Minis and the odd rally with a Morris Oxford. *"The night navigation events were absolutely brilliant and we knocked down a shitload of fences."*

Cleland's first race was at Ingliston with his Cooper Mini which he entered alongside his friend Hugh McKinnon. *"The race, I think, was twelve laps and we did thirteen because we hadn't seen the flag, we were having so much fun. I remember going down the back straight. Hugh and I were hard on it. We passed Andy Barton and Sedric Bell and thought there was something wrong with them. Of course when we arrived at Arena bend they had already opened the gates to let the public to the inside of the track and we nearly killed a hundred spectators: I remember getting a serious bollocking for that! I think I was fourth and Hugh was fifth. Actually I only ever did one race a year because my father would not let me do any more.*

John Cleland's first true racing car was this Chevron B8 seen at Doune Hill Climb. The car was later sold to Stirling Moss

we could continue running. We knew nothing about how they would heat up or how the car would handle and I just went off at the esses. That was my first big learning experience of f.....g up. After that incident I never again put a scratch on that car in all the hill climbs I did. Eventually the engine went to Bob Leckie and the chassis went to London. I have traced the car back to France and one of those days I might run down to France and buy it. I would have liked to have kept it but due to the deal with my father it had to be sold so we could move on. I remember thinking at the time he was a tight old bastard but it was actually a really good discipline. I remember once coming back from a hill climb at Rumster, where we slept in the back of the van. We took a detour over the Kincardine Bridge to get home because I ran out of money and my dad wouldn't pay the toll on the Forth Road Bridge."

By now Bill Cleland had sold his British Leyland dealership at Bogside to the Appleyard group and John worked as a salesman for Appleyard. However, there was no way Bill Cleland could keep out of the motor trade and he was later back in business when he bought a derelict garage in Peebles. John was then fired by Appleyards so he joined his father and the Clelands were back in business, this time with a Colt dealership. As there was no advantage racing a Colt, John went back to rallying in a Colt Lancer. However, everything changed when they took on an Opel franchise. They ran an Opel Kadett in the Scottish hill climb championship and won the road car class. *"Again, I only did one race that year (1976) and that was at Ingliston to help Graham Birrell win the road car championship. They brought some hard nuts over from Ireland to try and beat Graham and I was in there trying to protect him and his Opel."*

This led to Dealer Opel Team in which Bill Cleland was a guiding light and in turn led to the development of Vauxhall's highly successful rally and racing programme. Because of Cleland's success they were able to buy the team Opel Ascona 2000 and talk to the right people. John began in the official Opel team driving Tony Lanfranchi's car and this led to his deeper involvement, one that was to last for most of his competition career.

During his racing he won the Thundersaloons series twice, with Vince Woodman in a Senator, which was an Australian Holden Commodore, and then in a Vauxhall Carlton. *"That was my first proper factory drive where I was paid £500 a round and was the first stage of me becoming a professional driver who turned up with a crash helmet and nothing else. In 1989 I was doing the Thundersaloon championship in the Commodore and the BTCC with the Vauxhall Astra."* That year John became British touring car champion. In 1995 John won the British touring car championship again, this time under the Ecurie Ecosse banner with Hugh McCaig and Ray Mallock.

In 1992, Alan Gow, Peter Brock's manager, gave John the chance to go to Australia and race at Bathurst in one of Peter Brock's Holden Commodores. On every occasion after that he drove Holdens until recent years when he has raced Ford Falcons in Australia. He is the longest serving British driver still competing at Bathurst.

Throughout his career John Cleland has raced cars other than saloons. He had two races with TVR Tuscans and the only time he ever drove single seater racing cars were in hill climbs; Doune, and Prescott. Mike Pilbeam had been doing work on the suspension of the Vauxhalls and had the idea that, as John had started out in hill climbs, it would be an idea to offer him a Pilbeam hill climb car for a bit of publicity. He was entered at Prescott as a second driver to Alistair Douglas Osborne the former hill climb champion. *"I had never been in a single seater in my puff and in my first practice broke the class record. Douglas Osborne went out and went quicker and we kept doing this all through the event; it was brilliant. Pilbeam was so excited he entered me for Doune. Kenny Allan was the kiddie at the time and I kicked Kenny's arse.*

"The deal with my father always was that the old man would buy the car, I would find the money to run it and then I had to return the same money with profit on the race car. He never took money out of the company and he never said ' here's the money son crack on and do it'. "

John's first real racing car was a Chevron B8 his father bought from Tony Charnell for £1400 complete with trailer and spare wheels. Even then, John was still only allowed to do one race with the car - the rest were hill climbs and sprints. *"At the end of the season I sold the car for £2,000 and it eventually ended up in the hands of Stirling Moss. We had to sell the B8 to buy the Chevron B23 formerly raced by John Burton of Red Rose Racing. My father, in his true style, swopped an automatic Reliant Scimitar for the Chevron"*

John's racing inexperience caught up with him when driving this Chevron B23 at an Ingliston test day." *Norrie Galbraith pulled across in front of me at the hairpin and I skiffed the back of the Ginetta which broke a wheel. As we didn't have a spare we put a set of wets on the back so*

Then Kenny got me but he had to pull all the stops out. That was the only single seater I ever drove competitively and I loved it. During my racing it had never occurred to me to try single seaters."

John Cleland brought a breath of fresh air to British motor racing. Not for him the press releases and guarded comments. He was outspoken and a terror of club nights, where he would mercilessly and humorously attack his fellow competitors. At times on the track, however, he could be a bit of a loose canon and had some memorable battles.

However, when all the talk stopped, John Cleland produced the goods and continues to do so.

ANGUS CLYDESDALE
(The Duke of Hamilton.)

Angus Clydesdale was a driver who first came to everyone's attention driving a Lola sports car but as early as 1960 he made his motor racing debut at Charterhall in a Ford Popular! He was a commissioned officer in the Royal Air Force at the time and so had to fit his racing in with his day-to-day work of flying Canberra bombers.

Some time later he moved into historic racing with a Maserati 250F (C/n 2526) which was an interesting car. It was the second of the 250Fs with offset transmission to bring the driver lower in the body and had been raced in the Italian GP by Jean Behra. When he stopped racing, the car was sold to Bobby Bell of Bell & Colvill and finally ended up in the Schlumph collection in France.

Within the past years Angus has been back at the wheel setting up high-speed endurance records for diesel engined cars at Millbrook with Audi and Skoda models.

Today he runs a company in the South of England building specialised vehicles.

Angus Clydesdale at the wheel of his Maserati 250F which he brought to Ingliston.

ALASTAIR CORMACK

Alastair Cormack was an extremely shy and modest man who was not only well known as a racing driver but as a pilot in the years before the War.

He was born into the family owners of the Cormack Shipping Line in Leith that traded mainly with Russia and Latvia. Despite the fact they lost a large number of their ships during the first World War, business was strong in the 1930s but during the second World War they again lost more ships, the Russian trade virtually collapsed and the company was wound up.

Remembering his father, son Sandy Cormack remarks *"He was very reticent to talk about his racing or his flying but occasionally he would reveal small bits to my brother David and I, like landing a Liberator at Prestwick airport with no engines as his co-pilot had made a mistake.*

"Dad was fortunate in that the Cormack shipping line provided a fair bit if money for the Cormack family and therefore he was able to afford to practice his hobby, which was cars. He got into flying the same way and had his own aeroplane. Indeed when the War started the RAF had an act passed in Parliament whereby all private aircraft were taken over by the government and so they commandeered dad's aeroplane. During the War he became a test pilot for the Ministry of Aviation and Production and things developed from then. He became the first British pilot to be cleared to fly American aircraft, Bostons, Liberators and Flying Fortresses. As he was too old for combat flying he set up the training scheme to teach British pilots how to fly the American planes."

Alastair Cormack's motor sport began in 1933 on the sands at Kirkcaldy where he won the event outright with a Speed 20 Rover Meteor Coupe.

Cormack made his first sortie abroad in 1933 with his friend Harry Jardine-Stuart on the Austrian Alpine Trial and they won the Austrian Alps Trophy as the furthest travelled competitors. Years later Jardine-Stuart was a key figure in the Scottish Sporting Car Club and was starter for the Rest and Be Thankful hill climb.

In 1934 Alastair Cormack bought an 1100cc supercharged Alta with the Edinburgh registration number FS 8673 and broke the 1100cc Mountain record. This proved to be an exciting experience as it was set up at Brooklands as a single record attempt. They were delayed and it began to get dark. Alastair was not achieving the appropriate lap times so "Griff" Griffiths, the Alta works manager who was standing at one of the key corners with a torch, decided to move his position forward. Then a few laps later moved forward again so that Cormack did not realise his braking point was getting less and less. Only afterwards was it discovered that Geoffrey Taylor had been doing the same thing at another of the corners so it must have been an exciting run for Alastair. In that same year Alastair entered for the famous Klausen hill climb and as usual he was meticulous in his preparation. His drawing of the climb and notes as to the road surface, which seemed to switch from tarmac to concrete, are still in the family archives. Amongst his fellow competitors was future Auto Union driver Ernst von Delius in a Zoller car and Hugh Hamilton with an MG Magnette. The full Mercedes Benz and Auto Union teams competed in the same event. Cormack ended up third in the 1100cc class behind Hugh Hamilton and the factory Austin 7 racer of Ernst Burgaller.

Cormack raced at many circuits including Dieppe in 1935 and in October 1935 he broke Prince Bira's Brooklands lap record with the Alta. He then became a factory driver for Alta in the 1936 season. Cormack also had his own racing car transporter built and amongst his correspondence is an invoice from Henry Alexander, the Edinburgh Ford dealers, dated March 1935 reading:*"Fordson forward control chassis with engine £250 One van body to carry a motor car with a rear ramp"*. He was also meticulous with his preparation reflected in a letter he wrote to the competitions manager of the Anglo American Oil Company - later called Esso.

Dear Sir
You may have noticed in the Circuit of Dieppe in 1935 I was a non-starter entirely attributable to the fuel supplied to me by your associated company in France. I was running on an NG2 and tuned this car on the track before leaving here. I had six laps in practice and the car ran exceedingly well and was one of the fastest cars there. As soon as the French fuel, which I understand was made up from your formula, was introduced it started burning out plugs. At first I suspected fuel starvation so cleaned out the whole system finding nothing wrong. Eventually by going up in mixture strength from a weaker strength of RN4 to a stronger mixture of RN7 and filing down the needle the mixture was nearly correct. However the fuel consumption had increased to such an extent my fuel supply system could not handle the extra necessary and therefore I was obliged to scratch. To make sure the fuel was to blame, immediately I returned to this country I took the car down to the track I put in two cans and tried the car at its normal mixture strength. The car functioned perfectly. As this occurrence has put me to considerable trouble and expense all for nothing I shall be glad to know what steps you are proposing to take to ensure that this will not occur again. It is possible I will be be leaving this country on Monday for the Grossglockner hill climb in Austria and I have already entered for the Coppa Acerbo in Italy.

Yours faithfully.

Reply from C Walton of the Anglo American Oil Company :

We regret to note your problems but we are bound to say, however,. the alcohol in France was to a different specification due to their laws. Another driver congratulated us on the excellent performance of the fuel NG2 4BIS used by him . We cannot guarantee mixtures.

One of Cormack's most interesting races was the 1936 Prince Ranier Cup. This was the first running of the event that was for Voiturettes and was the support race for the Monaco Grand Prix. It was also Alta's first continental entry and Alastair Cormack was the driver. In this race Cormack was faced with many of the great racing drivers of the day like Luigi Villoresi and Prince Bira .There were six ERAs entered and no fewer than nine Maseratis including the prototype 6CM entered for Gino Rovere. (A car which ended up in Scotland with Ray Fielding.)

Later, with the supercharged 1500cc Alta Cormack, tied as fastest 1.5 litre driver at the Brighton Speed Trials.

After the war Alastair Cormack became involved with Scottish Aviation, which opened up commercial flying in Scotland using converted Liberator bombers. Cormack was invaluable to the new company as he not only had a first class pilot's licence but a navigators and engineers licence also. This was particularly useful when Scottish Aviation had special flights, such as when they tried out their first Prestwick - New York flight, on which Cormack was the navigator. It meant that if a pilot became tired Alastair could take over!

His father-in-law was James Ross whose family had a successful car dealership in Edinburgh and he was asked to come over to Edinburgh and literally take over the business which he not only did but developed it into one of the major Rootes distributors in Scotland. He later became President of the Scottish Motor Trade Association. He was not totally finished with motor sport because he began rallying Sunbeam Talbots in events like the Scottish Rally. Also, he was a friend of David Murray of Ecurie Ecosse. When the Ecurie Ecosse Association commissioned the building of the famous Ecurie Ecosse transporter, Alastair Cormack gifted the Commer chassis to the team.

Of Alastair Cormack's two sons Sandy was the one who followed in his father's footsteps in a modest way racing a much-modified Hillman Avenger at Ingliston. He was also instrumental in David Murray's decision to use Hillman Imp engines in the Ecosse-Imp Formula 3 cars.

DAVID COULTHARD

David Coulthard was born on March 27 1971 in Dumfries. His father, Duncan, was partner in a thriving contracting business - Haydon-Coulthard - and their trucks were active all over the country. Another product of the karting school, David started in karts at the age of 11. He and Allan McNish raced together and like McNish he joined up with David Leslie Senior to run a Van Diemen-Scholar RF89 in Formula Ford with backing from Eternit and his father's business. Right from the start he raced in the National championships starting, in 1989 with the Dunlop Star of Tomorrow and P & O European Ferries series where he became the season's sensation. Though he had many tussles with Kelvin Burt, by June, Paul Lawrence in Autosport, reporting on a round at Mallory Park, concluded. "....a race that proved beyond doubt that Coulthard can win from behind as well as in front." Both Coulthard and Burt were excluded after a wheel banging incident at Donington but by August Coulthard had virtually confirmed the Dunlop title. The next month David Leslie entered him for the main Esso Senior British championship round at Oulton Park where he qualified third fastest and took second place overall; the head hunters started to move in with offers of Formula Three and 3000.

As a mature 18 year old he commented at the end of the season." The Leslie family definitely helped with impressing sponsors. If you don't do these things professionally, you aren't going to be as successful as you possibly can be." Coulthard was named British Club driver of the year at the Autosport Awards which saw him win a Formula Three test as well as a drive in one of Ron Dennis' McLaren grand prix cars. Little were we to know this first link with Ron Dennis was to lead to his main grand prix drives in the future.

One of the people impressed by Coulthard was Jackie Stewart - who never hesitates to wave the Scottish flag - so it was no surprise when David was brought into the Paul Stewart Racing team of Formula Vauxhall Lotuses in 1990 with sponsorship from Camel. His team-mate was Gil de Ferran and in the opening round at Donington Coulthard took an impressive second place to Vincenzo Sospiri. He then won the second round at Silverstone. In the European series he was less successful trailing in fourth place behind the leader Rubens Barrichello. He returned to Scotland for the Knockhill round but was out of luck retiring in the race. Indeed it was very much an up and down season which saw him end up fourth in the championship

behind Sospiri, his team mate de Ferran and Kurt Luby. During that season David also raced a factory Vauxhall Cavalier in the British Touring Car Championship a few times.

As promised, Coulthard was given a test in the McLaren Honda V10 grand prix car at Silverstone in December: this after just one season of Junior Formula Ford and one in Vauxhall Lotus. A special seat was made for him as Jonathan Palmer's seat was too close to the steering wheel and Gerhard Berger's seat was too far away. Silverstone was damp and Coulthard wisely took things easy. Afterwards he commented *"it shows amazing trust from them! How can I thank Ron Dennis? It was nice to come here and see a McLaren with 'Coulthard' on the side..........hopefully, in a few years, my name will be there again"*. It was.

At the end of the season he sat down with Paul and Jackie Stewart and it was decided he would move into the PSR Formula 3 team for the 1991 racing season driving a Ralt. Tom Farmer of Kwik-Fit in Edinburgh rallied to the cause and was one of PSR's sponsors that year, a rare occurrence for a Scottish company at that level of racing. Later, Highland Spring the mineral water company were also to help sponsor Coulthard.

Despite the fact the Reynard was clearly the chassis to have in Formula 3 that year, Coulthard challenged the early championship leader Rikard Rydell and, with Rubens Barrichello, those three proved to be the ones to beat.

When he won the Marlboro Masters at Zandvoort he was promised an F3000 test drive but his efforts in the British F3 Championship literally fell apart. He went off on the first corner at Donington, letting Barrichello win and then at the final round at Thruxton he clashed with Hideki Noda and had to retire. This allowed Barrichello to become Champion with Coulthard second.

For 1992 the PSR Formula 3000 team had an all Scottish lineup, both Paul Stewart and David Coulthard moved into the Formula. Coulthard's first race in 3000 was not exactly a great success. Indeed he had a bitter sweet incident at the end of qualifying when a snap rain shower spun him off the road and on to the Silverstone mud. He ended up with his car alongside Allan McNish in another 3000 who had done exactly the same

During his season with Paul Stewart Racing in Formula Vauxhall Lotus, David Coulthard came back to Scotland to race at Knockhill with the Camel sponsored car.

thing. Relegated to the back of the grid by the incident, Coulthard was faced with a struggle but he fought back to seventh, passing his team-mate Paul Stewart on the way. A lot of the problem centred round the Judd engine which was only to show its potential later in the season when David mopped up two third places to end ninth in the championship.

On David's departure from the team he and his father, Duncan, were able to get a Reynard drive with Mike Earle's Pacific Racing in 1993. Again, the season started out badly with an engine evacuating all its oil but in the next round at Silverstone he climbed from ninth place to fifth on the first lap. He then had to deal with his former boss, Paul Stewart, and, after a cat and mouse affair that saw Paul bobble it on a corner, Coulthard moved into third. A win at Enna saw him take third place in the F3000 Championship. That year also brought a diversion for him when he received a telephone call from Tom Walkinshaw offering him a drive at Le Mans. The car he was offered was not an XJR but one of the three XJ220s running in the GT class. His fellow drivers were Dane John Nielsen and Australian David Brabham. He had the satisfaction of winning the GT class despite the car spending an hour in the pits. *"He's very inexperienced but he's learning all the time and he's doing a really good job "* said David Brabham of his team mate. New and satisfying though the experience was, his aim was to get into Formula 1. During the year he had been doing occasional testing for Williams and for 1994 had a full testing contract with them, which at least got him into the grand prix milieu. His elevation to the actual team came about, however, in tragic circumstances. Because his Williams contract was only for testing he fished around for a drive in F3000 and found a place with Vortex and on May 2 1994 he finished second to Frank Lagorce in the opening round at Silverstone. It was also his last F3000 race for, on the previous day, Ayrton Senna was killed at the San Marino Grand Prix at Imola. Ten days later David Coulthard was given Ayrton Senna's seat alongside Damon Hill in the Williams team. It was not a full contract, as he was displaced by Nigel Mansell in four grand prix races, but he was a full member of the team for the 1995 season. At one of the grand prix races towards the end of the season when sidelined by Nigel Mansell, Ron Dennis and he had a long conversation. As a result David was invited to join McLaren Mercedes where he has remained until the end of 2004.

David Coulthard's first grand prix win was in the Portuguese Grand Prix in 1995 where he headed both Michael Schumacher (Benetton) and Damon Hill (Williams). Since then he has won thirteen grand prix races, but in many ways has always been in the shadow of his two main Finnish team-mates Mika Hakkinen and Kimi Raikkonen. On his day, and with the car running well, David Coulthard is world championship material and came close to his goal with McLaren.

ANDREW COWAN

To most people, Andrew Cowan is a rally driver, two-time winner of the London-Sydney Marathon and factory driver for Rootes and Ford amongst others. Born in Duns on December 13 1936, Andrew is another pupil of the Berwick and District Motor Club school of motor sport personalities. A farmer, like his near neighbour and friend Jim Clark, he farmed Blackadder West and at weekends rallied first a Volkswagen Beetle with his brother Willie and then a Sunbeam Rapier.

Andrew first raced his Sunbeam Rapier at Charterhall and Ian Scott Watson gave him

his road-going Lotus Elan to race at the first ever race meeting at Ingliston where Andrew finished fourth. This was not the end of Andrew's racing, however, as David Murray of Ecurie Ecosse entered him for a number of races in the Ecurie Ecosse Tojeiro-Buick but his heart was still in rallying.

By 1966 Jim Clark was well established at Lotus and, impressed with Andrew's driving, persuaded Colin Chapman that Andrew should be given a test drive in a Formula 3 Lotus. Such was the power of Jim Clark's hold over Colin Chapman, the cheeky chappie agreed and the next thing Andrew knew he was at the wheel of a Lotus. *"This is one aspect of Jimmy Clark which is not generally known, and that is the influence he had in setting up trial drives for people and genuinely trying to help his friends if he thought they had a chance in racing"* said Cowan at the time. (Clark was to do exactly the same for Jackie Stewart when he persuaded Chapman to let Stewart drive a grand prix car for the first time.)

Despite *"driving over a field of winter wheat and diving into a ploughed field"* in the test, Chapman offered Cowan a race. It is amusing to think that on both occasions he raced a factory Lotus in Formula Formula 3 car he was entered as A N Other and nobody appeared to bother to ask the real name of the driver!

I remember, after his second race, Andrew telling me that he missed a gear leaving the start at Goodwood and half the field passed him into the first corner. He felt racing was not for him - *"I was honestly petrified and not the slightest bit relaxed"* - and though Colin was quite keen to let him continue, Andrew drew a line under it. There was an amusing follow up to this when Colin asked Andrew at the motor show in 1960 if he would like to race a Formula 5000 Lotus the following year. They both had a laugh about this.

Today Andrew Cowan is the successful director of motorsport for Mitsubishi in Europe and has a string of world championships to his belt.

JIM CRAWFORD

Jim Crawford was a Fifer born in Dunfermline in February 1948. He later moved to Bolton in Lancashire and his accent became more Bolton than Dunfermline. He got into motor racing in 1973 when he became mechanic for his friend Steve Choularton. Choularton had bought a new March 73B for the Formula Atlantic series that year. As a reward for all the work he had done on the car, Steve gave him a drive at Croft and he promptly went out and won the libre race, breaking the outright circuit record. Thus was born Jim Crawford the racing driver. A few weeks later in the actual Championship event held at Croft David Purley set up fastest lap but was not as quick as Crawford who won the race.

Neil Edwards, who had worked with Chevron, took Jim to a local pub in Bolton where he knew Derek Bennett of Chevron would hang out. They ambushed Bennett and, rather than commit himself, Derek suggested that Jim come to a test session at Aintree. Such was his performance that, in the pub after the test session Bennett offered him the factory Atlantic Chevron for the rest of the season. The next day Jim turned up at Chevron. Derek Bennett didn't even recognise him, then the penny dropped and he handed Jim Crawford a suspension unit from a B25 and said *"Make yourself a car."*

Some of the bits for this car came from the wreckage of Gerry Birrell's Chevron in which he had his fatal accident at Rouen. Jim was loaned the works engine by Race Engine Services and Jim raced it for the first time in a libre event at Aintree to see that it worked: he won.

His first official race in the Atlantic championship was at Oulton Park near the end of the season and set off from the start leaving the rest for dead. He broke the lap record and then, near the end, John Nicholson in the Lyncar passed him. Derek Bennett was never one to show his feelings and when Jim handed the car back to him at the end of the season, nothing was said. Obviously miffed, Jim, with the help of his friend Steve Choularton built up a second March 73B for the 1974 season. This led to an amusing incident at a general test session when Jim met up with Derek Bennett again. Puzzled, he asked Bennett why he had not offered him a Chevron for that season and was completely floored when Bennett replied *"Why didn't you ask for one ?"*.

To make life complete, Jim Crawford was offered a testing contract with the Lotus Formula 1 team. He was also offered his first Formula 2 drive with Team Harper in a Chevron B27 BMW at Nogaro and finished fifth. The man who finished fourth in that race was French newcomer Rene Arnoux and Crawford was not impressed when he heard that Arnoux had also been offered a Lotus testing contract. Jim Crawford ended the year as BP Superman of the Year.

Despite having only raced for a year, Crawford was now in the thick of things. He had a factory supported Chevron B29 for 1975 season and again finished second in the Atlantic championship but was given two grand prix races in the Lotus 72E in the British and Italian GPs.

On his F1 debut at Silverstone he spun off in the rain and then at Monza he finished down the field. His racing career now stalled and we only saw him at his best in the Aurora AFX championship in 1980 when he won the F2 class with a Chevron.

By 1982 he had decided to go to the United States and see what he could do over there. He immediately became successful in the SCCA sports car series, finishing second in the championship in both 1983 and 1984 before moving into Indy car racing.

There are two lovely stories told about Crawford when he went to the USA with a March-DFV Can-Am car. He read the Can-Am rules closely and saw it was mandatory to have two fuel stops. He realised the March could do the race on one tank of fuel so he set up his pit alongside the start and finish line. After his first pit stop he was in the lead but knew the American V8s would soon overtake him. He pressed on whilst the US cars made their second stop and then on the last lap he dashed into the pits, took on a couple of litres of fuel then drove out across the line which was alongside his pit. He claimed that the finish line was a line extending not only across the circuit but the entire racing area including the pit lane. Paul Newman, whose Lola looked destined to win, protested but the protest was finally thrown out and it is alleged that Newman got his name in the papers by throwing a punch at Jim Crawford. It made Crawford's name in the States and helped him establish himself.

The other story concerns Crawford and his team manager going into a bar in Dallas, Texas, to discuss plans for Indycar racing. At the bar they befriended four guys in Stetsons and plaid shirts and a discussion started about racing Indycars. One of the four said to Jim *"Hey, what would it cost to run at Indy?"*. When Jim told them, he got very excited and said *"Hey, guys, that's just a million dollars each."* and three of them wrote cheques for a million dollars each and handed them to Crawford. The fourth one was clearly embarrassed and said that he didn't have his chequebook with him but gave Jim a million dollar cheque the very next day!

The Indianapolis 500 was Crawford's favourite race and he made his debut there in 1984 but didn't qualify. His best result was sixth in 1988 driving Kenny Bernstein's Lola-Buick. Jim continued to run at Indianapolis into the 1990s and qualified every year until his last two attempts in 1994 and 1995 when he sadly did not qualify. He was the last Scot to race at Indianapolis until Dario Franchitti in 2002. He retired from racing to run a fishing boat and died at the early age of 54 in August 2002.

NICOLL CUTHBERT

Nicoll Cuthbert's introduction to motor sporting madness came during his schooldays at Edinburgh Academy where his fellow MG Car Club member friends were John Milne and George Gibson. The fact that George's father owned the MG dealership in Edinburgh meant that Milne and Gibson had brand new MG TDs but were then banned from bringing them to school for doing hand brake turns and spraying the masters' cars!

Nicoll was less fortunate, but his father bought him a 1934 supercharged MG Magnette that promptly blew its supercharger to bits on the Queensferry Road in Edinburgh. John Brown at Eastern Motors helped get the car repaired but it was later traded for a used Healey Silverstone.

In between MG Car Club events he raced the Healey at Crimond, Winfield and Turnberry against Jimmy Stewart. *"The trouble was that we couldn't touch Jimmy on the track and were told later his Riley engine had been tweeked up by Freddy Dixon the great Riley racing driver and expert."* (Jimmy Stewart finds this remark hysterically funny as he prepared his own car)

When Nicoll married Mary, he gave up racing but in 1965 was persuaded to return but this time as an entrant. He bought Trevor Twaites' Lotus Elan for Bill Dryden to drive but realised it was not competitive. He sold it and bought a new lightweight competition Elan which Dryden raced successfully at Ingliston and elsewhere. He later sold the car to his brother Norman Cuthbert who went on to have more success with the car in England.

Then came the moment he visited the Paris Motor Show and saw the Ford GT40 for the first time. *"I just had a rush of blood to the head and fell in love with the car on the spot."*. He ordered one (Chassis P/1022, now in the USA) and it was delivered to the family construction company. Nicoll asked Eric Liddell to race the car and it was Eric's big break in International racing. He had two good seasons with the car. At the BOAC 500 event at Brands Hatch in 1966 Eric shared it with Peter Sutcliffe and in 1967 he shared it with Peter Gethin. However, around this time, Nicoll was being chivvied by the Portuguese driver Carlos Gaspar to sell him the GT 40. Eventually he got his way and the Ford went off to Portugal.

Cuthbert was then approached by the rugged Australian Paul Hawkins. It was agreed that Nicoll would buy a new Lola T70 (Chassis SL76/142) and form a team with Jackie Epstein and Paul Hawkins. The arrangement was that Epstein and Hawkins would run the car in the same colour scheme Nicoll had used for the Ford, red with a white stripe up the centre, and Nicoll would take a back seat. Through his friendship with George Heaney of Terex in Glasgow, the GM subsidiary, Nicoll was able to order two spare Traco engines as the plan was to do Le Mans. Sadly, Paul Hawkins was killed in the car at Oulton Park and it was totally destroyed.

Not only was this a tragic thing to happen but Nicoll found the car had not been insured and so he lost everything save his transporter and the two spare engines. What riles him to this day is the fact that there are now two Lolas running with his chassis number and yet he had instructed, after the Oulton Park accident, the remains of his car were to be cut up and buried.

Nicoll explains what happened next. *"Jackie Epstein suggested that a joint venture be formed between Lola - who would supply a T142 F5000 chassis, mechanic, workshop space etc.- and ourselves. I would supply the two engines, which were modified to suit, and Mike Hailwood would drive for the rest of the season. Mike only won one race but we finished third in the Championship due to Mike's liking for the T142. However, in 1970 the partnership ceased due to the fact that both engines were destroyed and I lost interest - not to mention money."*

RYAN DALZIEL

Ryan, born in Lanarkshire, graduated to motor racing from karting and won a number of championships as a teenager. He was 1998 British Winter Series karting champion before moving into the Formula Vauxhall championship in 1999 where he scored three wins and was a finalist in the McLaren Autosport Young Driver Award. After a toe-dipping season in Scottish racing, Ryan won the Ecurie Ecosse Trophy for the most impressive young Scottish driver of the year.

Dalziel chose the British Formula Renault Championship in 2000. He finished second behind a promising Finnish newcomer called Kimi Raikkonen. Ryan then raced in the British F3 championship in 2001 but had a middling time of it, missing four rounds of the championship. His best outing saw fourth place in the British GP F3 support race.

Ryan decided to move to the United States and try his luck in the Toyota Formula Atlantic Championship in 2002. He was offered a seat with Michael Shank racing and on his debut took second place in Mexico and had a further six top ten finishes. His car was a Swift 014A. Towards the end of the season, when lying in fifth place in the Rookie of the Year standings, he switched teams to Hylton Motorsports for the last two races of the season at Montreal (3rd) and Denver Colorado (2nd).

For 2003 he stayed in the Toyota Atlantic Championship, joining the Sierra Enterprises team where he won twice and ended as runner-up in the Championship. This led to him testing for Walker Racing in December of that year in a Champ Car which led to him signing for the team in 2004. The owner of the team, Derrick Walker, is himself a Scot from Leven in Fife. He formed his Champ car team in 1989 after working with Penske Racing.

NORMAN DICKSON

It was no surprise when Tommy Dickson's son Norman came into motor racing. It was a modest beginning with a Hillman Imp at Ingliston in 1973. In 1974,however, he moved into Formula Ford and became Scottish Champion. Moving up a scale he then raced a March 752 in the Scottish Formula Libre Championship which he also won.

Norman spread his wings in 1976 with a Formula Atlantic Modus running in the British Aurora Championship. He won the Atlantic class and also competed at Ingliston.

In 1977, with backing from British Caledonian Airways, he went into Formula 2 with a March 772. By now his father had developed Gleneagle Helicopters and they were one of the major sponsors. With very little experience, but with the loyal support of an ex-Team Lotus mechanic, Colin Bennett, he joined the hardest school of all at that time. It is interesting to look back and see the opposition Dickson had in that first year : Rene Arnoux, Didier Pironi, Clay Reggazoni, Riccardo Patrese, Alan Jones, Keke Rosberg, Jacques Lafitte, Derek Daly and Eddie Cheever. All of them graduated to Formula 1 and two became world champions. It was no surprise that Norman found it tough qualifying that first season.

After a second season in 1978 where he struggled but won the F2 class in the British Aurora Championship and in 1979 with a March 792 as well as the Scottish Championship. For 1980, his last season, he went the whole hog and bought a Lotus 78 from Spanish driver Emilio Villota and took two second and one third place in the British Championship before retiring to prepare to take over his father's business. His son Niki - named after Lauda - also took up motor racing and was well placed in Scottish events during the 2001 racing season.

TOMMY DICKSON

My first sighting of Tommy Dickson came when I was a trainee journalist in the Edinburgh Evening Dispatch. The art editor was a quirky character who had a glass eye and would scrutinise the piles of photos of the days news by pulling each one until it was about an inch from his good eye and then decide which ones he would use. One day I was looking over his shoulder when a photograph of an odd little guy in a leather RAF flying jacket three times too big for him, fell on his desk. It had been sent by a local stringer in Perth with a caption along the lines of *"Scotland's new racing hope "*. The car was the world's oldest Mark IV Cooper-JAP. He went on to bigger and better things including an Erskine Staride 500cc racer, one of the top cars at that time.

Tom suffered from bad eyesight and wore glasses with thick lenses but it never stopped him from being a very fast driver. My favourite story of Tommy was at Oulton Park in the British Empire Trophy when he was running his Hugh Shannon-prepared Lotus Eleven. He finished his heat in

Some of Tommy Dickson's great successes came in a series of Lotus Elevens, here racing in Ireland's Leinster Trophy.

second place behind Graham Hill in the factory Lotus Eleven. Arriving back in the paddock hot and bothered he said to Hugh, *"Who was that guy I was racing against ?"* He could not even recognise it was Hill who was in front of him.

After winning a major trophy at Oulton Park in 1959, now with a Lotus XV, Tommy was approached by David Murray and offered a test with an Ecurie Ecosse D type Jaguar. Tommy's reply was typical *"All right David, it's a comfortable car but it is too old fashioned ; I could go faster than that in my Lotus!"* He slightly fell out with Murray but was persuaded back by Wilkie Wilkinson. As Tommy remarked at the time *"I found it easier to talk to Wilkie than to David."* Wilkie Wilkinson asked Dickson's opinion on what car Ecosse should buy to replace the D types and he told them a Lotus. Again David Murray disagreed with him *"....they break down a lot don't they"*. Murray went out and bought a Cooper Monaco and it was Dickson who drove it. After his first race with the car he said *"....the Monaco was designed as an oversteer special for Roy Salvadori...it was like driving my old Erskine Staride".* Later, when Ecosse did not have the money to buy a 2.5 litre Coventry Climax engine for their first Tojeiro-Climax Coupe it was Tommy Dickson who loaned them the engine. Tommy retired from racing in 1961 to spend more time on his fast developing motor business. As time went by, Dicksons of Perth were big time Mercedes Benz and Saab dealers.

PAUL DI RESTA

Paul is certainly the youngest of the drivers listed but his career in karting from an early age demonstrated that he had absorbed some of his skill and determination of his father, Louis di Resta. In 2003 at the age of 17, he was committed to a full British Formula Renault championship season with Manor Motor Sport. At the end of 2003 he was given a test in Formula Renault by John Village.

Behind the scenes his father, Louis who raced successfully in Formula Ford in Scotland and the south but was handicapped by developing his own business at the time. His enthusiasm has now been switched to Paul and along with uncles, Dario and Marino Franchitti, he has had plenty of advice and shows great promise.

DENYS DOBBIE

Denys Dobbie is the son of a former Edinburgh chartered accountant and clearly the plan was that he should follow in the footsteps of his father. He was also a great motor sport enthusiast and started out in minor driving tests and rallies in a BMW Isetta bubble car and later a Morris Minor. In the midst of cramming for his accountancy exams, he rashly bought Archie Craig's supercharged MG special but kept it hidden from his family and was looking forward to having some fun. However, when larking about with his younger brother, he fell through a plate glass window and severed the nerves in his left wrist . When he was recuperating, David Murray asked him to become the first Secretary of the Ecurie Ecosse Association and he travelled around with the team. Having sold the Supercharged MG Special - the Bongazoo - to Peter Mossman, one of the Ecurie Ecosse mechanics, he had planned to buy a Lotus Eleven with another young enthusiast, Bill Turnbull but this came to nothing.

In 1960 he passed his CA exams, took one look at the standard rates CA apprentices were paid and promptly flew off to Vancouver in Canada where he was offered much more money. He later came back to Scotland, married and had a son, but once more he decided the wages were not good enough

and this time went to Nassau in the Bahamas as an accountant with Peat Marwick Mitchell and Co. He moved on to become a partner in a stock broking firm which he sold out to Slater Walker in 1967. Thus enriched he set up his own trust company with an Australian and as a result was in on the legendary boom in an Australian stock called Poseidon. When he sold out his partnership to a Bahamian bank in 1970 he returned to Scotland in some style with his own Perthshire mansion.

He went on to found DART (Dobbie Automobile Racing Team) with various Chevrons. At the Racing Car Show in 1972 the new GRD 2 litre sports car appeared on the stand finished in dark blue and with DART on the side however he was to pull out of running a racing team. Instead he invested in the fledgling Knockhill Racing Circuit, ensured that the job was done properly and the track was launched in 1975. The economic situation was not wonderful and Dobbie later sold his interest in the track and has had little or nothing to do with motor racing ever since.

BILL DOBSON

Bill Dobson is probably best known as one of the founder team members of Ecurie Ecosse. He had always been interested in cars and bought a BMW 328 from London racing driver John Young. Many years later Young confided that he didn't tell Bill that he had rolled the car in a huge accident but it gave Dobson a lot of success. When David Murray later took over the ex-Peter Whitehead short-wheelbase Ferrari F2 car he offered it to Bill Dobson to race and Dobson had a number of successes. When Bill bought his Jaguar XK120 he was recruited by David Murray, along with Ian Stewart and Sir James Scott Douglas, into the new Ecurie Ecosse team. Dobson was forced to retire from racing at the end of the 1952 season due to the pressures of the family business,

BILL DRYDEN

Though best known as a saloon car driver, particularly with Vauxhalls, Bill Dryden also dabbled in single seaters and then became a backer and sponsor of a number of young Scottish drivers.

Bill's father was a key figure in the Scottish motor trade as managing director of SMT Sales & Service Co. Ltd, the largest Vauxhall dealers in Great Britain at the time. It was clear that Bill and his brother Dennis were destined for the motor trade but whereas Dennis went into regular car sales with SMT's Volkswagen dealership in Glasgow, Bill decided to stick to the commercial vehicle business and Bedfords in particular.

His first race was with a Vauxhall VX 4/90 at the last ever race meeting at Charterhall but when Ingliston started he was prominent in the saloon car classes and became Scottish champion with his Vauxhall Firenza. Drafted into the Dealer Team Vauxhall team he raced all over Britain. Back home his main rival was Douglas Niven with a variety of cars and Graham Birrell with Ford Escorts. Interspersed with this was a drive with John Romanes' Martin-Lotus at Ingliston, Nicoll Cuthbert's Lotus Elan and a few drives in Formula Vee and for Ecurie Ecosse driving the Ecosse-Imp.

His most memorable result, however, was in the Super Stock saloon race at the original Nurburgring which ran alongside the Interseries Race. He was driving his Vauxhall Firenza and had a great battle with German Walter Brun in a BMW CSL Coupe. In the end he finished second to Brun in the Super Stock class.

Eventually business caused him to stop racing and once he formed his own company, SDL, in Falkirk, he was instrumental in helping out not only British rally champion Jimmy McRae with a Vauxhall Chevette but his young son Colin who had just started out in rallying. On the racing side he assisted both Peter Dumbreck and Allan McNish in Formula Vauxhall Lotus. Since selling his business he spends his time on his motorcycles and continuing to follow motor racing.

DAVID DUFFIELD

David Duffield is one of the shy men of Scottish motor racing. Never one to boast about his exploits he was the true working racing driver. In the early days he raced karts and became friendly with another karter, Hugh McCaig. When David wanted to move into Formula Ford he received some support from Royal Court whisky but it was when McCaig took him under his wing that he really began to shine. He moved seamlessly from Formula Ford into the Formula Atlantic Ralt run by one of McCaig's companies, Money Concepts, and became Formula Libre Champion and Ingliston lap record holder. It was only natural that when, in 1984, McCaig reformed Ecurie Ecosse, David Duffield would be one of his drivers and Duffield shared the Ecosse-Ford with Mike Wilds and Ray Mallock at Silverstone. However, at Le Mans he just could not get to grips with driving a 200 mph car in the dark and made a decision to retire from racing. It was typical of David that he would be honest with himself and come to what must have been a tough decision. Everyone who knows him respected him for it. David, however, became one of the Ecosse team members and from then on has put back into motor racing far more than he ever took out of it by helping younger drivers. He briefly came back into racing in the 1970s with a Formula Ford 2000 to show he had not lost his touch but he typically once more moved back into the shadows to help other up and coming drivers.

PETER DUMBRECK

Peter Dumbreck is one of the most modest and unassuming of all of Scotland's international racing drivers. He has had more success, in the various classes in which he has competed, than most and yet he could never be accused of trading on his success. Born in Kirkcaldy, his father was a mushroom farmer who took Peter and his brother on holiday to Majorca one year when Peter was 11 and he tried his hand on the local kart track. He was bitten by the bug and on their return to Fife they looked into the karting scene, went to Crail to watch a meeting and bought a kart. As he explains, he never had any great ambition to become world champion or anything like that but after karting he went down to Donington to take part in the Jim Russell Racing School run by fellow Scot John Kirkpatrick. He won the course and got a drive with the Formula Vauxhall Junior running out winner of the School championship that year. Money was tight so he moved into the new Formula First class and came second in the Winter Series to Darren Turner.

The crunch had arrived: what to do next. With the help of his father and brother and a Trust Fund set up by his grandfather, Peter blew the lot on the Formula Vauxhall Junior championship which he won in 1994. This led to him joining Martin Donnelly's Formula Vauxhall Lotus team for 1995 but this was not a success. At this point Jackie Stewart stepped in and he was brought into the Paul Stewart Racing Formula Vauxhall Lotus team and

proceeded to win ten of his fourteen races becoming FVL Champion. This led to a move with the Stewarts into Formula 3 in 1997 where he finished third in the championship.

Dumbreck then made a shrewd move, he went to Japan and won the Japanese Formula 3 Championship with eight wins out of ten and the Macau Grand Prix. Now he was noticed by Mercedes Benz who signed him for their Le Mans team but they allowed him to go back to Japan and run in the Formula Nippon championship. At Le Mans that year he and Mark Webber both had flying incidents, Dumbreck lucky to be unhurt in a horrifying accident which threw his Mercedes into the trees. Mercedes, however, stuck with him for one of their DTM teams in 2000 before joining the main factory team where he was to finish third in the Championship in 2001, behind his team mate Bernt Schneider.

For 2002 he was moved to the Persson team and raced a year-old car which brought him no success. As a result Peter signed for the factory Opel team for the 2003 season and became the only Opel driver to seriously challenge the dominant Mercedes team. As a result he signed a full contract with Opel for the 2004 championship.

THE EARL OF ELGIN & KINCARDINE.

Andrew Bruce, the Earl of Elgin, can trace his family roots directly back to King Robert the Bruce. Another ancestor brought the famous "Elgin Marbles" from Greece to Britain.

Throughout his life he has been enthusiastic about cars and became Pesident of the Royal Scottish Automobile Club. In the 1950s he competed in a number of rallies with his Triumph TR2 painted in the mustard yellow family colours. With the development of Ecurie Ecosse he became President of the Ecurie Ecosse Association and was the driving force behind the formation of Friends of Scotland, surely one of the first groups put together to raise sponsorship for the team. When the Association was wound up in the 1970s he became custodian of the title "Ecurie Ecosse" until it was passed on to Hugh McCaig in 1983.

In the 1960s Lord Bruce, as he was then, headed up at least three developments aimed at creating a new motor racing circuit in Scotland, including one in the grounds of his family seat at Broomhall near Dunfermline.

RAYMOND FIELDING

Ray Fielding was one of the leading British Hill Climb championship drivers in the 1950s and 1960s.

His first racing car was a Bugatti but for the 1953 season he bought the HWM that had been raced by John Brown in various sports car events. However, with the birth of his daughter, he decided to forsake circuit racing for hill climbs and had an impressive array of cars that he normally shared with his wife Doreen.

Ray's father-in-law was Peter S Nicholson who opened a garage business in Forres near Inverness and built up a successful British Leyland franchise. Ray took over the running of the company and expanded it taking in Citroen, BMW and, at one time, was Maserati distributor for Scotland. He had a good service team around him and became heavily involved in the historic racing car scene which brought him back to the circuits.

It was Ray who not only restored some of the many cars owned by Lord Doune - later the Earl of Moray - but built up an admirable collection of his own. He had at least three interesting Maserati racing cars. One of them was the interim A6G/250F with the cigar shaped body raced by Harry Schell. He also bought a pre-war Maserati and a rare Maserati-Milan based on the Maserati 4CLT. During his hill climb days he and his wife Doreen used to share the cars in hill climbs all over Britain. Amongst those cars were a Bobtail Cooper-Climax, an HWM-Jaguar, an HWM-Alta and even a BRM grand prix car. Once he had given up hill climbing, he and his friend Martin Grant-Peterkin went historic motor racing with the Maseratis and also the 1929 grand prix Maserati owned by Lord Doune. He later took up sailing and died in the early 1990s after a long illness.

GREGOR FISKEN

Born and brought up in Forfar Gregor Fisken moved to London and started up his very successful business selling classic sports and racing cars. In order to promote the business he started racing historic cars and was notably successful with a Cooper Bristol. He later went on to race cars for a number of people and is a regular competitor in historic meetings around the world. Two years ago he also moved into modern cars and raced a Porsche at Sebring and Nurburgring.

ANDREW MANSEL TALBOT FLETCHER

It is safe to say that Andrew Fletcher was Scotland's first-ever serious racing driver as the records show he was a regular competitor as early as 1903. One of his forebears was a famous Scot, Andrew Fletcher of Saltoun, who figured large in Scottish history at the time of the Union of Scotland and England in the 17th century.

Andrew Fletcher was an enthusiastic pioneer motorist, friend of the Hon. Charles Rolls and indeed a photo exists of Fletcher at the wheel of Rolls' Mors racing car at the Southport Speed Trials of 1903. Fletcher would arrive at events not only in Britain but in Europe with his chauffeur/mechanic John Henry Parrott. Later Parrott decided he did not want to be a chauffeur any longer, stole one of Fletcher's cars and sold it to a dealer in London. He used the money to buy two tickets to New York with his girl friend. The dastardly deed was discovered and Parrott was arrested when the boat docked and sent back to London where he was put in jail!

Andrew Fletcher had considerable wealth and as his grandson, also Andrew Fletcher, remarks. *"...grandfather, in that era of 1904 and 1905 had no idea what the word business meant. He only knew what the words playboy, shooting, fishing, gambling, drinking and womanising meant. Then he saw his friend Rolls was moving into aeroplanes so grandfather turned to his man and said ' go to France and buy some aeroplanes'. He came back with six Bleriots which were imported into England and I can find no record of what actually happened to them."*

Andrew Fletcher certainly was a character and a newspaper report in 1903 recorded *"...Mr Andrew Fletcher of Saltoun Hall, was fined £10 and costs for driving a 60 hp racing car on the Great North Road at Retford at an excessive speed.....an innkeeper on the road said that between thirty and forty cars passed his inn daily but he had never seen anything go so fast, not even a railway train!"*

Bearing in mind the state of roads in those days, Andrew Fletcher raced all over Europe including Germany and the Circuit of the Ardennes in Belgium. He was sixth at the La Turbie hill climb and was clearly well known to the Mercedes factory because a report appeared in one of the motoring magazines to say *"We have it on the authority of Mr Jellinek (Mercedes director whose daughter Mercedes gave the marque its name.) that Mercedes cars will not be entering officially for the Circuit des Ardennes. It is probable that the 90 hp Mercedes of Mr Andrew Fletcher of the Life Guards, will be the only Mercedes driven in this race."*

ANDREW D T FLETCHER

Andrew Fletcher is a gifted amateur driver who raced mainly Brabham and Chevron cars in the late 1960s and early 1970s. Andrew Mansel Talbot Fletcher, above, was his grandfather.

Andrew has his own small collection of interesting cars including an Alfa Romeo Tipo 33, one of the first private Alta Formula 2 cars and the Chevron B16 he used to race.

He was brought up on a farm in Fife before moving to part of the former family estate at East Saltoun in East Lothian where there is a fountain to commemorate one of his notable ancestors.

As his father had been killed during the war, his mother was the guiding light in his life and it was she who later encouraged him to race. His first introduction to racing came from the Templeton brothers, neighbouring farmers in Fife, who were speedway riders. Doug Templeton was Captain of the Glasgow Tigers speedway team and so was something of a legend at the time. The brothers built their own dirt track on the farm and used to practice there, watched by Andrew and his best friend. Later they offered Andrew a bike to try out and his mother offered to buy him a bike to race but Andrew decided he would rather wait and race cars. The first of these was an aged Gemini with which he never shone.

He was one of the first drivers to race at Ingliston and had some good results with various Brabhams. In an F2 race at Snetterton in 1966 he was involved in an accident, when John Hine swerved to avoid Jackie Stewarts slow starting car, and pulled all the tendons in one hand. He then moved into sports cars and had much more success in 2 litre sports car racing not only in his own Chevrons but with his friend Nigel Morrison in a Chevron B8. Andrew later bought Paul Hawkins' Ford GT40 (Chassis P/1019) and bravely took it up Doune Hill Climb but it was sold on to a Belgian driver. Today he occasionally appears at historic events with his Frazer Nash Le Mans Replica (Chassis : 21/100/127) that had originally been raced by Roy Salvadori. Later, in 1953, the car came to Scotland and was raced by Peter Kenneth from Argyll. Kenneth then sold the car to Andrew Fletcher so that it has been in Scotland for the past fifty years.

RON FLOCKHART

In contemporary terms, Ron Flockhart would be the Martin Brundle of his day, a fast, thoughtful racing driver who was more successful in sports cars than he ever was in grand prix cars. He was an all-rounder and even competed in the Monte Carlo Rally one year in a Ford Pilot with his long time friend, and early racing partner, Alastair Birrell and fellow Scottish racing driver Ian Stewart. Had he not been killed in a flying accident in 1962, he would have been 81 years of age today (2004) and able to look back on a motor racing career that had its successes and great disappointments.

He might, for instance, have regretted the fact he spent so much time at BRM trying to sort out the problems associated with that original V16 engined car, or the fact that he chose not to join David Murray when Ecurie Ecosse originally started. But at the same time he would have relished his two victories in successive years at Le Mans, 1956 and 1957. Also he was one of the three *"Tartan Musketeers"* at the French Grand Prix at Reims in 1960 when Colin Chapman's three factory Lotus 18s were raced by three Scots, Jim Clark, Ron Flockhart and Innes Ireland finishing fifth, sixth and seventh.

Ron Flockhart was born on June 16 1923 in Edinburgh. His parents sent him to Daniel Stewarts College where he was sufficiently bright to pass his *"Highers"* and move on to Edinburgh University in 1940 where he studied engineering. As there was a war on, Ron had thoughts of becoming a pilot and at one time wanted to leave his studies and join the Royal Air Force but his parents dissuaded him. However, he was one of the students who helped form the Edinburgh University Flying Club; which didn't actually do any flying because of the war!

In those days there was an active *"Home Guard"* and Ron decided to do his bit by becoming a motor cycle despatch rider though, to be frank, there was very little German activity over Edinburgh so he must have had a relatively quiet time. By 1943 he had his BSc in Engineering and changed his mind about the Air Force as his skills might have kept him on the ground rather than in the air. So he joined the Royal Electrical and Mechanical Engineers. Before he knew it, he was up to his ears in the war during the Italian campaign where he spent his time dodging land mines and booby traps. There was one happy element about the Italian sojurn. He and some of his soldier buddies came to an arrangement, which, if discovered, would have found him in serious trouble. They did a deal with some South African Air Force pilots based nearby, that in exchange for the Brits loaning them a Jeep and a Utility vehicle, the South Africans would lend them a Piper Cub to fly!

Being in the REME, Flockhart's interest and skill on motor cycles was called upon and later, when posted to the Middle East, his life was punctuated by sand races, motocross and impromptu speedway racing.

Demobbed in 1947, he returned to Edinburgh and engineering but his escapades on motor-cycles led him to move on to an MG TC with which he started his motor sport career. Despite his interest in flying, Flockhart did not actually possess a pilot's licence so he got down to it seriously, passing glider licences and then on to his pilot's licence with a Tiger Moth.

With the MG, Flockhart was able to join the rest of the post-war Scottish motor sports enthusiasts. Up to that time, Scotland had never held a motor

race meeting, a subject Ron and his friends discussed endlessly. When the Lothian Car Club managed to get permission to lay out a circuit on the sandy beach beside the legendary St Andrews golf course, Flockhart was not only one of the first to enter but he actually won his first race there, a handicap affair. By now Flockhart's MG had been ministered to, was pretty quick and was used for rallies, driving tests and anything sporting.

By 1950 the bug had really bitten and Ron contacted a Scots engineer, Joe Potts, who was best known for tuning and racing motor cycles but in the process of building his first racing car, the JP. Ron was not interested in a 500cc version as he preferred Formula Libre, so he fitted a Vincent Black Lightning 1,000cc twin into his JP chassis and went racing wherever he could get an entry.

His most important race was the Ulster Trophy meeting at Dundrod in 1951, a big International event back in those days. Indeed that year it was won by World Champion, Guiseppe Farina in an Alfa Romeo 158. Ron, however, was entered in the separate race for 1300cc racing cars in which two young English drivers, who were also to become quite famous, were taking part. Peter Collins was driving an 1100cc Cooper and Mike Hawthorn was driving a Riley Brooklands. As the race was run in two sections, Scratch and Handicap, Flockhart ran out the overall winner with the JP-Vincent and Hawthorn won the Handicap.

In his early days Ron Flockhart competed in anything. His brave passenger in this MG Car Club driving test meeting is Nicoll Cuthbert who was later to run a Ford GT40 for Eric Liddell.

At the end of the season, Ron sold the JP-Vincent to Marshall Watson and persuaded a friend of his - Alastair Birrell who was an electrical engineer - to share the cost of buying an ERA. They needed a team name and as David Murray had only just chosen the name Ecurie Ecosse, Flockhart and Birrell chose the team name "Alba Union". Alba was the ancient name for Scotland and Union because it was a partnership.

The car they bought from David Hampshire was the original ERA, R1A. It was Alastair Birrell who gave it its first two outings, at the opening race meeting at Charterhall in April 1952 when he finished 3rd in the Formula Libre race and a month later at the opening race meeting at Crimond, near Aberdeen where he was second in the Formula Libre event. A week later Ron ran the car at Charterhall but retired. There was then a great rush to get the car prepared for the Ulster Trophy where, this time, Flockhart was racing against the big boys like Fangio and Moss in BRMs, Taruffi in the Thinwall Special Ferrari and even Mike Hawthorn in the Cooper Bristol. In this race Flockhart was absolutely brilliant and was lying in third place behind Piero Taruffi and Mike Hawthorn when the ERA ran out of fuel. He and Birrell hadn't worked out the fuel consumption properly! One of Ron's great friends, the late Archie Craig, was persuaded to spend his honeymoon with his new wife Betty, helping Flockhart and Birrell at this event. Archie recalled that Ron created consternation in Donegal Square, in the centre of Belfast, when he started up the ERA and drove it through town and out to the circuit!

Around this time Flockhart met Raymond Mays and was given the chance to buy probably the most famous ERA racing car, R4D. The car was offered with both a 1.5 litre and 2. Litre engines and the price seemed right. I remember this day well as I had a telephone call from an excited Flockhart asking me to rush up to his house and see what he had just bought. When I got there he proudly flung open the doors of the garage and there was a rather dirty and decrepit looking R4D ERA.

Alastair Birrell bought Ron's share of R1A and continued racing the car into the 1955 season when his business began to take up too much of his time. He offered the car for sale at £400 (Sic) and it was sold to Bill Moss.

Meanwhile Flockhart took 5th place in the Formula Libre race that accompanied the British Grand Prix with his new mount. By now he had been fortunate to meet up with a real Scottish character in Willie McVee who was normally a chauffeur but was a natural racing mechanic. He became Ron's right hand man from then on. With Formula 1 adopting a 2 litre format there were plenty of old 4.5 litre and 1.5 litre supercharged racing cars around and so there were plenty of Formula

Libre events in which Flockhart's twenty-year-old racing car was still competitive.

At the beginning of 1952 Ron had been approached by David Murray to buy a Jaguar XK120 and join the new Ecurie Ecosse team. Ron was insistent, however, that if he drove for Ecurie Ecosse it would be with his new ERA and he was not about to sell it to buy an XK120. As a result they reached stalemate and there was a coolness between Flockhart and Murray for a couple of years. Flockhart continued as a private entrant with his ERA.

He was offered the chance to race a Connaught at his home circuit, Charterhall, and was given the Hillborn-Travers fuel injected car to drive. In a voice tinged with irony he described the race as follows. *"Making a poor getaway, I added to my shame by spinning on the wettish track coming out of a slow right-hander. However, I managed to keep out of the way - which was not very difficult as the major part of the field was in front - and for the first time in a motor race I was possessed of a cold fighting mood".*

Flockhart was good and it was no surprise when John Wyer of Aston Martin offered him a factory DB3S to race at Snetterton. He won the race and came second in the unlimited event against the bigger Jaguars but it was the only drive he ever had in a factory Aston Martin, for other things were in the wings.

One day late in the season, Ron was invited to Goodwood to try out the Mark 1 16-cylinder BRM. He was surprised and shaken by the sheer noise of the car. *"I was quite deaf for 24 hours after driving the car. I felt convinced the rev counter was not working. I gave the throttle pedal a jab that would have damaged the engine of the ERA and the rev counter shot up to 7,500 rpm"*

Flockhart was then offered the chance to join the Owen Organisation and take charge of their Birmingham-based company Charles Clark Ltd as well as becoming driver and test engineer. He advertised the ERA for sale at

The car that brought Ron Flockhart to BRM's attention was the famous ERA R4D. The photo shows the car at Charterhall shortly after he bought it in the early 1950s.

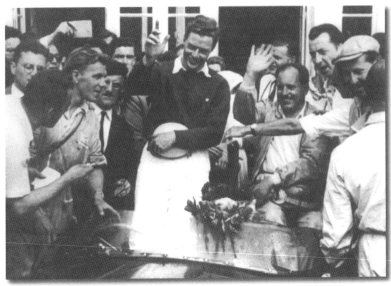

Flockhart again, this time with Ivor Bueb after winning Le Mans in 1957.

£1500, which was a good price for such a car, and it went to Ken Wharton - who was a fellow BRM driver. I asked Ron about the car at the time and he remarked: *"As I see it, the D type ERA represents about the maximum performance with stamina that can be obtained with a racing car capable of being maintained on a spare-time basis with the limited facilities at my disposal."*

His racing debut with BRM was Easter Monday Goodwood 1954 where he spun at the first bend but recovered to finish fourth and equalled the fastest lap in the race. His next race was at Snetterton where there was a poor entry and Flockhart, ever the realist, remarked *"...When you bring the bulldozer they expect you to push over the molehills"*. He need not have worried as he not only won the race but set a new outright Snetterton lap record at over 91 mph. Flockhart was also supposed to make his Le Mans debut in 1954 driving a factory Austin Healey 100 with the great Louis Chiron. Healey withdrew from the race and so Flockhart made his Le Mans debut a year later, sharing a factory Lotus IX with Colin Chapman; they were disqualified.

The year 1954 turned out to be a great one for Flockhart as he was asked to be reserve driver to Prince Bira in the British Grand Prix with a Maserati 250F. Bira was suffering from malarial fever and during the race pulled into the pits for Ron to take over. It was short lived as the de Dion tube broke at Silverstone's Copse Corner on his very first lap and Flockhart was lucky not to be badly injured when the car rolled.

In 1956 he raced for the Owen Organisation in a Grand Prix for the first time when he took the wheel of a 2.5 litre BRM P25 for the British Grand Prix at Silverstone. Unfortunately his engine expired in the race and he was out. He was then offered a drive in the Connaught factory team for the Italian Grand Prix that same year and BRM allowed him to take the drive. He drove a storming race to finish 3rd behind Stirling Moss' winning Maserati 250F and the Juan Manuel Fangio/ Peter Collins Lancia Ferrari D50. Reminiscing with Mike Oliver, Connaught's technical director, many years later Mike admitted that he missed out on what was probably Connaught's greatest achievement at Monza. *"I didn't go to that race because when Rodney (Clark) asked me if I thought the engines would last for 300 miles on such a very fast circuit I said ' no, most unlikely, forget it'. However we were offered so much starting money*

Rodney couldn't resist the offer and decided to go. As I was so pessimistic about our chances he thought he would go instead. Connaughts finished 3rd and 5th!"

Ron Flockhart was one of motor racing's nice guys. True, he could be stubborn at times, but his temperament always appeared to be relaxed and he always seemed to be in control. We kept up a correspondence during the two years I spent in National Service and he kept me up to date with his testing of the short nosed Mk II BRM. It gave him a few frights but it is generally accepted that Flockhart played a big part in making the original V16 at least manageable. Sadly it was far too late for the car to make any further impact in International motor racing. In a sense, Ron's racing was somewhat curtailed but in 1955 Geoff Healey offered Flockhart one of the new factory Austin Healey 100Ss which he ran in British events. Healey then entered Flockhart for the Mille Miglia that year.

Driving on his own, Ron was involved in a bizarre and serious accident with the car. Out in the countryside he arrived at a tight right hand corner across a stone bridge with low parapets. In true fashion Flockhart slid the car through the bend but at that moment a little boy threw a rolled up ball of paper on to the road in front of him and Flockhart swerved, hitting the bridge parapet and going right through it. The Healey overturned in mid-air throwing Flockhart into the river. The car landed upside down with a huge splash. The spectators were horrified and rushed down the bank to try and save the driver, who they thought was trapped under the car. Meanwhile Ron, who had a huge bruise on his head, surfaced in the river only to be "rescued" by a couple of Italians. Ron was quite naturally a bit dazed but could not believe his ears when he heard his rescuers say to each other. *"Where do you think he keeps his money?"* The other remarked *"...In his hip-pocket I should think."* At this Flockhart, who had learned a bit of Italian during his army stint, jumped to his feet and gave them an earful of colloquial Italian.

Two years later, in 1957, Flockhart was back at the Mille Miglia this time in an Ecurie Ecosse D-type Jaguar. Ron borrowed David Murray's road Jaguar to drive around the route. He originally wanted to do the event with Swiss journalist Hans Tanner in the passenger's seat but nothing came of this and Flockhart set off on his own once more. Any doubts that Flockhart could hold his own were dispelled on the fast opening stages to Pescara where the roads suited the D-type. At one stage he was in seventh place overall in an ageing car with no fewer than five Ferraris running ahead of him but it was not to last. The D-type was a pretty good car for smooth road surfaces but on the open roads of Italy, it began to break up. When the fuel tank worked its way loose, Ron stopped beside a field and "borrowed" some wire from a fence and wired up the fuel tank but it was only a temporary measure and he retired the car soon afterwards.

This eventual partnership between Flockhart and David Murray proved to be fruitful for both of them. According to my records, Flockhart's first race with Ecurie Ecosse was at Snetterton on March 25 1956 driving D-type (XKD561). He won one race and finished second in another. A week later he was at Goodwood with the same car and won again and took third at Oulton Park the following weekend. It was a good start and for the Aintree event Ron was switched to XKD502 and then finally David Murray put him into XKD501 where he took a first and second place in two races.

Murray was offered the chance to race at Le Mans as a place was left vacant. With the help of Lofty England of Jaguar, who persuaded the organisers that Murray's team was very professional, they were allowed to enter one car, XKD501 and Murray chose Ron Flockhart and Ninian Sanderson to be

Ron Flockhart's last race in Scotland was at Charterhall with the Border Reivers DBR1 Aston Martin in 1960.

the drivers. Looking back now it was an odd choice as Sanderson thought Flockhart was far too posh because he came from Edinburgh and there was a fair bit of needling between them.

The race gave David Murray and Ecurie Ecosse world-wide fame as the two Scots won the event, and in a sense saved Jaguar's bacon. When they went back the following year, this time with two cars, David Murray decided to be diplomatic and split the pairing with Flockhart going with Ivor Bueb and Sanderson driving with Aberdonian Jock Lawrence. This time they finished first and second in the D types.

Part of the reason for splitting Sanderson and Flockhart could have been influenced by a typically outrageous incident involving Sanderson and Flockhart. It took place in the United States consulate in Edinburgh when they were applying for visas to go to Sebring in 1957. The ever-diplomatic David Murray and his chief mechanic Wilkie Wilkinson took Flockhart and Sanderson to the consulate and they were all ushered into a room where each was questioned in turn. Historians will recall that the US was particularly sensitive to communist activity and when Sanderson was called before the consular official and was asked the standard question. *"Are you*

or have you ever been a member of the communist party?" Sanderson replied *"No, not me, but Flockhart has!"*. At this there was a stunned silence and Murray had to step in and explain to the stony-faced official that Sanderson had a typically cruel Glasgow sense of humour and, of course, Flockhart was not and never had been a communist.

Away from his work at Rubery Owen and his testing, Ron Flockhart enjoyed his flying. Once he had qualified as a pilot in 1954 he bought an Auster which he used to fly to most of the race meetings. He had very simple tastes and enjoyed hill walking and even highland dancing. He never forgot his early days in club racing and was keen to attend the most modest club events. He felt it was the normal club members who were the real enthusiasts, who kept racing going and he was always grateful for their support. Flockhart was also good at judging the mood of contemporary racing. In an interview back in 1960 he came out with the following remark. *"...To my way of thinking the best method (of finding the world champion.) is that used by the American professionals. A sponsor, driver and mechanics to go through the season as a team and it is the team that wins the title. This wouldn't work over here, unfortunately"*. Little was he to know what would happen just eight years later with the arrival of John Player in Formula 1.

Ron Flockhart's last race for Ecurie Ecosse was Le Mans in 1960 when he was entered in one of the team's ageing Jaguar D types with his friend Bruce Halford. That year Ron had met Gillian Tatlow a British Overseas Airways air-hostess and they became engaged. Ironically, Bruce Halford had become engaged to one of Gillian's BOAC hostess friends.

During the late 1950s Ron Flockhart formed himself into a limited company, AREF Ltd, with his friend Hugh Langrishe and they both tried to influence David Murray to dispose of the D-type Jaguars long before he eventually did. Indeed as early as 1958, in a letter to Murray, Hugh Langrishe had recommended a 2-litre Lotus XV as the ideal car to race. Also, there was the matter of money. David Murray was never one to lash out when it was not necessary. Langrishe pointed out that Ron's agreement with John Coombs to race a Lotus 11 during the 1957 season had turned out to be more profitable than his season racing D-types with Ecurie Ecosse. There is a telling line in one particular letter to Murray, which reads *"...Ron also mentioned to you our concern to conclude this year's agreement in writing, however repugnant this may seem. I am sure you will appreciate our point of view"*.

Though there were some fairly pointed remarks thrown back and forth between Hugh Langrishe and David Murray, Murray clearly had great respect for him. Some years later, after Ron Flockhart had been killed, Murray wrote to him asking his assistance in helping form a private company - "along the same lines as the one Ron had for his motor racing" - for a young driver who wished Murray to help him. Nothing came of this: the young driver was Jackie Stewart!

In 1956 Flockhart took third place in the Oulton Park Gold Cup driving John Coombs' Lotus 11 finishing ahead of Colin Chapman in the works car.

Whilst a parade of other drivers came and went at BRM, Flockhart doggedly continued with the odd alarming incident and wins in events such as the 1959 Lady Wigram Trophy. It was the end of the original BRM saga. By now he and Hugh Langrishe had their own garage business and for the 1960 season Alan Brown offered him a drive in his Formula 2 Cooper. He also had two races in grand prix cars that year, for Lotus at Reims, as mentioned earlier - filling in for an absent John Surtees - and in the US Grand Prix driving for Cooper when he retired with transmission trouble. He ran his own Lotus 18 over the winter of 1961/62 in the Tasman series.

By now he was 37 years old and had become even more interested in aircraft and had his eye on an obscure record. This was the record time from Australia to England in a single piston-engined aircraft. Sadly on April 12 1962 it was to lead to tragedy in the Dandenong Ranges near Melbourne, Australia.

I am grateful to Roy Williams of Geelong in Australia who has supplied me with a huge amount of detail on what happened in Flockhart's fatal accident. Roy is a Maserati enthusiast, has a great admiration for Ron Flockhart and went to great lengths to trace all the minute facts from the inquest and in subsequent conversations with other pilots.

Ron Flockhart held British pilot's licence (No.29579) issued on 3rd August 1954 and valid until the 18th of May 1964. This enabled him to fly single-engined aircraft under 12,500lbs in weight. By the time of his crash in 1962 he was an experienced pilot who had logged 961 flying hours, 60 of those in Mustangs. His original Mustang was only the fifth to have been built under licence in Australia and was registered G-ARKD. Part of the money for the plane came from the banking company United Dominions Trust as they were sponsors, along with BP, for the record breaking attempt from Australia to London.

In 1961 he had first attempted to break this record with his Mustang and was ahead of time when he arrived to refuel in Greece. However the attempt ended in frustration and disappointment because the authorities held him on the tarmac while they tried to untangle red tape. The engine overheated, and the bid finished there - virtually on the last lap. Then there came another set-back when the new engine was being fitted to the plane. A mechanic set fire to the plane and it burned out. A second Mustang was obtained, a Mark XXI registered G-ARUK, and this was prepared for a second bid for the record.

In 1962 he returned to Australia with his new wife Gillian. He was there to go motor racing (Former Ecurie Ecosse mechanic Ron Gaudion prepared his Cooper-Climax and crewed for him), and to fly his new Mustang P51 in which he would again attempt to break the record.

Roy Williams has been frustrated by the varying, but unexplained stories surrounding Ron Flockhart's sudden tragic death in Melbourne nearly forty years ago. Many have blamed the instruments, others have put it down to pilot error - but the following is the most accurate report anybody is likely to furnish. Most of the details have come from the official reports and eyewitness accounts from the time.

His particular Mustang P51D MkXXI was built in 1948. Its serial number was CAI8/1438, and was fitted with a Rolls Royce Merlin Packard engine bearing the serial number #33031. On the 12th of April 1962 it was placed on British registration with the Certificate of Registration #7481/1, and given the registration number G-ARUK. AREF LTD., Ron Flockhart's company in England, owned the Mustang at this stage. In Melbourne it had had all of the instruments rebuilt by Smiths and Sons. These had been refitted, but not tested and additional fuel tanks were fitted to enable extra flying time and distance to be achieved,

On the 12th of April 1962, Ron submitted an abridged flight plan to Moorabbin Airport for a flight from Moorabbin to Bankstown in N.S.W. The purpose of this flight was to check fuel consumption and have work carried out on radio and navigation equipment. Ron advised the Chief Engineer of Brookes Aviation that he would make a circuit of the aerodrome before departing, and land if he found any serviceability problems with the aircraft.

He took off at 1015 hours. After satisfactorily completing one circuit of the aerodrome, a course was set for Lilydale at 1018 hours.

At 1023 hours, Ron reported to Moorabbin Tower from over Lilydale, and one minute later advised them he was unable to proceed visually due to cloud, and therefore would return to Moorabbin.

At 1027 hours he advised he was having trouble, had lost his compass and was in cloud at 3000 feet. He was further instructed to maintain 3000 feet and home in on Moorabbin, Ron acknowledged this message.

At 1029 hours the pilot was requested to confirm that he was homing on the non-directional beacon, but no further response was received.

What follows is an abridged version of Roy Williams' theory of what happened having read the reports of witnesses and inter-departmental correspondence.

"I have also spoken to Paul Moxham, who apart from his extensive interest in historic motor racing and sports cars, was until recently, a Captain with Qantas and responsible for the training of pilots in all types of aircraft including 747's. Paul became acquainted with Ron Flockhart during his time at the Royal Aero

This publicity photograph of Ron Flockhart with his Mustang fighter, was taken in Australia prior to his final tests when he crashed fatally.

Club at Bankstown NSW, and offered to give him both instrument and night flying experience, but this offer was not taken up.

"On taking off, Flockhart flew towards Lilydale via the Dandenong Ranges of which he was not conversant, therefore he was not aware of the low cloud/ mists that often cover them. The weather that day was described as fine and hazy, with a visibility of 15 miles and only slight turbulence.

"It appears the Mustang circled Kallista at low altitude, in part cloud, and emerged at 1300 ft, - (the hills at that point were 1200 ft. above sea level, plus the height of trees at another 100 ft. above that!). The plane carried out a left turn, possibly to avoid higher terrain. In the course of this turn the nose dropped sharply, and the aircraft struck the trees at 200 m.p.h. plus and approximately 55 ft. above the ground.

"Ron's Rolex Oyster Perpetual GMT master watch stopped at 0028 hours GMT. The plane was broken into forty parts..

"The conclusion reached by the Ministry of Aviation on 20th of May 1963 (over a year later) was - "The possibility that the pilot temporarily lost control of the aircraft whilst circling in cloud, and that it subsequently stalled during the recovery turn to avoid high terrain cannot be excluded thus, there is insufficient evidence to conclusively establish the cause of the accident".

Ron Flockhart's great friend Mike Oliver of Connaught - who was a well known wartime test pilot - summed it all up when he remarked. *"I understood that Ron was a victim of the oldest mistake in the game 'flying in clouds with hard centres'. I am afraid it happens just as often today as it did when I was flying."*

Ron died at a period in his life when he was very happy. His motor racing career had all but ended, and certainly would have done at the end of that season. His business was going well and he had just married Gillian.

As soon as the news reached David Murray he wrote a touching letter to Gillian and remarked, quite honestly, *"...Although we did not always see eye-to-eye at all times I admired his guts and tenacity. He was a tremendous factor in the rise of Ecurie Ecosse"*

A number of years later Gillian married Alan Fosler, a merchant banker. They moved to Hong Kong with Alan's business and had two daughters during their 25 years in that country. Since Hong Kong has returned to Chinese ownership they have re-settled in the South of England. From time to time Gillian appears at events and at Donington in 1992 she handed over the Ron Flockhart trophy at an historic event.

Ron Flockhart was a credit to his fellow Scots racing drivers. Always polite, always considerate,very fast when the car and conditions allowed, and greatly underrated in International motor racing.

IAN FORREST.

Few Scots have been more involved with motor racing than Ian Forrest, first as a driver and today as an administrator and organiser. Most of his motor racing has been in Scotland where he became multiple 1000cc saloon champion in a variety of Hillman Imps and a Davrian before going up market and competing in the British Touring Car Championship in the 1990s with a BMW M3. He became the leading private entrant on one particular year and with the M3 he also raced in Sweden.

DARIO FRANCHITTI

Like Allan McNish before him, Dario Franchitti seemed destined to go motor racing. His father, George Franchitti, had been a regular and successful racer in Formula Ford in Scotland but retired to devote all his time to nurturing Dario's, natural talent for motor racing. Also, like McNish, he had been racing karts and when, at the age of 17, he decided to move into motor racing the original idea was to take the normal route of Formula Ford. George Franchitti had words with David Leslie Snr and instead they decided to enter the new Formula Vauxhall Junior class in 1991. By round five Dario had scored his first win at Thruxton. Throughout the early part of the season he ran second in the championship to his team mate David Cuff.

The coveted McLaren Young Driver of the Year award was presented to Dario at the end of the 1992 racing season and things were looking up. By 1994 he was with Paul Stewart Racing alongside Jan Magnusson and was slightly overshadowed by the Dutchman.

In 1995 Dario made one of those sideways moves that was hard to figure out at the time. He and Jan Magnusson joined Mercedes Benz to compete in the prestigious International Touring Car Championship and was to stay there for two seasons. In December that year he was given a 40 lap test in a McLaren-Mercedes at Jerez which came to nothing. After some good results in Touring Cars including a win at Suzuka, the whole Championship was put into turmoil when Alfa Romeo and Opel withdrew. This left him technically without a drive. However all this changed towards the end of 1996 with a move that put Dario in the direction he has followed for the past six seasons.

It was all a bit of a rush, really, Carl Hogan in America decided to create a new team to compete in the 1997 CART series. Hogan, with Mercedes Benz and the co-operation of Reynard, formed his team and was offered

Dario ran successfully in Formula Vauxhall Junior, skipping the usual Formula Ford route, with David Leslie's team.

Dario as a driver by Mercedes. By the end of January, only a few weeks after the team was formed, Dario was off to the Homestead circuit in Miami for his first test. The chassis was a 1996 Reynard whilst the new chassis was prepared and Dario. In his first season Franchitti was quick enough to be picked up by Barry Green for his KOOL Green CART team in 1998. He quickly fitted in to what was a happy team and won seven times for Team Green and in 1999 tied for the Championship with a young Columbian called Juan Pablo Montoya and was unfortunate to lose the crown on the only occasion a tie-breaker has been used in the CART series.

In 2002 Team Green ran with Dario at Indianapolis where Dario finished 19th in his Rookie Year. Then for 2003 Team Green left CART and moved into the Indy Racing League series. Sadly Dario lost the best part of eight months out of the cockpit when he suffered a motor cycle accident back in Scotland. This ruined his chance of running in IRL that year. However, by the start of 2004 he was back at the wheel seeming as quick as ever at the wheel of his Andretti Green Dallara-Honda. In July 2004 he was back on the top of the podium.

MARINO FRANCHITTI

Meet Marino Franchitti once and you will never forget him. Unlike his brother Dario, Marino is finger-snapping chirpy, extremely self-confident and a great laugh. He was born on July 7 1978 in Broxburn and was the youngest of the three children of George Franchitti and his wife Marina - the third child is their daughter Carla who is probably the brothers' greatest fan and a great motor racing enthusiast.

He virtually followed a similar early career path to his brother Dario starting out in karts at the age of 9. However, he realised that Dario's success meant that he would have to push himself forward. He became Scottish Open Karting Champion in 1988 and then won the Scottish Pro-kart championship four years later.

He signed up with the Jim Russell Racing School and went on to compete in a number of rounds in the Formula Vauxhall championship aided in this by sponsorship from Dario. At the age of 18 he was approached by Alfa Romeo to do some test driving with their touring car but his first serious season came in 2000 and the British Formula Ford Championship with the Aztec International team. He had some reasonable results and qualified as an up and coming driver in the Autosport awards. This led to him being offered a drive in the British GT Championship for 2001 in the GTO class. Porsche GB were behind the plan and they wisely paired the flamboyant Marino with the seasoned Kelvin Burt. It was during this season that Marino matured considerably and proved himself adept in GT cars. It resulted in the Franchitti/Burt pairing winning the GTO class outright. During 2001 he had the chance to race at Spa in the DD Racing Porsche GT3-R. Throughout his racing he has been adopted by former Toyota Formula 1 driver Allan McNish and was prepared to listen and act on Allan's advice more so than he would have done had Dario been doing the same thing !

In April 2002 Franchitti had his first US drive in an out and out prototype, the Lola-Nissan of Rand Racing. Two months later with Niclas Johnsson and William Rand he finished third in the Watkins Glen Six-Hours. He continued to race in the United States and Europe in 2003 always seeking a top line drive.

JOHN FYDA

Though he did not race much outside Scotland, John Fyda was one of the most successful Scottish drivers in the 1970s and '80s first with Hillman Imps and then with a string of Mallock and Vision Clubmans cars. He won the championships on a number of occasions and even took his Mallock to Zandvoort in 1985 and had a brilliant win. He then joined forces with Laurence Jacobsen and they raced Jacobsen's Ecosse Group C2 car in a number of British events. In 1987 he and Jacobsen were joined by the London based Italian "Stingbrace" to race a Tiga-Ford Turbo in the Brands Hatch 1000kms race but they had a lot of trouble with the car even though they finished the race. John became Chairman of Scottish Motor Racing Club and eventually retired from racing to concentrate on his AGRA Engineering business in Dundee. However, in 2003 he returned this time to historic racing with a Mallock U2.

JOHN EASON GIBSON

John Eason Gibson with his son Neil and an Alfa Romeo Monza.

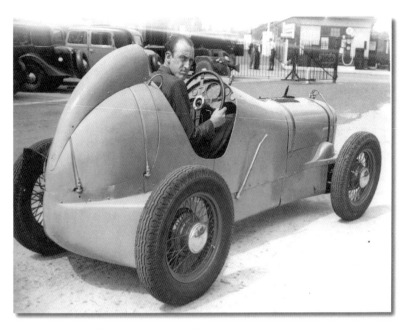

Eason Gibson at the wheel of a Riley Special he prepared and raced at Brooklands before the war.(Photo Neil Eason Gibson)

John Eason Gibson became one of the best-known Scottish characters in motor racing. Though he had a fascinating racing career as a driver in the 1930s he later became an administrator of considerable skill. His role as Secretary of the British Racing Drivers Club saw him rule the Silverstone events with a rod of steel. Behind it all, however, there lurked a great sense of humour.

John was born in Nithsdale Road, Glasgow in 1905. Whilst there he bought his first racing car, a 1928 chain-gang Frazer-Nash. After moving to Clapham in London, to run Beecholme Motor Company, he bought a Brooklands Riley and took part in the first ever race at the Donington circuit in 1932. He was offered the number 13 but refused it and ran his Riley with the number "12A". The Riley was replaced with an off-set single seater Riley and he was also offered drives in Ken Hutchinson's Zoller-supercharged single-seater Ford Special. Eason Gibson built three Ford Specials called the Jaberwocks for the RAC Rally and beat the Ford factory team.

At the outbreak of war Lord Howe, President of the British Racing Drivers Club suggested to the Minister of War that BRDC members should be offered commissions in the armed services and this was agreed. John was an ammunitions officer in the 1st Guards Brigade of the Sixth Armoured Division. Immediately after the war he came straight back into motor racing not only testing cars but acting as team manager for Aston Martin in the 1947 Spa 24 Hour race and later at Le Mans in 1949.

In 1949 John Eason Gibson was manager of the Aston Martin team at Spa. Amongst the group are racing drivers Lance Macklin and Leslie Johnston.

During this period he took some of the photographs for the BRDC yearbooks. In 1957 he took over from Desmond Scannell as BRDC Secretary, retiring ten years later. Much of the development of BRDC after the war was due to the organisational work behind the scenes by John Eason Gibson.

He is survived by his son Neil Eason Gibson who was also involved in motor sport administration and was for many years a senior official with the RAC before briefly becoming historian of the British Racing Drivers Club.

BOB GIBSON-JARVIE

The first of the finance companies to become prominent sponsors in motor racing was United Dominions Trust, owned by the Scots-born Gibson-Jarvie family. Gibson-Jarvie had always been interested in motor racing and accompanied David Murray and Ecurie Ecosse to their famous Le Mans victories. However, thanks to the persuasion of Ken Gregory they agreed to sponsor a team of Lotus Formula 1 cars finished in the pale green colours of UDT. There is an interesting story relating to the strange band painted across the nose of the UDT-Laystall Lotuses. Eventually the design was traced to the family tartan of the Gibson-Jarvie family.

GRAHAM HAMILTON AND GORDON DALZELL

Graham Hamilton and Gordon Dalzell apart from racing various cars - Graham more so than Gordon - took over the running of the Ingliston circuit at the beginning of 1978 and ran the circuit with a fair degree of showbusiness for five seasons.

Graham Hamilton was born in South Africa and saw his first motor race at Kyalami. When his father died his mother brought him back to Scotland where he settled down. One of his first jobs was working in Graham Birrell's motor sport shop in St Vincent Street. He later met Douglas Macdonald Shand who ran a carpet business in Dumfries with his nephew Gordon Dalzell. Thanks to Douglas, a Van Diemen was bought for Graham to race at Ingliston. Later another car was bought which was occasionally raced by Gordon Dalzell but generally the racing was left to Graham. When McDonald Shand decided to go into Formula 3, Hamilton was the driver and he raced in a number of F3 Championship races. This link was to assist Graham and Gordon Dalzell later when they took over Scotcircuits Ltd and ran the motor racing at Ingliston. On the death of his mother, Graham Hamilton was able to buy the Balmoral Hotel in Moffat. During their early days at Ingliston, they invested in a Surtees-Cosworth which started a trend that saw a few other ex-grand prix cars come north to Scotland. After Hamilton and Dalzell transferred their Ingliston franchise to Hugh McCaig at the end of 1982 they moved to London and run a specialised chauffeur drive business for their many friends in show business.

LORD ALEXANDER HESKETH

Thomas, Alexander Fermor-Hesketh brought to grand prix racing in the 1970s a breath of fresh air. At a time when serious money was bringing in serious sponsors and curbing the somewhat cavalier attitude of racing drivers and owners, along came Hesketh with his troup of equally enthusiastic partners, Bubbles Horsley, Harvey Posthlewaite and driver James Hunt. Suddenly we had something to smile about and though Hesketh was perceived as a bit of a clown he very quickly demonstrated that he was serious about his racing and had considerable success even though he did not have the budgets other teams had to spend.

Alexander Hesketh's mother, Kirsty, came from a long established Border family who still have holdings in the area but his family home is the 7,000 acre Easton Neston just a few miles from Silverstone circuit. Sadly his father died when Alexander was five years old and his mother was a strong influence in his life. From his early days he avidly read Motor Sport magazine even though nobody in the family was the slightest bit interested in motor racing. What changed all this was a chance meeting, at the wedding of Formula 3 driver Charlie Lucas, with Anthony Horsley - normally called "Bubbles". In turn he became friendly with Piers Courage and Frank Williams and he found it all very exciting.

Hesketh left school at 16 and surprised everyone by becoming a car salesman before getting himself closer to a real job with a stint as a stockbroker with Dean-Witter in San Francisco and a ship broker in Hong Kong. This experience was to serve him well for on reaching 21 he inherited a lot of money and set up Hesketh Finance.

Then motor racing came back into the equation and he and Horsley bought a Formula 3 car for Horsley to race and the pair spent the season on the European F3 circus. When once asked why he didn't race himself, Hesketh replied that after a couple of rallies and being taken round Silverstone by Jackie Stewart *"...no amount of money, no woman, nothing in the world would make me go around Woodcote at 165 mph"*

Sometime in 1972 Hesketh bought a second car, this time for a young driver called James Hunt. When both cars were written off at Silverstone Horsley retired from racing but Hesketh moved up to Formula 2 with a Brabham and Hunt as the exclusive driver. However, by the end of that season they had the idea of going into Formula 1 and rented a Surtees TS9 from John Surtees to use in the Race of Champions at Brands Hatch in 1973. To everyones surprise, Hunt finished third. That was it. A March 721G (03) that had been raced at the end of the previous season by Ronnie Petersen was bought and Hesketh racing and James Hunt appeared in their first World Championship race at Monaco.

For 1974 Harvey Postlethwaite designed a completely new car, the Hesketh, (See Racing Cars) and Hesketh racing ran their own GP car for two seasons proudly emblazoned with the St Andrews flag of Scotland on the airbox. When Hesketh pulled out of Formula 1 at the end of 1975 he went on to many other pursuits including the development of a sensational new motor cycle. Later still he became President of the BRDC before resigning.

It could be said that present day grand prix racing would get a jab in the arm if a modern day Alexander Hesketh were to come along but in these cynical times Hesketh's sheer politically incorrect fun and enthusiasm would probably fall on deaf ears : more's the pity.

BARRY HORNE

Barry Horne is one of the typical new breed of Scottish drivers who initially started driving locally in Scottish events and then leapt into the maelstrom of British racing in an effort to make his mark and be seen. He struggled for a number of years but was rewarded in 2003 when he won the British Porsche Carrera Cup Championship.

BERNARD HUNTER

Bernard Hunter was always slightly larger than life. He came into racing through stock cars, which was appropriate as the family business was Bernard Hunter Plant Hire so there were plenty of donor vehicles out in the yard. He built his own stock car with a BMC 1200 engine and in 1967 was third in the Scottish Championship and qualified for the world championships. Even though his father was not keen on him racing, he gave up stock cars and bought a Lotus 51 Formula Ford to finish third in the Scottish FF Championship, won that year (1968) by Tom Walkinshaw.

He went on to race a Merlyn and a Hawke but had to stop when his father took seriously ill and subsequently died.

Bernie completely transformed the family business and by 1977 he had bought a Hawke DL17 and was back racing at Ingliston. The Hawke was changed for a Van Diemen and then he left Formula Ford. He bought Iain McLaren's Chevron F2 car and drove it both in Scotland and at Croft. The familiar team of Bernie with Edinburgh traffic policeman-cum-racing mechanic, Stevie Carroll and Jimmy Rafferty always brought a laugh to the paddock.

Bernie decided to go into National racing and bought a Ralt for the Hitachi Atlantic Championship. To Bernard's surprise, he won his first race with the car, an Atlantic event at Croft, but even then he commented that he was very much a weekend racer and could not do the testing everyone else did. However, at Mallory Park he almost pulled off a wonderful move. When the rain started he quickly pitted for wets and was off but the Clerk of the Course stopped the race so that everyone could change to wets and he lost his advantage. Still, he finished third in one part and his overall position was fifth. For the 1980 season he linked up with Colin Bennett and raced a March 80B but he was always a private entrant in a world that was dominated by big budgets and testing.

After he retired from car racing, Bernie tried truck racing and today still keeps in touch by turning up at events.

COMISH HUNTER

Comish Hunter was born in Wishaw, trained as an engineer and came to prominence when he joined his father-in-law's business, Atlantic Engine Company that specialised in diesel engines. He joined the RAF during the war and afterwards joined his brothers in the family business T Hunter and Sons Ltd.

His first involvement with motor sport came in dirt track speedway racing in the 1930s but he gave that up after an accident. In 1947 he joined forces with Pat Prosser and Joe Potts and all three of them bought Cooper 500s. His crowning glory was to win the first Formula 3

race at the opening Winfield race meeting driving a Scottish-built JP 500. He also competed in the Alpine Rally with Carlisle racing driver Bob Dickson in a Morgan. In 1953 he moved from Scotland to South Africa and never raced again.

INNES IRELAND

When it comes to talking about Innes Ireland it is difficult to know where to start. As far as the outside world is concerned he is remembered as a tough and brave racing driver and by his amusing anecdotal biographies which were very popular and listed many of his escapades. But that was not the real Innes Ireland.

As with many people who like to joke and clown about, he always seemed to be jousting with himself and had enormous highs and terrible lows. I always thought he had wasted many opportunities in his life and sadly, he realised it, even though at times he was too stubborn and proud to admit it. He was very Scottish and the Scots can often be their own worst enemies. Yet he was one of the best friends you could have because under that hard leathery exterior there remained a thoroughly likeable guy with a heart of gold. Ironically he also aimed to extract as much enjoyment and entertainment out of life as he could.

Robert McGregor Innes Ireland was actually born near Todmorden in Yorkshire but his Scots father, a veterinary surgeon, moved to Kirkcudbrightshire where Innes was brought up. His mother was an accomplished singer. What became clear very early on was that Innes was not going follow his father and end up with his arm up the backside of an Aberdeen Angus. *"I had actually thought seriously about becoming a vet - that is until I made enquiries into the course. It appeared that at the Veterinary College in Edinburgh the course was as difficult - if not as arduous - as the university course for ordinary doctors. This knowledge turned my thoughts sharply away from the academic life. Since my early school days I had been firmly against the principles of learning and I did not see why I should abandon my deep convictions at this juncture."*

His brother Alan was the real athlete in the family but Innes was something of a gymnast and an enthusiastic rugby player: he was twice chosen to represent Scotland in the national Air Training Corps championships.

His first personal link with cars came at the age of 12 through his friendship with an old lady in Newton Stewart who had two old Bentleys and a chauffeur. Innes used to work on the cars and sneak the odd run up and down the drive in them. She sent him Tim Birkins book "Full Throttle" as a Christmans present and that was it, Innes was hooked.

At the age of 18 Innes' father gave up any hope of Innes as a fellow vet and enrolled him as an apprentice with the Aero Division of Rolls Royce Ltd at Hillington in Glasgow and he stayed there for three years before being transferred to London.

The first motor sport event he saw was the Bo'ness hill climb in 1947 and was impressed by Sydney Allard in action with his big Allard. He was also impressed by George Abecassis and sent his precious Birkin book to Abecassis to autograph for him. Four years later, when based in London, he went to Silverstone and saw Reg Parnell win the Daily Express Trophy and this made him even more enthusiastic. Little did he realise fate was about

Innes Ireland was given his chance to race the new Ecurie Ecosse Tojeiro-Jaguar at Charterhall where he won one of his two races against Jim Clark and Ron Flockhart.

to touch him with its magic wand. The old lady he had befriended died and left him one of the 4.5 litre Bentleys in her will. By now he had been called up to join the Kings Own Scottish Borderers for his two year National Service. He was posted to Berwick on Tweed which just happened to be convenient to the new circuit of Charterhall. His first race with the Bentley had been at Boreham but he raced a few times at Charterhall, taking a second place in the vintage class on one occasion.

Whilst a soldier at Berwick, Innes was refused permission to run his Bentley in a rally in Glasgow. Being Innes he went "over the wall", with the connivance of his father and competed in the event getting back to the barracks unseen. Unfortunately his platoon sergeant was sent the local Edinburgh newspaper that reported on a certain Robert McGregor Innes Ireland having won his class driving a Bentley. Needless to say Innes was marched in front of the Commanding Officer but he talked his way out of trouble by offering to give the C.O. a ride in the Bentley!

His father, meanwhile, travelled around the south of Scotland attending to his veterinary duties which included visits to James Clark's farm and the farm of Alec Calder, his son-in-law, in Chirnside. Alec was an original member of the Border Reivers and had a fast Brooklands Riley 9. Meanwhile, Innes had left the army and joined a friend, John Mason, in a garage business. As Innes had recently sold a big Packard for a good price he was able to buy Alec Calders Riley and this is what set Innes off on his successful career in racing. The Riley brought him to the attention of people like Bill Boddy and Denis Jenkinson of Motor Sport who had already seen another British driver, Mike Hawthorn, come to the fore in a Brooklands Riley.

His big break, however, came when his brother introduced him to an army friend, Major Rupert Robinson, who bought a new Lotus Eleven sports car for Innes to race in 1956. He was to continue racing the car for the next two seasons. Now Innes had the goods and he quickly delivered the job by winning the Motor Sport Brooklands Memorial Trophy and coming to

the attention of Colin Chapman. He became a factory sports car driver for Lotus in 1957 but kept racing his own Lotus 11 in British events.

Around this time David Murray of Ecurie Ecosse received a letter from a great Borders motor sport enthusiast called Douglas Wilson. Douglas, despite a disability, used to rally fiercely in a little Standard 10 and was Innes' major Scottish promoter. In the letter Wilson almost begged Murray to give his friend Innes a drive for the team but cautioned *"....I do believe this boy (he is 27) has a future but I don't want to have him rushed."*

A year later Innes was given his first Ecurie Ecosse drive in a D-type Jaguar at the support race to the British Grand Prix. The car he raced was the famous XKD606 which had won Le Mans in 1957 and was an ex-factory long-nose D-type. This was very much the third car in the team on that occasion as Ivor Bueb had been entered in Ecurie Ecosse's new Tojeiro-Jaguar and Masten Gregory had the Lister-Jaguar but Innes drove wisely and finished 9th. That evening, back at the hotel, Innes gently asked David Murray if there was any chance of some prize money. Murray thought for a moment, looked at his new driver and said *"Would a packet of fags be OK?".*

David Murray liked his new recruit as he enjoyed life and Innes was a tonic in any team, so he offered him a contract for 1959; the plan being that Innes would drive the new Tojeiro-Jaguar Ecurie Ecosse were building for that year. But there was a problem. Innes had signed to drive a factory Lotus with Colin Chapman and had been promised a Formula 1 drive. It was typical of Innes then, and later, that despite what he may have appeared from the outside, he was intensely loyal to people; something which was to cause him to lose out when things went wrong at Lotus. However, Innes had a word with Colin Chapman and was allowed to drive with Ecosse in any events that would not clash with his Lotus grand prix and sports car races. When he wrote to Murray telling him this, Innes was quick to justify his decision with Lotus by remarking *"...it will be in my own best interests in the long run."*

Innes Ireland was no stranger to accidents. From Bill Colson's archives comes this photo of Innes receiving attention at Brands Hatch when his Lotus XV was in collision with Chris Bristows Cooper Monaco.

As it transpired, Innes only raced twice for Ecurie Ecosse in 1959 but, being equally loyal to Colin Chapman, he tried to talk Colin into selling Ecurie Ecosse two Lotus 19s to run as a semi-factory team. Nothing came of this even though Ron Flockhart also tried to get Murray to buy a Lotus 19 the following year.

Innes was always a very brave driver and a man who could also laugh at himself. When David Murray wanted to set some obscure world records with the team's new Tojeiro-Climax Coupe at Monza the first person he turned to was Innes. However, by that time Innes was driving for BRP and Ken Gregory, the team manager, would not let him drive for Ecosse as the Scots team was supported by Esso and this clashed with BRP's fuel supplier. Innes' loyalty to Ecurie Ecosse was underlined in a letter he wrote to David Murray about having to decline the chance to set the records. *"I am greatly distressed about this as you can imagine because of my association with the team and it would have been wonderful to have pulled off these two record attempts together. I feel as though I am letting you down, although it is because of circumstances which are entirely beyond my own control."*

When Donald Campbell was killed attempting the world water speed record in Bluebird, Innes was quick to step in and offer to pick up the gauntlet and go for the record. Innes loved sailing and one of his unsuccessful businesses came about when he moved back to the South of Scotland in the 1960s and bought a fishing boat. He reasoned there was a growing demand for lobsters and I remember visiting him during this period and asking how business was going. He went to great lengths to explain that the best lobsters were in amongst the rocks and it was costing him a fortune repairing his boat as he kept spearing the hull on the rocks in his quest for lobsters.

One of Innes Ireland's most spectacular accidents came in practice for the Monaco Grand Prix in 1961 when he lost control coming out of the tunnel. Innes always owned up to his mistakes and he went to a lot of trouble to explain exactly what happened.

"During practice that year I had been trying three different gearboxes in the Lotus; two five speeds and a four speed. The two five speed boxes had different

shift patterns. With all this chopping and changing it came to the last practice and I realised I had to go out and set a qualifying time. We chose what we thought was the right car with the best gearbox for the circuit. I was in the tunnel going flat out in third gear and changed up to fourth. As I put the lever into the slot and let the clutch out I just knew it was wrong but in the fraction of a second it took, there was just no way I could do anything about it. I shot out of the tunnel and into the barriers at high speed."

Innes was no stranger to accidents and he suffered a monumental one in the United States when racing the Team Rosebud Lotus 19. Team Rosebud was formed by Tom O'Connor and Don Miles who were not only major Texas ranchers but oilmen into the bargain. They decided to go motor racing and eventually ran the efficient Team Rosebud with Scotsman Jock Ross as team manager and chief engineer. Jock had earlier worked with Border Reivers.

Innes was very good at cultivating rich entrants and it was no surprise when he raced for O'Conner as his star driver alongside Pete Lovely. The car was originally raced by Innes for BRP but after being raced with the usual 2.5 litre Coventry Climax engine, it was converted to Ferrari power with a V12 beautifully fitted into the back of the Lotus 19. Innes was engaged to test the car at Watkins Glen before the sports car grand prix. On one of the uphill sections the car broke away and slewed across the circuit. As it was a test day there was none of the normal race day discipline and a marshal had parked his car beside the circuit. Innes hit the car with the Lotus, ending up with multiple injuries. Ever cheerful, however, he wrote to David Murray of Ecurie Ecosse from hospital where he was in traction. "....being flat on my back doesn't make writing too easy - although it is particularly suited to other activities - unfortunately that too is denied me."

His incidents were not confined to racing cars, however, and as an enthusiastic pilot he got into trouble relying on Colin Chapman. Once, when he planned to fly to Goodwood, he asked Colin for help. "Colin agreed to park his car on the runway at Goodwood pointing into the wind so that I knew which way to land. Unfortunately he had forgot and had just parked it any old way. As a result I landed with the wind, flew down the runway and took my plane straight through a hedge and into a field. Obviously I couldn't stay there so I turned the plane round and drove it back through the hedge"

When I was preparing my biography of Jim Clark after Jim's tragic death in 1968 I again visited Innes in the South of Scotland and raised the subject of his long standing rift with Jim Clark.

This blot in the relationship between Jim Clark and Innes Ireland needs some explanation.

As team mates in Team Lotus, Jim Clark and Innes Ireland got on very well and Innes was helpful to his fellow Scot during Clark's first season in Formula 1.

No one could ever deny that Innes Ireland was quick and he could be phenomenally fast. The trouble was consistency in racing situations and there were times when it could be said that Innes was too emotional in a race rather than coldly calculating. All seemed fine at Team Lotus until after the US Grand Prix in 1961 where Innes gave Team Lotus their first world championship win. Two weeks later he was fired from Lotus and there have been many versions of the story. A few days after his firing Innes came to Scotland. At the time I was the motoring correspondent of Scottish Television and interviewed him on the subject. It was fresh in his memory and untarnished by brooding.

Innes had gone to the London Motor Show shortly after winning the US Grand Prix, the highlight of his career and a great landmark in the life of Team Lotus. He bumped into Geoff Murdoch the Esso competitions manager and casually asked him about plans for the 1962 season and in particular the Springbok winter series in South Africa. Murdoch was taken aback and asked if Innes had spoken to Colin Chapman. Puzzled, Innes said he had not and repaired to the Lotus stand. Innes takes up the story: "I saw Colin and asked him about the plans for 1962 and Colin told me he was taking Jimmy and Trevor Taylor to South Africa and my services would no longer be required. I was stunned, I couldn't think of anything to say and then Colin remarked ' it's a right bastards trick' and I just walked away."

Innes at the time appeared to have accepted the situation even though he was very upset about it. Only later was Innes' attitude to change. Many years later in a deeply reflective mood he told me that he had begun to remember Jim Clark and Colin talking and was convinced that Jim Clark had persuaded Colin Chapman to fire him. This became a constant torment for Innes and left Jim Clark totally perplexed at Innes' new attitude towards him. Shortly after Clark was killed I sat with Innes in his house talking about Clark and at one point he got up and strolled over to the window almost in tears. He turned round and said "...you know, I made my peace with Trevor Taylor over the whole thing and now Jimmy is dead and I can never make my peace with him." Innes wrote one of the most moving obituaries to Jim Clark to those of us who knew him; he had made his own peace.

There were times when Innes' quick temper flared up and if it happened it was wise to melt into the background. I was caught out quite innocently on one occasion and could not avoid what happened next. Back in the 1950s and '60s there was a great rapport between drivers, marshals and journalists and as a result I had a private arrangement with a number of drivers, one of whom was Innes. It was the sports car race run alongside the British Grand Prix at Aintree and, as was the case in those days, many GP drivers also raced sports cars at the same meeting. Innes was driving the UDT-Laystall Lotus 19 Climax. I was out on the circuit taking photos as usual and Innes won the race. On the last lap I went to the edge of the track and gave Innes the thumbs sign as he came past and he nodded. This meant that on his slowing down lap he would stop and give me a lift back to the paddock. This he duly did and I jumped into the roasting Lotus. As he accelerated away he shouted whether he had broken the lap record? I hadn't a clue, so I shouted back I didn't know. At this he lost his temper, slammed the Lotus into a lower gear and accelerated flat out through the gears. He tore down the long back straight and I was fighting for breath as there was no screen to protect the passenger. He flicked the Lotus through the esses at the end and arrived back in the pits to find that he had, in fact, broken the lap record.

After the Team Lotus affair Innes was too good a driver to be idle and was quickly picked up by UDT-Laystall. But the damage had been done, and the highest placing he ever had after that was fourth place at the Dutch Grand Prix in 1963 in a Lotus-BRM. His last grand prix was the Mexican GP in 1966 in a privately entered BRM P261 where the gearbox broke and he retired.

It was a sad end to Innes' grand prix career because he had all the determination and will to win. Another team, like BRM, should have picked him up. All of this was a great pity as Innes Ireland, on his day, was every bit as fast as Jim Clark. This was proved time and time again in non-championship races where he could win in outclassed machinery. This was also the case in GT racing where his handling of the Aston Martin DB4GT and Ferrari GTO was brilliant. In both cases, however, he was with team managers who could be firm and knew what they wanted from their driver.

As if to emphasise this, he was brought into the Ford team to race the Ford GT40 and took fifth place at Spa with Chris Amon.

The last time I met him racing was as late as 1984. I had arrived at Daytona for the 24-hour race and was walking down the pit lane when all of a sudden there was an iron grip round my neck. It was Innes fully suited up. When I asked him what in heavens name he was doing there - he was 54 years of age by that time - he confirmed he was racing a modest Porsche 924 Carrera entered by an American pal Paul Gentilozzi. He was as pleased as punch to be racing, and this nearly twenty years after his last grand prix. But this was the spirit of Innes Ireland. He then asked if I had heard anyone playing bagpipes in the Daytona paddock. I told him there was a sandy-haired American, who looked like Popeye with a kilt, wandering about. Innes asked me to seek him out and bring him to the car. This slightly bemused Scots-American arrived beside the Porsche to serenade Innes. *"..listen matey, get your bagpipes in gear as we're the only two real Scotsmen in this place; give us the Flower of Scotland."* This was met with a quizzical look from Popeye. Innes and I then had to hum Flower of Scotland to him as he had never heard it before!

Innes was also a very good writer and rightly deserved to become Sports Editor of Autocar magazine. He also wrote for the American magazine Road and Track. Then there were the pranks and the jokes, which on many occasions bordered on the criminal. Certainly in these politically correct days Ireland's conduct at times went beyond the pale. He was an expert at driving rental cars into hotel swimming pools. On one occasion Innes and Roy Salvadori were flying from Honolulu to New Zealand on New Year's Eve and clearly Innes was in high spirits. At one stage the captain of the plane called the hostesses and asked for a cup of coffee. At this Innes persuaded one of the hostesses to take off her uniform and he squeezed into it, complete with padding up front. The other hostesses got out their make up bags and at the end of it Salvadori claims Innes Ireland looked pretty good. At this he took a tray of coffee to the cockpit. Everyone was rolling in the isles but the captain was not amused and gave the hostess a dressing down over the intercom. At this Innes switched to his diplomatic mode and calmed the captain down.

Innes suffered many tragedies in his life. His first marriage broke up and then towards the end of his life he was diagnosed with terminal cancer. As if this were not enough, his only son committed suicide leaving Innes a long personal note explaining his feelings about life. This really tore the heart out of him. Around this time he had met up with Jean Howarth, who he had known back in the 1950s when she was engaged to Mike Hawthorn. After Mike died she remarried but now, in the 1990s, she and Innes met again and he married Jean not long before he died.

Even at end, when he was suffering greatly, he was still keen to work. When the whole debacle surrounding Tom Walkinshaw and the British Racing Drivers Club came to a head, Innes took over the Presidency and threw his whole heart into the job. He proved an effective leader at a difficult time for the Club.

He had also become a close friend of Hugh McCaig of Ecurie Ecosse and Hugh used to have him out sailing on his boat on the West Coast on many occasions during his last years and they had many happy and uproarious times.

In 1993 Innes was invited to Duns to present a sculpture of Jim Clark that had been created by an East European sculptor. He flew to Edinburgh airport and Bernard Buss of SMRC arranged for racing driver/doctor Hugh Chalmers to pick him up so that he had a doctor with him at all times. Hugh later explained that Innes was obviously in great pain but shrugged it off in his usual way. Three months later he was dead.

In the final reckoning Innes Ireland deserved better out of his grand prix career and could have won more grand prix races but the fates, and Colin Chapman, decided otherwise.

LAURENCE JACOBSEN

Laurence Jacobsen's father was a successful engineer and his Kelvin Construction company was involved in a number of important projects. In turn, his son Laurence chose to go into architecture and was one of the most successful students when he was at university. Small, dapper and outspoken he nonetheless has a great sense of humour. Highly professional in everything he does, Jacobsen's first racing Hillman Imp was one of the best-prepared cars on the grid. He then moved on with a Chevron sports car and then an Atlantic Chevron that he converted into a special saloon with a lightweight glass fibre body. He was one of the first people to recognise and encourage Bryce Wilson's talent when Bryce was just a teenager. He had no hesitation in running Bryce with the Chevron when it was still an Atlantic car and Wilson's success in the car led to Laurence renting the Jan Lammers European F3 championship winning March for Wilson to drive at Thruxton in a non-championship event. He continued to support Bryce Wilson throughout Wilson's hectic career.

In the early 1980s Jacobsen and his close friend Robin Smith bought the Chevron racing car company from the liquidator and started building Sports 2000 models in Scotland before selling Chevron to Roger Andreason. During that time he built himself a Chevron B16 that he raced occasionally. He then bought one of the ex-Ecurie Ecosse Ecosse-Ford Group C2 cars and ran it in the British Championship. He also developed a number of other cars including a Can-Am car based on a Reynard F3000.

GLEN KIDSTON

It might seem surprising to find that one of the famous Bentley Boys, who so dominated Le Mans in the 1920s was, in fact, a Scot and a member of the Glasgow family whose fortune was made from A G Kidston & Co the Glasgow metal and machinery merchants. Glen Kidston was born in 1899 and was the son of A Glen Kidston a captain in the Black Watch.

Kidston was probably one of the most charismatic members of the Bentley team and got into all sorts of scrapes both in his racing and in his flying career. This included being the only survivor of a plane crash in which he kicked his way out, with his overcoat in flames and rolled about on the grass to put the flames out! Sadly he was not so lucky some years later when his plane crashed in the mountains north of Johannesburg in South Africa and he was killed.

Kidston finished second in his first Le Mans race (1929) in a 4 1/2 litre Bentley partnering Jack Dunfee and followed this up with a win in 1930 with Bentley financier Woolf Barnato in a 6 1/2 litre.

Today Kidston's nephew, Simon Kidston, runs the European end of Bonhams the auctioneers.

NATHAN KINCH

Though a relative newcomer to the scene, teenager Nathan Kinch has made a name for himself not only in historic racing where he drove a TWR Jaguar but in GTs. He first came to notice in the Ferrari Challenge series where he was one of Britain's most successful competitors in a competition where the Italians tend to dominate. During 2002 he appeared in one of Graham Nash's Saleen S7R. Clearly he is still feeling his way before deciding what direction to take in his racing. His plans were thwarted somewhat when he broke his wrist playing with the family Doberman. With the help of his father, who is a successful entrepreneur in Aberdeen, Nathan moved on in 2003 into the FIA GT Championship sharing one of the factory Lister Storms with Jamie Campbell Walter.

ANDREW KIRKALDY

The fact that motor racing can be tough is amply illustrated by the talented Andrew Kirkaldy. He was one of Scotland's leading kart drivers from 1989 to 1993 and became Scottish Champion.

He then took the normal entry into racing by moving into Formula Ford in 1995 and won eight out of fourteen races. Clearly he was an emerging talent. For 1996 Jackie Stewart gave him the chance to race in Formula Vauxhall Junior and with four wins he finished fifth in the championship. The following year he was second and was named the BRDC McLaren Autosport Young Driver of the Year but had difficulty progressing. A year in Formula Opel in 1998 saw him take another 2nd place in the Championship. He received sponsorship from Sandy Watson and Irvine Laidlaw, who are both successful historic racing drivers, and as part of the deal he also raced Laidlaw's Porsche 906 in historic events.

In 1999 he moved into Formula 3 and was given the chance to test a McLaren MP4-14 but this did not lead to anything special and he has been struggling for drives along with many other talented racers. He had a good season in the Renault Clio Cup series and his prospects looked better late in 2002 when he took over Calum Lockie's drive in the Veloqx Team in the British GT Championship.

JOHN KIRKPATRICK

One of the most capable and modest Scots in motor racing is John Kirkpatrick, for long the man who ran the Jim Russell Racing School at Snetterton and then at Donington. At the same time John has helped and encouraged many young Scots along the way.

John was born in Annan in the South west of Scotland where his father was a livestock auctioneer. His father used to sell sheep to Jim Clark and so here was another driver inspired by Clark. Early in his career John Kirkpatrick worked with Graham Wylie who used to race at Charterhall and Ingliston and occasionally ran an F3 Titan. He moved to the Russell School in 1972 as an instructor but his flair for organisation led to him running the School. At one stage he formed his own team, John Kirkpatrick Racing, and ran Anthony Reid in Formula Ford with a Van Diemen in 1980. John was also a leading light in the Racing For Britain scheme that raised money to help young and talented Britons. Amongst those helped at that time were David Leslie, Johnny Herbert and Nigel Mansell.

LORD LAIDLAW

Irvine Laidlaw, who was born in Keith, is a successful businessman who was enobled in April 2004. He is best known for his exploits in the past eight years in historic motor racing all over the world but not many people know that as a young man he hill climbed and raced a Morgan 4/4 specially built with a space frame chassis. Then he decided that if he wanted to continue to race he would need to earn some money. Eventually his company, which sets up conferences all over the world, allowed him to do this. Today he has a collection of historic racing and rally cars including a pre-war Maserati 6CM, Lotus 69 and Porsche 904/6. He races most of them at the major events. In rally events his wife Lady Christine drives her Ferrari 250 GT SWB and BMW 328. In 2003 Laidlaw, one of the richest men in Scotland, set up the Laidlaw Youth Project and plans to give £20 million a year to charity from 2006 onwards.

JOHN "JOCK" LAWRENCE

Though everyone associates Jock Lawrence with Aberdeen, he was actually born on July 10 1921 at Thinacre Lodge, Hamilton. The family moved to Aberdeenshire and he was educated at Cullen and Fordyce Academy. He always wanted to work with cars and on leaving school moved to Edinburgh to serve his apprenticeship. The war came along so he joined the Royal Navy at the age of 19 and won both the DSM and BEM for bravery whilst serving on motor torpedo boats.

When he was demobbed he started his own motor business in Cullen in 1947. Later he was also involved with the Wakes hotel in Cullen.

With the arrival of Crimond racing circuit he acquired an early Cooper-MG and immediately started winning with the car. After a successful 1952 season he was entered in a number of races by Jack Hunter from Newcastle who had bought one of the ex-Ecurie Ecosse C type Jaguars. This led to him being approached by David Murray to join Ecurie Ecosse. He had many successes with the team, his finest moment coming at Le Mans in 1957 when he finished second with Ninian Sanderson in an Ecosse D type Jaguar and behind his team mates Ron Flockhart and Ivor Bueb in the winning Ecosse D type. After retiring from racing, he found it tough to develop his motor business and left Scotland for Australia. He returned to Britain in the late 1980s settling in the South of England where he could dabble in his favourite hobby of sailing. He died in the 1990s.

DAVID LESLIE Snr.

David Leslie, or "old David" as he is affectionately called in Scotland, was one of Scotland's earliest kart drivers and was instrumental in developing kart racing. He then threw himself into helping his son, also David, firstly in karting and then in motor racing. David is quiet spoken and shy but he was instrumental in launching the racing careers of three of Scotland's leading racing drivers of today, David Coulthard, Allan McNish and Dario Franchitti.

Allan McNish probably speaks for all three when he comments *"...David has the ability to bring the best out of you and he got me into a position* to become a professional racing driver. I, personally, will forever be in his debt." Leslie ran both David Coulthard and Allan McNish in their Formula Ford years and encouraged them to move on. With Dario he ran a two-car team in Formula Vauxhall Junior. Though he no longer runs his own team, he still attends the race meetings and is always willing to help out young drivers.

DAVID LESLIE

David is another graduate from the karting school and was helped along his way by the fact his father was not only a good engineer but a good kart racer. The family had moved from Dumfries to Carlisle where David senior had a Fiat dealership. He first came to our notice at Ingliston when he and his father took part in a series of kart races supporting the race meetings in the mid-1970s. He then started racing Formula Fords supported by Crossflags Garage. In 1978 he became BARC Formula Ford champion and later Shellsport Martini Champion in Formula Ford 2000. When the British Formula Atlantic series took off, David Leslie won the 1980 series and by now was getting better known. He was one of the few drivers to race the Grand Prix Chevron but this was in the British Championship rather than in a grand prix. The car was virtually undeveloped, never raced or was even entered in a world championship grand prix.

If David Leslie's career seemed to stall in the early 1980s it was perhaps because of his relative shyness. Whilst many of his colleagues talked their way into drives David seemed destined to be left on the shelf. Then, in 1984, Hugh McCaig reformed the Ecurie Ecosse team and chose David Leslie to share the driving of the original Ecosse-Ford with Ray Mallock and David Duffield. When Duffield decided to pull out of racing the Leslie/Mallock team had a number of successes.

In 1984 David was offered the chance to race in a couple of Can-Am events at Detroit and Dallas but the car he was to drive, a Frisbee, was in bits when he arrived and he helped to build the car. In one event he had an oil pipe break and in the other he was forced off the road.

In 1986 David, along with Ray Mallock and Belgian driver Marc Duez, won the world Group C2 Championship for Ecurie Ecosse in the Rover V6-engined Ecosse. This was to open many doors for him.

In 1988 Ecurie Ecosse ran an Opel in the British Thundersaloons championship with Hugh Chalmers where they were runners up and in the same year Leslie drove for Mazda at Le Mans. During the early 1990s Leslie continued to race for Ecurie Ecosse in the British Touring Car Championship before switching to Mazda and then Honda. He came back to the Ecosse team with the Nissan Primera and was runner up in the 1999 British Touring Car Championship.

As with many drivers, David Leslie has made a successful career out of his racing.

ERIC LIDDELL

Eric Liddell started out on motorcycles as a speedway rider for Glasgow Giants. His talent, however, was lost in speedway and he moved into cars. Amongst his early cars was a Lola Formula Junior but, as with many other

Eric Liddell poses with the new Ford GT 40 he raced for Nicoll Cuthbert.

Scots drivers, he found it hard going raising the finance to race. In 1964 he bought one of the Emeryson Formula 1 cars and brought it to Charterhall for his first race with it. In practice the car caught fire and though Eric managed to bring it to a stop he had to stand and watch his new car burn.

Eric was given a test by David Murray's Ecurie Ecosse team driving the Tojeiro-Buick Coupe but he turned down the chance to race for the team as he was offered the break that really transformed his racing career. Former MG car club member and enthusiast, Nicoll Cuthbert, invested in a brand new Ford GT 40 (Chassis P/1022) for Eric to drive. This was Eric's introduction to the highest levels of GT racing and was to go on to race for a number of teams driving Lola T70s, and Ferraris with his friend Paul Hawkins all over the world. He was one of the most successful Scottish drivers in GT and sports car racing in the 1970s before retiring from racing. He then played a major part in encouraging his son Robin in the 1990s.

ROBIN LIDDELL

Though he is probably less well known at the moment, Robin Liddell has had as dogged and determined a career in racing as his father had thirty years before. When Robin showed an interest, Eric used his experience to put him on the right track with proper race training and it all paid off. After racing in various minor formulae he moved up to GT cars in the 2000s almost exactly the same racing career course taken by his father.

In May 2002, Robin Liddell had his first taste of the fabulous Le Mans circuit when he was given a drive with PK Sport in a Porsche 911 GT3-RS. His lap time of 4 minutes 12 seconds put him in second place in the GT class during this test day. Later in the season he had the chance to race one of Graham Nash Motorsports Saleen S7Rs in the final round of the American Le Mans Series having earlier won his first race in one of Nash's Saleens at Snetterton. He was back at Le Mans driving a Porsche for PK in 2003.

Robin launched 2004 with a fine second place overall at the Daytona 24 Hour Race sharing Orbit Racings Porsche GT3RS with Mike Fitzgerald, Johnny Mowlem and the Policastro brothers.

The Hon. PATRICK LINDSAY

The Honourable Patrick Lindsay was the second son of the Earl of Crawford and Balcarres and so came from a famous Fife aristocratic family. Patrick was very knowledgeable on cars and became a Director of auctioneers, Christies, where he was a natural to become the specialist voice of car auctioneering. His first racing car was bought in 1953 and was an ex factory HWM-Alta - similar to the car John Brown used to race. He raced the car for two years before marrying Lady Annabel York and leaving racing: but not for long. In 1957 he bought Remus the well-known ERA raced by Prince Bira which he drove with verve and vigour. He once said that he preferred to finish a happy second rather than a frightened first. He really forced forward the concept of historic motor racing in Britain and towards that end he started to build up his own collection. His ex-John Cobb Alfa Romeo Monza was followed by two 250F Maseratis. He had a huge accident in one of them at Thruxton and sold the remains to Innes Ireland.

One of Jim Clark's greatest memories was when he ran in the French Grand Prix at Rouen. There was a supporting historic race and Patrick Lindsay was running his ERA. As usual Jim was fascinated and asked if he could *"..have a shot"*. As Lindsay remarked later, after about four laps Clark was quicker than he was and he had been driving the difficult car for years. He added to his collection the ex John Cobb Napier Railton which had held the outright lap record at Brooklands and then had been used to test parachutes. Then came the aeroplanes, his Stearman bi-plane, the Stampe and the Sopwith Triplane replica amongst others; and of course his Spitfire. Patrick was a very cultured man, his father having been a great art collector. Indeed in 1970 Patrick hit all the newspapers when, at one of Christies sales, he sold Mantegna's "Adoration of the Magi" for a then astounding sum of £8.1 million.

Sadly Lindsay was struck down by cancer and he died in 1981 at the age of 57. His mantle for historic racing was taken up by his three sons Ludovic, James and Valentine who still own many of the cars and some of the aeroplanes their father left them.

ALASDAIR McCAIG

Alasdair McCaig was brought up amidst motor racing thanks to his father's involvement with Ingliston circuit and Ecurie Ecosse, so it was no surprise when he and Michael Mallock, son of Ray Mallock who raced for Ecurie Ecosse in the 1980s were sent to the Paul Ricard circuit in France to take part in the Winfield Racing School. They were both 15 years of age and by far the youngest in the group of drivers from all over the world who took part in the course. At the end they proved to be the two quickest. The School manager, Simon de Latour, apologised and told them that they would not qualify for the school's annual finals day as the Elf contract, for a year's sponsored racing in French Formula Renault, was only open to drivers over the age of 18.

Since then both have moved into motor racing, with Alasdair having to fit his racing in with his studies at Newcastle University. However, though quiet and modest away from a racing car he has proved to be a determined and skilful driver with a variety of cars including a Lotus VII and now a Radical sports car. At the age of 19 his father entered him for a historic race at Knockhill circuit in the Ecosse-Rover that had won the Group C2 World

Championship in 1986 and he promptly won first time out. He had proved he could handle the horsepower and in August 2002 was entered for the Group C Historic event at Nurburgring and finished second in the Group C2 class to one of the Ecosse-DFVs. At the same meeting he was invited to share the driving of John Clark's Cooper Bobtail and they won the historic sports car race over the aggregate of two heats, which bodes well for his future. University and the Mini Cooper Challenge kept him busy in 2003 but in his first drive of 2004 in the Radical he took a promising second place.

HUGH McCAIG

Hugh McCaig's father was a miner who worked hard and eventually had his own open cast coal mines and brick works in Central Scotland. Hugh started racing karts in the 1970s where he met his long time friend David Duffield from Kirkliston. Duffield moved on to racing a Formula Ford Dulon backed by McCaig. This in turn led to McCaig buying a Formula Atlantic car for Duffield. From time to time Hugh pulled out his road car and raced in road saloon races at Ingliston but a big accident, when he rolled his Jaguar XK120 drophead at Ingliston, gave him time to think again.

McCaig has been, and still is, one of the most committed supporters of motor racing in Scotland. Never afraid to put his money where his formidable mouth is he not only regenerated Ingliston in the early 1980s but reformed Ecurie Ecosse and took the team back to Le Mans and success as World Group C2 Champions in 1986. Then followed Ecurie Ecosse's success in the British Touring Car Championship with Vauxhall and Nissan. Indeed, it could be said that McCaig revitalised Scottish motor sport and, today, still manages to send the odd fox into the chicken coop that is Scottish motor racing.

BILL MACKAY

Bill Mackay's career in motor racing was very short and in a sense he was thrown in at the deep end. As a salesman with Hillhead Automobile Company in Glasgow he was required to race an Austin Healey 100S they had just bought from Carlaw Cars and had been raced by Ted Evans. This was only a few months after passing his driving test but he became enthusiastic for racing. He raced the car at Charterhall, Ouston, Thornaby and at one of the Winfield sprints before it was sold. The car that replaced it was an Aston Martin DB3S and Mackay also raced this car. He came to the notice of David Murray of Ecurie Ecosse and drove for the team in the last days of the D-type Jaguar. He was nominated, alongside Ninian Sanderson, to race the team's ex-factory Austin Healey Sprite at Le Mans in 1961. However, Mackay had a huge accident at White House in which he was seriously injured. He might have lost his arm but for the fact his father, a Glasgow surgeon, had him flown directly to Glasgow where his father looked on as his arm was saved. Mackay never raced again but returned to his favourite sport, sailing, where he became one of Scotland's best racing skippers. Today he is still engaged to skipper yachts all over the world.

JIMMY MACKAY

One of the most under-rated of all Scottish racing drivers is Jimmy Mackay from Scrabster in the far north of Scotland. Jimmy thought nothing about setting off for Brands Hatch with his Lotus Eleven on a trailer even though faced with a 1200 mile round trip.

Born at Skinnet in Caithness in September 1916, his grandfather was a farmer and his father was "boots" in the Pentland Hotel in Thurso. In 1925 his father bought the Scrabster Hotel but he died in the 1930s and Jimmy's mother ran the hotel on her own with his sister Babs. After leaving school, Jimmy was a shipping clerk but was a volunteer when war broke out and served in the 5th Seaforth Highlanders. He and his wife set up a fish haulage business, which he later sold due to his wife's illness. In the late 1950s he took over control of the Scrabster Hotel from his mother.

His first "racing" car was an MG PB which he entered for his first meeting at Charterhall. At the end of a 300 mile drive to the circuit he had not brought a crash helmet and the officials wouldn't let him start. David Murray of Ecurie Ecosse loaned Jimmy his crash helmet so he could race.

Early in 1956 he bought Lewis Fraser's Lotus Six fitted with a Ford Consul engine and was successful with it. Today the car is owned by the Edmonton Tool and Engineering Company that used to make parts for Colin Chapman in his early days.

The Lotus Six was replaced with a Lotus Eleven but in 1957 he bought a new Series 2 Lotus Eleven and registered it SK 6003. His son John still has the receipt for the car in his collection of Jimmy Mackay memorabilia. Jimmy's local mechanic was Sinclair "Clair" Calder but Hugh Shannon, who prepared Tommy Dickson's cars, usually tuned the engines and made the various modifications to them. It was natural that Jimmy and Tommy Dickson became close friends and they used to share Tommy's bus and trailer to take their cars to circuits. They also used to share each others cars, which provided a few headaches for those of us who were trying to keep track of who drove what. It was with the Series 2 Eleven that Hugh Shannon was given rein to make various modifications. He changed the de Dion rear axle into a fully independent arrangement and from then on the car became known as the Shannon-Climax. Later still, in the 1960s, Hugh took the car a stage further and added a hard top and it became the Lotus Eleven GT.

Around this time Jimmy's son John Mackay bought a well-used Lotus Eleven from another northern Scot, Nairn Ferrier, and so now we had two J Mackays racing, which created a lot of confusion.

Not content with racing in Britain, Jimmy embarked on a trip to Roskilde Ring in Denmark with his Lotus Eleven on a trailer behind his faithful Simca Aronde. He was friendly with all the leading British drivers of the time, particularly Paul Hawkins. His reaction to Paul's death *"Such is the way sometimes in this game and you feel queer for a while but then you are out and at it again."* Like Jim Clark he was a good tactician, such as at Roakilde Ring in 1962 when he was on pole against Hawkins, Bob Hicks, Tony Lanfranchi and a number of quick continental drivers. *"To get this fastest practice time I just sat in the paddock till the rest of the field had done their best and loaded their cars on to their transporters. I then went out knowing just how fast I had to go to qualify for the number one place on the grid. This I managed, much to the surprise of the English team who were sure that nothing could touch their new Lotus 23 with their professional driver (Hawkins). Although I had an accident in the race, at least I made the fastest time and in the process put Stirling Moss in the shade."*

Jimmy Mackay had many successes and he was proud of the fact that he held and still holds the 1100cc lap record on the original Brands Hatch short circuit before all the changes were made. He proved to be something of a special visitor at Brands. Jimmy Mackay died of a heart attack in the 1970s just before his 55th birthday but will always be remembered as the gritty little Scot with the permanent five-o-clock shadow who raced like a terrier and never gave up. One of his great friends was Jim Clark who early on recognised Jimmy's talents. In a postscript to one of Jim Clark's letters to Jimmy Mackay he wrote *"They tell me you were going well on Sunday"* showing that even after he had become world champion Clark still remembered his old friend. It is also touching that his son John Mackay was able to trace his father's best known Lotus Eleven - SK 6003 - and buy it from the owner. It resides to this day in Scrabster

RONNIE MACKAY

Ronnie Mackay was always a quiet and contemplative person when you met him but he had the determination to stretch his racing beyond Scotland. It was assumed in the 1960s he was a member of the Mackay family - Jimmy and John - but this was not the case.

In 1970 he decided to try his luck in the Formula 2 Trophy race at Mantorp Park in Sweden where he was up against all the stars, Regazzoni, Stommelen, Attwood, Cevert, Bonnier and Petersen. Whereas most of the Brabham drivers were in the latest BT30s Ronnie took his BT21. It was a sad introduction to the tough world of Formula 2 as he did not qualify. He had better luck at Phoenix Park in September when he finished a strong fourth behind Alan Rollinson, Richard Scott and Brian Nelson.

For the following season he was entered for the Speed International Trophy at Mallory Park in one of the Irish Racing Cars Brabham BT30 but was unplaced. He had entered for other Formula 2 events that year but circumstances contrived to find him a non-starter on the other occasions.

CAMPBELL McLAREN

Campbell McLaren is one of the great Jaguar enthusiasts and yet he did not race for the first time until 1978. His father was in the construction business in Glasgow and at one time was Vice-Chairman of Glasgow Rangers Football Club. The first car he raced, however, was not a Jaguar but an Opel Kadett which his friend Graham Birrell had persuaded him to buy. At the end of the year he entered and raced his Jaguar XKSS in the historic event and for good measure entered Graham Birrell in his Aston Martin DB4 Zagato in the same race. By now Campbell began what was to be one of the finest Jaguar collections in Scotland. He bought a C type Jaguar from the United States and then managed to find one of Briggs Cunningham's lightweight E-type Jaguars (5116 WK) which he also raced at Ingliston. He always wanted a proper D type Jaguar but one never came his way. I remember him passing a remark in the early 1980s to the effect that *"....a short-nosed D type is now commanding something like £60,000 and that is right out of my league."* In 1998 the ex-Ecurie Ecosse Le Mans winning short-nose D type sold for £1.7 million! His most famous Jaguar was "Chassis No.8" the first Jaguar factory racing car based on an SS100.

When business took a downturn Campbell sold his Jaguar collection and in recent years has come back into historic racing with a very rare racing Jaguar. This is the sole Jaguar XK150 developed by the company for racing but never actually raced. Campbell used the car to win the Jaguar Historic Championship in 2001 and is likely to continue racing it.

IAIN McLAREN

Iain McLaren was a stalwart at Ingliston throughout the 1970s and '80s. He built up a successful British Leyland dealership in West Lothian and

expanded with an additional dealership in Bo'ness, where he was born. Needless to say Iain used to go to the Bo'ness hill climb when he was a little boy and thought the racing people were very odd, never realising that one day he would be doing the same thing. He started out as a motor cycle trials rider but dropped this to study as a civil engineer.

In 1968 he admits he did not know much about motor racing but a number of his pals were interested so he bought Ian Cochrane's Lotus 7 for the princely sum of £345, then decided to go hill climbing. Next he bought a Vauxhall Viva into which he fitted a 1650cc Ford race engine. It was not the greatest car and was sold to buy the ex-Gerry Birrell Singer Chamois. Then he decided to go into single seaters buying Tony Charnell's Lola T55. After scaring himself silly in the car he opined : *"That car had even worse handling than my old Viva and had a nasty habit of changing ends without any provocation."* Moving on, McLaren sold the Lola and bought a Chevron B8 which he loved and then returned to the Scottish Hill Climb Championship in 1971 with the ex Cyd Williams B15 Chevron F3 car which turned out to be one of his most successful cars, winning the championship. When he sold the Chevron to Kenny Allan, Iain decided to go for broke and bought Sir Nicholas Williamson's Brabham BT35X winning the Scottish hill climb championship again. This Brabham was exchanged for a newer Brabham BT36 and won the hill climb championship yet again in 1973.

By now the hill climb people were fed up with McLaren winning everything and were happy when he bought Ron Dennis' Rondel Formula 2 car for a serious attempt at the Scottish Libre Championship in 1974. One of the keys to Iain McLaren's success was the meticulour's preparation of his cars. He had a planned pattern of replacing parts at set periods rather than waiting for them to wear out. He won the Northern Formula Libre Championship with the Rondel and closed the season by winning at Ingliston with Campbell Graham's Chevron B25. He never had any aspirations to become a professional racing driver but presented his cars as though he had. In 1976 he bought the famous factory Chevron "Chocolate Drop" and finished second in the official RAC Gp6 National Championship just one point behind outright winner John Lepp in the factory March. There followed the ex-Klaus Ludwig Chevron Formula 2 car and then a new Chevron B36 sports car. At one time he contemplated buying a Shadow Formula 1 car for Ingliston but thought better of it and eventually finished his career racing, appropriately, a McLaren M26 which he was able to buy through his long time friendship with Ron Dennis.

Whilst he was still young enough to enjoy himself he sold out his British Leyland businesses and retired to Ayrshire to take up sailing. A happy man, and another unsung hero of Scottish motor racing.

DONALD MACLEOD

Donald MacLeod, at the time of writing, is the only winner of the Formula Ford Festival at Brands Hatch in a car constructed by himself and also the only person who has won the Festival twice.

Donald moved from Scotland to London. He raced in the second ever Formula Ford Festival, in 1973, and won the event outright. He hoped this would be a step up into Formula 2 or Formula 3 but after a few rides in Formula Atlantic and Formula 3 he and his brother Hamish moved on to take over the Sark racing car project - see Scottish Racing Cars chapter - and run the Sark FF2000. During that year, 1979, he and his brother designed and built a brand new Formula Ford 1600 Sark and Donald decided to have it ready for the Formula Ford Festival that year. Bear in mind the car had not fully turned a wheel before the Festival,and also that Donald by then was 32 years of age. Lined up against him were all the hotshots of the day, many of whom were to go on to race in Formula 1 and sports cars. They included Roberto Moreno, Julian Bailey, David Sears, Tommy Byrne and Thierry Tassin. Donald was king of Brands in the wet. On the Saturday he easily qualifyied for the quarter finals on the Sunday. However on the Sunday the engine acted up in the wet and he could only finished fourth. In the semi-finals he then shone and won his heat, so qualifying on pole position for the final. Despite being hit by Ric Morris at Clearways on the opening lap, McLeod took second place and set off after the leader, Terry Gray. As the Sark was magic in the wet, McLeod surprised everyone passing Gray by taking a path through a puddle and into the lead. It was probably the greatest moment in Donald's career and he won his second Formula Ford Festival this time in his own car, the Sark. He did one more Festival, a year later, which was to be his last ever motor race but the racing car market had collapsed and he shortly got rid of Sark and retired.

ALLAN McNISH

Allan McNish was a natural racing driver from the very start. Not only was he frighteningly quick in karts but even as a teenager, he had developed a way of analysing not only his performance, but his race strategy: the mark of a future champion.

Allan was born in Dumfries where his father, Bert, owned Crossflags Motors, today a progressive BMW dealership. Bert McNish was very friendly with David Leslie, father of today's racing driver, and Bert was a mechanic and helper for David when his son first started racing. As a result of this young Allan has been embroiled in motor racing all his life.

Allan McNish was something of a child prodigy. At the age of 11 his father bought him a kart in order to satisfy his enthusiasm to race. Exactly one year later at the age of 12 he became Scottish Champion.

By the age of 15 Allan was not only British Super One champion but finished third in the World Championships, the highest-ever placing by a Scot. When he moved into Seniors at 16 he immediately became British Champion. He was factory driver for Fullarton whose PCR engines were developed in Italy. By then he was fully committed to coming into Formula Ford as soon as he was seventeen and could get a full driving licence.

During his initial racing season in Formula Ford, Allan McNish raced the David Leslie Racing Van Diemen at Knockhill.

Bert McNish and Hugh McCaig were friends, Hugh being a customer of the McNish garage, and it was no surprise when Hugh, under the Ecurie Ecosse banner, helped Allan through his karting years with sponsorship.

When, at the age of 17, it came to a move into Formula Ford David Leslie Sr, took Allan under his wing and provided the kind of solid-as-a-rock support that any driver needs at that age. That season, 1987, McNish in his Van Diemen RF87 was the man to beat in the Townsend Thoreson Junior Championship. Ironically he was racing that year against another Scot who would later employ him as a driver, Paul Stewart. By August that year, McNish moved up to the senior class and the Snetterton round in the Owen Brown RAC British Championship. Here he stunned everyone by winning first time out against all the leading drivers. Even championship leader, Eddie Irvine, was demoted to seventh place. In the Formula Ford Festival, that showcase for new drivers, McNish finished fifth overall behind winner Eddie Irvine. At that same event he raced against two Finnish newcomers who would play a part in his future racing career, Mikka Hakkinen and Mikka Salo.

At the end of the season Marlboro organised a driver testing session at Donington Park and invited a number of up and coming young drivers to take part, including Eddie Irvine, Allan McNish, Mikka Hakkinen and Martin Donnelly. The judging panel included James Hunt, Ron Dennis and Mike Earle and the stars of the session were Hakkinen and McNish with the Finn just 0.8 seconds a lap quicker than the Scot in FF2000s. This was made more remarkable by the fact that McNish was driving a 2000 for the first time. Marlboro decided to plump for the pair as their team for 1988. The original plan was to run in the Formula Ford 1600 series as the works Van Diemen team but the announcement of the new Formula Vauxhall Junior class saw Marlboro switch to this with McNish and Hakkinen.

Marlboro broke with tradition and announced their new team at Ingliston before dashing off for the first round of the championship at Thruxton. Here McNish did not put a wheel wrong and won the inaugural FVL race out of the park with his team mate Hakkinen in second place. It was no surprise when the McNish/Hakinen duo dominated FVL in that opening season, Allan becoming British Champion and Mikka becoming European Champion.

By now Allan McNish was coming to the attention of the important people and he moved smoothly into 1990 with continued help from Marlboro and signed up with the DAMS-Lola team alongside Frenchman Eric Comas.

"For once the Auld Alliance didn't help me." Remarks McNish about his first turbulent year with the French based team. It became clear that most of the effort would go to the Frenchman but McNish was within three points of Comas in the F3000 Championship. The car proved unreliable and Allan and the team owner simply did not see eye to eye. Though Marlboro tried to switch him to Pacific Racing for the 1991 season, he stayed with DAMS and Lola and it was a further disaster as the team decided to switch from

Allan McNish wins the first Formula Vauxhall Lotus race with his team mate Mika Hakkinen in second place.

crossply to radial tyres and the Lola was not the best chassis for the Avons. However, during the season Allan was able secure a testing contract with McLaren thanks to winning the Cellnet award. Then came his Donington Park accident. At the F3000 race at Donington he decided to start the race from the pit lane and chose slicks rather than intermediate tyres. As the weather improved he began hauling his way up the field and came up behind Emanuelle Naspetti.

"At the end of the straight leading to the chicane I dived for the inside and I honestly think Naspetti didn't see me. He squeezed me and my car slid off the road and hit the barrier hard, killing a mechanic"

At the end of the season his future looked uncertain. He signed for Mike Earle to drive a Reynard in the F3000 championship but the team pulled out part way through the season. There was little testing around so McNish was on the look out for a drive in 1993. However, fate stepped in when he contracted a debilitating virus that hit him like a poleaxe. He visited a number of specialists but they could not isolate the virus and it was Professor Syd Watkins who suggested that it had probably come from some rice he had eaten in Thailand two years before and the virus had remained dormant. McNish was incapable of driving a racing car as it had weakened his body. As part of his recuperation he had two lumps of lead bolted on to an old crash helmet and would wear this contraption at home

whilst watching television rocking his head from side to side to strengthen his neck muscles.

Tom Walkinshaw, who had bought into Benetton, approached Allan and offered him a full time testing contract with Benetton which got him back into racing trim again. *"You know"* he reflects *"that testing deal with Tom was done on the strength of a handshake"*

Allan McNish's professional racing career appeared to be off the rails. In 1994 he drove for Middlebridge Racing and then for Paul Stewart Racing in 1995. *"Paul (Stewart) had decided to retire from racing and Jackie offered me the drive but we had a lot of problems with reliability"*

Clearly Allan was getting nowhere. There were no prospects of a full season in Formula One and he had spent five uncomfortable seasons in Formula 3000. America looked like a possibility when he was invited by Bruce McCaw's PacWest team to go to America and take part in a test session for a place in their CART team. However, despite the fact that McNish was the quickest of the drivers, McCaw chose former grand prix driver Mark Blundell, so leaving the Scot virtually on the shelf for the 1996 racing season. The small opportunities to come his way, however, included a few drives in the VIP car in the Porsche Supercup series. It was to totally transform his career.

During 1997 Porsche came back to McNish. In the United States they had been running a car for an American team but wanted to clinch the title and sent McNish over to the USA for the final three rounds with a GT1 to play with. As a result he scored two wins and a second place and Porsche were champions. He was then brought into the Porsche team for 1998 with Le Mans as the goal. Talking of Porsche, McNish has nothing but praise. *"I think Porsche as a team appreciate what you can do more than any other team. They are very inclusive and they have a kind of family atmosphere and are very supportive."* In 1998 McNish, with Laurent Aiello and Stephane Ortelli led home their sister car by a lap so becoming, along with such as Ron Flockhart, Ninian Sanderson and Johnny Dumfries a Scottish Le Mans winner.

At the end of that year Porsche withdrew from racing but McNish was kept on a Porsche retainer throughout 1999. When he was approached by Toyota to race at Le Mans that year Porsche graciously allowed their driver to take part and he and Thierry Boutsen were lying in second place to the winning BMW when Boutsen did a quick overtake of a Porsche GT2 into the Dunlop Curves. The Porsche's steel brakes could not slow it quickly enough and it punted Boutsen's Toyota into the barriers and out of the race.

During 1999 Porsche had developed a new prototype racer with a V10 engine and Bob Wollek tested the car on Porsche's Weissach circuit. It proved to be very much on the pace and McNish had hopes of running with Porsche again but the Porsche board ruled out racing in 2000 to concentrate on their new Cheyenne road car. Despite having a three-year contract, McNish left Porsche and signed for their great rivals, Audi, in sports car racing.

He was entered for Le Mans with his French friends, Aiello and Ortelli and after leading, the car hit trouble. McNish put on the pressure and galloped back up the field to finish second overall to his team mates with the third Audi behind him. McNish was also contracted to compete in the American Le Mans Series and won that outright for Audi. He was on the crest of a wave.

Meanwhile, on the other side of the world, Toyota were planning to enter grand prix racing and approached Allan McNish about rejoining them.

Everything McNish had beavered for all those years looked like coming to fruition. When the official announcement was made it was McNish and Mika Salo who were named as test drivers for the 2001 season with the planned move into grand prix racing in 2002. For McNish the first three months testing were all his as Salo was recovering from injuries in an accident early in the season. As usual, McNish threw himself into the task proving once more to be a dedicated test driver of great ability. When the 2002 season came around he was confirmed as one of the drivers alongside Mika Salo.

Throughout 2002 McNish was always there, or thereabouts, but his finishing record was poor, mainly due to problems with the new car and when it was announced, near the end of the season, that both he and Salo would be dropped - a decision which came from Japan rather than from team boss Ove Andersson - it created quite a stir. Not one to dwell too much on the perfidiousness of life in motor racing, Allan once more started looking around. He was offered a couple of drives in sports cars for 2003 and even tested an Indycar though there was never any direct indication he would take this route.

However, McNish was approached by Flavio Briatore to join Renault as their F1 test driver in 2003 and he accepted right away. As he remarked, philosophically, *"I will be in the paddock, under race conditions and as well as that, every minute spent on the circuit will be important."* Whether this leads to a full time return to grand prix racing remains to be seen.

Allan McNish, however, is the embodiment of the Scottish racing driver, determined, diligent and with a thoroughly intelligent approach to his career. He is also quick to give credit where credit is due. He credits Belgian driver Thierry Boutsen for teaching him *"how to win races out of the car as well as in it.".*

"TASO" MATHIESON

Thomas Alastair Sutherland Ogilvie Mathieson, to give him his full name, was rarely called anything but Taso though within the family he was known as Alastair. Born in 1909 he had three great loves in his life, motor racing, the French way of life, and Bugattis. He originally trained as an engineer and served his apprenticeship at Thornycrofts where he joined at the age of 21. It was whilst there that he made friends with two amateur racers who persuaded him to be their passenger in a relay race. The story is told of him taking part in this race at Brooklands without one of the broad bodybelts drivers used in those days in cars with virtually no suspension to speak of. For days after the race his stomach muscles ached. He was now hooked on motor racing and shortly after this bought a supercharged Italian OM and won his first ever race at Brooklands in 1931. He then started his great love for Bugattis when he bought a Type 37 followed by a string of others. In 1934 he bought a brand new Type 51 Bugatti from the factory but his health was not good and his parents were beginning to put on some pressure. Mathieson entered it for Chris Staniland to drive. That same year he gave up engineering and returned to Glasgow to join the family business that made small hand tools. This lasted just four years before he moved back south of the Border in 1938 and continued his racing. In the Spring of that year he made a sudden decision to enter for the 1938 Le Mans 24 Hour race and bought a 4 litre Talbot-Darracq T150C from the Frenchman Mahe who had a confirmed entry for the race. Mathieson roped in Freddie Clifford as his

co-driver and they had an eventful race, the car catching fire no fewer than four times. The last time saw Mathieson abandon it at White House where it burned to a cinder. The only relic TASO saved was the tachometer which he kept as a souvenir!. A year later and he was back at Le Mans with a Talbot T26 partnered by none other than Luigi Chinetti who had already won Le Mans in 1932 and 1934 driving for Alfa Romeo. Chinetti was also to be the man who persuaded Enzo Ferrari to build road cars and became Ferrari's East Coast distributor in the United States. The Mathieson car, though entered privately, was in fact a factory car. During the night a tyre tread came off and the car slid into a sand bank. Mathieson kept digging and eventually got the car back to the pits but the steering was broken and it was retired.

Mathieson had served in the Territorial Army so was called up for war service. He spent two years with the Highland Light Infantry and landed on the Normandy beachhead on D-day plus 3.

After the War Mathieson was quickly back into racing with the ex-Tim Birkin Maserati 8C he had bought just prior but had not raced. He ran in June 1946 at St Cloud in France and three weeks later at the Grand Prix of Roussillon where he finished sixth against such opposition as Louis Chiron, Raymond Sommer and Giuseppe Farina. This car he later converted into a road car that he eventually sold to Mike Oliver of Connaught fame. In 1946 he was an investor, with his fellow Scot Lord Selsdon in the HRG sports car firm and then bought a Maserati A6GCS with Argentinean driver Roberto Mieres. Mathieson went back to Le Mans in 1949 with an Aston Martin DB2 but the car retired and in 1950, his last Le Mans race, he had his best result finishing 9th in a Frazer Nash Mille Miglia with Dickie Stoop. That same year he took delivery of a Frazer Nash Le Mans Replica that had been broken up after the 1949 Mille Miglia. This car came back into Scotland in the early 1990s when John Romanes of Scotcircuits bought it and raced it in a few historic events. One of Mathiesons last races was the 1952 Targa Florio where he raced a Ferrari 195S and finished a remarkable sixth overall behind three factory Lancia Aurelia B20s.

In 1946 at the age of 38 TASO decided he would retire when he reached 40 but he cheated a little, retiring at 43.

He wrote various articles and an important book Grand Prix Racing 1906-1914 which was illustrated with photographs from his amazing collection, most of which came from the French photographer Marius Branger.

Later, in reviewing his racing life, he admitted he shuddered whenever he thought how much it had cost but *"...it was worth every dime."*

JOHN EADIE MILNE

For most of his competition career, John Milne was a rally driver and became a member of the official BMC factory team driving a variety of cars including Austin Westminsters and MGs. A few days after surviving a huge accident on the Liege-Sofia-Liege, he was forced off the road just outside Glasgow in his modest Ford Prefect and sustained a broken neck. He not only recovered but continued with the odd rally. He quietly bought one of the handful of Dick Jacobs MG Midget Coupes and this was a mark of the man. Having trained as a lawyer, he inherited the family whisky and restaurant business, Eadie Cairns, and was always very secretive about his cars. He began racing the Midget at Charterhall and Ingliston as well as one of the factory MGAs that had been prepared and raced at Le Mans. Once, at Nurburgring with the Midget Coupe, John drove like a man possessed and when he passed the pits at the end of the lap his friend and co-driver John Williamson held out a sign saying *"F....g Schnell!"*. The Midget Coupe is still in Scotland after over forty years and is raced by Milne's stepson, James Willis. Ironically Willis and Lance Gauld went back to Nurburgring with the car in August 2004.

COLIN and JIMMY McRAE

Rally driver Colin McRae and his father Jimmy, who was a multiple winner of the British Rally Championship, are probably not normally associated with motor racing but both of them have appeared on the tracks. In the 1980s, when Ecurie Ecosse was reformed, one of the cars raced by the team was a Vauxhall Chevette and Jimmy McRae was offered a drive with the car at the Ingliston circuit. His performance brought the crowd to their feet with his power slides through the corners. As he was busy at the time helping to promote the careers of his two sons Colin and Alastair in International rallying he did not have the time to continue in racing but he proved, as other successful rally drivers have done in the past, that he could have made a career out of motor racing.

Colin McRae has always enjoyed driving different cars and at the wheel of a TVR Tuscan in the Tuscan championship in the early 1990s he provided a lot of excitement with his forceful driving. In 1992 his then rally boss at Prodrive, David Richards, prepared a BMW 318 for him to drive in the Knockhill round of the British Touring Car Championship. He confounded all his critics by finishing eighth in the first race. In the second heat he and Matt Neal clashed and as a result he was excluded from the race results.

He was given a drive in a Jordan GP car in a publicity stunt and proved that he was no slouch. He was then offered the chance by Ford to race a Ford Taurus in the ASCAR championship on the Rockingham oval. He qualified 11th and finished 8th overall.

McRae now has thoughts of going back into motor racing and has his eye on a drive in the legendary Australian event at Bathurst and Le Mans. The latter was confirmed early in 2004 with the announcement of his drive in a Ferrari 550 Maranello at the 24 Hour event.

NIGEL MORRISON

Glaswegian Nigel Morrison first raced with his brother Ronnie's Triumph TR3A lightweight but this came to an end when he rolled the car at Rufforth. He continued to drive the car but kept the flattened bonnet hinges which had been ground down as the car slid along the track. He then invested in Jimmy Mackay's Lotus XI which he drove spasmodically until 1968 when he bought a Chevron B8. He raced the Chevron in the European 2 litre sports car championship rounds at Karlskoga in Sweden and Jullyandsring in Denmark which had the same circuit length as Ingliston. At the end of the 1989 season, Nigel sold the car to Andrew Fletcher and it subsequently went to Canada before returning to Britain.

DAVID MURRAY

Nearly fifty years ago, in June 1956, the motor racing world was shocked when a relatively unknown private team from Scotland won the Le Mans 24 with a two year old D-type Jaguar on their first appearance at the track. It is a feat unlikely to happen these days and was even surprising back then, but the team, Ecurie Ecosse, were to go back to Le Mans in 1957, this time with two cars, and finished first and second!

The man behind this team with the French name was a modest Edinburgh accountant called David Murray. Murray first raced in middle-age with a Maserati 4CL grand prix car that had been owned by his friend Reg Parnell, and then, in 1951, with a 4CLT Maserati. His racing at this level came to an end at the German Grand Prix that year when he went off the road. He walked part of the way back to the pits before being given a lift by a member of the public. By now his wife, back at the pits, had feared the worst and when he finally appeared, uninjured, she insisted that he gave up motor racing. Which he did.

It was only when he moved to London for a brief spell that he saw motor racing for the first time, at Brooklands. He was captivated and bought an MG but there was no motor racing in Scotland and so did a few rallies and hill climbs with it. However, six years later, in 1949, he took part in a few sprints in Scotland before buying R1A, the very first ERA racing car.

As anyone in racing will tell you, it is difficult to get rid of the racing bug and after the Nurburgring accident, Murray, who now had a small garage in Edinburgh with his partner Wilkie Wilkinson, could not resist trying to get back into motor racing. With one of his customers, a young farmer and racing driver Ian Stewart, he had the idea of forming a team of cars to race under the Scottish flag. Reg Tanner, the competitions manager of Esso petroleum, offered to help if Murray could form a team with three identical sports cars. The amount of money he offered - £5,000 (or around £100,000 in today's value) - was enough to get Murray thinking. Ian Stewart was racing one of the new Jaguar XK120s and Murray had sold his own identical car to another young driver called Bill Dobson. Now he had two identical cars and needed a third. He had hoped to persuade his wife to let him buy another Jaguar for himself but she refused to budge so he found a young Scottish nobleman, Sir James Scott Douglas, who was keen to race with his Jaguar XK120. Now they had their team of three drivers and cars and Esso, true to their word, provided the much-needed money to set the team on its way.

David Murray wanted to underline the fact the team was Scottish and so called it Ecurie Ecosse. (from the French meaning Team Scotland.) The reason for the French name was two-fold. Firstly Murray had a great love of France and was later to open an up-market wine shop in Edinburgh specialising in French wines. Secondly, the shrewd Murray felt that by giving the team a French name he might get better starting money when racing in Europe.

The team became very successful with the influx of new talent such as Jimmy Stewart and Ninian Sanderson and Ecurie Ecosse were feared wherever they raced. The familiar Jaguars, with their unique metallic dark blue colours, raced all over Europe with a lot of success against factory opposition. At the same time the Jaguar factory were quick to realise that success by a private team with their cars was worth more publicity than when a factory car won and gave considerable help to the team. Indeed for the 1954 racing season Ecurie Ecosse bought the factory disc-braked C-type Jaguars including the car with which Duncan Hamilton and Tony Rolt had won Le Mans in 1953. This continued in 1955 and 1956 with Ecurie Ecosse taking over the factory D-type Jaguars.

Though David Murray had always dreamed of racing at Le Mans there was one problem. At that time you were invited to compete at Le Mans, you did not just sent in an entry form. When the Belgian racing team, Equipe National Belge, could not take up one of their entries for 1956, Lofty England, the famous Jaguar team manager, suggested to the organisers that David Murray should be invited to enter one of his Ecurie Ecosse D-type Jaguars. England assured the French that Murray would *"put up a good show."*

The team that went out to Le Mans was mainly a bunch of friends of the drivers to handle timekeeping and pit signalling and the most David Murray expected was to finish the race. However, as time went on the factory Jaguars dropped out as well as most of the Ferraris and Maseratis and to their total astonishment Ecurie Ecosse found themselves leading the greatest long distance motor race in the world. The victory was so impressive that the English magazine Autosport printed their front cover in blue in honour of the Scottish team's success. When, a year later, Murray, now on the invitation list, ran two D-type Jaguars and finished first and second Ecurie Ecosse were at the peak of their success. That same year, 1957, the American Indianapolis drivers challenged the European grand prix teams to a race between Grand Prix and Indycars round the banked Monza circuit. The European teams were reluctant to compete but David Murray entered three of his D-type Jaguars for the race believing that they might do well against the Indy cars and that Europe had to be represented in the race. As it turned out the D-types with their four speed gearboxes led the race in the early stages whilst the two-speed high-geared Indycars picked up speed. Though the Jaguars were swamped and beaten Ecurie Ecosse became the toast of America for at least challenging the Indycars. There was even talk of the D types racing at Indianapolis. This was intoxicating stuff and many years later David Murray confessed that he had let all this success go to his head.

For a start David Murray was convinced that the six-cylinder Jaguar engine would continue to be competitive but other teams and engines were coming along. Lotus and Cooper both produced lightweight sports cars with Coventry Climax engines and were defeating the big and lumbering Jaguar-powered Jaguars and their Lister and Tojeiro derivatives. Indeed, Ecurie Ecosse, were the last team to race a D type Jaguar at Le Mans. This was in 1960 when the design was already over six years old. The only bright spark came in 1963 when David Murray offered a drive of the team's Cooper-Monaco and Tojeiro-Buick Coupe to Jackie Stewart, the younger brother of his former team member Jimmy Stewart.

Ecurie Ecosse was to continue in racing until 1971 but they never repeated the giant-killing success they had in the 1950s. As for David Murray, even his skill as an accountant could not keep up with the teams debts and business concerns. In 1968 he fled Scotland for the Canary Islands when faced with tax bills. Now living in relative poverty and working behind a bar he was involved in a road accident and when in hospital suffered a massive heart attack and died. His team, Ecurie Ecosse, had been left in the hands of its supporters club, the Ecurie Ecosse Association but in 1971 they stopped racing after an unsuccessful two seasons in Formula 2 with Brabham and March racing cars.

Today Jackie Stewart continues to acknowledge the debt he owed David Murray for giving him the chance to race for Ecurie Ecosse and though his life was to end so sadly, David Murray is still remembered in Scotland as the foundation stone of what was to become something of a revolution in young Scottish drivers.

DAVID H MURRAY

Not to be confused with the founder of Ecurie Ecosse, David Hugh Murray, also came from Edinburgh but moved to London and set up a garage in Pinner. He was always a great Frazer-Nash enthusiast and in June 1934 he bought his first Meadows-engined Byfleet model. Two years later Frazer Nash had problems. David Murray was persuaded to invest in the company

and he bought 10% of the equity. When FN came to an agreement with BMW to build the legendary 328 model, marketing it as the Frazer-Nash BMW (Note the addition of a hyphen.) It is interesting to note that the first three cars were sold to Scots - John Flint, Johnny Millar and Tom Miekle. The fourth car also went to a Scot, David Murray. He entered the car with ERA driver Pat Fairfield for Le Mans in 1937. As Fairfield was an experienced driver and one of the finest of the day it was agreed he should take the first driving stint. However there was a multiple crash at Arnage corner and Fairfield arrived on the scene to find the road blocked by crashed cars. He skidded off the road. The car went end over end and Fairfield was taken to hospital where he died. The car was repaired and Murray raced it in the Tourist Trophy at Donington Park but retired after spinning off. During the War Murray sold his shares in Frazer Nash to the Aldington family but continued to be a staunch supporter.

In 1950 the Tourist Trophy found a new home at Dundrod and as David Murray still had his Frazer-Nash BMW he entered it for the first post-war TT and finished fourth in his class. He then bought one of the new Le Mans Replicas (Chassis 133) and raced this in Britain. He raced in some of the early Scottish meetings causing great confusion with two Edinburgh born David Murrays in racing.

RICHARD NOBLE

Richard Noble set up the World Land Speed Record in October 1983 with his Thrust 2. It was set on the Black Rock desert in Nevada and he reached over 633 mph. Richard was born in Edinburgh and also held the British land speed record of 263 mph at Greenham Common in 1980.

SASHA PEARL

Very few people, even in Scotland, might have heard of Sasha Pearl as she raced for comparatively few seasons. Daughter of a Perthshire farmer, Sasha, was determined to become a racing driver and after some initial races in Scotland she raced in the first year of Formula Vauxhall Junior where she was remarkably quick. At Thruxton in June 1991, for example, she finished fifth overall just behind David Cuff and Kevin McGarrity. With some decent sponsorship, rather than family financial help, she might well have developed in all areas of motor racing.

ANTHONY REID

Anthony Reid was the first of a new group of Scottish racing drivers to appear on the scene in the early 1980s. Born in Glasgow in 1957, his father was an architect and his mother a pianist. He was educated at Loretto in Musselburgh, where Jim Clark was a former pupil, and Clark was always Anthony's hero.

He originally took a course at the Jim Russell Racing School in 1975. He was a good pupil and two years later he entered the Jim Russell World Scholarship with another 150 entrants. The prize was a works drive with the school in the 1978 season. Anthony ran out the winner and had his season of racing. But how to earn sufficient money to carry on was the problem. He decided that the fledgling oil industry was the answer and for two years he lived in a tent and worked at the Sullom-Voe oil terminal in the Shetlands.

In 1981 he qualified for the Marlboro Formula Ford World Cup with his three year old car. He was a member of the Scottish team and finished

10th overall out of the 250 entrants. The following year, still on a miniscule budget, he finished fourth in the RAC Championship and sixth in the Townsend Thoresen. At this he was snapped up by Argo to race their factory FF2000 in the 1982 season. He was to finish fourth in the Championship and capped a successful season with a strong second place at the BBC Grandstand Trophy as well as a Grovewood Award. Then Argo fell apart and he missed most of the next season. Glasgow hi-fi company Linn Products supported him for the Grandstand series and just lost out to Martin Donnelly.

The normally mild-mannered Reid could be a complete terror in a racing car. For 1985 Reid moved into uncharted waters by driving not only a new car, the first carbon-fibre chassis F3 Reynard, but coupled to an in-line four cylinder SAAB engine. SAAB had shown initial enthusiasm. It was an Indian summer and they were out of Formula 3 at the end of that season but not before Anthony gave them a spectacular induction at Silverstone when he cartwheeled the new car in front of the television cameras!

He continued in Formula 3 but when Formula Vauxhall Lotus came along in 1989 he finished third in the Championship. He then moved to Japan and ran in the World Sports Car Championship for the first time with a Porsche 962C taking a stunning third at Le Mans that year with David Sears and Tiff Needell in the Japanese entered car.

Between 1990 and 1995 he concentrated on racing in Japan and in 1992 was Japanese Formula 3 Champion with a Ralt powered by a Mugen-Honda engine. His career took off again in 1994 when he ran an Opel Cavalier in Japan, winning at Macau as well as racing Porsches and a Vauxhall in the FIA World Cup. From now much of Anthony's racing centred around touring cars including a Nissan Primera in the German Super Touring Cup and for Nissan in the BTCC alongside David Leslie. To keep his hand in with sports cars he had a couple of drives with the Lister Storm in 1997 but from then until now he has been a stalwart in the BTCC firstly with Team Ford Mondeo - where he finished runner-up to Alain Menu in the 2000 series - and more recently with MG where he was fourth in 2002. This also brought him into the MG racing team for Le Mans in 2002 when *"We were lying third overall and were splitting the Audis but we knew the cars would not last and after eight and a half hours we were out."*

During 2003 and in 2004 he raced for the factory MG team in the British Touring Car Championship.

JOHN ROMANES

John Romanes can be credited with changing the whole direction of motor racing in Scotland and kicking it into shape with the launch of Ingliston. Forceful, yet charming, he ruled Ingliston with a rod of iron and was generally respected by everyone who had any dealings with him. He was straight-forward and positive even if his answer was not what you wanted to hear. He also had a thirst for motor racing that remained unquenched up to his passing in January 2003 after a serious illness.

I first met John shortly after he had returned to Edinburgh to run the family business, Lothian Chemical Company Ltd. He was a next-door neighbour to Archie Craig, another inveterate enthusiast who was racing the ex-Cliff Davis Cooper-MG at the time. It was the mid-1950s and Archie took me next door to meet John and his wife Doris who were struggling with a

Lotus Eleven kit bought new from Colin Chapman. Though John Romanes was one of Chapman's greatest supporters he did not feel so enthusiastic when he discovered, like most other people who bought Lotus Elevens in kit form in those days, that the car may have looked nice once it was built but stringing it together was a nightmare. John was to persevere and began racing the Lotus at Charterhall alongside a number of fellow Lotus Eleven drivers like Jimmy Mackay and Tommy Dickson. He then moved into single seaters with a Lotus 18 and later a Lotus 35 fitted with one of Ray Martin's engines. This engine was not a great success and by then John was fully committed running Ingliston. He loaned the car to Bill Dryden to race and then switched to Andrew Fletcher. By this time the Martin engine had been sold and a 2.5 litre Coventry Climax took its place. During the time Bill Dryden drove the car seat belts had been fitted which was fortunate for at Croft Fletcher had a rose joint break on the straight. The Lotus hit the bank at an angle and rolled over, trapping Fletcher under the car. As he later explained the seatbelts saved his life.

John was so shocked at what had happened he cancelled his plans for the following year, which were to run a Brabham Formula 2 car with Fletcher as the driver. He took the wreck of the Lotus from Croft back to Edinburgh, cut it up into little bits and destroyed it.

John had always been interested in racing cars and as a young man in 1946 he moved to England to work with Anthony Crook on his 2.9 litre Alfa Romeo. This car was later bought by Major Thompson, the Ecurie Ecosse benefactor, and it stayed in Scotland for many years. John then looked after Raymond Mays ERA hill climb car, the Bugatti and K3 MG of Peter Monkhouse, the Maserati of Ian Connell and Dudley Folland's 2 litre Aston Martin. He then worked in Paris in the workshops of the famous French racing driver Raymond Sommer before moving briefly to work at BRM.

On returning to Edinburgh he took over the running of the family business, Lothian Chemical Company, and developed it into a very successful enterprise. When Scotcircuits Ltd., was formed he became Managing Director alongside his fellow directors Ian Scott Watson and Jim Clark. In the late 1970s he passed Scotcircuits Ltd. on to Graham Hamilton and Gordon Dalzell and from then on became the senior Scottish Motor Racing Club Steward. He became Chairman of SMRC when the original chairman, Willum Stewart, retired and later was made an honorary member of the club. He was also a member of the British Racing Drivers Club. John was a very modest man who did not like to talk about his enterprises. For example few people in Scotland knew that he was one of the financial backers of Brian Hart when he developed his various engines including the fabulous Hart F2 engine.

In the late 1980s John decided to try his hand at racing again in the historic class and bought the famous Frazer-Nash Le Mans Replica (Chassis: 421/100/121) formerly owned by a fellow Scot TASO Mathieson (See above.). After Mathieson owned it, the car came to Scotland and was raced by Jimmy Neilsen from Largs who was tragically killed in the car at the British Empire Trophy in the Isle of Man. Nearly forty years later it came back to Scotland in John Romanes' hands but after a few races he sold the car and retired from racing completely, save for visits to Knockhill as a Club Steward.

JOCK ROSS

The name of Jock Ross is probably unfamiliar to most people as he only spent a short time as a mechanic with Border Reivers before leaving for the United States to seek fame and fortune. He set up his own shop but also worked with Lotus in California. He was recruited by Texan Tom O'Connor to run his Rosebud Racing Team. He prepared the ex BRP Lotus 19 the team had bought and whose drivers included Pete Lovely and Innes Ireland. It was in this car, later fitted with a Ferrari engine, that Innes Ireland had his huge testing accident in the USA. Jock also had time to race the Team Rosebud Formula Juniors.

JOCK RUSSELL

There has rarely been a more spectacular or controversial Scottish racing driver than Jock Russell. Born in Bathgate a member of the well-known family which ran a large transport business, Jock never quite fitted in with the family business. He was given an allowance and told to go and make his own way in life. Naturally at that time it meant motor racing and he started out with an Austin A35. When Colin Chapman produced his first Lotus Elite Jock bought one and had some wild runs with the car. Jock was never a stylish racing driver but he was brave, fast and determined. Indeed when Jock had a Lotus XV sports car he used to give Jim Clark a run for his money in the Border Reivers Aston Martin. Clark often said that Jock

Russell and Tommy Dickson were the two toughest competitors he had when he raced in Scotland. Moving on, Jock bought an ex-factory Lotus into which he squeezed a Ford V8 engine and was one of the first to do this. It was never a great success and it didn't help that someone poured a pint of beer down the air trumpets after an Ingliston race meeting.

Jock went on to buy the Lotus 43 chassis that Jim Clark used to win the US Grand Prix but it came without an engine: when Clark drove it it had a BRM engine. Jock approached David Murray about the Ford Shelby V8 engine that had been in the Ecosse-Ford spyder crashed heavily by Bill Stein at Brands Hatch. He fitted this engine into the Lotus and had a good second place finish in a Spanish F5000 race. This was followed by a Lotus 70 Formula 5000 car that Jock raced a number of times before buying a McRae F5000. Though he held on to the Lotus 70 he decided to modify the McRae to his own ideas and called it the Russell F5000.

Jock lived the life of a hermit in his big house near Bathgate surrounded by his racing cars and from time to time ran various businesses. He briefly returned to racing at Ingliston when a series for 2CV Citroens was launched and finally raced a Scania truck at Donington in one of the truck racing events.

NINIAN SANDERSON

Had Ninian Sanderson ever sat down to write about his motor racing career it could have been something of a hooligans charter to motor racing. As his widow Dorothy once said "...he was a rebel". Like all rebels he gathered around him a cast of similar characters. Notwithstanding, he was one of the most successful Scottish racing drivers. Who knows, had he been just a little more compliant, he might well have gone to greater heights but the rebel in him precluded that. Perhaps this is why he was never offered a factory drive with Jaguar. Mind you, a team with Ninian Sanderson and Duncan Hamilton in it would surely have created a whole heap of problems for team manager Lofty England.

Ninian started out with a Cooper 500 he bought from Joe Potts and painted it yellow. He was not only fast but revelled in the cut and thrust of Formula 3. He soon outpaced most of the other Scots in that class. A trip to Luxembourg netted him a sixth place against all the stars in a newer

Cooper but he sold this and bought an Erskine Staride which he took to more events south of the Border.

At the end of the 1952 season his father bought a C type Jaguar so that Ninian could join David Murray's Ecurie Ecosse. Throughout his racing career he was loyally supported not only by his father Bob but by his quiet and gentle wife Dorothy, normally called "Blackie" because of her jet black hair. Sanderson was a tough, gritty driver who perhaps did not have the artistry of Ron Flockhart but had the determination of a hungry rotweiller. Mind you, he had a thing about Flockhart who, because he came from Edinburgh, was judged to be too posh for Ninian. But they both had their greatest victory actually sharing an Ecurie Ecosse D-type Jaguar at Le Mans in 1956 and winning. He followed it up with second place the following year. Later, he raced a variety of cars at Le Mans including the factory ACs and Triumphs and also raced the Ecurie Ecosse Cooper-Bristol from time to time.

After retirement he developed the family car businesses firstly with Fiat and then with Citroen until the advanced stages of cancer caught up with him.

Despite his "attitude", deep down Ninian Sanderson was one of the nicest and kindest people you could meet but he went to great lengths to hide this side of his remarkable character.

ARCHIE SCOTT BROWN

Anyone who ever watched William Archibald Scott Brown drive a racing car and then met him face to face, simply had to marvel at his phenomenal car control. It was only when you met him you realised that he had no right hand - in most photographs he managed to cover the stump of his right hand with his left arm! Added to that he had a badly deformed leg that caused him to walk awkwardly.

The Scott Browns were well known in Paisley where his father had a garage on the main Glasgow/Paisley road. Archie moved south to Cambridge where he worked with a famous company flogging Dobies Four Square tobacco. He was heavily involved with the Cambridge University motor club people where he became friendly with both Brian Lister and Peter Hughes. Indeed, after seeing Archie's skill at the wheel of an MG in sprints, Lister suggested he might like to drive his Tojeiro-JAP special. This was John Tojeiro's first proper racing car commissioned by Lister with a fearsome JAP-twin motor cycle engine hung out front. In later years Lister admitted the cars handling was horrendous but Archie Scott Brown found it child's play. Lister then sold the car to Peter Hughes who brought it to Scotland and raced it for a couple of years: it has only recently be found somewhere in England.

Lister was so impressed he entered Archie for the 1954 British Empire Trophy Race at Oulton Park with his first Lister-Bristol but another entrant questioned Archie's disability with the stewards and his competition licence was taken away from him. All was not lost however as a group of important people including Stirling Moss, Earl Howe and fellow Scot Gregor Grant of Autosport put forward a strong case as to his driving ability and the RAC allowed him to re-apply for a racing licence. Robert Edwards in his superb

book "Archie & The Listers" tells how the famous Dr Benjafield *"...cleverly arranged that all the RAC Stewards shake Archie by the hand to test his strength. He had little to lose so squeezed as hard as he could. This was a major ordeal for the unsuspecting committeemen, however much it may have amused Benjafield"*

A year later, Archie Scott Brown won the same British Empire Trophy at Oulton Park in the Lister-Bristol and was on his way. He drove Listers and also for the Connaught team in Formula 1, finishing second to Stirling Moss' Vanwall and ahead of Roy Salvadori's Maserati in the Daily Express International Trophy at Silverstone. He was delighted when David Murray offered him a drive with Ecurie Ecosse in a D-type Jaguar and by 1958 was on top of the world. The new Lister-Jaguar was proving to be a world beater and Archie was entered by Brian Lister for the Spa world championship sports car race that year. Archie took the lead and was flying but a snap shower of rain soaked part of the circuit on the far side. Scott Brown's Lister skidded at high speed and hit a kilometre stone. In the resultant accident and fire Scott Brown was killed. Obviously there were those who blamed his infirmity but Jim Clark - who was driving in his first International event at that same Spa meeting - was in do doubt that the changing conditions put Scott-Brown in a situation he could not have avoided.

Archie Scott Brown was not only a tough competitor but a highly amusing character and a great ladies' man. He proved that man's fortitude can overcome defects of birth that would have totally demoralised most of us.

SIR JAMES SCOTT DOUGLAS

Though born at Sherston in Wiltshire, Jamie Scott Douglas came from strong Kelso stock, the family home being Springwood Park in Kelso. Big, boisterous and great fun to be with, Jamie had a way with money: he spent it! I remember being told he went through two fortunes before being forced to get a real job and was in the advertising department of the Daily Express towards the end of his life.

He had done a couple of club races in an MG before he was "discovered" by David Murray, desperate to find a third person with a Jaguar XK120 to join the nescent Ecurie Ecosse team. Jamie Scott Douglas was a much better driver than most people believed and on some occasions saved Ecurie Ecosse's bacon with a third place at Spa for example. When the team switched to C type Jaguars in 1953, with Ian Stewart, Ninian Sanderson and Jimmy Stewart, Jamie went out and bought his own C type which also raced under Ecosse colours. He occasionally drove the team's Connaught F2 car but never the Cooper Bristol which was much too small for him. At the end of the season he sold the C type to Berwyn Baxter as money was tight. Ian Stewart remembers bumping into Jamie in Argentina in January 1954 when he was on his way to tap some friends in Argentina for money. Then another relative died and he was able to return in triumph and live the lush life with a yacht in Monaco, a Ferrari forever in the Modena service department, and a suite in the Real Fini Hotel. Ever gullible - he lost money on a deal with Harry Schell which went wrong - he admitted to having tried to sell some guns to the Algerian patriots during the France/Algeria war. Typically he smuggled the guns aboard his yacht and sailed for the bars of Algiers. When he couldn't find anyone interested in buying them, he tossed them over the side of his yacht on the way back to Marseilles as he would have ended up in jail had he brought them back to France.

Jamie Scott Douglas was a breath of fresh air but he was never a very fit man and he died of a heart attack almost penniless. He deserved better.

RICHARD SCOTT

Richard Scott was born in Aberdeen on November 18 1946. Though the family business was building contracting he was keen to become a racing driver and felt the best way to get there was to become a mechanic. He was one of many Scots attracted to motor racing when the Ingliston circuit opened up in 1965 and his mentor was Willie Forbes. When Forbes bought his Formula 5000 Lola, Scott bought the Forbes Elva-BMW sports car and was immediately quick winning a number of races.

In order to get on, he decided to move to England and contacted Frank Williams who at the time supplied spare parts to most of the privateers running in motor racing. Frank immediately offered him a job as a mechanic.

Richard is probably proudest of his achievements in British F3 during the 1970 season when he had his own Brabham BT21 with the right Firestone tyres and a Richardson prepared engine. That year he scored more pole positions in F3 than any other driver in the championship *"...but I was pretty hopeless in the races and realised then that I did not have what it took to be in the top line."*

In 1970 he also had his first Formula 2 race in the European Championship event at Mantorp Park, driving for Albert Obrist's MRE Brabham team with a BT30 (Chassis 20). He managed to put the car on the fifth row of the grid and was just behind Reine Wisell. In the first heat he ran himself in and finished a steady 14th and in the second he finished 10th. He was given 10th place on aggregate times. At Crystal Palace he took second in a small field but then had the setback of not qualifying at Imola in Obrist's other Brabham (Chassis 24).

In 1971 Richard joined the LIRA Team Lotus squad along with Reine Wisell but the Lotus 69 was not the chassis to have that year. At Hockenheim he was well back on the grid alongside John Watson's Brabham BT30 but he broke a valve and was out and from then on it was all downhill. Before the season finished the LIRA team was disbanded.

It was tough getting a drive for 1972 but with sponsorship from Uniacke Chemicals, Richard was able to field the winningest car, a Brabham BT36 and set off for Mallory Park's opening round of the European F2 Championship. It looked like being a repeat of 1971. In the third Round at Thruxton, when he had switched to a brand new Brabham BT38 (Chassis 09) he took a strong fifth place in the first heat behind Nicki Lauda, Gerry Birrell, Jody Scheckter and John Surtees and ahead of Peter Gethin and Carlos Pace but he crashed in the final. By Hockenheim, he was entering the car himself and had a good placing on the grid but broke the gearbox. At the Nurburgring he had an amazing practice session. He was third on the grid behind Derek Bell and Jochen Mass and took a third place finish and at Crystal Palace he was third behind Carlos Reutemann and Vic Elford and ahead of drivers like John Watson and Jean Pierre Beltoise. These were his best Formula 2 results.

Then Richard had the idea of building his own car, the Scott. He had the misfortune to crash out in practice, first time out at Mallory. He only ran part of the season before the finances ran low. His best result in the Scott was 7th place at the Nurburgring, outstanding for such a new and untried car. Almost inevitably he ran out of money and the car was sold in June

1974 to Bob Howlings.Today the one and only Scott Formula 2 car is still around.

Scott raced the Durex sponsored Formula 5000 car without much success. For the 1976 season he was invited to join the Formula 2 team run by Dicksons of Perth alongside Norman Dickson. They drove Modus Formula 2 cars in Formula Atlantic championship. The cars were upgraded to Formula 2 and ran in the European Formula 5000 Championship that had a class for Formula 2 cars. By mid season Scott was holding 5th place in the championship and Norman Dickson 13th. Shortly after this he retired from racing. He and his wife set up shop in Huntingdon. A short spell with Barry Bland's Motor Racing Consultants followed but as he explains, it underlined that he was really not very good at paperwork.

He and his wife contemplated moving their shop to Cambridge but with the oil boom in full force, opted to return, instead, to Aberdeen.

Richard's son, Simon Scott, spent a couple of years in 100cc karting and then moved into the quick 125 Great Britain class with gearboxes and went on to win the British Championship in this class. *"I was very proud of the fact that as Simon's mechanic we had almost 100% engine reliability that season."*

IAN SCOTT WATSON

Many years ago I described Ian Scott Watson as the perfect embodiment of Mr Toad in Toad of Toad Hall. Show Ian some gadget, or something new, and his eyes light up with that "must have it" look and nothing stops him. He became a motor sport enthusiast after joining Berwick and District Motor Club with his MG which was used on various rallies and was replaced with a self-built Buckler. It was never the greatest car he owned but he was greatly attached to it.

Around 1954, however, AFN Ltd., who not only built Frazer Nash cars but were the British importers for Porsche, brought into the country the DKW-Sonderklasse front wheel drive saloon. Powered by a three-cylinder two-stroke engine - a version of which was later to power the Saab - Scott Watson fell upon the concept that being a two-stroke three cylinder meant something like six cylinder power and immediately bought his first DKW. This car was used mainly for rallies and occasionally Jim Clark would navigate for him. This led to the famous incident when Clark spread the maps out on the back seat of the car and read out the instructions. After going wrong a couple of times they realised that, as he was looking backwards, every time Clark said to turn left he really meant turn right!

This particular DKW was rolled by Scott Watson's co-driver, Alan Cury, on the 1955 Scottish Rally and was replaced by another DKW Sonderklasse. It was in this DKW that Scott Watson first tried racing. It was the same car he persuaded Jim Clark to drive in his first race at Crimond in Aberdeenshire.

Scott Watson then bought a Porsche 1600 Super, previously owned by bandleader Billy Cotton, and with this car Jim Clark won the first BMRC Trophy race at Charterhall. Now Scott Watson diverted all his attention to promoting Jim Clark and persuaded Jock McBain of Border Reivers to buy the ex- Murkett Brothers D type Jaguar which was on the market.

Scott Watson started his own house design company and then had a penchant for circuit design. Many of the Scottish circuits, proposed from the 1960s to the 1980s, were designed by Scott Watson. Unfortunately none actually came into being, save Ingliston. He, along with John Romanes, was a guiding light behind the circuit. Today he is still designing houses, some for racing driver friends like John Cleland.

LORD SELSDON
(PETER MITCHELL-THOMSON)

Patrick William Malcolm Mitchell-Thomson was born in 1913 and was a descendant of three Scottish families, the Mitchells and Thomsons of Alloa and Edinburgh and the McEacharns of Islay. Though his true Christian name was Patrick he was always called "Peter". His grandfather was Lord Provost of Edinburgh at the turn of the century and his maternal grandfather Sir Malcolm McEacharn was the first Lord Mayor of Melbourne in Australia and founder of "The Scottish Line" shipping group. Peter's father Sir William Mitchell-Thomson was a member of Parliament for Glasgow and later a cabinet member.

At Winchester he was a keen sportsman and enjoyed boxing and wrestling. In the latter pursuit he wrestled in the professional business under the name "White Eagle" and any prize money he earned he gave to charity.

He became passionate about motor racing and, supported by his mother and inherited wealth, he had the means to finance his racing. He won Le Mans when he shared his Ferrari 166 with Luigi Chinetti in 1949. His son, Malcolm, the present Lord Selsdon, tells a lovely story about his father about whom he knew very little as his mother and father were divorced when he was quite young. One Monday at his prep school, the French master announced to the class in French that Malcolm's father had won the Le Mans 24 Hour Race. As Malcolm comments. *"...it was only years after his death that I began to realise the extent of the motor racing activity he had pursued and felt able to delve into the past."*

Peter Mitchell-Thomson's first two racing cars were Frazer-Nashes including the first single-seater Nash built by the factory. His mother bought a 1903 Mercedes and a 1904 Panhard which she and her son would enter for VSCC events including the London to Brighton run.

Peter also raced the Mercedes at Brooklands and was a great friend of Dick Seaman the British driver who raced for Mercedes Benz before the War.

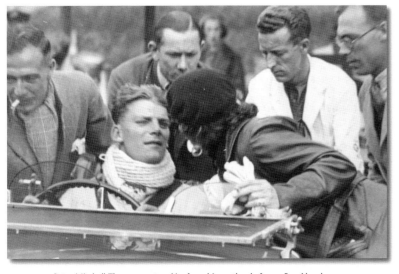

Peter Mitchell Thomson gets a kiss from his mother before a Brooklands race.
(Lord Selsdon Archive)

When he retired from motor racing in 1950, after running at Le Mans with another Ferrari 166, he became an important figure in the BRDC and was always interested in motor racing safety. He had also been an investor and shareholder in both Frazer-Nash and HRG. His last competition appearance was in the 1952 Monte Carlo Rally in a Daimler with journalist Tommy Wisdom. Eleven years later, when in poor health, he died on board the cargo ship Baron Garioch on his way to New Zealand and was buried at sea.

RYAN SHARP

One of the most promising young Scottish racing drivers to suddenly emerge in recent times is Ryan Sharp. He came to everyone's notice in 2002 when he drove in the British Formula Renault championship. He took a gamble and chose to race abroad in 2003. He joined the Swiss team Jenzer Motorsport and competed in the German Formula Renault Championship. This was a wise move and he romped home as 2003 champion. This led to him being one of the six young British drivers chosen for the McLaren Autosport BRDC award alongside his fellow Scot, Susie Stoddart. Though he did not win he came to the attention of Jackie Stewart who gave him a lot of helpful advice.

Born in Newtonhill, between Aberdeen and Stonehaven, Ryan admits he came into racing late - in his early 20s - but his determination to succeed is obvious. Added to this he is a good communicator and had no hesitation in signing up with Jenzer Motorsport for the Eurocup Formula Renault V6 championship in 2004. In the opening round at Monza in March, Sharp was third in the first heat, despite being rammed in a first corner incident and stalling the engine, and won the second heat. He took the lead in the championship. Clearly Sharp is someone to keep a look out for in the future.

ANDY SIM

Andy Sim was reared on karting as he lived not far from the Larkhall kart circuit. He was a determined driver but his story is one often repeated in this book; that of the promising driver without the financial support needed to get over the major hurdles. At times he tried desperately hard, too hard, and had a notable incident at Ingliston in Formula Ford when he was seriously challenging champion Cameron Binnie but crashed. By virtue of hard work and moving south to work at Reynard, Andy was rewarded with a drive in the initial season of Formula Vauxhall Lotus. He was only just beaten by Allan McNish at Knockhill and finished second ahead of Justin Bell. Sadly, the breaks never came and Andy was destined to drift out of motor racing.

BILLY SKELLY

Billy Skelly was born into the motor trade, his father having started a small garage business in Motherwell just outside Glasgow. Thanks to Billy's drive and the support of his father and brothers, Skellys of Motherwell became one of the strongest Ford dealers in Scotland. In the beginning they had sub-dealerships for Morris and Lea Francis and went on to become Scottish distributors for Alvis but the eventual link with Ford saw the company thrive. Billy's brother Ian Skelly was sales director and his youngest brother Sherwood

Skelly became service director. Ian did a little racing with an MG TF and brother Sherwood was always more interested in rallying and competed in a number of International events.

Billy was born in 1931 and so grew up during the War, helping his father. He was apprenticed to Lea Francis where he became very friendly with their Chief Engineer Albert Ludgate. When the motor racing bug struck him Billy decided to build a very special Lea Francis single seater and Albert Ludgate enthusiastically joined in and helped him. Indeed the engine Skelly used in his car was a very special Lea Francis engine Ludgate had developed for American dirt track racing. This engine was further developed and became the mainstay of the Connaught racing car.

Billy Skelly built up and raced this Lea Francis Special when serving his apprenticeship with Lea Francis. It was superseded by one of only three Frazer-Nash Formula 2 cars built.

During his period at Coventry Technical College, Billy raced the Lea Francis all over and also raced a Jowett Jupiter in sports car events.

The Lea-Francis was raced a number of times but was replaced by a rare single seater Frazer-Nash (Chassis: 421/200/180S). This was one of only three Frazer Nash Formula 2 cars built and Billy raced it until the end of the 1952 season. He might have ended up as a driver with Ecurie Ecosse as David Murray tried persuading Mr Skelly senior that he should buy a Jaguar for Billy to race with the team. Today Billy Skelly honestly admits *"I preferred to do my own thing because I was racing as much for my interest in the cars as for racing for racing's sake. I had no illusions about my own driving."*

However, back in Motherwell his father took seriously ill. As the oldest son, Billy was expected to carry most of the burden of developing the company and he retired from racing. He has never lost his interest in motor racing and was a regular visitor to Oulton Park and Silverstone and kept in close contact with his good friend Roy Salvadori.

BILL SMITH

Bill Smith's career in motor racing was short lived, terminating in a flaming pyre at the Dundrod Tourist Trophy race in 1955. Bill was born in 1934 in Largs where his father was a doctor working at Greenock Royal Infirmary. As is often the case, the family moved about the country, first to Cheshire and finally to Lincoln. The family prospered and owned a farm in Suffolk

and it became clear that Bill's destiny would be towards farming - or motor racing.

When still quite young, Bill joined the Eastern Counties Motor Club and first raced at the age of 17 with his father's Jowett Jupiter at the AMOC race meeting at Snetterton. This led to him being loaned a Tojeiro-MG by Eric Ridley. At 18 he joined the RAF for his two year National service. Despite opposition from his mother, he was able to persuade his father to buy the ex-Ecurie Ecosse C type Jaguar (LSF420) which had previously won Le Mans with Duncan Hamilton and Tony Rolt at the wheel. Whilst on leave from the RAF, he took it to Dundrod and the Ulster Trophy meeting which was run on handicap. Smith was given a lap over scratch man and Dundrod specialist, Desmond Titterington in an Ecosse D-type and Smith not only achieved his handicap target but won the race. Clearly Bill Smith was an exceptional driver and later that year, 1955, he was given a factory HWM-Jaguar to share with Lance Macklin.

Both John Wyer of Aston Martin and David Murray of Ecurie Ecosse offered Bill Smith drives and the youngster came to Crimond and raced an Ecosse D-type for the first time. David Murray was so enthusiastic he signed Bill Smith for the 1956 racing season. At the same time Lofty England of Jaguar had expressed an interest in Smith so the doors were beginning to open for him. In September 1955 Smith had been approached to race a DKW saloon at the Tourist Trophy but then Ken McAlpine, the backer of Connaught, announced his retirement and his place in the works Connaught sports car was offered to Smith as co-driver to John Young.

In those days the TT featured a Le Mans start where the drivers ran from one side of the road to their cars and then set off. No seat belts in those days! Not only that but the cars were lined up in cubic capacity rather than lap times so the Connaught was well back in the field. As I was nearing the end of my own National Service in the RAF, and was based in Belfast, I attended the race as a journalist. Bill Smith had a tough time on the opening lap trying to pass slower cars as Dundrod is very narrow and has high earth banks which allowed no mistakes. A very slow Mercedes Benz 300SL driven by Vicompte de Barry had started at the front due to its engine capacity and was getting in everyone's way. On the second lap Jim Mayers in the factory Cooper-Climax had to swerve to avoid the Merc and hit a stone gatepost and was killed instantly, the car becoming a blazing wreck with burning fuel running over the road. Ken Wharton in a Frazer Nash did not hesitate and drove straight through the flames but Smith, coming up next, could not avoid the wreckage and he was killed. He was only twenty years of age.

MURRAY SMITH

Murray Smith is another racing driver probably not well known in Scotland. Born in Largs, he grew up to become an advertising man and moved to London joining the famous agency, Coleman Prentice & Varley. He then moved to the United States where he ran CSS Promotions over there. In turn the US branch was absorbed until finally Murray arrived as a Director of Octagon, the US based multinational sports marketing company which not only took over Brands Hatch Circuits (Brands, Mallory Park, Oulton Park and Snetterton) but also the franchise to organise the British Grand Prix. Despite all this Murray, still based in the United States, manages to fit in his motor racing.

He started out in a modest way with an Austin Ulster at Brands Hatch and then, when based in Greece, he took part in rallies and was a regular on the Acropolis Rally. When he moved to the USA he bought an OSCA from Stan Nowak and then went into bigger events with an IMSA Chevrolet Camaro. This was followed by a Lola and a Porsche 962. He always enjoyed racing older cars and is best known today as a historic racer with his Lotus 15, Brabham BT42 and pre-war Invicta. He became involved with Skip Barber and Laguna Seca organiser Steve Earle in the re-organisation of the big historic race meeting at Lime Rock in Connecticut. Though he may have the swagger and the slight American accent, he usually slips back into the West of Scotland patois when with his many Scottish racing friends.

ROBIN SMITH

Robin Smith is one of those mechanics who was a frustrated racing driver and got down to the job of achieving his aim. This he did successfully and had many years of racing before settling down to developing and preparing racing cars - usually sports cars - which he continues to do to this day.

Robin was born in Ayrshire and after his apprenticeship he joined Murray Reid at the Four Square Garage in Airdrie. This was in the mid-1960s and Robin was keen to build his first racing car. This was the legendary Project. He looked around for anything he could find and after building the space frame a Porsche 1500 engine was available but was quickly discarded for a Ford. The real problem was the chassis as the wheelbase was a bit short. The handling was described by his friend Alan Muir, who drove it, as *"different, very different"*. Then along came the chance to move south and join Alan Mann. He was involved in converting the Ford Falcon Futura Sprints from rally cars into racing cars and was also involved with the Len Terry designed Ford F3L. Needless to say Robin used the experience to develop his skills in fabrication. Then he went to Austria to work on a team of Formula Fords that had been sent there to establish the Formula in that country. He still wanted to race, however, so he returned to Scotland and joined forces with his pals Bobby Deans and Alan Muir who had formed Bardene Automotive under the arches by the River Clyde. The old Project was dusted down. and Robin and Alan fitted a Ford Twin-Cam engine

and cut a hole in the roof so that Alan could drive it. However, they both finally agreed the car was an utter disaster. Robin then demonstrated his great bargaining skills by trading it for the legendary Atilla-Chevrolet one of the first of the big American engined sports cars built in Britain. This also proved to be a disaster, particularly at Ingliston, where the car had a marked tendency to go where it wanted to go rather than where the driver intended.

The next move was to join forces with what was called the "Falkirk Mafia" consisting of Tony Evangelisti, Robin Traill, George Stuart and Robbie Callander and between them they bought a Chevron B8 which started Robin's great love affair with Chevrons. Tony was big and ebullient and he was nominated to drive the car at Silverstone where he totalled it. The bits were literally shovelled on to the trailer and brought back to Scotland where Robin bought the remains. He sent the chassis down to Arch Motors to be straightened and then decided it would be better as a Spyder and so Robin's first Chevron was an original Chevron B8 Spyder. He raced the car and in 1972 decided, with his then wife Jane, to do a season on the Continent with a Lola T212. For 1973 they changed this for a Chevron B23 and set off to live in the car park at Nurburgring. He kept checking with promoter Barry Bland to see what race circuits offered the best starting money and off they would go: anywhere !

In 1975 Robin had his greatest ever success, finishing second overall with his Chevron B26 in the European Interseries Championship to the winning 3 litre Porsche. For 1976 he bought the ex-Clive Santo Lola T142 F5000 car but changed this for a March 742 which he and Richard Jones used in the Aurora Championship. In turn they moved up and bought an Ensign Formula 1 car crashed by Jones at Snetterton. The bits were sold and replaced by a Surtees. At Le Mans in 1979 he and Tony Charnell won the 2 litre class and were highest placed British entrants. When Jackie Stewart wanted to demonstrate his famous Tyrrell at Ingliston it was Robin who hauled it out of Glasgow Transport Museum in a terrible condition. He was pleased as punch when Jackie publicly praised him for his efforts. Then he and Laurence Jacobsen bought Chevron - see under Chevron in the Scottish Racing Cars chapter.

Robin continued to race with a variety of cars including a DFV engined Chevron B36 and a Ferrari. Since moving south of the Border, Robin still develops racing cars and occasionally races them. He is certainly one of Scotland's great racing characters.

JIMMY AND JOHN SOMMERVAIL

The Sommervail brothers, Jimmy and John were border farmers swept into the general enthusiasm for motor racing in the early 1950s. Jimmy Sommervail bought the famous ERA racing car "Hanuman" which had originally been owned and raced by Prince Bira. The car came into his hands in August 1951 and he finished second in his first race with it at Turnberry in Ayrshire. The car had previously been owned by Ecurie Ecosse owner David Murray and David Hampshire. It was eventually sold in 1954 to D G Owen. He replaced the ERA with the Cooper-Bristol originally raced by Reg Parnell and ran it as a Border Reivers car. His next move was to a Lotus Eleven and finally, in 1958, Border Reivers decided to buy a D-type Jaguar to be shared by Jimmy Sommervail and the young Border farmer Jim Clark. Jimmy Sommervail realised the first time they tested the D type at Charterhall, Clark had far more natural talent as a racing driver and quietly retired from motor racing. His brother John did not race as much as Jimmy but at one time ordered a new Austin Healey 100S which raced as a Border Reivers car. He crashed and badly damaged it on its first outing at Snetterton and shortly after that the car was sold and John retired from racing.

BILL STEIN

Bill Stein's father had a small Rootes agency in Edinburgh. Bill caught the racing bug and bought a Lotus VII. He was very successful with the car and progressed to a Lotus 23 and then a Lotus 23B.

It was when driving the latter car that he came to David Murray's attention. Bill was well placed in the sports car race at Oulton Park where Jackie Stewart has his accident in the Cooper Monaco. He was tested for Ecurie Ecosse with Eric Liddell and Andrew Cowan in the Ecosse Tojeiro Buick and then raced the single seater Ecosse-Climax at the opening race meeting at Ingliston. He also tested the single seater at Silverstone with racing veteran John Coundley. The car was impressive on the circuit but was never raced at any event outside Ingliston.

When Ecurie Ecosse converted their Tojeiro-Ford coupe into a spyder, it was Bill Stein who raced it for the first time at Silverstone but he broke the crown wheel and pinion at Abbey Curve. In the race the crown wheel broke again.

He then was entered for the support race to the British Grand Prix at Brands Hatch in 1966 where he had a huge accident at Paddock Bend that nearly cost him his life. The car simply understeered off the road and into the banking and folded in two trapping Bill inside. Fuel was everywhere and the race was not stopped. Eventually, by using two breakdown trucks, the car was gently straightened out and Stein was rushed to hospital.

Bill never returned to motor racing as a driver but was made Clerk of the Course at Ingliston a post he held until he moved to Spain.

ANDREW KEIR STEVENSON

A K Stevenson - no one ever called him Andrew - literally created and sustained motor sport in Scotland. He was born in Girvan but lived most of his life in Kilwinning. When he left school he wanted to become an apprentice chartered accountant and managed to get two interviews in Glasgow. One appointment was with Mitchell and Smith and one at S Eason Simmers. *"I came up to Glasgow and was interviewed by Mr Mitchell. After the interview they said they would let me know. Then I went to see Mr Simmers,*

grandfather of Brian Simmers the Scottish International rugby player. On the Friday morning I received a letter from Mitchell and Smith telling me to start at nine o clock on the Monday morning. When I got back home there was another letter from S Eason Simmers asking me to start on the Monday at the same time. One of them had put a 5p stamp on it and I often wondered what would have happened if I had received the two together ; what decision would I have made? Had I accepted the Simmers invitation it would have altered my whole life; I might have been a millionaire by now." Said AK when in his eighties.

AK became the protégé of Robert Smith who had accepted the post of Secretary of the Scottish Automobile Club and was thrown into motoring originally addressed envelopes so never qualified as a CA.

When planning the first Scottish Rallies his boss, R.G.Smith, would take him along to write the route book. However in those days you did not have a mileometer so he had to guess mileages from a contour road map *"We would come to a junction. He would stop, look about, and say "White cottage ivy growing on the front, turn right.".* This also led to some amusing incidents such as when they were preparing a rally route some years later. *"We were going up Loch Lochay and at the end of the Loch, near Laggan Bridge, the road rises for a mile on the side of the hill. On that bit there were nine river fords. Mr Smith told me to put down 'water courses'. He took my route book home and rewrote it and sent it to Hay Nisbet for printing. When the road book came out it said "Beware caochan" in italics. (Caochan is the ancient gaelic word for a small stream or rivulet.) That night I overheard two of the drivers talking and one said 'Did you see the caochan today? We were told in the book to beware of them'. The other one said ' Oh I didn't see that' To which the first speaker said "Oh you missed one of the greatest sights of your life, they were the ugliest beasts I have ever seen."*
When an approach came from the Automobile Club of Monaco for a British start to the Monte Carlo rally Stevenson, the enthusiast, was quick to step in and offer to organise it on behalf of the Automobile Club of Monaco. So the tradition of Scottish starts for the Monte began for which Stevenson was given a high honour by the AC de Monaco later in life. Anything to do with motor sport was latched on to by Stevenson and promoted for what it was worth. He was behind the initial Bo'ness hill climb and of course negotiated on behalf of the RSAC the lease to run hill climbs at Rest and Be Thankful. He was also foremost in easing through the permits for all the original Scottish motor racing circuits right up to Ingliston.

A.K. Stevenson was an enthusiast to his last breath and probably did more to promote motor sport in Scotland than anyone else.

IAN STEWART

Ian Stewart retired from motor racing in 1954 after an accident in the 1000kms race at Beunos Aires in Argentina. He was sharing one of the ex-factory C-type Jaguars with Jimmy Stewart (No relation) that had been sold to Ecurie Ecosse. Coming up to lap a slower Porsche the driver started to overtake an even slower car without looking in his mirror. Stewart was in a position of either hitting the Porsche or going off the road. He chose the latter, hit a wall and ended up in hospital with a broken collar bone. His father was a prominent Scottish cattle breeder."Stewart of Millhills" cattle had a world-wide reputation, particularly in the Argentine and Ian's father made frequent trips there. One trip ended just before the fateful race but he was so much against Ian's racing that he refused to stay on the extra few days to see him. He was actually sailing back to Britain when the accident happened. Due to some false information he was told on ship that Ian had been killed in the accident. Clearly, when he got back to Scotland and found Ian had not been killed he gave him an ultimatum, stop racing or the equivalent of 'go and never darken my doorstep again'. Ian chose to retire from racing which was a great pity as he was a stylist in the manner of Stirling Moss. Indeed three years before Moss had noticed Stewart's talent and had tipped off Jaguar team manager Lofty England to look out for this guy which resulted in Ian sharing a Jaguar C type at Le Mans in 1952 with Peter Whitehead. This was the year Jaguar tried a streamlined low nose on the C types which stangled the air passing to the radiators and all of the cars retired with overheating trouble. The following year at Le Mans he was again paired with Peter Whitehead in a factory C type Jaguar and finished 4th overall.

The Stewart family was mainly based in Perthshire and Ian's branch resulted from his great-grandfather marrying Christian McCallum whose father and uncle were true entrepreneurs and founded the D & J McCallum Perfection Scotch Whisky company. Their son Duncan Stewart - Ian's grandfather - was also successful and inherited everything when he was middle-aged and proceeded to build a family tomb in Kenmore. He also developed a successful herd of shorthorn cattle and it was the whisky and cattle businesses that Ian's father inherited. In 1936 when Ian was just seven years of age his father sold the D & J McCallum whisky business to a new group called Distillers Company Ltd for the unheard of sum of £1 million. Talking about this fifteen years ago Ian remarked of his father "...the bloody fool fell for it and sold it." In the early part of the war Ian Stewart was sent to Canada and when he came back he was sent to boarding school at Repton. His interest in motor racing was sparked by visiting the 1949 British Grand Prix at Silvefrstone. His first car was an MG TA and he started motor sport in 1949 with the TC at Bo'ness and Rest and Be Thankful hill climbs as well as in trials. One day whilst walking his dog he met Noel Bean who was a boffin with Wimpey,the contracting firm. Bean happened to sprint a Jaguar SS100 and Ian bought a half share in the car. He later bought out Noel's half and ran the SS 100 at the hill climbs and sprints, as there was nothing else at the time. At the end of 1950, however, he bought a Healey Silverstone just in time to enter it for the first-ever motor race meeting in Scotland at Winfield. This was for him, and he immediately arranged to sell the Healey. He ordered one of the new Jaguar XK120's for the 1951 season and drove it in a number of events which brought him to the eye of David Murray and Wilkie Wilkinson at Merchiston Motors. When Murray had the idea of forming a team of cars for the 1952 season he called on Ian and so Ecurie Ecosse was formed.

He was called up to race for Jaguar and in 1952 as a factory driver he had the chance to buy one of the first production C-type Jaguars. The car he bought was chassis number 006 and it was quickly made ready for the Jersey Road Race of 1952. Despite the fact that he ran the car in on the drive down to the ferry for Jersey Ian went out and won the race. At that time the car was running in its original dark British Racing Green but the car was soon repainted Ecurie Ecosse blue and was the first C type raced by Ecurie Ecosse. It is interesting to note that during the 1952 British racing season Ian Stewart took part in nine races with the C type and won every single one of them save at Boreham when he crashed. His greatest race was at his home circuit of Charterhall on October 11 that year when he faced up to Stirling Moss in Tommy Wisdom's C type Jaguar. The Wisdom car had been fitted with disc brakes whilst Stewart's C type was still on drum brakes. The race was an epic with Stewart beating Moss to the flag. The Stewart C type was eventually sold to Dutchman Hans Davids and today the car is owned by David Lake whose father bought it in 1974.

In addition to the Jaguar, Ian raced the team's Connaught A type that he drove in his only Grand Prix, the British Grand Prix of 1953 at Silverstone. The car retired.

Since retiring from racing in 1954 Ian has kept a watching brief on current motor racing and he and his wife Alex were also able to persuade their sons David and Christian that perhaps motor racing was not such a great idea. At one time Ian was distributor for Ferrari in Scotland but very much on a personal relationship.

SIR JACKIE STEWART

As with Jim Clark and David Coulthard the Jackie Stewart story has been told in books and at great length. As a result it is only necessary here to give an overview of a career and influence in motor racing greater than any other driver up to this time.

Jackie Stewart is the perfect example of talent fulfilled by hard work and sacrifice. The hard work came in the beginning. There had already been one member of the Stewart family involved in motor racing, his brother Jimmy, and by the time Jackie began to have the pangs his mother left him in no doubt that she really did not want to go through all of that again. His father, Bob Stewart, was a genial man and one could see that not only had he been proud of Jimmy - and justifiably so - but that he was to give Jackie encouragement where he could. The sacrifice came when he left the comfortable family business and moved to England to become a professional racing driver.

Those who knew Jackie back at the beginning know that on the way back from Rest and Be Thankful, when you stopped at Dumbuck Garage for petrol, it was probably Jackie who would serve you. Behind the scenes in the workshop he worked on customers cars which of course led him to Barry Filer. Barry is always mentioned as a kind of afterthought but he not only gave Jackie the chance to try his AC-Bristol which Jackie was preparing for another driver, Jimmy McInnes, to drive, but immediately saw that Jackie was something special and virtually bought the Marcos which brought Stewart to everyones notice.

From that moment onwards, and until he signed for BRM, Jackie virtually drove anything and everything offered to him. For example he was extremely proud when Eric Brown offered him his modified Jaguar XK120

Brand new and ready to race, Barry Filers Marcos attracted a lot of attention in the paddock. The driver was A N Other – otherwise Jackie Stewart wih his first serious racing car.

to race, a car which would appear to have been below the talents of this young man. At Charterhall a friend of his offered him his 3.8 litre Jaguar saloon to race and he jumped at the idea.

All of this, if we could only have realised at the time, was Jackie, in his usual meticulous way, sniffing out all the options. When David Murray of Ecurie Ecosse offered him a season in 1963 driving the Ecosse Cooper Monaco and Tojeiro Buick Coupe he had achieved his first goal. He still talks today about how amazed he was to be asked if he wanted the pedals adjusted for him. For Jackie this was the big time and yet within 12 months he had completed the balance sheet and from January 1965 Jackie Stewart knew where he was going. Ecurie Ecosse chief mechanic Stan Sproat, however, is in no doubt as to the value of having Jackie Stewart, however briefly, in the team. Commenting on the relatively unloved Tojeiro-Buick and Tojeiro Ford Coupes Sproat admitted *"Things broke more often with Jackie driving. He drove the car hard and considering the gearboxes we had at the time he did well. John Tojeiro once produced a couple of extra wide wheels at Oulton Park and one rim split so Jackie was not happy about that"*

It is interesting that Jackie's original contract with David Murray gave Murray the option to retain his services in 1965 but when BRM came along

The car that launched Jackie Stewarts career was the Marcos built by Jem Marsh using wood laminates. It was light and had phenomenal handling which allowed Stewart to sweep round the outside of Ronnie Morrison's E type Jaguar at Charterhall.

Murray gladly waived this option and became one of Jackies greatest fans. Indeed not long after David Murray died of a heart attack on the Canary Islands, Jackie won his first world championship and said at the time that he would have liked David to have seen his crowning moment.

Throughout his racing career Jackie Stewart would analyse everything and could accept advice provided it came from someone he respected. In this area he almost worshipped Jim Clark. Indeed they made a perfect foil for each other. Jimmy, quiet and reserved at parties listening to Jackie pontificate and joke and then on the track it was different. One of the most touching stories ever told to me by Jim Clark was shortly after the Belgian Grand Prix in 1965 in which the rain had poured down making this dangerous track even more so. Clark hated Spa. In his first race there Archie Scott Brown had been killed and so he always treated it with respect. Now here was his young friend Jackie Stewart out in a BRM and it was raining. The story Clark told was how, when about 48 seconds in the lead in his Lotus, he had begun to ease off so that when passing back markers he could take his time and do it as safely as possible. He noticed from the pit signals that not only was Jackie in second place but that his lead had been considerably reduced. On one lap at the end of the straight he noticed Jackie in his mirrors, still a bit back, but immediately began to get worried. I now paraphrase roughly what Clark had to say. *"It suddenly struck me that Jackie could probably see me up ahead and I was worried that he would try too hard to catch me and as he didn't know Spa he might get carried away. So I put in three or four quick laps and put the gap back up to 48 seconds."* Not only does this illustrate his concern for Jackie on his first visit to the track Clark hated, but also some idea of Clark's through process and ability to adjust his pace seemingly at ease. Many years later I told Jackie this story and he admitted *"I did see Jimmy up ahead but thought there was something wrong with his car ".*

Jackie Stewart's greatest contribution to motor racing was his crusade for better track safety. He was the first grand prix driver to insist on having seat belts in his car and he was one of the first to use Bell's new fully closed crash helmet - Jacky Ickx was, I think, the first. But not only that, he began to look at the circuits themselves and started to speak out on the stupidity of straw bales, for example, which had a terrible habit of catching fire and indeed it was this which caused the death of Lorenzo Bandini at Monaco. He also wanted to see medical facilities improved and was backed up by his team boss, Louis Stanley of BRM who opened the first Grand Prix Medical Centre.

Jackie began to be quoted everywhere but some people were actually against his campaign. One of those was the legendary motoring journalist Denis Jenkinson who did not agree with what Stewart was saying and he was not alone. In 1968,however, Jim Clark was killed at Hockenheim, ironically as Jackie was inspecting the safety barriers and facilities at Jarama in Spain. The fact that Jim Clark could be killed in racing was bad enough but to realise that if barriers had been placed at that part of Hockenheim circuit he probably would not have been killed was too much. It was a tragic wake-up call but from that moment on Stewart had won the cause and motor racing has never looked back.

It was also typical of Jackie that he planned his retirement from racing nine months in advance and not even his wife Helen knew he had made the irrevocable decision to retire at the end of the 1973 grand prix season. As usual his figuring out was impeccable. The last race of the season was the US GP at Watkins Glen and it would have been his 100th grand prix: a nice figure on which to end a remarkable career. By the time the race came around he was already 1973 world champion - his third championship - and he had broken Jim Clark's record number of grand prix wins. An ideal prelude to telling Helen after the race that he had retired from grand prix

racing. But it was not to be. His team-mate, Francois Cevert, was killed when his Tyrrell crashed on to the barriers and Jackie and Ken Tyrrell withdrew Stewarts car. So the records show that he only competed in 99 grand prix races.

By now Stewart had a clutch of consultancies and he settled down to that until he came back into active motor racing with Paul Stewart Racing. Though he gave Paul plenty of encouragement he was also firm to the extent that many felt Jackie was placing too much pressure on Paul. However, once Paul retired from racing father and son went on to run one of the most successful teams in motor racing. All the time they never forgot their native Scotland. Jackie was involved in the frustrating business of trying to create a green field motor racing circuit beside Edinburgh Airport but in this he came up against local authority politics and had to walk away. He had also brought on three young Scots who have become the best Scottish racing drivers of today, Allan McNish, David Coulthard and Dario Franchitti.

Not content with this punishing schedule the Stewarts moved into Formula 1 with their own team backed by Ford. Remarkably, in view of the progress of teams which have come to Formula 1 since, Stewart Formula 1 was a success and they did, after all, win a Grand Prix within their short lifetime before selling out to Jaguar. Others, like Minardi, Sauber, BAR and now Jaguar still - at the time of writing - have to break their duck. Once more Stewart had made a shrewd move.

In his early racing career Jackie Stewart would race almost any car such as this 3.4litre Jaguar owned by a friend of his in Glasgow.

Today he has at last shown signs of coming down off that adrenalin cloud. Twice the family have been hit by cancer, first with Paul and secondly with Helen. Then he, too, was diagnosed with skin cancer and this has caused Stewart to step back a trifle and take note of life flying by. His other son, Mark, was going to become an actor - he even temporarily changed his name to Matt Stewart as Equity already had a Mark Stewart - but that did not last. He has now developed his own film company not just to make motor racing films but he has branched out and made films for National Geographic amongst others.

As President of the British Racing Drivers Club Jackie has still not avoided controversy and his battles with Bernie Ecclestone to keep the British Grand Prix at Silverstone have dominated 2004.

However, the Stewarts are a close and happy family and nobody can deny Jackie Stewart has changed grand prix racing from a safety standpoint as much as Bernie Ecclestone has changed it from a commercial standpoint.

JIMMY STEWART

Bob Stewart had a small garage at Dumbuck near Dumbarton and had always wanted to work on cars. His father had been a gamekeeper on Lord Weir's estate and Lord Weir encouraged young Stewart in his chosen interest. One great advantage for trade was that the garage stood on the fork where the main Loch Lomond road and the road into Dumbarton met and so there was a lot of passing trade. He was able to buy the bungalow next to the garage and it was here that his two sons James (Jimmy) Stewart and John Young (Jackie) Stewart were born. By the early 1950s Bob had an agency for Austin cars and a sub-agency for Jaguar. His elder son Jimmy started work as salesman in the garage whilst his younger son, Jackie, was still in short pants at school. Bob's wife was keen on sports cars and was the early tearaway in the family and she clearly passed on this interest to her two sons.

Jimmy Stewart started competing in hill climbs with an old MG TC and then graduated to a Healey Silverstone. At the same time down in England Tony Brooks had also started racing a Silverstone and it was a good entry-level car for motor racing. During the 1952 season Jimmy proved to be quick and could more than match the pace of the Frazer-Nash Le Mans Replicas in Scotland at the time so he clearly had talent.

His father was enthusiastic about Jimmy's racing career and needed little persuasion from David Murray of Ecurie Ecosse to order and buy a C type Jaguar for him to race with the team. This car, Chassis 041 was run by the team until July 1954 when it was sold. The car had a chequered history and in 1976 was sold to the Australian enthusiast John Blanden. In August 2000 Scots historic car dealer Gregor Fisken was able to persuade Blanden to sell him the car and Gregors father, Ian, proudly brought it back to Scotland where it resides today in Forfar.

Jimmy Stewart clearly had talent and he desperately wanted to race for the Jaguar factory team. When he was approached by John Wyer in 1953 to race an Aston Martin DB3S Coupe at Le Mans he accepted the drive even though he had wanted Jaguar to choose him. The race was a disaster as both Coupe's crashed, Prince Bira in one and Jimmy Stewart in the other. Jimmy recalls being thrown out of the car at White House corner and sliding along the edge of the track on his backside watching the car destroy itself in a series of pirouettes.

In the 1954 British Grand Prix Jimmy Stewart raced the Ecurie Ecosse Cooper-Bristol and was holding sixth place when one of the wheels collapsed and he came to rest in a three wheel car.

As with most young men Stewart had to serve two years National Service in the army but had a sympathetic commanding officer who even helped him go all the way to the War Office to get leave to race in Argentina! Eventually he was given the chance he had always dreamed of, to share a factory D type Jaguar with Mike Hawthorn in the 1955 Le Mans 24 Hour race. Sadly Jimmy crashed an Ecosse D type at Nurburgring and damaged an arm he had originally hurt in the Aston Martin accident and had to pull out of the Le Mans squad. In 1955 Mike Hawthorn, now partnered by Ivor Bueb, won Le Mans after the tragic Mercedes Benz accident to Pierre Levegh which took so many lives.

On retirement Jimmy went back to the family garage business which was later taken over by his brother Jackie. Today Jimmy Stewart is still a regular spectator at Silverstone and often travels with Jackie to grand prix events.

PAUL STEWART

To be in the shadow of a famous father can sometimes condemn you to partial obscurity. In a sense this is what happened to Paul Stewart. When last did anyone talk to you about Paul Stewart the racing driver rather than Paul Stewart the racing team owner?

The fact of the matter is that Paul Stewart was a much better racing driver than was ever acknowledged. For example there must be few racing drivers who, from starting out at a racing drivers school, I goes on to win his first National Formula 3 race after only 35 race starts in total. That takes ability and his father, Jackie, did not make it easy for him.

Jackie and Helen Stewart, I am sure, had hoped that neither of their sons, Paul or Mark, would take up motor racing. Indeed I remember Jackie's joy when, as young children, both sons decided not to go to watch dad race the Monaco Grand Prix. Instead they chose to spend the time learning to be clowns at the circus that had its winter lodgings near their house in Begnins, Switzerland.

But it didn't last, Paul became keen and so Jackie insisted that if he wanted to race he had to do the Brands Hatch Racing School course - such a thing did not exist in Jackie's day. So at the age of 19, and when studying political science at Duke University in North Carolina, Paul enrolled at Brands Hatch School as "Robin Congdon" to hide his true identity. He moved into Formula Ford 1600 in 1987, Formula Ford 2000 in 1988 and Formula 3 in 1989.

In his season of Formula Ford 1600 he met up with and raced against another young Scot, Allan McNish, whose description of Paul is apt even today. *"Paul really is a nice guy but oh, my goodness, the number of times I have shut my eyes and thought ' is that Paul or Jackie talking?' He sounds the same, he says the same things and acts the same: Jackie Junior he really is!"*

No matter what the cynics may say about privilege, you still have to go out and perform and no amount of money or influence can change what happens on the track.

The real problem Paul faced was that nobody could treat Paul as an individual. He was always seen as Jackie's son. It was therefore secretly demanded of him that something of a motor racing gene transplant had taken place and he was Jackie reborn. Paul Stewart was as good as any Scottish racing driver to come along, apart from the ones who graduated to Formula 1. One gets the feeling that, as with many other drivers, his milieu in racing could have been outside single-seaters as his win in the IMSA GTO class at the Daytona 24 hour race in a Rousch Racing Mercury Cougar, indicated: but we will never know.

By 1988, he and his father had formed Paul Stewart Racing and were offering a step ladder for promising talent by running teams in various categories. In their heaviest season, 1991, they ran a two-car team in Formula 3000, two in Formula Three and two in the Vauxhall Lotus Championship. In all of this Paul Stewart played an important role and yet still had time to race in the Formula 3000 series. Tom Walkinshaw offered him a Formula One test in a

Footwork Arrows but at the end of that season he retired from motor racing to concentrate on the successful Paul Stewart Racing team.

Early in 2000 Paul Stewart, at the age of 34, found he had contracted cancer in his lymphatic system. His treatment at the Mayo clinic was successful and today Paul is rebuilding his life with his wife and family.

LORD DAVID STRATHCARRON

David Strathcarron is another of the great Scottish motor racing characters. He still rides to the House of Lords on his high-powered motor-cycle and was a pioneer post-war racing driver.

Strathcarron is a Macpherson whose family hails from the Newtonmore area. He was born and had lived in London for most of his 80 years until recently moving to Beaulieu.

After being educated at Eton and Cambridge he joined the RAF and flew Stirling and Warwick bombers during the war. He then joined Car-Mart in London as a salesman. He bought one of the first Marwyn 500cc racing cars that was made in a small garage in Dorset and was asked to be the factory driver.

"The Marwyn was badly designed for on the original 19 inch wheels it tended to turn over and killed one particular customer. I was practicing at Thruxton before it became an official circuit when I gained first hand knowledge of this fault. An eye-witness said my car looped the loop and rolled three times. I was thrown out with no helmet and luckily landed on the wet grass rather than the concrete. I was unhurt except I lost my memory for a day. The car was later put on 15 inch wheels and this solved the problem. In the early days most of us used the dirt track JAP. engine, which cost £75 new, and spare parts were cheap. I used to run the car on an 80/10/10 mix of alcohol, petrol and benzole and a 14:1 compression ratio. The richer drivers discovered that the Manx Norton engine was more powerful but they cost £400 each. Those drivers would then probably send it to Francis Beart or Steve Lancefield for tuning: another £60. This was a huge price to pay for a 500cc single cylinder engine in 1947.

Lord Strathcarron was the works driver for the Marwyn Formula 3 team. He also hill climbed the car such as here at Shelsley Walsh.

"Colin Strang and I drove the original Kiefts which were so slow and heavy we had difficuty keeping up on the warming-up lap at Silverstone. The successful Kiefts were the later Ray Martin design and quite different.

"I drove at the opening meetings at Silverstone, Goodwood and Brands Hatch without distinction and have also competed in vintage Alfa Romeos, a Brooklands Riley, a Talbot 105 and an Austin Healey Sprite.

ROB WALKER

Though he was not born in Scotland, Rob Walker was a Scot through and through. His father, Campbell Walker, was the heir to the Johnny Walker scotch whisky empire and died at the young age of 32. (Rob Walker was the great-great grandson of the founder.) Rob's mother, another Scot, Mary Ramsay, remarried so Rob was brought up on the family estate near Warminster.

Robert Ramsay Campbell Walker was born on August 14 1917 and was first exposed to motor racing at the age of 7 when he was taken to see the Boulogne Grand Prix. Later, at Cambridge, he obtained his private pilots licence but did not hold on to it for very long as he proceeded to show off at a point-to-point meeting taking all the jumps on the course in his Tiger Month biplane!

His first events were sprints and speed trials with a Lea Francis but he had his excitement away from racing too. He used to tell a wonderful story about running into Lady Denbeigh with his car as she was getting into hers. *"She rushed up to me and claimed that she'd had both a shock and a fit and that she was suing me for £100, That was quite a lot of money in those days and it didn't go down well with my mother or with our insurance company. Besides, the accident put a hole in my radiator"*

He started racing at Brooklands with a Delahaye formerly owned by Prince Bira and used to bet on himself with the trackside bookies to increase his prize money! His finest moment came in the Le Mans 24 hour race in 1938 when he and Ian Connell took 8th place.

During the war he joined the navy as an able seaman but became a pilot and flew a variety of seaplanes. His good friend, journalist Doug Nye, tells the story of Walker being flown out to Alexandria sitting behind the pilot of a Fairy Swordfish. Walker had spent the whole journey sipping from a bottle of gin - he never drank whisky ! - and as there was a strong wind blowing he decided that when they landed he would jump out of the plane and hold on to the lower wing so that it would not be blown over. *"...unfortunately I made two serious mistakes. I jumped out before it had landed and on the wrong side. By the time I'd rolled down the runway I was unconscious and trouserless as the tail wheel had caught my belt buckle and ripped them off. I ended up in a hospital and was amazed to find I had no broken bones. I was still pretty tight, though, and I was very fortunate that the doctor was a friend of mine. He wrote in his report, "...Multiple contusions and abrasions; patient partially anaesthetised at time of accident."*

To most people Rob Walker was famous as the man who provided a lot of race winning cars for Stirling Moss to drive. He was the first private owner in Formula 1 to win a world championship grand prix - the 1958 Argentine

GP, Moss with a Cooper-Climax - as well as the last world championship grand prix by a private owner ten years later - the 1968 British Grand Prix, Jo Siffert with a Lotus 49B Cosworth.

He also ran Moss in GT events winning the Tourist Trophy race twice in a row with Moss driving 250GT SWB Ferraris.

After he stopped as an entrant he continued to help out other teams and also turned his hand to writing as European correspondent to the American magazine Road and Track. Rob was always willing to help anyone out. When the writer organised, with Jackie Stewart, one of the first auctions of motor racing memorabilia in aid of the Scottish Dyslexia Trust I telephoned Rob. I asked him if he had anything which might be of interest. He sadly explained he had disposed of nearly everything once he stopped racing in Formula 1 but said he would ring back. True to form he rang to say that he had found in the back of the garage the pit board his mechanics had taken down from his pit at the 1968 Monaco Grand Prix where he ran Jo Siffert in a Lotus 49. He immediately despatched it to Edinburgh where it was sold for over £600 to a Siffert collector.

TOM WALKINSHAW.

Tom Walkinshaw has a little bit of everything. He is a tough nut when it comes to business, an amusing companion when you can get him away from business, an inveterate risk taker and a positve charmer when he feels like it. All of this combined to make him one of the most successful and controversial Scots businessmen; and all from fairly humble beginnings. Then came the Arrows disaster and today Tom Walkinshaw awaits his fate with the prospect of further law suits to add to the loss of the companies from which he had prospered in the past.

You could say that Tom Walkinshaw has always been a driven man. Whether it be in developing his business or in racing cars, he appeared at times a man possessed. The family market garden business in Prestonpans - just outside Edinburgh and on the River Forth coastline - had been developed by his father William Walkinshaw and Tom was automatically roped in as soon as possible to help out.

Tom was born in Lanark on August 14 1946 where his father had a farm. However when Tom was 10 the family moved to Prestonpans and he was educated at Preston Lodge School in Prestonpans. He once listed his hobbies as rough shooting, swimming and power-boating but he has always had little time for any of these sports in his pursuit of business.

Tom went to Edinburgh commercial college, so his business acumen was not totally developed at a street level,but it was clear from the start he was determined to do well. A few years later, when he was running Rover's development programme, he was asked about his attitudes towards business. *"You have to lay down certain lines of management and then employ the people to get on with it. I may be idealistic, but too many British managers do not have the commitment and believe in what they are doing. It is worth communicating with people and explaining what you, and therefore they, are trying to achieve."*

He raced for the first time at Ingliston in an MG Midget - that was in 1966 when he finished third in his first race - but the thing which got him thinking was the announcement, late in 1977, of a new single

seater class powered by Ford engines to be called Formula Ford. His mentor at that time was Bill Borrowman who, with his father, ran a small garage near Prestonpans and raced Mini Coopers with great success. Bill had links with Lotus as a sub-dealer in the Edinburgh area and Walkinshaw decided to sell the Midget and invest in a Lotus 51, the first Lotus Formula Ford model.

Even in his first seasons in Scottish Formula Ford, Tom became controversial. It was not helped by the fact that in one of his early races he put the Lotus into the barriers and was shocked to receive a bill from Circuit owner John Romanes for the repairs to the barrier! For many years the subject still came up when the two of them met.

Then there was the highly amusing, to those who were onlookers, battle of wits between young Tom and Glasgow driver Campbell Graham.

Campbell Graham's family business was founded by his grandfather and they were builders merchants. If you ever visited their huge building in Glasgow he would point out thick bolts about three feet long which at one time had been used in the shipbuilding industry. He added that they had been in stock for years and that the family never consigned anything to the dump, it was kept just in case someone needed it. As a result anyone making or building anything and needing some obscure set of nuts, screws, bolts or whatever, would go there knowing that they would still have them in stock.

Like Walkinshaw, Campbell Graham was a no holds barred motor racing enthusiast and he too was racing in Formula Ford; a Crossle at that time. In one of their early races Graham shot off the road at a high rate of knots and suspected Tom had delivered the coupe de gras. What followed was a vicious argument in the paddock. They nearly came to blows and a few days later, in explanation, Campbell told what had transpired. He had told Tom Walkinshaw that if he wanted to play that game it was alright by him and he was quite prepared to write off Toms car if it meant getting the point home. As it turned out it was a bit of a storm in a teacup.

In those days Tom had an engineering bent and was not familiar with racing cars but it didn't take him long to learn. Walkinshaw had little luck in his first meetings but was in the first four in all his subsequent races. Dave Lazenby at Lotus offered Tom their prototype Formula Ford for 1969 but his racing was curtailed after a big road accident in April that year. However, he returned and won the Scottish Formula Ford Championship with a Hawke. This resulted in being chosen as a member of the British team in the British United Airways Formula Ford Torneio in Brazil. He bought the ex-Emerson Fittipaldi Formula 3 Lotus but quickly switched to a March 703 in 1970 with support from Petonyer Racing.

Walkinshaw eventually became Scottish Formula Ford champion and he was approached by Ecurie Ecosse, now being run by the Ecurie Ecosse Association.

The team were running on a shoe string and an agreement was reached whereby Ecurie Ecosse bit the bullet and bought a March 712 for Walkinshaw to drive in a joint sponsorship deal with Petonyer Racing, his sponsor.

It was a disaster. Tom had arrived in Formula 2 when some of the greatest future racing drivers, including Niki Lauda, dominated the category. Tom tried hard and some of his practice positions were impressive, bearing in mind the miniscule resources of the team, but they pulled out in mid-season and the Ecurie Ecosse team was disbanded completely only to re-emerge twelve years later.

As for Tom Walkinshaw he had learned a lot about race-car engineering and management and clearly had decided he would be better off doing it himself. *"Scots have a habit of proving themselves when they leave Scotland"* he later remarked and so it was with Tom.

Early in 1973 at the age of 25 he was hired by Ford to develop their Capri's and Escorts. Whilst being engaged by Ford as a driver Tom set aside enough money to set up his own engineering shop which he called Tom Walkinshaw Racing: the era of TWR had begun.

Tom worked hard developing his company and honing his skills. With typical Walkinshaw brashness he went to British Leyland, who were running a team of Rovers, and bluntly challenged them, inferring that he could produce a real race winner for them. B-L to their credit, had nothing to lose and let Walkinshaw get on with it. As a result the TWR Rover went two seconds a lap faster than the factory cars and he got his first long-term factory contract for TWR: to manage and develop Rover's racing programme. By now Walkinshaw was firing on all cylinders driving, managing and alternately haranguing and charming everyone. Indeed his success with Rover saw the company build the Rover Vitesse road car and not for the first time were Walkinshaw's short term aims of building racing cars to have a long term production link with the manufacturers for whom he was employed.

Within a year he had Mazda and Audi as clients. His work with Mazda in particular was very successful, so much so that TWR ran a lucrative sideline selling Mazda tuning kits to Japan. He also broadened the scope of his companies. Amongst his early small enterprises was as British distributor for French Motul oil products and the British distributorship for AGV crash helmets.

Meanwhile, up in Coventry, Jaguar's forceful chief executive, the ebullient John Egan, contacted Walkinshaw and posed the question as to whether the company's new Jaguar XJS coupe could be developed for the European Touring Car Championship. Tom was in there like a shot. Within two years the European Championship was won by Jaguar. Meanwhile in America Bob Tullius had been developing his Group 44 racing Jaguars but Egan had been impressed and turned over Jaguar's racing programme to Tom Walkinshaw who brought in Tony Southgate to develop the XJR-6

By 1985 TWR had become a magnificent success with a turnover of £30 million of which only 15% came from the racing developments. For example, there was his Compac machinery company which made chipboard out of fibrous waste like straw and sugar cane and was a ready seller in India and other Third World countries. He was the man who developed, manufactured and distributed plastic components for the motor industry including the ubiquitous Herbie Clip, a nylon version of a Jublilee clip. Add to that five car dealerships with Jaguar, Mazda and BMW and Walkinshaw soon had no time to go motor racing, so he retired.

One of his engineering businesses was doing a lot of secret development work for manufacturers. He went into production himself in a small way with his TWR XJS's. For this he had Egan's approval and a nice little worldwide contract to sell them.

In 1990 Tom Walkinshaw made big changes within his company. He expanded the technical department but Tony Southgate did not fancy taking over an entire department of fifteen people. By a strange quirk of fate Tony joined the Aston Martin AMR1 Group C project in which Hugh McCaig was involved. However, this did not last as the whole project was torpedoed by the Jaguar hierarchy.

The man Tom Walkinshaw brought in to head his new techinal department was a young bespectacled Englishman called Ross Brawn who had been working on the Arrows. At the time Walkinshaw remarked of Brawn *"..he is one of the top four Formula 1 designers"* how right he was: and that was in 1990! With Walkinshaw now virtually developing everything on the car within TWR, it led to a telling quote illustrating the pressures he was under with the Jaguar programme at that time. *"Life would be a lot easier if a little man turned up on Friday night with 18 engines in the back of a truck and said ' use these this weekend' And then all we'd have to do was screw one in and make the thing go round for two and a half hours . Then afterwards we would figure how to make the chassis and gearbox go together better and have the little man take his 18 engines off and figure out what he had to do. The breadth of involvement is beneficial, but also it creates a lot of pressure for us"*

By this time Tom was running 28 companies employing a total of 1500 people and had a turnover of £100 million. However, around the very same time Tom got himself into the first major brouhaha of his career that still simmers under the surface. He was elected President of the BRDC and in his usual fashion took the job very seriously. The whole affair is so complicated and confused that even to attempt to unravel it would be virtually impossible. Suffice to say that the financial affairs of the BRDC were turned upside down. In short time, Tom was out, and there were losses on both sides. It is an episode Walkinshaw and the BRDC would rather forget.

Tom Walkinshaw has never been short of ambition and Formula 1 was clearly the ultimate goal. He first of all looked at Lotus when the team were on the ragged edge in 1993 and left Formula 1 shortly afterwards. When Lotus did not work out he started talking to Jackie Oliver about buying the Arrows team. Oliver was willing to sell but there were complications over the possible use of Ford engines and the deal fell through. Then Flavio Briatore got into negotiations to buy Ligier from Guy Ligier. He wanted to buy the team 50/50 with Walkinshaw but this was not in Tom's plan so he told Briatore that if he ever wanted to sell the team he would be interested. At the end of 1994 the call came and a deal was signed whereby Walkinshaw would buy Ligier with a completion date at the end of 1995. However, there was a slight complication, Briatore had only bought 85% of the shareholding and Guy Ligier had kept 15%. Though Ligier had agreed to sell his share he later changed his mind and as far as Tom was concerned the deal was off, and he had wasted a lot of valuable time on the whole Ligier situation.

Now Tom was sure of what he wanted to do and decided that, come what may, he would create his own team in time for the 1997 season. Then, at Melbourne in 1996, Bernie Ecclestone entered the picture and suggested that Tom make another bid for Arrows as they might be in difficulties. The Arrows deal was done quickly with founders Jackie Oliver and Alan Rees maintaining a link with the team: a year later Walkinshaw would become the sole owner of the team. The Arrows team was moved to Tom's massive 35-acre site at Leafield.

Meanwhile, back at the ranch, TWR had won Le Mans with a Porsche developed by them and now they were involved with Volvo and the C70 and a venture with Renault and the Clio V6 supercar for RenaultSport.

Walkinshaw's Arrows project looked good as he secured an engine deal with Yamaha, a tyre contract with Bridgestone and had signed Damon Hill as his driver. But then there was talk of financial difficulties at Arrows and a mysterious Nigerian Prince suddenly appeared on the scene as the alleged saviour of the team. The fact that he just as quickly evaporated from the scene, never to be heard of again, simply added to the mystery. Then came a breakthrough sponsorship deal with mobile phone group Orange for the 2000 season. It was not a successful season but for 2001 Tom seemed to have come up with the goods and a contract to run Cosworth engines for 2002. Though the cars appeared at the early races financial problems reared their ugly heads and Arrows simply could not pay for their engines. This, despite the fact a large stake in the Arrows team had been sold to an investment bank. What happened next falls into an area where the courts will decide who did what to whom and why. The claim was that Walkinshaw had tried to negotiate the sale of the team to a Swiss-based company over the head of the investment bank. Whatever facts will emerge, the results were quick, dramatic and devastating for Walkinshaw. The entire TWR Group was offered for sale in February 2003. When the 2002 Arrows racing cars came up for auction they were bought by Minardi's Paul Stoddart. Everything, it seemed, must go, including Walkinshaw's own treasured private collection of racing cars.

Obviously, Tom Walkinshaw does not need to look far to find critics or enemies, he has cultivated them over the years. Part of the problem is that Tom, at times, is like grabbing at a cloud of smoke. He may talk but says little, particularly about himself or his business. When it comes to money he is very much down to earth: *"You have to remember, even if you write off something unsuccessful, it is still real cash and not monopoly money. It is probably a Scottish trait looking after the pennies as well as the pounds."* At the time of writing Tom's comments may turn out to be profound and sadly he may be left with just that, pennies rather than pounds.

SANDY WATSON

Sandy Watson had his first race at Oulton Park in July 1965 driving a Mark III Mallock Clubmans car that he later raced at Ingliston. Sandy was a dyed in the wool Mallock enthusiast. Whilst starting up his own scrap business he managed to get through a Mallock 8 in 1969, a Mallock 11B in 1971, and then became Uniflo British Clubmans Champion in 1972 after which he retired from racing to concentrate on his business.

Three years later and Sandy was back again, this time with a Gryphon that he bought from Norrie Galbraith. However, the lure of Mallocks saw him return to the marque with a Mark 18B, a Mk 20, Andy Smith's Mk 21 and finally the Mark 34 Thundersports car. He rolled the car with disasterous results at Ingliston and was persuaded by Paul Gibson to buy a Vision which he used until he retired yet again in 1986.

Sandy did not stay out of racing for long, however, as he helped Andrew Kirkcaldy in his early days with some sponsorship. In 1995 he bought a Chevron B8 - the car had been converted into a Gropa but was then rebuilt as a B8. It is this car he races in modern historic racing. This led to Sandy winning the 2001 European Historic Sports Prototype Trophy, a series organised by Jonathan Baker. To win this Sandy, driving his Zul-Racing prepared car, outdrove regular 2 litre sports car winner Andrew Schryver who had to settle for second place with another Chevron B8. Sandy won his class in no fewer than eight of the ten qualifying events taking place all over Europe. He has now added a Chevron B16 and a Lotus to his stable of historic racing cars.

HARTLEY W WHYTE

Though not a serious racing driver, Hartley Waddington Whyte was one of Scotland's great motoring benefactors. Small of stature and looking like a retired Army major with his small bristling moustache, Hartley and his wife

Sheila were true enthusiasts. His grandfather was the founder of Whyte & Mackay's scotch whisky but Hartley was a very modest man who gathered an interesting collection of cars. Both he and his wife Sheila hill climbed and raced a fierce Cadillac-Allard but sold it after they loaned it to Ian Struthers who was was killed driving it at Bo'ness. Hartley once said he tended not to sell any of his cars, which is why he owned, late into his life, his very original Jaguar XK120 and even his salmon pink Triumph TR2 which he and Sheila used to share at Bo'ness and Rest and Be Thankfull hill climbs: Sheila usually being the quicker driver! He owned a former factory Aston Martin DB2 that had been raced by Dennis Poore and later, one of the most famous Aston Martin DB4 Zagatos that had been raced by Jim Clark. The latter car was sold to Nick Cussins and it remains today in Nick's collection on the Isle of Man. Hartley was also a great Bentley fan and was a personal friend of Woolf Barnato who owned Bentley before the war.

On July 3 1936, thanks to his friendship with Woolf Barnato, he bought a very controversial 8 litre Bentley which had won the 1931 Brooklands 500 Mile Race. Prior to this, fitted with a 6.5 litre engine and a sports body, this car had been Old Number 1, the first ever Speed Six Bentley which won Le Mans in 1929 and 1930. In 1932, after it had been converted into a single seater it was crashed at Brooklands and the driver, Clive Dunfee, was killed. The damaged car was rebuilt as an 8-litre saloon and this was the car Hartley Whyte bought. In 1939 he sold it back to his friend Barnatto. After the war Hartley tried to buy the car back but it was not for sale and he had to be content with another 8 litre Bentley tourer which he used to run on various events.

He presented to Scottish Motor Racing Club a magnificent gold trophy and his wife an equally magnificent silver trophy along with cash awards to be presented to Scotland's promising young racing drivers. To this day the Hartley Whyte Trust continues to honour the agreement long after his passing.

BRYCE WILSON

The Bryce Wilson saga is a case study in how not to go about promoting a natural talent into ultimate success. Bryce was a truly great prospect with a promising motor racing career before him but he was young, foolhardy and unable to adapt to the disciplines of self-control and articulateness that are part and parcel of modern marketing-inspired motor racing

In the past, you really only needed personal money to go motor racing which resulted in some mediocre talent making its way to the top.

All that had changed by the 1970s. True, you still needed money but that money could be raised through sponsorship from a company that wanted to promote its products. To do this the driver was duty bound to help the company in every way to make the sponsorship work. This change of emphasis democratised motor racing by placing the emphasis on the talent rather than the bank balance. To assist this, there were a number of people who looked out for potential talent and then helped to promote that talent, sometimes, for money but in Bryce Wilson's case, simply to give him the opportunity to show his true potential. The man who saw this in him was Laurence Jacobsen, himself a racer with a disciplined but magnanimous approach to his motor racing. In the late 1970s Bryce Wilson was the king of Scottish karters. He was a multiple Champion but was eager to get into motor racing. Laurence had seen Bryce karting and determined to help him along. Bryce, who was born in Fife, came from a very modest family background but he truly shone in karts even though his style was aggressive. It is even said that in one race when battling side by side with an opponent he reached over and pulled his challengers plug lead off in the middle of a race!

In January 1978 Laurence took Bryce to Knockhill and let him drive his Chevron B23 sports car which was a considerable act of faith as Bryce was only 17 at the time. Jacobsen's faith in Wilson was such that he did not go out and buy a Formula Ford, which was standard practice, but instead bought the ex-Jim Crawford factory Chevron B29 Formula 2 car and put him straight into it for a race meeting at Croft where Andy Barton was king. Bryce not only put the car on pole position but won the race. At the end of the season Jacobsen hired the best F3 car around - the car Jan Lammers used to win the European F3 Championship - for Wilson to drive at Thruxton and he was a sensation..

No great offers came forward but a friend of Jacobsens was Dr Erlich, who had built the Erlich Formula 3 car, and he offered the "works" drive for the 1970 racing season to Bryce. He borrowed a caravan and small motor cycle and set off for his first year in the big time, the British Formula 3 Championship. There was no way even a talent like Bryce Wilson was going to win the championship but this was his entrée into an arena where he might surprise a few people. This he did in his very first race at Snetterton when he was well down the grid after practice but came storming up the field on the first lap and was battling with Mike Thackwell when the cars touched and both went off the road. For some reason Bryce chose this as a reason to stop racing, return to Scotland and marry his girl friend. He was not yet 20 ! Clearly it was a disappointment to everyone who had helped him and that was it.

Some time later Jacobsen still ran Bryce in a Chevron Sports 2000 but his main chance had gone.Many years later still, Bryce developed into a successful businessman and came back into minor national racing winning the Renault Spyder Cup. By now he was a changed man who could never understand how stupid he had been in his youth and at all the chances that had lain before him. However, he has continued to race and, what is more, help young and coming drivers. No one can live on what might have been but those who saw Bryce at his best realised that the man had great talent but could not understand the personal concessions which have to be made in modern commercial motor racing.

Chapter 12

Scottish Racing Cars

There were very few racing cars built in Scotland but some of them deserve a place in the history of Scottish motor racing.

BEARDMORE

Though Beardmore is best known for making passenger cars in the 1920s, the designer of the car, Alexander "Alf" Francis got to work on his own car and in August 1922 ran it in the Western Speed Trials at Inchinnan. He won four classes and the half mile sprint in 39 seconds. This led Sir William Beardmore, now Lord Invernairn, to build two Super Sports versions with aluminium torpedo bodies and Rudge wire wheels. The engine was now 1800ccs and Francis drove Lord Invernairn's own car at the Dalgain Brae hill climb near Sorn in Ayrshire and made fastest time of the day. Well-known English racing driver Cyril Paul drove the second of these Super Sports cars. That season the car had fourteen first places. As a follow up to this a small production run of Super Sports was sold, each with a certificate to say that it had lapped Brooklands at 70 mph with a passenger on board. Cyril Paul personally tested every Super Sport at Brooklands in order to substantiate the certificates.

In 1924 a lightweight version was even faster and Cyril Paul won Shelsley Walsh hill climb outright as well as setting a new course record. He even defeated Raymond Mays in the Brescia Bugatti and Humphrey Cook in the TT Vauxhall.

CHEVRON

To link Derek Bennett's successful racing car company with Scotland might appear to be stretching a point but following Bennett's death - in a hang gliding accident - the company went down hill and was eventually bought by Laurence Jacobsen, Leslie Cuthbertson and Robin Smith in May 1980.

As with most small racing car companies Bennett's Chevron concern had had great success, particularly with their 2 litre sports cars, the B8, B19, B23 and B36. Their single seaters were perhaps less successful so it was surprising when Bennett dipped a tentative toe into Formula 1 with the Chevron B 41. This car, however, never competed in a world championship grand prix but was raced in a non-championship event at Zolder where Tiff Needell finished second to David Kennedy's Wolf. It was also driven in the Aurora series by David Leslie, Ray Mallock and Mike Wilds who were later to be the driving strength for the Ecosse-Ford.

Then there was the Can-Am car, the Chevron B50 that was shipped straight to America for Bobby Rahal to test for the Newman-Freeman team led by film star Paul Newman. This car was a bit of a lash up and was never raced. It was then tied up in various legal wrangles regarding payments to the company which shipped the car to the USA and little or nothing is known of what happened to it.

Eventually Bennett's sisters made tentative attempts to sell the company. One person interested in the project was Florida racing driver Peter Gregg who ran the Brumos Porsche outfit. He discussed the idea with his friend and former Cunningham driver John Gordon Bennett and Gordon Bennett told me that he was considering buying the company for its name so that he could build Chevron Indy cars. However this whole scenario fell apart when Gregg committed suicide.

Laurence Jacobsen and Robin Smith had both been racing Chevron sports cars and Jacobsen was particularly successful with a Chevron B19 in Scotland whereas Smith had been a member of the Chevron B36 crew that won the Motor trophy for the highest British car at Le Mans in 1979.

Jacobsen first met Smith when Robin used to spend the winter as a partner in a small garage called Bardene Autos that operated out of archway premises under one of the Clyde bridges in Glasgow. During the summer Robin would camp out at Nurburgring with his Chevron and lead the gipsy-racing driver kind of life for the season. Indeed Laurence gave Robin £50 to help him with his racing before he set off on one of his pilgrimages - it was the only sponsorship Robin had received up to that time.

Both Jacobsen and Smith knew the two active members of Chevron, Nigel Dickson and Paul Owens who had kept it going after Bennett's death.

With the additional financial help of Leslie Cuthbertson - whose company Rosetta had sponsored Bryce Wilson in Jacobsen's Chevron Formula Atlantic car in 1980- they bought Chevron Cars Ltd.

Chevron had just embarked on a new Sports 2000 design, the B52. When Jacobsen and Smith bought what was left of the company it including the almost completed prototype B52, some tubs, a Formula Atlantic car that was later built into a hill climb car for Gary Gibson, and a veritable mountain of spares.

The whole lot was transported in three or four 40 foot articulated trucks to Newmains Car Auctions just outside Glasgow where Jacobsen and Smith had rented a huge upper floor.

Everything was unloaded into this space to be sorted out and some of the stuff was very valuable as spares for existing Chevrons; but not all.

As Laurence explained *"..having been successful, Chevron had developed something of the big company mentality of ordering large batches of spares. I seem to remember we had something like 5,000 of the little rollers for the sliding skirts Chevron once used on the single seaters but which were now totally unsaleable when skirts were banned"*

Meanwhile the partially completed tubs were moved to Robin's farm at Newmains where the cars were built.

Obiously they were keen to start getting some money in so they started out with the B52 Sports 2000.

"It wasn't a bad little car. It was built to a price but we inherited something that was pretty wobbly as far as the structure was concerned." Remarked Jacobsen.

"Given the experience I now have I would probably have started all over from scratch but we continued with the original design." As an architect Jacobsen was used to creating structures and had a natural ability in this direction.

"Robin is a wonderful engineer but I would say that, structurally, Robin is a disaster. He has a fantastic feel for mechanical things and for many years he went motor racing by adapting bits other people were throwing away. I must say I have never been let down by Robin on a mechanical thing. As far as structures are concerned he doesn't have a natural feel."

They started to build and modify the B52 which Jacobsen himself bought and raced in Scotland. Eventually this evolved into the B54 that had a slightly different nose to improve downforce and at the back they dropped the rake to balance up with what they had done at the front. "*I remember when we used to get questions from Americans about the B54. One asked Robin whether the car had been in the tunnel to which he replied ' aye, the Clyde Tunnel' which was a great joke but didn't really go down well with our American customers.*"

In their first year of operation the first B54 was sold to John Clark in Aberdeen, now well known in the historic racing field. It was subsequently bought, in 1983, by Hugh McCaig as the first racing car for the new Ecurie Ecosse. It was painted Ecurie Ecosse blue and raced by young Highlander Willie Hourie.

Another six B54's were sold to the United States, which was a pretty fair start and was mainly due to one of Phil Crighton's partners who acted as their US agent. However everything went pear-shaped when the partner joined the "Moonies". It totally changed his lifestyle, and he was no longer interested in racing.

This called for a rapid change of plan so Jacobsen and Smith contacted Mike Gue who asked for a car to be sent out to him.

As sales had dropped they had not been able to fully develop their new model, the B60, but had a mock-up that was cobbled together, finished off and sent to the States. As Jacobsen admits today, it was not a good example to send to Gue. The car that should have been sent was one even better than the production version. As a result they got off to a rocky start with the B60.

"*When we originally ran our own B52 down south with Yamaha backing and Bryce Wilson driving we were quite successful but I think that was due to Bryce's driving ability more than anything else. I then bought the first B54 and took it to Silverstone It was my first visit to the circuit and thought it was like driving in a car park so I stood down gave the car to Ian Flux to race.*

"*I then bought the prototype B60 and it was a great little car so much so I converted into a proper sports car by fitting a Cosworth BDG in the back of it. Compared to the 52 and the 54, the tub of the B60 was greatly strengthened and modified but the debacle in America had left us with virtually no income at all and it was clear that Chevron could not continue.*"

The initial investment in Chevron had been around £20,000 and though there had been no great profit in the selling of the Sports 2000s Robin had done a good job selling spare parts to other Chevron owners. Also Laurence Jacobsen partly funded the company by being the one who actually bought the prototype cars of the following year's design as though he were a customer. When business was slow he also got Robin Smith to build a Chevron B16. Even in Derek Bennett's days not all B16 chassis were built in Bolton; some were built by Brian Martin who also had a jig. Through Nigel Dickson, who was now working with Brian Martin on the Martin sports car, Jacobsen ordered a new B16 chassis. Using some of the spares they already had and some parts from a wrecked B17 Formula 2 car Robin Smith built up a B16. " My B16 was actually built out of a Formula 2 car which is why, when the car was eventually sold to America without any FIA papers it carried a chassis plate with B16 "R".

Once the dust had settled what remained of Chevron Cars was sold in 1983 to Roger Andreason who not only continues to run the company but has developed it considerably. It is interesting that Roger was a regular competitor at Ingliston when he raced his Marcos-Volvo.

ECOSSE-CLIMAX

This car was a Scottish special as the engine and gearbox were from the Ecurie Ecosse Cooper Monaco that had been built up out of a kit of parts

The Ecosse Climax

at the Cooper factory by Stan Sproat. The Monaco was originally raced by Tommy Dickson, Roy Salvadori, Jack Brabham and Jimmy Blumer and then by team newcomer Jackie Stewart in 1963. Following a crash earlier in its life the Monaco was never the same and Blumer commented that it was the worst of the three Cooper Monacos he ever raced. However In Stewart's hands the car was quite successful but then was crashed heavily at Oulton Park writing off the chassis completely. The remains were carted back to Edinburgh where they were left in a corner. With the announcement, in 1964, that there would be a new circuit in Edinburgh called Ingliston David Murray had the idea of rebuilding the Monaco remains into a single seater using the 2.5 litre Coventry Climax engine and run it in Formula Libre events in Scotland. Stan Sproat fabricated the chassis and had the new bodywork beaten out so that it appeared for the first time at a non-spectator test meeting before the opening of the Ingliston track. Bill Stein was to set the first outright lap record at Ingliston and had a number of wins with the car before it was retired into the collection of Major Thompson who supplied much of the finance for Ecurie Ecosse.

The Major then put the car up for auction at Gleneagles Hotel in 1970. The Ecosse Climax was the last car to come up for sale and there was no great interest in it. However, an American book publisher from Virginia, Alfred Peyton Jenkins, was staying at Gleneagles with his wife and 9-year-old son Todd. To Todd this was the greatest thing he had ever seen and with his father's permission he was able to bid up to £1,100 and at that figure bought the car! It was taken back to Virginia where it lay for a number of years. Todd, in his early twenties, had the idea of rebuilding it and running the Ecosse-Climax in historic events and did one or two but his long-term plan had always been to have the car restored with a new chassis as a Cooper Monaco. This task was eventually accomplished in the 1990s with the help of former American sports car driver Bob Aiken and today it looks exactly as it did when Jackie Stewart first raced it. In 2001 Todd Jenkins decided to sell the car. It was bought by Dick Skipworth who owns more ex-Ecurie Ecosse cars than anyone.

The Monaco was brought to Edinburgh in April 2002 for the 50th anniversary dinner of Ecurie Ecosse so making its return to its original home after thirty-two years.

ECOSSE-IMP

Despite the fact that the Ecosse Climax raced at Ingliston in the early part of 1966, it was handed back to Major Thompson for his collection. Meanwhile, elsewhere in Edinburgh, Sandy Cormack, whose father Alastair Cormack had been a factory driver for Alta before the War, was thinking

The rather spindly rear suspension system on the lightweight Ecosse Imp.

about building a special to go racing. As the family company was James Ross & Sons the Rootes distributors he looked at the lightweight Hillman Imp engine based on the Coventry Climax. He mentioned this to David Murray of Ecurie Ecosse and offered David a scrap Imp engine and gearbox with the idea of building a relatively inexpensive racing car.

The project was handed over to Stan Sproat who designed not only the chassis but a special cylinder head to take a Weber carburettor. This allowed for the fact that in the racing car the engine would be virtually vertical rather than at an angle as in the production road car. The attraction of the lightweight four-cylinder Hillman Imp engine appealed to Murray's patriotic nature - particularly as it was being built at the Rootes factory near Glasgow - and so the idea was to build a Formula 3 car using the 1,000cc engine. The first chassis was given the number EC-1-66. The car had a light tube chassis and double wishbone front suspension. When it was finished it was taken to Ingliston where Graham Birrell tested it with promising results and so the decision was taken to build a second chassis. The reason for this was that the original driver of the Ecosse-Imp was to have been Bill Stein but he had been seriously injured in the Ecosse Tojeiro spyder at Brands Hatch. Graham Birrell was much taller than Stein and had trouble fitting into the original car. The second chassis, EC-2-66, had a slightly longer wheelbase to accommodate Birrell. At the same time, Cooper uprights were bought and the second chassis was much more competitive than the first.

Sadly the concept of creating these cars as the basis for an inexpensive national formula petered out as Ecurie Ecosse did not have the money, or the political clout, to launch a series. To be honest the Ecosse-Imps never really set the heather on fire but David Murray let a number of young Scots up and coming drivers have a go. Though the cars never raced in a true Formula 3 event - though both Graham and his brother Gerry Birrell drove them at Mallory Park - they were light and nimble and were able to lap the Ingliston circuit quicker than the 2.5 litre Ecosse Climax. The major financial backing for the cars had come, as was normal, from Major Edward Thompson and when Ecurie Ecosse stopped using them they were technically returned to him. When David Murray left the country for exile in the Canary Islands Major Thompson signed over both chassis to the Ecurie Ecosse Association. One of them was sold to Sandy Cormack and Malcolm Parkin to run for fun and in turn it was sold to the Thompson brothers in Edinburgh who raced and hill climbed it. Later both cars were sold and competed in hill climb and sprint events but

were hacked about a bit. At least one of them is now in Tom McWhirter's collection in Nairn.

ECOSSE

In 1983 Hugh McCaig reformed the Ecurie Ecosse team. At the start it was a modest toe-dipping exercise and a Chevron B52 was bought from John Clark. for Orkney Islander Willie Hourie to drive. However, Hugh soon linked up with Ray Mallock and a plan was developed which might see Ecurie Ecosse back at Le Mans. This idea really fired up Hugh and a much-used De Cadenet sports car powered by a Ford DFV engine was bought and converted to meet the 1994 Group C2 rules for the world sports car championship. The shapely and aerodynamic bodywork was designed round the Nimrod-Aston Martins of previous years. When completed the car was called an Ecosse but right from the start it came under the eagle eye of the scrutineers who could not make up their minds about the cockpit dimensions. It culminated in something of a stand-off at Le Mans when the car was officially declared inelligible to continue in the World Championship. Rather than pension it off it was pressed into service in the Sports car race that supported the British Grand Prix in 1994 with David Leslie and Ray Mallock as the drivers. After an early battle Ray Mallock took the car into the lead only for the brakes to fail at Druids Bend, the car plunging head on into the banking catching fire. Ray Mallock was lucky not to be injured but the car was destroyed.

The decision was taken to go back to the drawing board and design a car from scratch which was very similar to the original Ecosse and powered by a Ford DFL (3.3litre) engine. Two of these were built for the 1985 season, the second car running at Le Mans as a rental deal with three amateur American drivers.

For 1986 an approach was made to Austin-Rover with a view to using the Rover V6R rally engine. This was not the most reliable engine but thanks to the introduction of race engineer Max Boxtrom to the Ecosse team strength, a total redesign of the pulley system brought reliability. For that season Austin-Rover offered their contracted driver Marc Duez and the Ecosse team finished the season as World Group C2 Champions. The first time a Scottish motor racing team had won a world championship.

In 1987 the team reverted to Ford DFL engines and had a reasonably good season but already an approach had been made by Peter Livanos, whose family were the major shareholders in Aston Martin, to produce an Aston Martin powered Group C1 challenger to the Porsches called the AMR1. This

The beautifully styled Ecosse-Rover raced by Ecurie Ecosse in 1986 which won the Group C2 World Sports Car Championship that year. The engine was the Metro 6R4 unit already developed for rallies.

car was built and developed by a separate company, Proteus Technology, in which Hugh McCaig and Ray Mallock were involved.

Ecosse Cars:

Chassis 01   Ecosse-Ford   Built March 1984 based on De Cadenet sports car.

1984

April 2 :	Monza	Ray Mallock/David Duffield/Mike Wilds	2nd Gp C2 8th overall.
May 12:	Silverstone	Mallock/Duffield	Retd.
June 14/15	Le Mans	Wilds/ David Leslie/ Duffield	Retd.
July 21	Brands Hatch	Mallock/Leslie	Car destroyed.

Chassis 02   Ecosse-Ford   (Henry) February 1985. Completely new car.

1985

April 28	Monza	Mallock/Wilds	2nd Gp C2, 10th overall.
May 12	Silverstone	Mallock/Wilds	1st C2 9th overall
June 15	Le Mans	Mallock/Wilds/Leslie	Disqualified.
July 14	Hockenheim	Mallock/Wilds/Leslie	1st C2 8th overall.
Sept 1	Spa	Mallock/Wilds/Leslie	4th C2 14th overall
Sept 22	Brands Hatch	Mallock/Wilds	1st C2 5th overall

1986

May 31	Le Mans	Les Delano/Andy Petery/John Hotchkis	4th C2.
	Sold to:	Martin Colvil	
	Sold to:	Laurence Jacobsen	
	Sold to:	John Pearson	

Chassis 03   Ecosse-Rover   Tub built February 1985 not raced until 1986 with Rover V6 engine

1986

May 5	Silverstone	Mallock/Wilds	Leading C2 retired.
May 31	Le Mans	Mallock/Wilds/Leslie	Disqualified
July 20	Brands Hatch	Mallock/Leslie	1st C2 7th overall
Aug 24	Nurburgring	Mallock/ Marc Duez	1st C2 5th overall.
Sept 14	Spa	Mallock/Duez	1st C2 13th overall.
Oct 10	Fuji	Mallock/Duez	1st C2 9th overall

WORLD CHAMPIONS GROUP C2.

1987   Car reverted to Cosworth DFL engine

March 22	Jarama	Mallock/Leslie	2nd C2 11th overall
March 29	Jerez	Mallock/Leslie	2nd C2 5th overall
April 12	Monza	Mallock/Leslie	2nd C2 8th overall
May 10	Silverstone	Johnny Dumfries/Wilds	3rd C2 8th overall
June 13/14	Le Mans	Wilds/Petery/Delano	Retired
June 28	Norisring	Wilds/Win Percy	Retired
July 25	Brands Hatch	Wilds/Duez	3rd C2 10th overall
Aug 30	Nurburgring	Wilds/Percy	
Sept 13	Spa	Wilds/Duez	2nd C2 12th overall
Sept 27	Fuji	Wilds/Duez	3rd C2 15th overall

Car now owned by Hugh McCaig with Rover V6 engine.

Chassis 04   Ecosse-Ford October 1986.

1987

May 10	Silverstone	Mallock/Leslie	1st C2 6th overall
June 13	Le Mans	Mallock/Leslie/Duez	2nd C2 8th overall
		Winner Index of Performance.	
June 28	Norisring	Mallock/Leslie	2nd C2 8th overall
July 25	Brands Hatch	Mallock/Leslie	1st C2 7th overall
Aug 30	Nurburgring	Mallock/Leslie	Retd.
Sept 13	Spa	Mallock/Leslie	3rd C2 13th overall
Sept 27	Fuji	Mallock/Leslie	2nd C2 14th overall
	Sold to:	Don Shead	
	Sold to:	Bryan Wingfield	

FISHER SPECIALS

Jack Fisher had a motor business in Edinburgh and was an inveterate Special builder.

If some of the Scottish specials tended to be heavier than they should have been Jack Fisher went in the opposite direction. For his original Fisher Special he used a Fiat 500 chassis which meant his eventual Special weighed a mere 9 cwts. This despite the fact that he used a Riley Sprite engine and gearbox which was not the lightest available. The trouble with this one was that it could not put its power on the road and so Jack built a new chassis of his own design but still used the Riley engine,

In 1964 Jack came up with another special this time based on a BMC Mini power train and a bodywork using bits from a damaged Lotus Elite and finally the Fisher-Lancia, a single seater which never really got going and it competed for only one season.

*Just one of the many Fisher Specials built by Edinburgh driver Jack Fisher.
The car occasionally appears in historic events driven by its owner John Foster.*

HAMMOND-GORDON SPECIAL

Peter was one of those characters who turn up in motor racing who have their own life agenda which is part reality and part fantasy. I believe that today he is somewhere in the Dordogne living as "Captain Gordon" You could not but like Peter Gordon as he was totally irrepressible.

Born in the northern town of Golspie "Flash" Gordon, as he was always called, was sent to Aberdeen to work in the sales department of a timber supplier at the docks. When racing started at Crimond he was hooked and managed to buy Ninian Sanderson's old "Yellow Peril" Cooper 500. Later after selling the Cooper to Doug Duncan, an Aberdeen bookie in Castle Gate, Peter had the idea of building his own Special. Meanwhile an Aberdeen architect called Gerald Hammond had been running an Allard and a Dellow in various events. He had a great passion for messing about in his workshop garage and one day he was approached by Peter Gordon to build the car which was to become the Hammond-Gordon Special. One of his other friends at the time was Edwin Whyte who described the conditions under which they worked on the Special as being "...worthy of a Tibetan yak ! It was little more than a dug out with a tin roof. As an apprentice I had used the machine shop at Rossleigh, the

Peter Gordon, centre, with Edwin Whyte, left, and Gerald Hammond with the fruits of their work.

Jaguar dealers in Aberdeen, and produced a variety of parts for the special. In fact many of the parts for this car were re-cycled from the company scrap heap. In its finished form the car looked spectacular but if John Garden, the scrutineer, really knew what lay under that aluminium paint the car would never have turned a wheel in anger."

The reason for this latter remark is that Peter and his crew had built the space frame chassis out of conventional seamed electrical conduit painted with aluminium paint and it managed to fool all the scrutineers. The car had old pre-war wheels off a van and cable brakes rebuilt to incorporate Morris hydraulic wheel cylinders. They ended up with a lightweight car that deserved to have an 1100cc Climax engine. Peter Gordon found out this would cost £250 so he settled for the reverse ported 1172cc side valve Ford engine with four Amal carburettors that Len Gibbs had developed .

The Special was registered NAV100 and raced all over the place with considerable lack of success. That was virtually the end of the Hammond-Gordon special.

HESKETH

To many people, the inclusion of the Hesketh grand prix car in a list of "Scottish" racing cars may be stretching a point but the man behind it, Lord Alexander Hesketh is quite rightly proud of his Scottish ancestry - his mother comes from the Scottish Borders - and carried the St Andrews cross on the car James Hunt raced.

Lord Hesketh came into Formula 1 in 1973 when he rented a Surtees TS9 for the Race of Champions. Hunt's third place in this event convinced Hesketh that they needed a better car and for the rest of 1973 and into 1974. Meanwhile their technical guru and designer, Harvey Postlethwaite was hard at work designing a new car, the Hesketh 308, which appeared for the first time as a test car at the Brazilian Grand Prix in 1974. However, at the Brands Hatch Race of Champions James Hunt put the Hesketh on pole position for its first actual race against the likes of Lauda, Fittipaldi, Regazzoni and Jacky Ickx but the car retired with handling problems after four laps.

The Hesketh looked different from most with a wedge-shape and a high airbox above the Cosworth 3 litre engine. Postlethwaite tried various suspension ideas including rubber cones but was usually on coil springs. Hunt drove a brilliant race at Silverstone to win the International Trophy. In Grand Prix racing they took a third in Sweden, Austria and the USA and a fourth in Canada. All of this was done with a pure white car with no commercial sponsorship. In the circumstances the results were very impressive but clearly there were financial pressures.

The team continued in 1975 with the original 308 but Postlethwaite was working on a new car with a completely new chassis and side radiators. This was the 308C and it made its debut at the "Swiss" Grand Prix at Dijon where it finished 8th. The car was not, however, a success and its best results were fourth place at the US GP and fifth in the Italian. By now the whole operation was costing Alexander Hesketh a fortune and despite selling off the previous years cars he called a halt to Hesketh Racing at the end of the 1985 season. True to a promise he made to the members of Scottish Motor Racing Club two years before, Hesketh brought a Hesketh grand prix car to Ingliston where Scotsman Richard Scott demonstrated it to the home crowd.

J.P.

The JP was the first true racing car built in limited production in Scotland. Like many other racing cars that proliferated during the 500cc Formula 3 period the JP was to fall by the wayside but it shone briefly with the success of Ron Flockhart.

During 1949 a Scots engineer best known for his exploits racing and tuning motorcycles, Joe Potts, bought a Cooper 500 and raced it but hankered after designing and building his own car. As a result in the winter of 1949 he and his chief mechanic Willie Rogerson got down to designing his own light chassis with a series of parallel main tubes and light tubular hoops to support the bodywork. The first car was started in the Spring of 1950 and then another Scot, Comish Hunter, who also raced a Cooper, liked what he saw and ordered chassis number two. Both cars were ready to test at Grangemouth airport by July 1950, Hunter choosing to use his 500CC JAP engine in his car whilst Potts put a 1,000cc Vincent HRD engine into his "works" car. It was completed just in time for the Ulster Trophy meeting where another Scot, Mirrlees Chassels was entered but the Irish circuit doctor thought his eysight was not good enough and Potts gave the car to Ron Flockhart to drive. On this occasion it retired when one of the two

Ron Flockhart with the 1000cc Vincent HRD-engined JP he used to win the Ulster Trophy handicap race at the Dundrod circuit.

Joe Potts was quick to capitalise on Ron Flockhart's win and advertised his racing cars in the sporting magazines.

cylinders collapsed. The Comish Hunter car also retired with a split fuel tank, the result of a hasty welding job.

Comish Hunter made his Silverstone debut with the 500cc version and ran well up the field before throwing a rod on the last lap. Later that season Comish Hunter gave the JP its first win at Winfield ahead of the Coopers.

Joe Potts' car seemed to have promise and no fewer than eight chassis were laid down for the 1951 season. Amongst those ordering cars was Ron Flockhart who also put a Vincent-HRD engine into his. Meanwhile the works car had been sold to Mirrlees Chassels. The only non-Scot to order one was Bob Dickson from Carlisle. During the season the great Reg Parnell was entered in a JP 500 for the support race to the British GP but was called up to drive the BRM and so did not actually drive the car. Generally speaking the JP's were hampered by the fact they were all owned by Scots who were hundreds of miles away from the action and so their engines never had the power of the better developed cars in the South.

Ron Flockhart then took his car to the Ulster Trophy meeting where he had practice problems with fuel starvation and plugs due to running on 80 octane fuel. In the race itself Peter Collins initially led in his Cooper but was passed by Flockhart at the end of lap 2, Flockhart being timed at 102 mph on the straight. Eventually Collins melted a piston in his Cooper. Flockhart went on to win the Ulster Trophy with the JP, his first major motor racing victory.

In 1952 Ron Flockhart sold his JP-Vincent to Irishman Marshall Watson whose son John Watson was to go on to drive grand prix McLarens in the 1980s. Another JP, owned by Ian Sutherland also went to Ireland, to Billy Leeper. By now Cliff Carter and Johny Higham had bought JP's to race in England but Joe Potts was advised by his doctor to stop his own motor racing.

By 1953 it was almost all over. Joe Potts was now heavily involved with his motorcycle racing preparation business and was concentrating on his two proteges Alastair King and the great Bobby McIntyre. Potts-Nortons became very competitive in the hands of McIntyre in particular and he went on to become a multiple TT winner before being killed in a racing accident. Joe Potts did, however, produce a new car for David Blane to race with a de Dion back axle but little more was heard of it.

In the 1960s a Scots enthusiast gave a very original JP to the Doune Motor Museum and another JP, heavily modified, was used for hill climbs and club races by Edinburgh enthusiast Tom Irvine in the 1980s. From time to time the odd JP turns up at events, a reminder of the start of motor racing in Scotland.

Some Early JP results.

1950

Aug 12 Ulster Trophy Race Dundrod

Dr Mirrlees Chassels entered a JP-Vincent. Ron Flockhart took over the Chassels entry when the circuit doctor would not let Mirrlees take part. After one lap Flockhart changed a plug. Flockhart set up 2nd fastest lap to Arthur Powys-Lybbe's Alfa Romeo. Car retired due to mixture problem.

Comish Hunter, JP 500. Hunter ran out of fuel due to a leaking tank. The two JP's were prototypes.

Aug 26 BRDC Daily Express trophy Silverstone

500cc Race: Joe Potts and Pat Prosser had their Coopers and Comish Hunter had the prototype JP. Potts was hit by Frank Atkins Iota-Triumph after having spun. Comish Hunter was ahead of Prosser but threw a rod on the last lap. Potts, shaken, toured round to the end.

Sept 30 SSCC Members Day Bo'ness

Comish Hunter logged a 42.31 compared to 42.69 with the Cooper at the June meeting.

Hunter sold his Cooper to Alex McGlashan to concentrate on his JP. David Swan (Cooper) beat Hunter into second place but Swan placed an order for a JP in 1951.

Winfield   October 7 The first Scottish race meeting.

Hunter recorded the JP's first win ahead of Pat Prosser and Bobby Leapingwell (Coopers) . Willie Rogerson was responsible for preparing the JPs. Potts drove a JP with a 500cc engine in the event for racing cars up to 1500ccs, which was won by Reg Parnell in the Maserati 4CLT from David Murray's 4CL Maserati. Potts finished a creditable 5th.

In the race for Racing cars up to 1100cc Hunter was penalised by one minute for a jump start. Then, catching up, was baulked by a slower car and hit the fuel cans at the side of the track.

The final version of the JP 500 in prototype form at its launch.

The wishbone front suspension on the new JP 500.

1951

In the Spring JPs were delivered to Ian Sutherland and Ron Flockhart, Joe Potts, Comish Hunter, George Brown, Bill Smith, David Swan, John Brown and Bob Dickson. Reg Parnell offered to drive one when available but this never took place.

Mirrlees Chassels took delivery of new Vincent-twin for the prototype JP and Comish Hunter's 1950 car was sold to David Blane. Ian Sutherlands car had a heavier chassis to take a 1000cc engine. The general opinion was that the JP was a bit heavy when compared to a contemporary Cooper.

June 30 Bo'ness hill climb.

There were six JP's entered for the 500cc class but Joe Potts' class record was broken no fewer than six times by Ken Whartons Cooper. Newcomer Ninian Sanderson was second fastest in the class with the ex-Pat Prosser Cooper " The Yellow peril"

Racing Cars up to 500ccs		Racing Cars 751-1100cc
4th	Comish Hunter	3rd Ron Flockhart JP Vincent
7th	Bob Dickson	
8th	David Swan	
10th	Ian Sutherland	
11th	David Blane	
12th	Bill Smith Triumph-engined.	

Rest and Be thankfull

Racing Cars up to 500ccs		Racing cars 751cc - 1100cc	
3rd	Comish Hunter	1st Ron Flockhart	
5th	Joe Potts	5th Mirrlees Chassels	
6th	David Blane	8th	D K Swan
10th	W J Smith Triumph engined		

British GP Silverstone

In the 500cc race David Swan and Ian Sutherland took part in their JP's. Reg Parnell entered a JP for the 500cc race but had to withdraw as he had a call from Bourne to drive a BRM. Parnell handed over the car to his friend John Green. The Scots did not do well as their engines did not have the power to match those who were racing every weekend in England.

June 2   Ulster Trophy Race Dundrod

Scratch race up to 1300ccs saw Ron Flockhart in his JP with a 998ccengine. Comish Hunter and Joe Potts also took part with their 500's. in the separate 500cc race. Potts put his car into a hedge to avoid a spinning car. Hunter broke a con-rod in practice and fitted his old sprint engine for the race.

Flockhart had trouble with fuel starvation and plugs then went on to win his first major International event.

In the 500cc event Hunter was holding second before the insulation cracked on the magneto and Hunter stopped at side of track.

In the handicap event Flockhart retired with gearchange problem.

Sept 1   Turnberry

In the 500cc race Comish Hunter, David Swan and Ian Sutherland retired with clutch trouble. Bill Smith finished third in his Triumph-engined car and Bob Dickson was fourth close race.

Bo'ness Club meeting

In the 500cc class Ninian Sanderson won with his Cooper with Davie Blane 2nd Comish Hunter, 3rd Bob Dickson 5th Joe Potts 7th Bill Smith 8th and Cliff Carter 9th all in JP's

1952

April 26   Beveridge Park, Kirkcaldy

Comish Hunter, Cliff Carter, Bob Dickson and Johnny Higham all had JP's. In the first heat Hunter retired with clutch trouble and in the final Hunter was 3rd and Bob Dickson 4th.

May 3rd   Turnberry

Joe Potts had an updated version of the JP for this event and finished 3rd . Joe also ran in the Formula Libre event but this was to be his last race as he was advised by his doctor to quit competitive racing.

May 10   Daily Express Trophy Silverstone

Comish Hunter ran his JP in the 500cc race but was unplaced.

Some idea of the workmanship Jot Potts put into his car can be seen here in the bare chassis of his last model.

LOCKHART SPECIAL

Gordon Lockhart is perhaps best known for racing his vintage Bentley but he built a remarkable little special using an Austin Seven chassis and an ABC-Twin engine fitted with a Shorrocks supercharger. This chain-driven special originally had the engine alongside the driver but later the driver sat in front. It weighed just 6 cwts but it was notoriously unreliable and was abandoned.

LWS

The LWS was the only Formula Junior car built in Scotland. When Formula Junior was announced in 1959 Edinburgh brothers David and Douglas Bertram took the original concept of Formula Ford to heart.

"When we saw this was being created as a low cost Formula we didn't think manufacturers like Lotus, Elva and Lola would run factory cars and so it seemed like an opening to create our own car"

The Bertram family business, James Bertram and Sons was founded in 1845 by the great grandfather of Douglas and David. It was an engineering company that specialised in designing and building paper making machines.

Both brothers started racing in the 1950s, David with a Triumph TR2 and Douglas with a Morgan. Though David was to race a total of three TR's Douglas also raced a Swallow Doretti and an AC Aceca.

They did a lot of racing in England and their favourite event was the 750 Motor Club relay race at Silverstone in which they competed on a number of occasions.

Eventually they decided to buy a proper racing sports car and were able to get a hold of Keith Hall's ex-factory Lotus 11 (4 DTM). After two seasons with the Lotus they had seen the success of Lola and so ordered a new Lola Sports car from Eric Broadley. Ironically both the Lotus 11 and the Lola were sold to the same American enthusiast in Wichitaw, Kansas.

It was now 1960 and the Formula Junior project was formed. The company's works and garages were in Edinburgh's Leith Walk and so the new car was called the LWS (Leith Walk Special.) The designer of the chassis was the company's chief mechanic Peter Beaton assisted by inveterate Edinburgh special builder Jack Fisher.

The design was very simple with a box section chassis and front mounted Ford engine. The Bertrams approached Eric Broadley and bought both the front and rear suspension systems from him as well as a Lola diff with inboard drum brakes.

The Leith Walk Special was the only Formula Junior car built in Scotland. David and Douglas Bertram of the Bertrams engineering company and designer Peter Beaton in Edinburgh were responsible for this professional looking car.

Though the car was raced for two seasons it was never terribly successful and so it was pensioned off. Later they added front and rear wings to the car to make it qualify as a sports car. It was raced in this form at the very first Ingliston race meeting by Bill Turnbull.

Eventually the Bertrams were approached by an enthusiast in the south west of Scotland, George McNay.He bought the LWS only to have a monumental accident with it and wrote it off. As far as is known it has not survived

SALTIRE

This car was built in 1956 by Ronnie Millar, the Chairman of the Motherwell Bridge company and fellow enthusiast Pat Melville, normally seen racing a Vauxhall 30/98 in Vintage events. Details of the car are sketchy but the engine was a Lea-Francis taken from Ian Hopper's Hopper Special. It had a fairly basic frame and an aluminium bodywork roughly similar to a Jaguar C-type. The car appeared only once, at Crimond, only to disappear. Not long afterwards Ronnie Millar ordered a Lister chassis which was sent to David Murray at Merchiston Mews to be built up as a Lister-Jaguar and is now in the ownership of David Ham.

The Saltire surfaced again in the hands of special builder Syd Ritchie but it came without its engine.

Syd Ritchie was a keen member of the 750 Motor Club and built a Wolseley Hornet Special followed by a Ford special. Jaguar specialist Bryan Wingfield points out that the original Saltire chassis had been based on an early single seater Ferrari 2 litre V12. It is probable that Miller and Melville actually bought the Formula 2 Ferrari David Murray of Ecurie Ecosse owned. What makes this more likely is that when Ritchie put an engine into the car it still had a Ferrari rear tranaxle. Certainly the Ferrari F2 that David Murray owned - originally the Peter Whitehead short wheelbase car - disappeared and the writer has no knowledge of it ever appearing again.

When Syd Ritchie bought the Saltire it came with no engine. The first engine Ritchie used was from an Austin Healey 100 with a three-speed gearbox and overdrive. The engine was claimed to be an "S" but it is more likely the engine came from a 100M as there were one or two of them in Scotland at the time. The handling of the car was "appalling" but Ritchie and Wingfield added extra dampers and modified the transverse leaf springs until it handled reasonably well. As the rear suspension was a swing axle arrangement, the car did tend to "jack up" at the rear when under stress. Ritchie then replaced the Healey engine with a Jaguar XK120C engine and it was in this form that he had his fatal accident at Charterhall. As mentioned in the text, he ran off the road and in trying to get back the car overturned.

SARK

Technically speaking the Sark was not a pure Scottish design but a project taken over by Donald MacLeod in 1978.

The Sark project was started in July 1974 by Gavin Hooper and was for the new Formula Ford 2000 class that started in 1975. It was originally called the Starfire and was designed by a very young Patrick Head, now best known for his work with Williams in grand prix racing. The Starfire failed to create any interest when shown at the racing car show and eventually the project was taken over by Richard Piper and Chris Parsons who had a workshop in Greenwich. They clearly did not want to continue with the Starfire since it had gone down like a damp squib. From their workshops they looked across to the famous Cutty Sark sailing ship at Greenwich and decided to rename it the Sark.

With the help of Patrick Head they made the car into a proper racing car and built a handful of them for sale to private entrants. Piper and Parsons laboured on but were getting nowhere and so sold the Sark project to Donald MacLeod. McLeod had tested the Sark in 1977 and, with his brother Hamish as the engineer, they decided to go into business as constructors. As the original car was an FF2000 Donald raced it but he and Hamish quickly decided that Formula Ford 1600 probably held out more promise and they developed a new car that had little in common with the F2000.

By slaving at the car they managed to get it finished in time for the 1978 Formula Ford Festival which was an ideal place to give any new car its debut in front of FF people from all over the world. As it turned out, the car was superb in the damp conditions. It was almost a dream start as McLeod won his heat and the quarter-final but a broken engine mount meant he finished fourth. This car had a very narrow track for straight line speed but it was not competitive on the fast circuits even though they had sold a few to customers. As a result Hamish re-designed it for the 1979 Festival.

Despite engine problems MacLeod qualified on pole for the final thanks to the phenomenal performance of the car in the wet. It did not, however, lead to sales and there was a recession on so the whole project was once more sold on. Donald McLeod achieved his dream and, as far as the writer is aware, is the only person to win the Formula Ford Festival in a car of his own construction.

SCOTT

It seems strange that a young Scottish racing driver, Richard Scott, should choose to build his own Formula 2 car in the early 1970s when Formula 2 was at its strongest; but there was logic in his decision.

"Back in those days Formula 2 cars were notoriously difficult to drive as everyone had copied Lotus and put the radiators at the sides. This meant that there was virtually no weight at the front. The cars understeered or else, if you pushed them hard, had violent oversteer. That was ok for drivers like Ronnie Petersen, who had the superb skill to handle a car like that, but I thought it would be better to produce a car with a more even front to rear balance than those cars. I spoke to my engine man Geoff Richardson about this and he felt

Richard Scott at the wheel of his Formula 2 Scott that was designed by a very young Patrick Head. The car is today owned by hill climb driver Peter Voigt.

he couldn't tackle it but he knew of a young freelance designer called Patrick Head and Patrick might take on the job. Patrick was only 26 at the time had achieved an honours degree at London University and worked at Weslake and Harry Ferguson research before moving to Lola. His father, Michael Head, had been a racing driver in the 1950s with a C type Jaguar.

"My plan had been to use my old Brabham BT38 and a whole pile of spare parts which were lying around and get Patrick to incorporate them into a new chassis design. Patrick said he would go away and think about it and then came back and told me to sell the lot and he would start from scratch. He saw it as an interesting challenge"

The car Patrick Head came up with was superb and everyone who saw it at its launch at Silverstone was impressed. There was nothing revolutionary and it was very straightforward. What caught the imagination at the time was that Patrick Head had designed a specially cast aluminium gearbox adaptor plate which put an extra five inches between the engine and gearbox and placing the driver much further forward in the cockpit. This had been tried in F5000 but was new in F2. The design was conventional in that the radiators were placed at the front of the 16swg aluminium monocoque. The nose had two air intakes ducted to the radiators and featured an alloy tray to act as a deformable structure in the event of an accident. The bodywork itself was clean and the interesting thing is that the car was developed and built for less than it would have cost Richard to buy a production car from Brabham or March. If major backing had come along the plan was to produce Atlantic and Formula B versions of the car.

That season the car always showed great promise and everything Richard Scott had hoped to achieve with his new car was gained at the Nurburgring in the wet where he finished seventh overall. *"In that race I gained championship points against all the factory competition. I felt that the car proved itself to be wonderful in those circumstances. We did not have the best engines and yet even with my limited skills, compared to the top drivers of the day, we had a very satisfying result".*

For the 1974 racing season the car was given a Richardson Formula Atlantic engine to compete in the British Championship and was successful until the funds ran out and the car was sold to Bob Howlings.

Today, the car is owned by former hill climb driver Peter Voigt.

Season 1973

SCOTT F2 CHASSIS 1-01

March 11 1973	Radio Luxembourg Formula 2 Trophy: Mallory Park
Richard Scott	Car crashed in practice, did not start. Best time 45.4 secs. Would have been on fifth row alongside Gethin and Schuppan.
April 08	VII Deutschland Trophae: Hockenheim
Richard Scott	11th row – Heat 2 – Finished 11th ahead of Vittorio Brambilla, Jody Scheckter and Mike Beuttler.
April 23	XXVIII BARC "200": Thruxton
Richard Scott	Heat 2 – 6th row alongside Silvio Moser. Retired after 7 laps with engine trouble.
April 29	XXXVI Eifelrennen: Nurburgring
Richard Scott	8th row alongside John Wingfield. Finished 7th overall behind Vittorio Brambilla.

May 05	XXXIII Grand Prix de Pau		
Richard Scott	Crashed in practice. Best time 1.18.5. *"Richard Scott crashed his car heavily"*		
May 20	III Swedish Gold Cup: Kinnekullering		
Richard Scott	Car entered but did not arrive.		

Race Record 1974 with Richardson Atlantic engine.

March 10	Mallory Atlantic	3rd overall	Richard Scott
March 17	Brands Atlantic	1st and fastest lap	Richard Scott
April 14	Snetterton Atlantic	1st overall	Richard Scott
May 5	Oulton Pk Atlantic	crash at Knickerbrook	Richard Scott

SEATON-RENAULT.

Bill Seaton was a Renault dealer based in Ayr but at the same time was a gifted engineer in his own right. His father founded a coachbuilding company in Ayr in the 1920s and young Bill was apprenticed to the company. After the war he satisfied his interest in tuning by working on a pre-war Riley Sprite and managed to coax 110 mph out of it but it was never used for racing.

In 1957 he took delivery of his first Renault Dauphine and immediately fell in love with the car and decided to specialise in the tuning of Renault Dauphines. He ran his Seaton-Dauphine in a number of sprints and hill climbs driven by former Lea Francis driver Freddy Stang and rally driver Kenny Moore.

Bill Seaton planned to go into serious production with his tuning kits which included his own suspension modifications - Dauphines had a bad habit of rolling when cornered fast - a four branch exhaust system and his own machined cylinder heads. His fastest mods would give a low-slung Dauphine a maximum speed of over 90 mph. A later model was timed early one morning on the Kilmarnock-Glasgow road at 117 m.p.h probably one of the fastest Renault Dauphines ever built. His kits were sent all over the world. He visited the French tuning firm, Ferry,that was building a Formula Junior car at the time and came back to Scotland determined to build an FJ car with a space frame chassis. This car was rear-engined and made a brief appearance but the project was shelved.

ROTOR

Stewart Roden had a mixture of success with the most competitive of the Rotor Formula Fords. On this occasion at Ingliston, however, he was caught out in the wet.

One of the few Rotor racing cars, the JT4 Formula Ford that was raced by Scott Ramsay.

The Rotor story is one which could be replicated all over Britain as there have been countless enthusiasts with little or no money who have sought to build their own racing cars. Colin Chapman was usually their mentor but few reached the giddy heights of Chapman. Graham Miller, on the other hand has never lost faith in his quest to build racing cars in Scotland.

As a child he was taken to see stock cars in action at the White City stadium in Glasgow and from then on cars and racing have dominated his life.

Eventually Graham Millar was able to buy a kart and when he sold it he took the money and enrolled in the Jim Russell race school at Snetterton where the school's teacher, John Kirkpatrick another Scot, gave Millar a lot of encouragement to keep at it.

Clearly Graham needed an income and joined the Fire Service to become a fireman. After three years rallying he was able to buy the Dulon MP17 which had been campaigned by Tom Brown and David Duffield. With his mechanic Tommy Donnachie he raced the car throughout 1979.

In 1980, encouraged by sponsorship from Lander Alarms, he swopped the Dulon for a more modern Hawke DL19 but this was damaged at Knockhill in 1981. Millar's racing had been run on a frayed shoestring and he couldn't afford to repair the Hawk. With his friend Jim Kennedy they decided to build their own car which turned out to be the Rotor JT1, a Formula Ford 1600.

The car made its race debut at Knockhill where it was actually quicker than the Hawke had been. To gauge how it could really perform Graham persuaded Roy Low, one of the most experienced Scottish Formula Ford drivers, to race it. His verdict confirmed that the chassis was good but the engine was on its last legs. Scotland's FF champion at the time, Tom Brown, then offered the use of his own engine. After a test at Knockhill Tom was impressed and agreed to race the car at Ingliston. It was a brave offer as he needed to clinch his Championship at that meeting. He put the car on pole position by 1.5 seconds and won the race from start to finish. It was the Rotor's greatest victory.

For 1984 two more Rotors were built but the team had no money for engines and so they missed the entire season and considered throwing in the towel. A new car was designed for 1985, the JT3. Eugine O'Brien and Scotsman Stewart Roden showed an interest in the design and eventually Roden agreed to buy a new engine to put in the car. Graham Millar would pay for the car and another friend, Sandy McEwan, would loan a gearbox. Roden wisely kept his Van Diemen RF84 so he had a bench-mark with which to gauge the performance of the new Rotor. In its first race it was lying third in the race before being damaged in a battle with the leaders. At the Formula Ford Festival at Brands Hatch in 1985 Roden looked set to qualify for the final but he spun and the car would not restart as a battery terminal had snapped. The car was sold to Kenny Brown.

The 1986 Rotor, the JT2 was built as an FF2000 for Harry Minty to race. Harry did well to finish second in the Scottish FF2000 championship to Tom Brown and Kenny Brown won three races with the FF 1600 car so Graham Miller had a lot to cheer him up.

In truth, the Rotor story was grinding to a halt. A company had been formed by Graham Millar and Sandy McEwen, a Glasgow lawyer, with the idea of building kit cars. This led to the design of a mid-engined sports car, the JT5, powered by an Audi Quattro engine. They found a workshop but the local council and the landlord created a lot of problems. Meanwhile the JT4 had been sold to Scott Ramsay, a novice who was initially out of his depth. He only kept the Rotor for one season. Scott sold the car to an enthusiast in Auchterarder whose later claim to fame was that he murdered his wife and two young children before committing suicide! The car disappeared never to be heard of again.

ROVER SPECIAL

The Gibbon family were the Rover main dealers in Glasgow and Jimmy Gibbon could reasonably be called the "wild one" of the family as he was passionate about sprints, hill climbs and racing. As a result he was to build a string of specials all powered by Rover engines and even developed a Marauder sports car for road rally events. His first special was the Girastro which he built with two friends, Jim Ramsay and Ken Starling. (Gibbon, Ramsay, Starling and Rover). He started on it in 1947 and it was ready for the 1948 season. The chassis came from a damaged Rover 12 shortened by two feet. It had Girling brakes and semi elliptic Rover springs and dampers at the rear. The engine was from a 1940 Rover 10 cylinder block bored out from 66.5 to 69mm and the head machined to give an 8.0:1 compression ratio. As Jim was to use the car as his normal transport two bodies were designed, one for touring and one for racing. They were easily detachable

Gibbon family in Glasgow were Rover distributors and Jimmy Gibbon raced a number of his Rover specials. This was the car in its final streamlined version.

and a lot of aluminium was used in their construction. It missed its first event because during testing Jim met a lorry head-on at Torrance Bridge and severely damaged the chassis. During the season the weight was trimmed by two cwts and it ran well but was still too heavy.

It was then fitted with an engine based on a Rover 90 block bored out to three litres to which Jim fitted a special cam shaft with higher lift and overlap supplied by Rover's experimental department. He then added 6 Amal T.T. carburettors. Girling made a set of front disc brakes with B.R.M. callipers which solved the problem Jim had had with the brakes.

Jim Gibbon's other great love was sailing and he crewed for his great friend and racing driver Ninian Sanderson on Sanderson's 8 metre cruiser between 1957 and 1960. Following his divorce he bought a yacht "Boonara" which he kept in Portugal and sailed all over the world with his second wife, Alice. Alice was a former rally driver and co-drove with Rosemary Smith in Rootes cars including the World Cup Rally. When Alice died in 1994 Jim continued his sailing life.

HOPPER SPECIAL

Ian Hopper was one of the great characters of post-war Scottish motor sport. The family business was in the motor trade and Ian usually competed wearing a natty line in tartan and chequered shirts. He had his own ideas of what a Special should be and it was not *"...a Ford 10 with a lump sawn out of the middle of the chassis and a bit of home-brewed bodywork placed thereon."*

Ian Hopper with his familiar tartan shirt storms up Bo'ness hill climb in his Lea-Francis engined Hopper Special in its final guise.

Ian's first special was built in 1929 from parts of an old Clover Leaf Mathis offered to him for a modest £4. As he pointed out many years later *"...my total assets at the time amounted to £3.16/- (£3.80) but having persuaded my father to advance me four shillings on account of pocket money I burned my boats and purchased the Mathis fully expecting to have it on the road in about two weeks time at a total cost of about £10. My enthusiasm in this instance was so great that it had not yet occurred to me where I was to lay my hands on the further £6 that would be necessary. However, by working on my wits, my friends' generosity, and credit, it was duly completed in about two months the final cost amounting to £18, which shook me considerably. It also shook my father, who was my biggest creditor"*

This Special was a disaster and was eventually sold. Some time later, when he was accepted into the family business, Ian started again on his next special which was shaped like an inverted bathtub. This was a genuine special by Ian's description as it contained a multitude of bits from every possible source. For example it had a Lancia Augusta front axle, Morris 25 steering gear turned upside down, a Riley Kestrel chassis, a Lancia Aprilia rear axle, Citroen radiator, Humber windscreen, a Ford V8 engine and a Triumph Dolomite gearbox. Part of the chassis cross members were made from refrigerator tubes.

As for the handling, let Hopper explain : *"...At first the road holding, over a road with series of dips and hollows was not too good as the rear independent suspension had more than a tendency to steer itself. I finally discovered this was due to the fact that the rear wheels had about 1 degree of positive camber. I subsequently altered this to 2 degrees of negative camber and the trouble was completely cured. This mistake gave me quite an inferiority complex at the time, but I felt much better when I finally found out that Enzo Ferrari had made the same mistake in his first series of rear independently sprung cars. This car was so low I could not mount the exhaust system in a conventional way and it was taken straight through the boot in an asbestos lined box and came out of the tail of the car."* He wisely added louvres to keep the petrol tank cool!

His last special was his most successful creation.

For this he went to Joe Potts in Bellshill who designed the chassis and the suspension. Like many constructors of the period, Ian chose a Lea Francis engine which he ran on a 9.5:1 compression ratio and a petrol/benzole mixture. With this he was producing a reputed 94 bhp and even though the car itself - for which Hopper had designed a body similar to a Healey Silverstone - weighed over 16 cwts.

CHASSELS SPECIAL

Dr Mirrlees Chassels was a burly and amusing doctor from Glasgow who, in 1938, bought a 1933 TT Replica Frazer Nash with a Meadows engine. He got to work polishing the cylinder head and ports and he ran it in Scottish sprint and hill climb events during the 1939 season. During the war he kept the Nash with him in the Royal Air Force. He broke the crank and bought a replacement engine for £2. it was with this car he continued his motor sport after 1945. With his brother Robbie he replaced the Meadows engine with a modified 1.5 litre Riley Sprite engine producing close on 80 bhp. Chassells tended to wrestle with rather than drive cars and he had fitted the strongest possible valve springs as he had a tendency to leave the line with plenty of revs.

For the 1948 sprint season he took out the Riley engine and put it into his road Riley saloon turning it into a genuine 100 mph tourer. Next, he fitted a Ford Mercury V8 engine which had originally been fitted to a wartime Bren gun carrier. Even though this engine produced around 100 bhp Chassells kept the chain drive of the original Frazer Nash which resulted in the chains breaking even more often than they did with the other engines. The system was replaced and Chassells added two Shorrocks superchargers for good measure. The car was very successful in sprints and hill climbs and during the 1949 season he was usually the fastest Scot in the major events. The Special has long since disappeared.

STEWART

Jackie Stewart himself could not have predicted that within 35 years of him starting out in racing he would be building and running his own grand prix car: but it happened and its success could be put down to his management and that of his son Paul.

In the development of the Stewart grand prix car too little emphasis has been paid to the role of Paul Stewart in pulling together all the divergent parts of such a complicated exercise. To have done it in nine months from signing the contract with Ford is even more impressive.

It was in March 1996 that the final go ahead was given by Ford Motor Company, who were the major backers of the entire project. The fact that Stewart had been a respected consultant to Ford worldwide for thirty years was a great help, but taking a concept into reality was something completely different.

What must be remembered, however, is that Paul Stewart Racing had been in existence for many years running racing cars in a variety of formulae from Formula Vauxhall Lotus right up to Formula 3000. In the early days, when he was not developing the business, Paul Stewart himself was racing the cars. Though he would be the first to admit he did not reach the great heights of his father, his racing performances were better than most of people who have come into the various series he contested.

Even in those days, however, the Paul Stewart Racing team was always on the lookout for new talent and had a very happy knack of choosing some truly up and coming stars who have proved themselves since. Maurizio Gugelmin, Rubens Barrichello, David Coulthard, Allan McNish, Kelvin Burt and Luciano Burti all came through the PSR school. It was a thoroughly professional outfit.

To design his grand prix car Jackie Stewart chose Alan Jenkins. Jenkins had worked with John Barnard in the development of the McLaren in the early 1980s and was senior engineer to both Alain Prost and John Watson. He then moved to Indycars and Penske Racing engineering the car Danny Sullivan used to win Indianapolis in 1985. Prior to joining Jackie Stewart he had spent six years with the Footwork Arrows team.

Most of the key posts in the new team, however, came from Jackie's team at Paul Stewart Racing. Dave Stubbs was moved from the F3000 team to become race team manager and Andy Miller became technical team manager.

Apart from the substantial backing from Ford, Jackie used his Scottish connections and secured sponsorship from the Hong Kong and Shanghai Banking Corporation, HSBC, Texaco, Sanyo and Hertz. He even had initial sponsorship from the Malaysian Government keen to develop a link with Grand Prix racing.

The project to design and build the car started with a clean sheet of paper and an empty room. As a result the entire car was designed and built using CAD (Computer Aided Design) the first grand prix car to be designed totally from scratch in this way. This speeded up the process and a 50% model was initially made and flown to the Swift wind tunnel in San Clemente, California.

The full size carbon fibre monocoque was then built up and the bodywork, though relatively conventional for the time, had been worked on using Ford CFD (Computational Fluid Dynamics) to make subtle and effective changes. The engine, meanwhile, was the Ford Zetec-R V10 of 2998 ccs coupled to a semi automatic six-speed gearbox mounted longitudinally. It featured a high -pressure hydraulic system for power shift and clutch and a choice of viscous or hydraulically assisted differentials. All of the engine work had been done at Cosworth Engineering.

Originally Ford and Cosworth embarked on the V10 programme in 1995. It was developed in just eight months and first ran in a racing car at Paul Ricard on January 16 1996. For the 1996 season the new engine was given to Peter Sauber's Sauber team but on the understanding that they would only have the engine for one season as Ford had other plans. Those plans, as we have seen, were to use 1996 as a development year prior to using the engine exclusively in the new Stewart.

The opening two rounds of the 1997 world championship saw first Jan Magnussen and then Barrichello suffer rear suspension failure in the Australian and Brazilian GPs but in the third round in Argentina Magnussen finished tenth. A disappointing start but at Monaco, probably Jackie's favourite circuit, it all came right and Rubens Barrichello split the two Ferraris of Michael Schumacher and Eddie Irvine to take a remarkable second place. In addition, Jan Magnussen finished seventh. Clearly the Stewart had promise but Monaco was merely an Indian summer.

We had to wait nearly two years before the Stewart team had their greatest success. Johnny Herbert, who had replaced Jan Magnusson in the team, won the European Grand Prix at the Nurburgring with Rubens Barrichello in third place. As a result of this they finished 4th in the 1999 Constructors Championship. Then, following an approach from Ford Motor Company, the entire Stewart team was sold to Ford, and renamed Jaguar.

TALON

The Talon company was formed in Brighton to build FF2000 cars in the 1980s but, as is common in motor racing, the company got into financial difficulties. A young Dutchman called Guy Czonka was working on the Scottish oil-rigs and occasionally raced a Formula Ford at Ingliston. He persuaded his friends David Chazen and Lance Gauld to go in with him and pick up the remains of Talon and build the cars in Scotland. When all the bits arrived in Scotland another Scot, Jim Irwin, was roped in to engineer the car. Various modifications were made to the chassis and rear suspension and Lance Gauld tested the new car but here the story ended. Guy Czonka left for the USA and the whole project was dropped.

Chapter 13
The Phantom Circuits

As in most countries in the world where motor racing has been held, people have sought new venues to race cars. As far as Scotland is concerned, some projects came to fruition but the majority of plans never progressed further than that; plans.

It is interesting that whenever articles are written about Ian Scott Watson he is usually referred to as the man who gave Jim Clark the chance to go motor racing but in fact he was the instigator and designer of more phantom motor race circuits in Scotland than anyone else. Not only that, but he was also approached about sites outside Scotland.

It is hard to describe Ian Scott Watson. Though self taught he wanted to specialise in designing farm buildings but quickly switched to timber-frame house design and was one of the earliest Scots in this field. This led to the formation of Celtic Homes where he was joined by Bernard Buss who had been assistant chief designer at Colt homes.

Ian Scott Watson's interest in designing motor racing circuits was given a chance to shine in the mid-1960s with the Polkemmet circuit and then Ingliston.

As has been written in the main text of the book, a number of circuits were developed mostly on the runways of World War II relief airfields. However, everyone in their heart of hearts truly wanted to see a proper custom built circuit somewhere. In the end Knockhill fulfilled that desire but even Knockhill was a tentative project until quite late in the day.

Amongst those interested in new circuits was Lord Bruce who was to become the Earl of Elgin & Kincardine on the death of his father. Lord Bruce was a great enthusiast in the 1950s and became President of the Royal Scottish Automobile Club. As he was very friendly with David Murray of Ecurie Ecosse, the team's success led him to consider building a circuit within the grounds of his family estate, Broomhall, near Dunfermline.

Towards that end he approached Edinburgh architects Alexander Gibb and Partners for a feasibility study in which David Murray gave valuable technical assistance. In the end it was decided there was not enough room for the project due to the fact that there were old mineral workings and a public road in the way. However, now armed with the knowledge of what was needed for the construction of a circuit, Bruce started to look around and as we have seen from the main text he was involved with the Dalkeith and Polkemmet projects.

When it became obvious that Charterhall, Scotland's only remaining race circuit, was not going to receive an RAC racing licence for the 1965 motor racing season, the race was on to find an alternative.

Despite the fact their efforts at the Duke of Buccleugh's estate at Dalkeith had to be abandoned, the same group, led by Lord Bruce, Caledonian Motor Racing Circuits Ltd., found a promising site in 1964 exactly half way between Glasgow and Edinburgh called Polkemmet and the project started off well.

The circuit itself was on land at Salsburgh under which there had been extensive mining at the beginning of the 20th century. It was close to the main A8 Edinburgh/Glasgow trunk road that passed straight through the

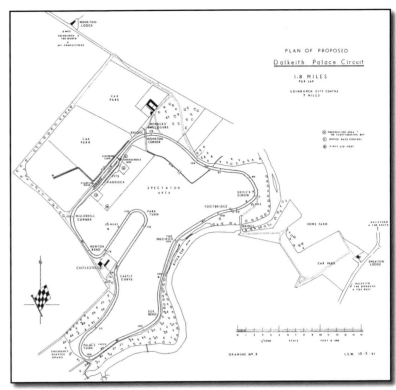

One of the first of a number of circuit plans that started in the 1960's as possible replacements to Charterhall was the Dalkeith Palace circuit in the grounds of the Duke of Buccleuch's estate just seven miles from Edinburgh. It would have been spectacular with the downhill sweep from the Precipice to Palace turn followed by the uphill to Park turn. The plan is dated May15 1961.

village and would have bounded the M8 motorway built some years later on the northern side.

The land itself had been owned by the Baillie family one of whom, Sir Gawaine Baillie, was one of Britain's best saloon car drivers in the late 1950s with 3.8 litre Jaguars. Some indication of the seriousness of this project was confirmed when John Hugenholtz, the well known Dutch circuit designer, was engaged, alongside Ian Scott Watson, to come up with ideas of how the circuit should look. John, whose greatest circuit design was Suzuka in Japan, was a great anglophile and relished the idea of designing a Scottish circuit. He came up with an interesting track that would have been something of a sensation had the project gone ahead. Hugenholtz's problem was that his design envisaged the building of two bridges across a small river running through the site. Scott Watson's alternative design was shorter in length and avoided this. The access to the site would have been superb as it was close to the existing main road that was to be superseded by the M8 motorway.

There then arose what appeared to be a serious problem regarding the site itself. The mineral rights for the land were allegedly still owned by the National Coal Board, which meant the NCB could come along sometime in the future and decide once more to dig for coal. This would have created serious problems for such a large commercial venture. As it turned out, a closer search revealed that the mineral rights were actually owned by a local brick works. The chances were that this would be no problem as brick making was in the doldrums at the time. The real bugbear was the usual one of finance. An approach was made to various concerns for help but the share capital of the development company was minimal and this slightly put off potential investors.

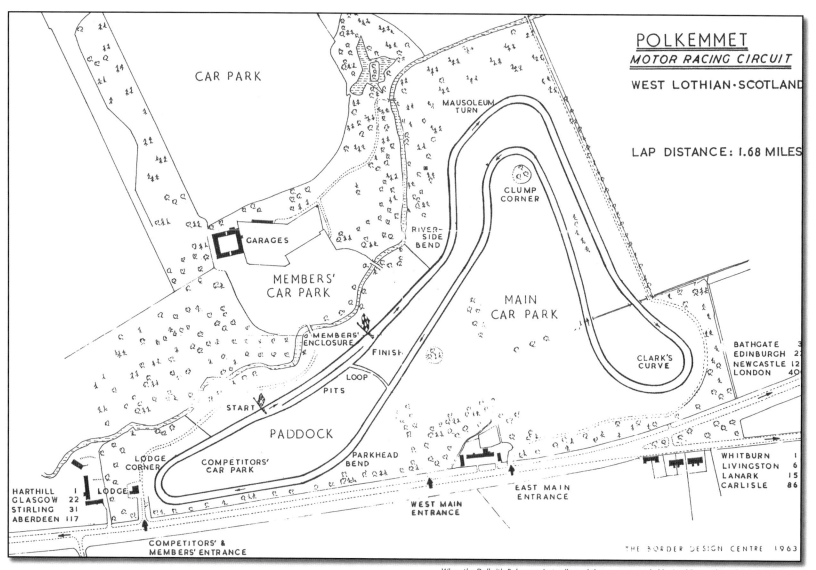

POLKEMMET
MOTOR RACING CIRCUIT
WEST LOTHIAN · SCOTLAND

LAP DISTANCE : 1.68 MILES

CAR PARK

MAUSOLEUM
TURN

CLUMP
CORNER

RIVER-
SIDE
BEND

GARAGES

MEMBERS'
CAR PARK

MAIN
CAR PARK

MEMBERS'
ENCLOSURE

FINISH

CLARK'S
CURVE

BATHGATE 3
EDINBURGH 2?
NEWCASTLE 12
LONDON 40

LOOP

PITS

START

PADDOCK

COMPETITORS'
CAR PARK

PARKHEAD
BEND

LODGE
CORNER

WHITBURN 1
LIVINGSTON 6
LANARK 15
CARLISLE 86

HARTHILL 1
GLASGOW 22
STIRLING 31
ABERDEEN 117

LODGE

EAST MAIN
ENTRANCE

WEST MAIN
ENTRANCE

COMPETITORS' &
MEMBERS' ENTRANCE

THE BORDER DESIGN CENTRE 1963

When the Dalkeith Palace project collapsed the same group, led by Lord Bruce - later the Earl of Elgin - found another site at Polkemmet alongside the old A8 road which was due to be bypassed by the M8. For this the Dutch circuit designer, John Hugenholtz was invited over to come up with his plan. At the same time Ian Scott Watson was also approached for his ideas. This is the Scott Watson design with its long sweeping bends but the lap distance was only 1.68 miles. A slightly larger plan was also drafted by Scott Watson.

During the development of the Polkemmet plan John Hugenholtz made a number of visits to Scotland. He is seen on the left with two of the directors of the promoting body, Noel Bean, centre, and Huw Carruthers.

Not content with letting the matter drop, Ian Scott Watson tried to interest Grovewood Securities - who owned Brands Hatch - in adding this new circuit to their Group. Rex Foster, who ran one of their circuits, Oulton Park, was very keen on the idea. Indeed Grovewood put their architect Chris Riley in touch with Ian Scott Watson to come up with more detailed plans that would have created a lot of excitement had they been taken up. For example they had gone to the extent of designing the circuit restaurant and toilets on a bridge across the track. It was a highly detailed plan for a 1.7 mile circuit but this was not the ultimate objective. Other sketch plans were aimed at extending the circuit length to 3 miles and even a possible future grand prix venue. But all the excitement was in vain. Grovewood had more than enough on its plate at the time as they were spending a lot of money on their keynote circuit, Brands Hatch, so the whole matter was shelved.

Polkemmet seemed promising but the intrepid Ian Scott Watson went the other route and sought an accommodation with the Royal Highland and

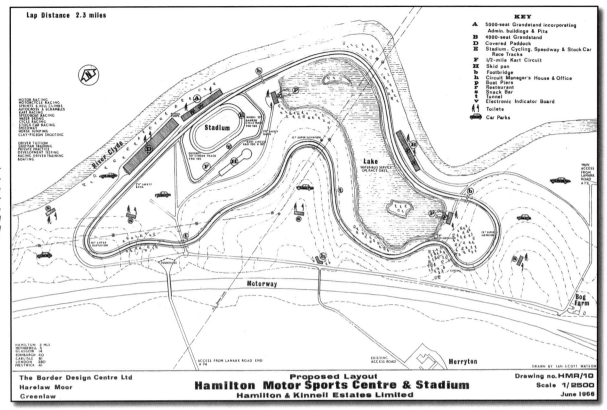

The need for land owners to landscape land utilised for public works led the Duke of Hamilton to approach the ubiquitous Ian Scott Watson to design a circuit utilising the landfill thown up by the building of the M8 near Hamilton. This was the first design complete with an artificial lake bordering the river Clyde (top) and including an athletic cinder track and a banked cycle track. The lap length was 2.3 miles.

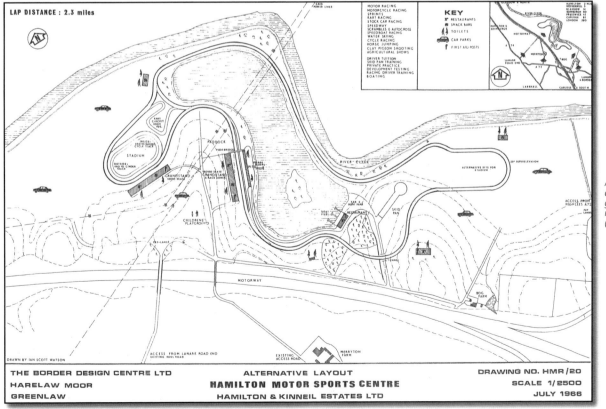

A month later Scott Watson came up with this modified design which separated the main racing circuit from the general sports facilities. On the extreme right the constant radius curve was designed with a 25 degree banking. (Daytona is more than 30 degrees.)

Agricultural Society for the building of a short circuit within their Ingliston headquarters. As this was their permanent showground, and was complete with a large grandstand, it seemed ideal and the original short circuit of less than a mile was drawn up and Scotcircuits Ltd., was formed to finance it. Many people at the time complained that the circuit was too small. Everybody involved knew that, but, in order to have some kind of circuit ready for the 1965 season, it was deemed that the short circuit would do for openers.

Even then, a slightly longer circuit, extending the upper straight into a tight hairpin and then coming back to rejoin the original, had been envisaged and this was built in time for the second season taking the length to just over one mile. It also allowed a few more competitors to start in each race as the maximum number of competitors allowed to start in a race is determined according to its lap length. However, even this small extension was actually a compromise as Scott Watson had designed a much larger circuit of 2.2 miles which took the cars out of the walled area and into what was the original car park.

Ian Scott Watson described it this way.

"The extension would have provided the existing original circuit, a separate circuit within the car park and a link to and from the original. The whole thing was that the car park circuit could have been used all year round for testing and there would be no need for a break for the Highland Show to take place. The whole thing was going to cost about £25,000"

It is worth pointing out here that one of the great problems of Ingliston was this break after the May race meeting until the July race meeting as the circuit arena had to be transformed with buildings and tents for the enormous Royal Highland Show. Where the competitors had their paddock - one of the few covered paddocks at a British circuit - was where the cattle were penned during the Highland Show and so the July and August meetings tended to be suffused with the agricultural aroma of cow dung!

In one sense it is a pity this much-enlarged Ingliston circuit did not go ahead - the directors felt it was too ambitious and expensive - but consider this. The great advantage of Ingliston, as it stood, concerned security. The small circuit was completely walled on all sides so making the necessary collection of spectator moneys an easy task. With the extended circuit there would have been two problems. One was that some very strong and high fencing would have been needed to stop spectators from seeing the racing for nothing. This would have been costly and probably unsightly. Secondly, the whole car park area was perfectly flat and so artificial spectator banking would have been necessary adding to the expense. This would, in turn, have created problems that would undoubtedly have cropped up as circuit safety requirements expanded considerably in the following years. It is my own opinion that the development would have become a constant nightmare in order to keep complying with RAC circuit safety plans. As it was, the existing Ingliston circuit, despite its remarkable safety record, was faced with having to make changes every year.

In 1966 road developments in the West of Scotland literally threw up another possible motor racing circuit, between Hamilton and Motherwell, at Merryton, part of the estate of the Duke of Hamilton.

The Scottish Office wanted to upgrade the A74 trunk road from Glasgow to the English border to motorway status. They planned to carve a new section of road to the north east of the existing A74 between it and the river Clyde. Work had begun on the motorway and the Duke allowed something like 1.75 million tons of excavated soil to be dumped on the haughs (A haugh is a flat piece of ground beside a river.) alongside the river

Clyde. The local planners, however, were pressing for this huge pile of earth to be landscaped along with proposals for its future use.

It so happened that the Duke of Hamilton's son, Lord Angus Clydesdale, was a serving officer in the Royal Air Force and had started motor racing. Angus, the present Duke of Hamilton, claims he had little or nothing to do with his father's concept of a motor racing circuit but it is hard to imagine such a project going further without some input from the young racing driver.

Ian Scott Watson was approached about the plan and was invited by the Dukes factor to go to Hamilton and discuss the solution to the problem. Scott Watson made two inspections and drew up two different plans.

Scott Watson's original visit led to his preliminary report on the Merryton site, as it was called, and here I quote some of the points he made to the Duke. Prior to this, Scott Watson had given some rough ideas as to what it would all cost. After this first proper report he pointed out it would cost considerably in excess of his initial estimate but he presented both the pros and cons of the scheme in a very balanced way.

Amongst the pros were two items mentioned earlier with regard to the Ingliston development plan. At the Merryton site you had the River Clyde on one side and the M74 motorway on the other so access could be reasonably well controlled. It was obviously convenient to the motorway to the south of England and, as it was virgin land with lots of infill, it could be designed as a multi-purpose area. Access would have been from the old A72 with an additional access using a farm road that joined the A74. Then there was the possibility of the river Clyde flooding at that point and placing the circuit under water.

The next problem arose in Scott Watson's second report where a specialist company had been brought in to investigate the mineral rights resulting in Scott Watson looking for an alternative to his original layout. It turned out that the contour maps,on which his original had been designed, had been radically changed by the infill dumping. In this report Scott Watson remarked *"...At first sight it may seem that the design of the circuit lacks a fast straight. This is deliberate. Speed is relative. At lower speeds it is safe to have the spectators closer to the circuit thus giving them a better view. This also gives the impression of greater speed without the consequent dangers. The length will allow 25 cars per race."*

A lake had been designed into the plan and the idea was to have a venue for speedboat racing and the like. A hotel or motel was also envisaged along with "low-cost" accommodation for competitors and their crews;which Scott Watson offered to design.

At the end of the day the estimated cost of it all, not including the hotel, would be between £600,000 and £700,000 which, in 1966, was a lot of money and would certainly have been the biggest motor racing development in Britain at the time.

Hamilton Estates commissioned a London company, Economic Consultants Ltd, to do an in-depth financial feasibility study of the plan and they produced a 140 page hard cover book which broadly came out in favour of the scheme but the Duke was concerned at the potential £600,000 cost. As mentioned in the main text of the book, the entire scheme was then offered to Grovewood Securities, which owned Brands Hatch at the time, and almost went ahead but they could not be convinced that there was a large enough local population to support it. As Ian Scott Watson ruefully remarked *"Their geographic knowledge of Scotland was woefully inadequate and they clearly did not realise there were 2.5 million people living little or no further from the site than Londoners were from Brands Hatch".*

Eventually the talks petered out and the site was redesigned with a sailing lake. Eventually part of this park was briefly used as a hill climb and sprint site but not for long. The course was also close to a large Motherwell and Wishaw council housing estate. Stubborn local residents tended to persist in walking in restricted areas saying that it was their public park and they could walk where they wished. Having been RAC Steward at two of the hill climbs I can confirm that local resident intransigence was a constant nightmare so it was no surprise when it was dropped as a site.

Earlier that year, in January 1966, Scott Watson was involved with a possible circuit on the outskirts of Kelso in the Scottish Borders. This was designed on the showground of the Border Union Agricultural Showground on the banks of the river Tweed. It is interesting to note that the BUA's headquarters were in Bridgend Park which had originally been the home of the Scott Douglas family. Sir James Scott Douglas, one of the founding drivers in Ecurie Ecosse was a member of that family and Bridgend was his grandfather's family home. It fell into disrepair and was taken over by the BUA as their headquarters.

With very limited space Scott Watson designed a shoe-shaped circuit that was even smaller than the original Ingliston and measured just 0.77 of a mile to the lap. There was no straight to speak off and the drivers had only one left hand bend before the start and finish line. This development got no further than the drawing board.

Scott Watson was involved in a number of other schemes including the John F Kennedy Raceway near Dublin. He had been introduced to the Irish-American "entrepreneur" involved by Jim Clark. Ian was flown to Dublin and immediately began to feel suspicious when the site turned out to be right in the middle of Ireland's main stud farm and horse race training area.

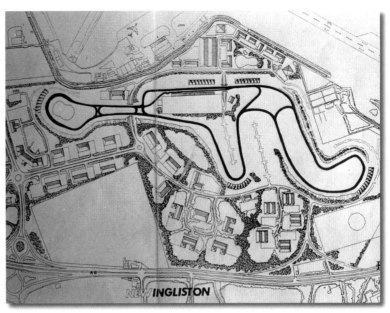

The design of Jackie Stewarts New Ingliston circuit offered a variety of different mini circuits that could be run at the same time and an industrial site for racing car and component companies.

The effusive developer assuaged Scott Watson's fears by saying that he had friends in high places - one of them was James Haughey who became Prime Minister of Ireland, and the other was later jailed for running guns to the IRA in Ulster! Once Ian had designed the circuit he was asked to submit his fee. *"...and then his cheque for my fee bounced back over the Irish Sea and I never got another penny. Although the same guy did phone after Harold Wilson de-valued the pound and asked me to add the 14% amount of the devaluation to my bill. 14% of nothing is still nothing, which is precisely what I got. It later transpired he had conned an engine out of Mike Hailwood and a complete car, without engine, out of Matra and was wanted by Interpol!"*

Another example was East Fortune airstrip to the East of Edinburgh that from time to time emerged as a possible racing circuit.

It was used for kart racing and the occasional sprint but in the 1990s Tom Brown had thoughts of developing the site when he took over a lease to run his Tom Brown Racing School. Nothing much has ever come of it, and years of wear and tear have made it a non-starter.

That same East Fortune site does, however, have a place in the history of aviation for back in 1919 the Daily Mail put up a prize of £10,000 for the first non-stop flight across the Atlantic that attracted pilots and machines from all over the world. One of these was the British-built dirigible the R-34 that was prepared for an attempt on the Atlantic crossing.

The 634-foot R-34 dirigible was commanded by Major G.H.Scott with the eccentric General E.M.Maitland who was head of the British Balloon Forces. They took off in their airship on July 2 1919 and, after a long silence, radioed Roosevelt Field in New York that they were running out of fuel somewhere off Massachusetts. They said they would be lucky to reach the tip of Long Island at Montauk Point. At this Frank Peckham of the US Navy was dispatched immediately to Montauk in a helter skelter drive that saw them nearly off the road twice. He arrived at the remote point at dawn in time to see the dirigible hove into sight. He waited for Scott and Maitland to valve off their spare helium and nose down to land but the intrepid pair flew right over their heads. Peckham immediately turned his

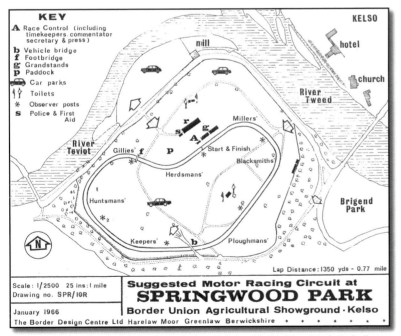

Probably the oddest circuit designed in Scotland was Springwood Park in Kelso, originally the family home of racing driver Sir James Scott Douglas. When the estate was taken over by the Border Union Agricultural Society it was used as their permanent showground. Scott Watson designed this tiny circuit measuring just over three quarters of a mile to the lap.

truck round and, with his crew, set off to chase the dirigible to Roosevelt Field. On the way they saw a parachute blossom beneath the dirigible and it was another member of the crew, Flight Lieutenant J.E.M.Pritchard who had been sent down to organise a landing party. But by the time Pritchard got to Roosevelt Field by road the dirigible had already arrived and was being hauled in, its fuel tanks almost dry. The R-34 therefore, had made the first air east-west crossing of the Atlantic in 108 hours and 12 minutes setting up a world's endurance record. They then discovered that a young soldier had crawled on board as a stowaway for the trip. Maitland used his influence to make sure he was let off with little or no punishment. Three days later they turned it round and flew it back to Peckham in England in seventy-four hours breaking more records and put Britain in a commanding position as the leader in the development of rigid dirigibles. It resulted in Britain being given a huge £2 million contract to build a dirigible for the United States Navy. And it all began at East Fortune!

Perhaps the biggest motor racing project Scotland has ever seen was New Ingliston, with no less a person than Jackie Stewart behind it. However, this one, despite its great potential, was scuppered by a variety of political problems from the largely left-wing Edinburgh city and Lothian regional councils.

The year was 1990, Ingliston was beginning to show its age and was running out of options to keep at bay the RAC safety inspectors who paid their annual visit. Scottish Race Promotions Ltd, who held the licence to run motor racing on the circuit, were finding it impossible to make a profit and the site owners, the Royal Highland and Agricultural Society were less enthusiastic at having racing cars pound round their Showground than once they had been

However, though it was not realised at the time, talks had started on what was the most promising and ambitious motor racing developments in Scotland's history. The people behind the project were Jackie Stewart and McGregor Holdings PLC.

Their concept was split into two parts. One was a well designed racing circuit which offered multiple useage, and the other a custom-built Autopark with space for eight motor dealerships as well as a leisure and tourist complex. The site was alongside the existing Ingliston circuit but on the Eastern side of the Edinburgh airport approach road.

McGregor Holdings PLC was a large and broad based property company involved in development and construction. It had been founded in the North of Scotland by John G McGregor and had a long track record of successful projects all over Britain including retirement homes in Brighton and hotels in the Highlands.

Work had started on the plans towards the end of 1989 and the concept was to develop the Autopark along the line of similar developments in the United States which sought to congregate all the key motor dealerships in one place away from crowded city-centre sites where parking was difficult. The general reaction from the motor trade was promising and Groups from South of the Border, keen to get into the Scottish market, also showed interest. Also, the site, within walking distance of Edinburgh airport so it seemed natural for further commercial development.

The entire £80 million project was planned on a 250 acre site on the edge of the A8 trunk road, the original road to Glasgow. At the time the section alongside the site was still in use as a link from the end of the existing M8 to the Edinburgh City Bypass and this was to be a slight bone of contention. Though a link from the M8 directly linking it to the Bypass, without passing Ingliston, had been planned, negotiations with the various landowners were still in hand and these were not expected to be completed until after the planned opening of the circuit.

The circuit itself was designed by Jackie Stewart with assistance from the late Derek Ongaro. Derek had for long been the RAC's circuit safety inspector and had been the regular inspector for the existing Ingliston circuit. Jackie had been asked to design circuits before, but had never committed himself to any specific project until now. He saw t he could develop his own ideas, from years of being a track safety advisor, not just for a safe circuit but for a circuit which could serve multiple purposes at the same time.

The concept of a compartmentalised circuit was not new but, in the case of New Ingliston, Stewart took it to greater lengths whereby, if pushed, four different disciplines could operate roughly at the same time. Explaining his philosophy Jackie made a telling remark : *"I'm not a great believer in fast race tracks. Every track becomes geographically obsolete as you increase the speed. There's no point in designing a 160 mph track, because 18 months later it'll be a 175 mph track. You won't see a lot of high speed corners either, because they would soon become straights. A corner designed for 130 mph will soon jump to 160 mph and no longer meet the safety requirements"*

At the launch of New Ingliston Jackie Stewart was joined by directors of McGregor Holdings, Alan O'Neil, left and Roddie Paterson

Scotlands new young guns in motor racing, Allan McNish and David Coulthard were present at the launch indicating Scotlands motor racing future.

As the circuit was also being planned for motor cycle racing it was designed with fewer sections of Armco type barrier but with big run off areas and sand traps.

The overall length of the full circuit was 2 miles to the lap but it also offered three other smaller circuits of .825 miles .675 miles and .285 miles. This last circuit, roughly oval in shape, was envisaged as a possible secondary school facility where pupils could be taught to drive in safety.

At the launch of the plan, Stewart was quizzed by the local newspapers as to whether this meant a Scottish Grand Prix. He fended this off by remarking that the way in which the circuit had been designed would make it suitable for Formula 3000 races and for Formula 1 testing, so theoretically could host a grand prix, but that eventuality certainly did not figure in the plans. This point about Formula 1 testing was an important one for there are relatively few circuits designed to grand prix standards where teams can test without falling foul of the FIA rulings regarding testing on existing grand prix circuits used for grand prix racing. In planning his circuit Stewart had consulted with various teams and component manufacturers and the indications were that it might be used by at least the British-based teams in Formula 1 for testing. Also, at least one tyre company had shown interest in a permanent unit at the circuit for the testing of racing tyres. Towards this end, Stewart had also done his homework and had in mind the installation of a very sophisticated track watering system where the track could be watered to specific depths to help tyre engineers develop both racing and road tyres.

The timetable envisaged work commencing at the end of 1991 and for the first race meeting to be held in the season of 1994.

No circuit plan in Scotland had been conceived in such detail as New Ingliston but of course the project was not simply going to Lothian Region and Edinburgh city planning on the basis of building solely a motor racing circuit. The circuit was part of a much more lavish complex which not only envisaged the Autocomplex but a luxury hotel, heritage museum, garden centre and even the opening of the site of an Iron Age fort that existed on the land, for archaeological study!

Under the original agreement, the management company, which would oversee the entire project, would be owned jointly by McGregor Holdings PLC and Jackie Stewart. Consequently formal planning permission was lodged with Graham Duncan, the Director of Planning for Edinburgh District Council, on August 22 1990.

The Scottish Development Agency for Edinburgh and Lothians gave their support to the project but planning permission in and around Edinburgh has always proved to be a stumbling block for any project. Apart from local governmental issues there are strong pressure groups including the Cockburn Society which was one of the objectors. The stumbling block was that the site lay on a strip of green belt land, around 600 metres wide, between the main A8 trunk road and Edinburgh airport and it was this which provided the main argument for the environmental groups.

There were many meetings and presentations with both Edinburgh District Council and the Lothian Regional Council. The Lothian Regional Council recommended to Edinburgh District Council that they refuse planning permission partly on the grounds of a very controversial report prepared by Dr John Bridge of the University of Wales and Dr Garel Rhys of Cardiff Business School.

The Regional council were also pressing for the circuit promoters to locate everything some miles away at Bathgate - presumably on the grounds

that bringing 2,700 jobs would help stem the labour gap caused some years before by the closing of BMC's Bathgate factory. In respect to this suggestion the Stewart and McGregor teams went to the proposed site at Bathgate but it just did not gell. Ironically, at the same time, another group had put forward the concept of a national football stadium on the actual site of the old BMC plant but another study showed that even locating a national football project there had little chance of success.

The Region then announced that "...development of the Ingliston site would be contrary to national, regional and local planning policies for the protection of the green belt"

This was not the end of the story because the development still had to be considered by the regional highways committee a few weeks later. Then the matter would finally be discussed by the entire Regional Council.

In the meantime Jackie Stewart took the opportunity to send out a personal letter to all the Regional Councillors in which his opening sentence was "I am very concerned that there is a real danger of the Regional Council refusing the New Ingliston planning application based upon inadequate and incorrect information."

He went on "The academic views expressed by Dr John Bridge and Professor Garel Rhys appear to provide a number of contradictory statements which I consider are based on inadequate briefing on the concept of New Ingliston, its industry functions and its financial equation. We have offered, on many occasions, to meet with both the Regional Council and Dr Bridge/Professor Rhys, simultaneously, in order to resolve these issues and I am at a loss to understand why it has been sought to avoid this meeting.

"The views of economists and academics, particularly if remote from day to day experience of a particular subject, can only be based upon the transmission of third party information and relies totally on the quality of the briefing they receive. It is therefore, I believe, relatively easy to understand how an incorrect conclusion can be reached".

But it was all in vain, the Regional Council refused planning permission and in turn so did Edinburgh District Council. If ever there was a reflection of the narrow and sometimes petty mindedness of Scottish local authority planning it was seen here and one cannot overlook the possible underlying political implications of a project which in some circles might have been seen as "elitist".

For Jackie Stewart it was a bitter blow as it would have been a laudable gesture on his part to take Scottish motor racing into the twenty first century.

Ten years later he reflected on the whole enterprise.

"The biggest problem of all was that it was on a green belt area that Lothian Regional Council were not keen to re-designate. We felt we could put together something that Scotland could be truly proud of, with all the landscaping and all of the aesthetic work that I believe would have been unique in the world.

"They carried out a study and got a University professor from Cardiff to make some statements to the effect that it could never make money, even though it was not their money that was being put up. We saw the opportunity to decentralise a lot of the motor companies out of the centre of Edinburgh and relocated them, as so many similar American motor sales parks have enjoyed great success. We were going to make it suitable for all forms of wet or dry weather testing and we certainly had both car companies and tyre companies interested in using the facilities.

"The motor sporting side, I think, would have been relatively easy. If you build a good race track with good new facilities it will certainly attract people and if you build around it some high tech industry opportunities the whole thing would, I feel, have been very successful.

"I was extremely discouraged by the Lothian Regional Councillors and their attitude. They missed a unique opportunity. I was so negatively affected by their attitude, and their way of doing business that when, later on, they wished to reopen the discussions I flatly refused."

Though other schemes have been put forward, this was the one with the financial clout of some heavy hitters and it was a setback that, in years to come, will still prove to be the one that got away.

A few months after this debacle an Autopark developer called Brian Sheridan expressed an interest in the New Ingliston concept and approached Roddy Paterson at McGregors who were behind the New Ingliston project. Strangely enough, Lothian Regional Council were mentioned in this context and a site "closer to Edinburgh" was hinted at but nothing came of it all.

There has always been a rivalry between the East and West of Scotland and whether this had anything to do with the emergence of a plan to develop a site next to the M8 Motorway between Glasgow and Edinburgh by Monklands District Council planning department, we will never know. The project began in the shadow of the New Ingliston dispute and whereas Lothian Region and Edinburgh District put up the barriers against Jackie Stewart's plans, here was a local district council actually in the driving seat; possibly the only occasion any circuit plan has been put forward from within a local authority rather than by private enterprise.

It all started innocently enough when Willie Miller the Planning Officer of Monklands District Council and another member of his staff, Marion Hopkins, discussed a local site at Forrestburn which was going to be put on the market. Willie is a great motor racing enthusiast and Marion was no stranger to motor sport as her husband, Brian Hopkins was a great supporter of historic racing with his chain-gang Frazer Nash and his Bentley. Stephen Kay, the curator at Summerlee kart circuit also helped to sketch out a plan. The group created their own car club, the Monklands Sporting Car Club, which would organise events on the circuit.

If you drive along the M8 Motorway from Glasgow to Edinburgh you reach the highest point, where both the BBC and ITV built their huge television masts. Now glance to your left and you will see a small valley with a

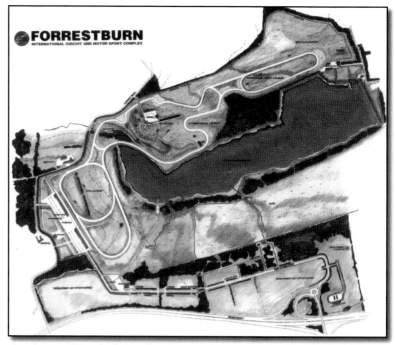

A much more ambitious plan for Forrestburn shows a much longer circuit with a greater facility to be split into different short test areas that could be run concurrently.

reservoir. This is Forrestburn. Ironically, the site was only a few miles from the original Polkemmet plan and by the end of 1991 proposals were being put forward within the council to develop the site as a *"substantial tourist facility...based primarily on a motor sports complex."* The first phase was to build a speed hill climb course on the high land to the northern shore of the reservoir financed by Monklands District Council and the Lanarkshire Development agency. Phase two was to develop a complete motor race circuit around the reservoir itself that *"...was to require major private sector investment as well as European Commission assistance."*

After considerable discussion, and the preparation of a number of reports, the District Council gave its approval in February 1993 for the construction of the hill climb. By July the climb had been built and the inaugural event was held on July 4 1993. As is customary with a new venue, the RACMSA insisted that the hill climb should be a closed event for club members with no spectators. It was such a success that the Scottish Hill Climb Championship committee looked forward to including Forrestburn as part of their hill climb championship. Towards that end they awarded the "Bob Hamilton Trophy" to the District Council in recognition of the Council's bold step to help promote motor sport in Scotland.

For the 1994 season two hill climbs on the site were proposed as counters in the Scottish Hill Climb Championship and various other small events were organised. Clearly everything appeared to be going well and, as is normal, the RAC made various recommendations to do with safety which, when completed, would result in Forrestburn receiving its Track Licence. These included improved safety banking for spectators and better pedestrian access to the spectator areas.

Whilst this was going on the District Council prepared to move on to phase two, the building of a proper motor racing circuit separate to the hill climb site in the picturesque valley surrounding the reservoir. The plan was for a 2.5 mile track with the facility to operate two different circuits at the same time. In addition there would be off-road facilities in the Paperthill Crags,

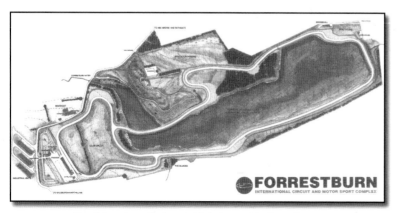

Though Forrestburn still exists as a hill climb venue the original plan was to have a motor racing circuit. This drawing shows the shorter Club circuit.

four-wheel drive areas, an RAC-licensed racing school and a learner driver training area with a skid pan. (An almost carbon copy of what had been proposed for New Ingliston.) One extra factor, however, was a 12-mile network of forestry tracks for use as rally special stages.

All the publicity that had surrounded the development was clearly not lost, for an approach was made to the council early in 1994 from a private group showing interest in developing the circuit. This group proposed to invest around £3 million subject to various conditions such as assistance with road access and land acquisition. Regarding access to the track there were plans to add a roundabout at Junction 5 of the Motorway with a slip road directly to the circuit.

By autumn the circuit plans had been modified to include both a 2.75 mile international circuit and a shorter 1.4 mile club circuit. The private developers were a company called Inreco Ltd., which included amongst its

principals Peter de Ritter, manager of Oulton Park, Adrian Chambers and former racing driver Sir Malcolm Guthrie. They had developed their plans to include not only a hotel but to take over the adjoining hill climb site. The rental set down for the site was £20,000 per year, all of this subject to planning permission for the entire development.

As with all such projects, costs began to spiral and the total cost of the work to be done was estimated at just over £6.5 million of which Inreco would provide the largest share with additional money from the Lanarkshire Development Agency, the District Council and an anticipated grant from European funds. Amongst the many elements that had to come together in order to go ahead was the purchase of two small farm holdings on the site and this fell into Inreco's domain. There was talk at the time that Tom Walkinshaw had been approached not only about purchasing the farms but also as a possible end user of the circuit for testing his Arrows grand prix cars.

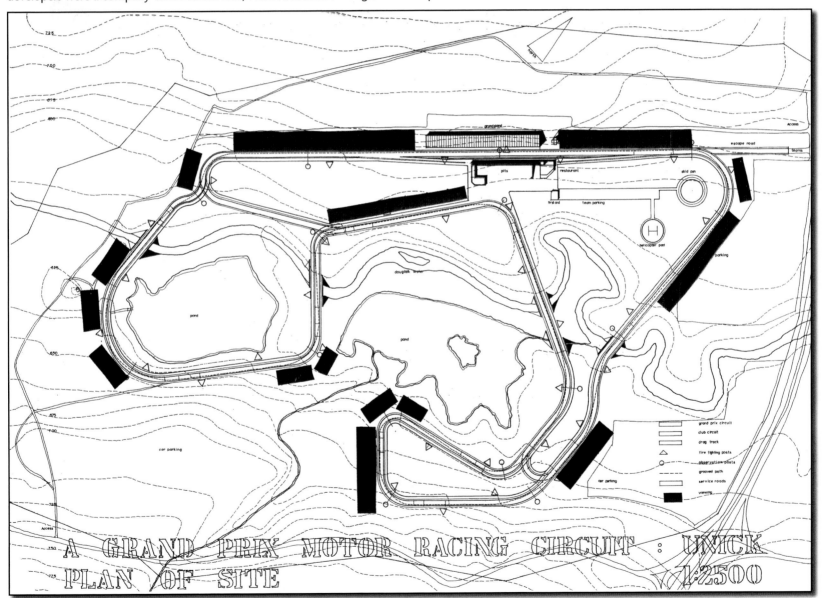

The only true phantom circuit, Jim Unick's hypothetical grand prix circuit project. The site actually exists just off the A74 road but was designed by Unick for his architectural exams. (Courtesy Jim Unick,)

In December 1994 planning permission was given for the project. To give some idea of the long drawn out process of this sort of development, it was not until the Spring of 1996 that work was due to commence on the building of the circuit. However, Adrian Chambers, the driving force behind Inreco died suddenly and the whole project began to crumble and fall apart. Today Forrestburn still exists and the Monklands Sporting Car Club still run the event with Brian and Marion Hopkins well to the fore.

Finally, the title of this chapter refers to "phantom circuits" but as can be seen each of the plans described above was envisaged as a potential going concern from the start. However, there is one truly phantom project which none but a handful of people know about, the Grand Prix circuit planned for a site at the junction of the A74 Glasgow to Carlisle road and the A70 Edinburgh to Ayr road near the town of Douglas. The actual circuit site encompassed the little valley between the junction and Douglas and features three small lochans.

The whole concept and design was thought up by Glasgow architectural student Jim Unick around 1972 when he chose the design of a grand prix motor racing circuit for his Part 2 examination in architecture to be presented to the Royal Institute of British Architects. Jim worked for two years on this plan and ended up with a ring-backed booklet over an inch thick and packed with the most detailed diagrams and costings for a full grand prix circuit.

Today Jim Unick and his wife are successful architects in Park Gate, Glasgow, and he laughs when he describes the work he put into a set of plans which, even in today's terms, could be translated into a proper circuit with the necessary safety updates that have come along in the past thirty years. In order to present his thesis he had to have a "Client" and he had to have a site. Though he was familiar with racing solely through television, he approached John Romanes of Scotcircuits Ltd who agreed to be his "Client" and Jim spent four months studying Ingliston to familiarise himself with what he needed to incorporate in his designs.

The proposed circuit length was 4.8 kms to make it long enough for grand prix racing and the remarkable thing about the design was the variety of fast corners and the fact that from the start there was a long constant radius curve leading into a short straight and left kink where the field could sort itself out. The design called for no fewer than four bridges to carry the track over the Douglas Water. There were two spur roads so that the entire area could be split into different layouts to suit grand prix and club race meetings. Even the main straight could have been used as a sprint course. If the circuit to that design existed today it would provide the kind of grand prix racing most of the fans have been hoping for. No doubt it would be deemed "too dangerous" as the speeds at the end of the main straight would exceed 200 mph.

In his presentation Jim Unick covered the technicalities of building the circuit to a remarkable degree down to the design of the grandstand seats and even a study showing the specific placements of the grandstands so that in any weather conditions they would not cast a shadow over the circuit itself. It was a true tour de force and it was little wonder he passed his exams with flying colours. Sadly, as far as Scotland is concerned, it was the only true phantom circuit: one that was never going to be built.

Appendix 1
Scots in Grand Prix Racing

The Grand Prix world championship was started in 1950, the same year Scotland held its first motor race meeting, and in the fifty four years since, many Scots drivers have not only competed but have been successful. We cannot forget that Jackie Stewart claimed three World Championships in 1969/1971 and 1973 or that Jim Clark won two before that, 1963 and 1965. Since then David Coulthard has come closest to becoming Scotland's sixth world champion with his second place to Michael Schumacher in 2001. The following is a list of Scots who have raced in world championship grand prix events.

Clark Jim:

Born March 4 1936, Kilmany, Fife. - Died April 7 1968 Hockenheim, Germany.

First world championship grand prix: Dutch Grand Prix 1960 driving Team Lotus Lotus 18 Climax. Retired with transmission trouble.

Last grand prix: 1968, South African Grand Prix driving John Player Special Lotus 49 Cosworth-Ford. Winner.

World Champion 1963 and 1965.

Coulthard David: *Born March 27 1971, Twynholm, Kirkcudbright.*

First world championship grand prix: Spanish Grand Prix 1994 driving Rothmans Williams FW16 Renault retired, electrics.

First Grand Prix Win: 1995 Portuguese Grand Prix.

Crawford Jim: *Born February 13 1948, Dunfermline - Died USA 2002.*

First world championship grand prix: British Grand Prix, Silverstone 1975 driving John Player Team Lotus Lotus 72E Cosworth. Spun off.

Last grand prix: Italian Grand Prix Monza 1975 driving John Player Team Lotus Lotus 72E Cosworth. 13th.

Dumfries Johnny: *Born April 26 1958, Rothesay, Isle of Bute.*

First world championship grand prix: Brazilian Grand Prix 1986 driving John Player Special Team Lotus 98T Renault. Finished 9th.

Last world championship grand prix Australian Grand Prix 1986 driving John Player Special Team Lotus 98T finished 6th.

Flockhart Ron: *Born June 16 1923, Edinburgh. - Died Flying Accident Australia*

First world championship grand prix: 1954 British Grand Prix, Silverstone driving Prince Bira's Maserati 250F crashed

Last world championship grand prix: 1960 US Grand prix driving a Cooper T51 Climax. Retired.

Ireland Innes: *Born June 12 1930 Todmorden, Yorks. Died November 1993*

First world championship grand prix: 1959 Dutch Grand Prix driving Team Lotus Lotus 16 Climax. Finished 4th.

Last world championship grand prix: 1966 Mexican Grand Prix driving BRM P261 V8, retired.

McNish Allan: *Born Dumfries*

First world championship grand prix: 2002 Australian Grand Prix driving for Toyota eliminated in first corner accident.

Murray David: *Born December 28 1909, Edinburgh - Died Canary Islands April 5 1975*

First world championship grand prix 1950 British Grand Prix, Silverstone, driving Maserati 4CLT/48. Retired engine.

Last world championship grand prix: 1952 British Grand Prix, Silverstone driving Ecurie Ecosse Cooper T20 Bristol. Retired with plug problems.

Scott-Brown Archie: *Born May 13 1927, Paisley. - Died in Lister-Jaguar at Spa in 1958.*

First and only world championship grand prix: 1956 British Grand Prix driving Connaught Alta B type. Retired, lost a wheel.

Stewart Ian: *Born July 15 1929. Edinburgh.*

First and only world championship grand prix: 1953 British Grand Prix, Silverstone driving Ecurie Ecosse Connaught A type. Retired with engine trouble.

Stewart Jimmy: *Born March 6 1931, Bowling, Dunbartonshire.*

First and only world championship grand prix: 1953 British Grand Prix, Silverstone driving Ecurie Ecosse Cooper T20 Bristol. Retired, lost wheel.

Stewart John Young (Jackie): *Born June 11 1939, Milton, Dunbartonshire*

First world championship grand prix: 1965 South African Grand Prix driving Owen Racing Organisation BRM P261 finished 6th.

Last world championship grand prix*: 1973 Canadian GP at Mosport Park driving Team Tyrrell Tyrrell 006 Cosworth. Finished 5th.

* Note that Stewart practiced for the 1973 US Grand prix but retired from grand prix racing on the death of his team mate in practice and did not compete in what would have been his 100th grand prix.

World Champion 1969, 1971,1973.

Thorne Leslie: *Born June 6 1916, Greenock.*

First and only world championship grand prix: 1952 British Grand Prix driving Ecurie Ecosse Connaught A type not classified.

Appendix 2

Scots at Le Mans

(Scottish drivers in bold face)

1929
Glen Kidston/Jack Dunfee — Bentley 4.5 litre — Finished 2nd.

1930
Glen Kidston/Woolf Barnato — Bentley 6.5 — Outright Winners.

1935
Margaret Allan/Colleen Eaton — MGPA 750 S. — Finished 26th
Michael Collier/**Peter Mitchell-Thomson*** — Frazer Nash TT Replica — Retired oil pump
* Later Lord Selsdon.

1937
David Hugh Murray/Pat Fairfield — Frazer-Nash BMW — Crashed 8th lap.

1938
T.A.S.O. Mathieson/ Freddie Clifford — Talbot T150C — Retired in 17th place.

1939
Lord Selsdon/Lord Waleran — Lagonda V12 — Finished 4th.
T.A.S.O. Mathieson/Luigi Chinetti — Talbot T26 — Retired after accident.
Rob Walker/Ian Connell — Delahaye 135S — 8th overall

1949
Lord Selsdon/Luigi Chinetti — Ferrari 166MM — Outright winner.
T.A.S.O. Mathieson/Pierre Marechal — Aston Martin DB2 — Retired 23rd hour accident.

1950
T.A.S.O. Mathieson/ Dickie Stoop — Frazer Nash Mille Miglia — 9th overall.
Jean Lucas/**Lord Selsdon** — Ferrari 195MM — Accident 17th hr.

1952
Ian Stewart/Peter Whitehead — Jaguar XK120C — Retired second hour engine.

1953
Ian Stewart/Peter Whitehead — Jaguar XK120C — 4th overall.

1954
Jimmy Stewart/Graham Whitehead — Aston Martin DB3S Coupe — Crash White House

1955
Ninian Sanderston/Bob Dickson — Triumph TR2 — 14th overall.
Ron Flockhart/Colin Chapman — Lotus II — Disqualified.

1956
Ron Flockhart/**Ninian Sanderson** — Jaguar D type Ecurie Ecosse — 1st overall

1957
Ron Flockhart/Ivor Bueb — Jaguar D type Ecurie Ecosse — 1st overall
Ninian Sanderson/Jock Lawrence — Jaguar D type Ecurie Ecosse — 2nd overall

1958
Tom Dickson/Alan Stacey — Lotus XI — 20th overall.
Innes Ireland/Michael Taylor — Lotus XI — Retired 20th hour.
Ninian Sanderson/Jock Lawrence — Jaguar D type Ecurie Ecosse — Retired engine.

1959
Jim Clark/John Whitmore — Lotus Elite Border Reivers — 10th overall.
Ninian Sanderson/Claude Dubois — Triumph TR3S — Retired 23rd hour radiator
Ron Flockhart/Jock Lawrence — Tojeiro-Jaguar Ecurie Ecosse — Retired engine.
Innes Ireland/Masten Gregory — Jaguar D type Ecurie Ecosse — Retired engine

1960
Jim Clark/Roy Salvadori — Aston Martin DBR1 Border Reivers — 3rd overall
Ninian Sanderson/Peter Bolton — Triumph TR4 — Not classified
Ron Flockhart/Bruce Halford — Jaguar D type Ecurie Ecosse — Retired engine

1961
Jim Clark/**Ron Flockhart** — Aston Martin DBR1 Border Reivers — Retired clutch.
Ninian Sanderson/Bill Mackay — Austin Healey Sprite Ecurie Ecosse — Retired Accident
Tommy Dickson/Bruce Halford — Cooper Monaco Ecurie Ecosse — Retired Accident

1962
Innes Ireland/Masten Gregory — Ferrari 250GTO UDT Laystall — Retired electrics
Tommy Dickson/Jack Fairman — Tojeiro-EE Ecurie Ecosse — Retired gearbox
Ninian Sanderson/Peter Bolton — TVR-MG — Retired water pump.

1963
Ninian Sanderson/Peter Bolton — AC Cobra — 7th overall
Innes Ireland/Bruce McLaren — Aston Martin DP214 — Retired engine

1964
Innes Ireland/Tony Maggs — Ferrari GTO Maranello Concess. — 6th overall

1965
Jackie Stewart/Graham Hill — Rover BRM Turbine — 10th overall
Innes Ireland/John Whitmore — Ford GT 40 F A V — Retired engine.

1966
Innes Ireland/Jochen Rindt — Ford GT40 Comstock Racing — Retired engine

1968
Eric Liddell/Peter Salmon — Ford GT40 — Retired gearbox.

1972
Gerry Birrell/Claude Bourgoignie — Ford Capri 2600RS — 10th overall

1973
Gerry Birrell/Helmut Koienigg — Ford Capri 2600LV — Retired engine.

1976
Tom Walkinshaw/John Fitzpatrick — BMW 3.5 CSL — Retired electrics
1977
Tom Walkinshaw/Eddy Joosen — BMW 3.00 CSL — Retired engine

1978
Robin Smith/Tony Charnell — Chevron B31 — Retired accident.
Tom Walkinshaw/ Dieter Quester — Osella PA6 — Retired Accident

1979
Robin Smith/Tony Charnell — Chevron B36 — 17th 1st in Class.

1981
Tom Walkinshaw/Tetsu Ikusawa — Mazda RX7 — Retired transmission

1982
Tom Walkinshaw/Peter Lovett — Maxda 254 Mazdaspeed. — Retired engine

1984
David Leslie/**David Duffield** — Ecosse C284 Ecurie Ecosse — Retired fuel pump

1985
David Leslie/Mike Wilds — Ecosse C285 Ecurie Ecosse — Retired engine.
Robin Smith/Richard Jones — Chevron B62 — Retired engine

1986
David Leslie/Ray Mallock — Ecosse C286 Ecurie Ecosse — Disqualified

1987
David Leslie/Marc Duez — Ecosse C287 Ecurie Ecosse — 8th overall.

| Johnny Dumfries/Chip Ganassi | Sauber C9 | Retired gearbox. |
| Robin Smith/Will Hoy | Argo JM 19 | Retired puncture |

1988

Johnny Dumfries/Jan Lammers	Jaguar XJR9 LM Silk Cut	1st overall.
David Leslie/Yoshimi Katayama	Mazda 767	17th.
Robin Smith/Martin Schanche	Argo JM 19C	25th.

1989

Robin Smith/"Stingbrace"	Tiga GC288	Retired Electrics
David Leslie/Ray Mallock	Aston Martin AMR1	Retired electrics
Johnny Dumfries/Geoff Lees	Toyota 89 C-V	Retired accident

1990

| David Leslie/ Alain Ferte | Jaguar XJR 12 | Water Pump |
| Johnny Dumfries/ Aguri Suzuki | Toyota 90 C-V | Retired accident/ |

1991

David Leslie/ Mauro Martini	Jaguar XJR 12	Retired transmission
Anthony Reid/ Franz Konrad	Porsche 962 C	Retired engine.
Johnny Dumfries/ Anders Olofsson	Cougar C26S	Retired 4th hr overheating.

1993

| David Coulthard/ John Nielsen | Jaguar XJ220C | Disqualified Exhaust |
| David Leslie/Win Percy | Jaguar XJ220C | Retired overheating |

1994

| Robin Smith/Stefano Sebastiani | Ferrari 348LM | Retired Clutch |

1995

| David Leslie/Chris Marsh | Marcos LM600 | Retired Electrics |

1996

| Anthony Reid/Geoff Lees | Lister Storm GTS | 19th |

1997

| Allan McNish/Stephane Ortelli | Porsche 911GT | Accident |

1998

| Allan McNish/Stephane Ortelli | Porsche 911GT98 | 1st. |

1999

| Peter Dumbreck/Nick Heidfeld | Mercedes CLR | Accident |
| Allan McNish/Thierry Boutsen | Toyota GT1 | Accident |

2000

| Allan McNish/Laurent Aiello | Audi R8R 2000 | 2nd |

2001

| Anthony Reid/Warren Hughes | MG | Retired |

2002

| Anthony Reid/Warren Hughes | MG | Retired in 4th place |
| Robin Liddell/Piers Masarati | Porsche 911 GT3-RS | |

2003

| Robin Liddell/D Warnock/P Masarati | Porsche 911 GT3-RS | 24th overall. |

Index